THE TAFTS

Other Titles by George W. Liebmann

Maryland District Court Law and Practice

Maryland Circuit Court Forms

The Little Platoons: Sub-Local Governments in Modern History

The Gallows in the Grove: Civil Society in American Law

Solving Problems Without Large Government, reprinted as *Neighborhood Futures*

Six Lost Leaders: Prophets of Civil Society

The Common Law Tradition: A Collective Portrait of Five Legal Scholars

Diplomacy Between the Wars: Five Diplomats and the Shaping of the Modern World

The Last American Diplomat: John D. Negroponte and His Times, 1960-2010

The Fall of the House of Speyer: The Story of a Banking Dynasty

America's Political Inventors: The Lost Art of Legislation

Vox Clamantis in Deserto: An Iconoclast Looks at Four Failed Administrations

Journal of Two Plague Years

THE TAFTS

George W. Liebmann

Twelve
Tables
Press

In Memoriam

Frederick W Brune IV
1894-1972

Mary Washington Keyser Brune
1899-1984

Contents

ACKNOWLEDGMENTS

Because the author writes from a provincial city and is not an academic, the usual array of dozens of acknowledgments can be omitted from this text. A number of persons have commented on the manuscript, including the late Ray Jenkins, one time editor of the *Montgomery (AL) Journal and Advertiser*; Dr. Frank Burd, a Taft biographer and former Director of the Baltimore Council on Foreign Affairs; Professor Jonathan White of Christopher Newport University; Professor Jean Yarbrough of Bowdoin College; and Professor Mary Ann Glendon of the Harvard Law School.

I have had the benefit of several conversations with members of the Taft family, including Governor Robert Taft III, William H. Taft IV, and John T. Taft. The views here expressed should not be attributed to them.

I am indebted to three earlier books on the Tafts, Henry Pringle's two volume biography of *William Howard Taft* (New York: Farrar and Rinehart, 1939); Robert Patterson's biography of *Robert A. Taft, Mr. Republican* (Boston: Houghton Mifflin, 1970); and Ishbel Ross's *The Tafts: An American Family* (Cleveland: World, 1964).

Taft documents are assembled in D. Burton (ed.), *The Collected Works of William Howard Taft* (Athens, OH: Ohio U., 2004) (8 vols.); C. Wunderlin (ed.), *The Papers of Robert A. Taft* (Kent, OH: Kent State U., 2001) (4 vols.), as well as in J. Vivian (ed.), *Collected Editorials of William Howard Taft, 1917-1921* (Westport, CT: Praeger, 1990).

Archival research has been easier than for most biographical subjects. The Tafts, with characteristic modesty, consigned their papers to the Library of Congress rather than, as said by Charley Taft, to "a mausoleum someplace else." The papers of William Howard Taft's closest aide, Gus Karger, are at the Cincinnati Museum Center.

I am grateful to my wife, Anne-Lise Liebmann for her forbearance; to the President and Fellows of Wolfson College, Cambridge and the Cambridge University Library for facilities there; and to Joseph W. Bennett, Librarian of the Library Company of the Baltimore Bar, for securing some needed publications.

George W. Liebmann
Baltimore
November 25, 2022

THE TAFTS

THE TAFTS

Alphonso Taft
1810-1891

Charles Taft	Peter R. Taft	William H. Taft	Horace Taft	Henry W. Taft
1843-1929	1846-1889	1857-1930	1861-1943	1859-1945

Children of Charles Taft

Hulbert Taft	Louise Taft Semple
1877-1959	1879-1961

Children of William H. Taft

Robert A. Taft	Helen Taft Manning	Charles Phelps Taft II
1889-1953	1891-1987	1897-1983

Children of Henry W. Taft

Walbridge Taft	William H. Taft II
1885-1951	1887-1952

Children of Robert A. Taft

William H. Taft III	Robert Taft Jr.	Lloyd Bowers Taft	Horace Dwight Taft
1915-1991	1917-1993	1923-1985	1925-1983

Children of Helen Taft Manning

Helen Taft Manning Hunter	Caroline Taft Manning
1921-2013	1925-2020

Children of Charles Phelps Taft II

Seth Taft	Lucia Taft	Cynthia Taft	Rosalyn Taft	Peter Rawson Taft III
1922-2013	1924-1955	1928-2013	1930-1941	1937-

Children of William H. Taft III

Maria Taft Clemow	William H. Taft IV	Martha Taft Golden	John T. Taft
1943-	1945-	1947-	1950-

Children of Robert Taft Jr.

Robert Taft III	Sarah Taft Jones	Deborah Taft Boutellis	Jonathan Taft
1942-	1943-	1946-	1954-

Children of Lloyd Taft

Louise Taft Cooke	Virginia Taft-Carabane	Julia Taft Jonathan	Rhonda Taft Jones	Patricia M. Taft
1949-	1950-	1958-2013	1984-	1984-

Children of Horace Dwight Taft

John G. Taft	Hugh Taft-Morales	Horace D. Taft-Ferguson
1955-	1957-	1963-

Children of Seth Taft

Frederick Taft	Thomas Taft	Cynthia Taft	Tucker Taft
1945-	1948-	1950-	1953-

Introduction

This is a book about five generations of the Taft family, America's longest-lived political dynasty but one that, unlike four generations of Adamses, three of Rockefellers and Kennedys, and two each of Oyster Bay and Hyde Park Roosevelts, has not captured the public's imagination.

Yet the impact of the Tafts on the present shape of American society may well be greater than that of any of the other political families. The book will interest conservative Republicans and independent voters who suspect that fashionable historians have provided them with only a partial and partisan version of twentieth-century history.

The Tafts' impact is unappreciated because, thanks to their unsympathetic biographers, William Howard Taft is thought of as a standpatter and fat plutocrat and his son Robert A. Taft as a blind isolationist and opponent of domestic reform.

This long-overdue reconsideration of the Tafts shows them to be far-sighted, fair-minded, and in many ways good guides in dealing with today's concerns.

William Howard Taft served in more significant and varied public offices than any other American: in his words, he always had his plate up when offices were being handed out. He was a collector of internal revenue, a state prosecutor, a state court trial judge, Solicitor General of the United States, a federal circuit judge, Governor General of the Philippines, Secretary of War, President of the United States, co-chairman of the War Labor Board under President Wilson, and Chief Justice of the United States. At various times, he was also a leader in the American Bar Association, a founder of the U.S. Chamber of Commerce, Chairman of the Board of the Hampton Institute, an historically black college, and Professor of Law at Yale.

Although identified with "dollar diplomacy," he was in fact an anti-imperialist opposed to Philippine annexation and unlike the Wilson administration avoided military adventures in Mexico. He brought an end to the Philippine Insurrection by bestowing state and local offices on its leaders; this perpetuated a landed oligarchy, reflecting Taft's profound and justified disbelief in the possibilities of democracy in an economy resting largely on plantation agriculture.

The present shape of antitrust and labor law owes more to his influence than to that of any other judge. He was one of the first judicial defenders of the right to organize and strike and was an opponent of "yellow dog" contracts ostracizing union members, while being vehemently opposed to secondary boycotts, mass picketing, and industry-wide bargaining. On the War Labor Board, he fostered minimum wages and plant-level employee organizations.

Among the Presidents, he was the leading trust-buster. Theodore Roosevelt, despite flaming rhetoric, was an exponent of regulated monopoly. Thurman Arnold's activity in the second Roosevelt administration was short-lived. He did much to de-concentrate wealth. He urged the Income Tax amendment, sponsored the first corporate income tax, favored federal chartering of the largest corporations, opposed federal incorporation of family foundations, set in motion banking reforms leading to creation of the Federal Reserve Board, supported the Hepburn and Clayton Acts, and urged the states to curb the duration of family trusts. He also mildly lowered most tariffs and secured the creation of the parcel post and postal savings systems.

He sought to conciliate the white South and bind up the wounds of the Civil War, viewing Southerners as a bulwark against collectivism. Unlike TR and Wilson, who were racists in the literal sense, he had much social intercourse with the leaders of black colleges, and sought to foster industrial education, a cause still warranting attention, in which he was opposed by white liberals and blacks like W.E.B. Du Bois who short-sightedly decried training for manual labor as a vestige of slavery. His Justice Department supported black voting rights, not without initial reluctance, in the

Grandfather Clause Cases; these did not enfranchise blacks but at least rendered their dis-enfranchisement illegitimate. He made more speeches to black audiences than most presidents, and, most remarkably, served for nearly 20 years as Chairman of the Board of the Hampton Institute, attending at least one board meeting a year and writing hundreds of letters in its behalf.

His breach with Theodore Roosevelt centered on his opposition to recall of judicial decisions and direct primaries and his view that Roosevelt's careless rhetoric made him a dangerous demagogue who would incite and not be able to curb a revolutionary spirit. He preserved the Republican Party as a conservative force.

He supported Wilson's League of Nations. While no militarist, he, like Theodore Roosevelt, favored a march to Berlin after the Armistice to crush German militarism and, like Churchill, an expeditionary force to strangle Bolshevism in its cradle.

As Chief Justice, he took a generous view of federal power over interstate commerce, which if continued would have mitigated many of the constitutional controversies of the 1930s and forestalled the federal grant in aid system. Although he was hostile to state legislation limiting business competition, he did not stand in the way of "welfare state" programs such as workmen's and unemployment compensation.

He greatly strengthened the Supreme Court, securing it its own building and control over its docket.

His son Senator Robert A. Taft was a realist, not an isolationist, in foreign policy. He was the leader in repealing the embargo legislation and in allowing Britain to buy arms in the United States during the first two years of World War II. He initially opposed lend-lease but proposed large loans to Britain, Canada, and Greece prior to American entry into the war.

He attached great importance to American control of the Caribbean, Central America, and Northern South America, a matter receiving little attention from some later presidents. He thought that the post-war Soviet Union had neither the desire nor the capacity to militarily invade Western Europe, a judgment borne out when the Soviet archives were briefly opened. He was virtually alone in seriously questioning the aggrandizement of presidential war-making powers that got us into Vietnam and Iraq.

His Taft–Hartley Act still governs American labor law and is the only important modern statute passed over a Presidential veto. It curbed secondary boycotts, mass picketing, and industry-wide strikes while preserving existing restrictions on private labor injunctions. He was active in dis-mantling wartime controls, thus sparing the United States "the British disease" with its labor unrest and economic stagnation.

He was also in important respects a progressive. He correctly predicted that abuse of the filibuster would bring Congress into disrepute, successfully sponsored a housing bill, and secured House passage but not enactment of a revenue-sharing bill without federal controls to assist black schools in the South. In response to President Truman's socialized medicine plan, he urged school health examinations, community health clinics, and subsidies to doctors establishing practices in poorer neighborhoods.

He was also a champion of civil liberties, and was the only official in all three branches of government to publicly oppose internment of Japanese-Americans. He also opposed conscription of labor, universal military training and the drafting of strikers and decried war crimes trials as acts of policy masked as judicial proceedings.

Later generations of Tafts functioned in a more competitive era but made important contributions. Senator Robert Taft Jr. was the first prominent politician to propose curbing "bracket creep" in the tax code to curb increases in the size of government. Ohio Governor Robert Taft III made himself unpopular with both parties in the Reagan era by fostering fiscal responsibility; he also has a continuing interest in science education. John T. Taft wrote meritorious books and television scripts criticizing the 1968 student disturbances and lack of American restraint in the Third World. John G. Taft sought to curb fiduciary abuses by brokers and fund managers and William H. Taft IV as Deputy Secretary of Defense curbed militarization of law enforcement and as counsel to the

Department of State in the second Bush administration "blew the whistle" on memoranda authorizing torture of prisoners.

The Tafts' success and influence was not based on personal wealth, though they had some, nor on a talent for personal publicity, for they were all notably self-effacing. Their influence rested more than anything else on the cultivation of academic excellence in each generation, and an ethic of self-denial that led them to marry intelligently and avoid alcohol, financial, and sex scandals. They were not the "foolish tawdry moths who fly into publicity's consuming fire" of whom Learned Hand wrote.

In an age whose politics rests on defamation, not information, and in which the capacity to frame legislation giving clear guides to private behavior has vanished, they furnish examples of responsible citizenship. This book undertakes to remove the bushel over their light, shining as long ago as 1838:

> "The race of Taft as a name has been remarkable for its habits of industry economy morality and good citizenship in Church and State affairs, as much so as any name among us. It is very rare that a Taft has been carried to the Poor-House, or been called before authority on criminal actions. Through the possession and exercise of those 'habits of industry, economy and morality,' this 'good citizenship in Church and State,' our citizens have subdued the wilderness, founded new empires, and made the American name and American institutions famous throughout the world. And if this republic shall ever perish, if our institutions shall be essentially changed in their character, it will be because of the deterioration of what, for want of a better form, may be called the great middle class of our people. So long as this class remains preserved by sound morals, by habits of industry and frugality from the degradation of poverty and vice—saved also in the good Providence of God from the perils and temptations of sudden, excessive wealth—earnest, enlightened,

conscientious in the assertion of their rights and the fulfilment of their duties, our future is secure."[1]

This is a work not of political but of intellectual history. Public knowledge of the Taft family centers on the lives of President and Chief Justice William Howard Taft and Senate Republican leader Robert A. Taft. Their biographies deal with politics in the narrow sense, particularly with the minutiae of the Republican political conventions that nominated the father and rejected the son. Their leading biographers—Henry Pringle in the first case and James T. Patterson in the second, were fundamentally out of sympathy with their subjects' political views. The commonalities between them are left unexplored, as is the extraordinary family ethos that has thus far produced five generations of significant political figures. In a permissive age dominated by self-indulgence among the well-to-do, the record of the Tafts is one of fidelity and sobriety. In an age of centralization they have worked in and upheld local and state institutions. In an age of increasing regulation, they have defended the private economy, competition and free collective bargaining. In a period of real or imagined external threats to the American policy, they have resisted needless foreign involvements and judged them in accordance with realism and national interest. In times of "interest-group liberalism" in which the welfare of classes dominates debate, their focus has been on opportunity for individuals.

In the age of Twitter and the tweet, where most politicians are "foolish, tawdy moths who fly into publicity's consuming fire," in Learned Hand's memorable phrase, it is useful to be reminded of a series of men who shunned personal publicity and glamour and who exerted great influence based on their breadth of knowledge and perceived good character.

---

[1] Letter of Frederick Taft, Esq., of Uxbridge, Massachusetts, in 1838, quoted by Henry W. Taft of Pittsfield at a Taft family reunion at Uxbridge, August 12, 1874, in L. Leonard, Life of Alphonso Taft (New York: Hawke Publishing, 1920), 234, 286.

Little is known by today's public of the paterfamilias Alphonso Taft, Attorney General and Secretary of War in the Grant Administration; of William Howard Taft's half-brothers, Charles P. Taft and Peter Ransom Taft, and of his brothers, Henry W. Taft and Horace Taft; of Robert Taft's siblings, Charles P. Taft II, and Helen Taft Manning; of Robert Taft's children, Robert Taft Jr., William Howard Taft III, Lloyd Taft, and Horace Dwight Taft; as well as of Charles Taft's sons, Seth Taft and Peter Taft and of a fifth generation including the financial executive John G. Taft, the historian John T. Taft, the lawyer William H. Taft IV, and former Ohio Governor Robert Taft III.

The Paterfamilias

Alphonso Taft (1810-1891)

It is generally conceded that Alphonso Taft was not a man of unusual brilliance, though he respected academic industry and learning, and demanded it of his children. His other great contribution to them derived from his having become a symbol of political integrity. This was in no small measure due to the manner of his entry into politics. President Ulysses S. Grant, following the impeachment for bribery of his Secretary of War, William Belknap, came to realize that he was surrounded by dubious associates and, like Diogenes, went in search of an honest man. He found him in the ample person of a hitherto little-known Ohio judge.

Alphonso Taft's era was dominated by the Civil War and its aftermath. He was an active participant both in the political controversies attendant upon Reconstruction and in those accompanying the explosion of Northern enterprise after the War, including the expansion and over-expansion of railroads and those arising from the arrival of new immigrant groups. He was described by his biographer as "the only American statesman who held two cabinet positions and two first-line foreign missions."[1]

He graduated from Yale College in 1832, the first of many generations of Tafts to be educated there, and was admitted to the Bar in 1838. He became a member of the Cincinnati City Council and the Union Board of High Schools. He, along with William Huntington Russell was a co-founder of the Skull and Bones Society, of which William Howard Taft and the senior Robert Taft, but not Robert Taft Jr., later became members. The Society was founded as a result of a dispute between two debating societies over Phi Beta

---

[1] L. Leonard, *Life of Alphonso Taft* (New York: Hawke Publishing 1920).

Alphonso Taft Secretary of War

Kappa awards. In his youth, he was a member of a literary club that included among its members a future president, Rutherford B. Hayes, and two future Supreme Court justices, Stanley Matthews and Salmon P. Chase.[2]

He declared: "I really never made any money practicing law. I maintained my family and educated my children and that was all." He secured a fine education through his own efforts and rose to distinction by means of his own ambition, industry and integrity. "I have worked hard, made some money, lost some and have a modest competency. But I am a working man."[3]

---

[2] J. Cole, "Ainsworth Spofford and the Copyright Law of 1830," 6 J. Library History 34 (1971).

[3] L. Leonard, 21.

He was credited with "integrity more than daring, character rather than genius." He described his over-populated native Vermont, where in the 1850s every inch of rocky soil was cultivated and stone walls ran to the tops of mountains, as "a noble place to emigrate from," and by-passed New York for what he saw as its consecration of greed, declaring that he had heard of a New England conscience, but not a New York or Philadelphia conscience.

He was an only child; an obituary of his father, Peter Rawson Taft, who was born in 1785 and died in 1867, noted that Peter had been "many times" a representative in the Vermont legislature; four years a probate judge and four years a county judge. "He was extensively trusted, confided in and consulted by his neighbours and fellow citizens of Windham County. He was universally regarded as a just and humane man, not grasping for gain nor ambitious for office, but rendering much useful service for modest compensation. Books have been a great resource in his old age. His historical knowledge was extensive and his familiarity with the Bible was truly remarkable."[4] The first American Taft, Robert Taft, a carpenter, emigrated to Braintree, Massachusetts, in 1678.[5]

As a lawyer, Alphonso Taft successfully defended the will creating the University of Cincinnati,[6] and played an important part in the success of the Cincinnati and Southern Railway.[7] He was the first President of the Cincinnati Bar Association in 1872, and was a member of the Yale Corporation from 1872 to 1882.

In his youth he declared: "I know not what could lead you to suppose me anything but a Whig."[8] He unsuccessfully supported

---

[4] "Death of a Venerable Citizen," Cincinnati Gazette, January 3, 1867, in WHT Papers, Library of Congress, Series 27: Additions, Part C.

[5] C. Anthony, Nellie Taft: The Unconventional First Lady of the Ragtime Era (New York: Morrow, 2005), 61.

[6] 165 U.S. 465 (1897).

[7] Walker v. Cincinnati, 1 Cin.Sup.Ct. 127, affirmed 21 Ohio St. 14 (1893).

[8] AT to Phelps, April 3, 1841.

Daniel Webster for the Whig nomination for president in 1852 and thereafter abandoned the Whigs and was at the founding convention of the new Republican Party in 1856 and was at the 1860 convention that nominated Abraham Lincoln. In a eulogy of Webster delivered in 1852, he declared that Webster, Clay, and Calhoun "rose above all their contemporaries early in life and retained their pre-eminence undisputed, to the end of it. They have each towered above the incumbents of the Presidential office." Of Calhoun, he said, "in logical power he was the superior of Mr. Clay and the equal of Mr. Webster, he was peculiar and original. We shall not see his like again." He compared Webster to Demosthenes and Cicero.[9]

Alphonso Taft was a local patriot in Cincinnati, urging railroad construction in all directions. "In this North American valley there can be sustained a population greater than the 300 million of China. The Atlantic states cannot compete with the States of this valley. It is not to be doubted that the domestic commerce of the country exceeds the foreign in a ratio of more than 10 to 1. Why then can it not build up greater cities?" Railroads, he declared, would cause Cincinnati to be "enthroned as Queen of the mighty West." "Wherever the rail-way track has been laid, it has yielded a profit to gladden the hearts of those who have struggled to accomplish its construction."[10]

His dreams were typical of American "boosters" of his period; particularly after the Civil War, the nation seriously over-built railways, and reorganizations of them were a large part of the business of investment bankers during the first half of the twentieth century.

---

[9] AT, Daniel Webster, December 18, 1852, in WHT, Papers, Library of Congress, Reel 593.

[10] AT, Cincinnati and Her Railroads (1850), 23, 52, in WHT, Papers, Library of Congress, Reel 593.

If Alphonso Taft's most grandiose aspirations were not realized, Cincinnati did come to be known as a "City of Factories."[11] Alice Roosevelt Longworth later said of it: "It was a town with a great sense of its own importance. Not a common, vulgar, Midwestern town at all. They were all terribly nice and civilized. They travelled to Europe and promenaded along with the Anglais and they got presented at Court and bought inferior pictures. They considered Boston and Philadelphia to be all right, but New York was just a place you sailed to Europe from."[12]

His views on education and family life were firmly declared in an address delivered at the dedication of the local House of Refuge or reform school, in 1850. He noted that the first reform school had been established in New York in 1825. He attributed the need for such schools to "want of family government," alluding to "that well-known race of 'third-generation' men who having wasted the wealth of their grandsires with riotous living have afterwards yielded to criminal temptations" because their youth was "wholly destitute of parental authority." "Chasten thy son while there is hope and let not thy soul spare of his crying." He demanded and got academic achievement from his own children, including his five remarkable sons.

Of disruptive students, he observed "their influence has contaminated others and has done much to injure the otherwise excellent characters of our free schools." Jails he regarded as institutions "whose professors are the most expert housebreakers and thieves." Reformatories were effective, he said, in three out of four cases; children are then prepared for work as indentured servants.

---

[11] C. Abbott, Population, Economic Thought and Occupational Structure: Three Middle Western Cities in the Ante-Bellum Decade, 1 J. Urban History 175 (1975).

[12] M. Teague (ed.), Mrs L: Conversations with Alice Roosevelt Longworth (London: Duckworth, 1987), 138.

"Rural pursuits have been found best suited to insure a permanent reform."[13] Today's juvenile justice institutions cannot indenture their charges, slavery having been abolished by the Thirteenth Amendment, but they might usefully consider the practice of Taft's day (and of Franklin Roosevelt's voluntary Civilian Conservation Corps), when efforts were made to get juvenile offenders away from the contaminating influences of the neighborhoods in which they had grown up.

He was an unsuccessful candidate for the federal House of Representatives in 1856 and for Governor of Ohio in 1875 and 1879. In the last two cases, his candidacy fell victim to discontent with his dissenting opinion in a case upholding reading of the King James Bible in Ohio public schools delivered during his tenure as an Ohio judge from 1865 to 1872. He viewed the statute as "contrary to the spirit of free schools intended for the children of parents of all religious sects and beliefs [upholding] a neutrality toward all the sects which could not be otherwise obtained and which had become essential to religious peace." His "strict separationist" view was upheld on appeal by the Supreme Court of Ohio,[14] and 90 years later by the Supreme Court of the United States in *Abington v. Schempp*, which quoted his opinion.[15]

In his view, people should "be satisfied to give religious instruction and enjoy religious marriage in the family and the church while the State with some impartiality shall perform its great duty of making education universal through the best system of common schools." Although rejecting sectarian instruction in the schools as offensive to Catholics and Jews, he was equally opposed to any division of the school fund or state support of religious schools. "If it were attempted the small sects and those who affiliate with no sect

---

[13]   AT, Address at the Opening of the Cincinnati House of Refuge, October 7, 1850, 14ff.

[14]   Minor v. Board of Education, 23 Ohio St. 211 (1872), *see* Leonard 148.

[15]   374 U.S. 203 (1963) (Clark, J.).

could hope for but little advantage from their share of the fund, and none of the fractional schools resulting from a division of the fund would have more than a mere semblance of the power and usefulness of the system in its present integrity." "They will have to learn in America that there is a divinity in the Republic as impregnable and more potent than any church organization can bring against it."[16] He was thus the prophet of the extreme laicism that today "has largely abandoned the role that was of such central importance for Horace Mann and his contemporaries: developing character and conveying moral principles for which there was a societal consensus,"[17] causing us "to have the most thoroughly secularized public schools in the Western world, excepting those of the [former] USSR."[18]

He was thus unsympathetic to the Catholic claims for parochial schools: "I now believe that the Catholic laity have it in their power to do their church and their country a most important service by refusing to bear so unnecessary a burden. In this country, the civil law must be supreme. The common school system in full operation will gradually disperse the clouds of ignorance and shed upon all the people the broad daylight of universal intelligence."[19] This seriously underrated the role of the Catholic schools in socializing immigrant groups, and the advantage they have today in their immunity from federal rules limiting school discipline in the interests of the disruptive and "disabled." Parish schools are not and were not dependent on remote bureaucracies and do not hire as closed shops. But in Alphonso Taft's day, the public school system had not become professionalized and bureaucratized and many of the

---

[16] "The Public Schools: Speech of Judge Taft of Ohio," New York Times, August 26, 1875.

[17] C. Glenn, The Myth of the Common School (Amherst: U. of Massachusetts, 1988), 288.

[18] L. Jorgenson, The State and the Non-Public School, 1825-1925 (Columbia: U. of Missouri, 1987), 221.

[19] AT, Speech at Cleveland, September 2, 1876, in WHT, Papers, Library of Congress, Reel 593.

graduates of the best colleges became public school teachers as per-manent careers, a phenomenon unknown in our time. (His vision of public schools was not shared by his son Horace, who referred to the newly established "normal schools" at which public school teachers came to be trained as places where subnormal students were taught by abnormal faculty.)

Alphonso's speech was decried in the *Catholic Telegraph* in uncompromising terms: "If any of the laity refuse to hear the Church when it prescribes Catholic education for Catholic children, they are acting as the heathen and the publican. The Church has spo-ken dogmatically and there is left neither to priest nor layman any choice between systems of education. He must accept the Christian and reject the pagan system which Judge Taft naturally favours."[20]

In 1875, the ultimately successful gubernatorial candidate was Rutherford B. Hayes, who wrote that "Taft had such a record on the Bible question in the schools that his nomination was impos-sible," though he was "an able and a good man. I did all I could to remove the prejudice against him and to aid in his nomination."[21] Ironically, 70 years later the anti-clerical Eleanor Roosevelt in her famous controversy with Cardinal Spellman, urged that Catholics should be satisfied with readings from the King James Bible in the public schools, which Taft and nineteenth-century secularists and anti-clericals had opposed. Bible readings "were the product of dis-crimination against minority groups by a still-dominant but fearful Protestant majority."[22]

In 1876, at least one article speculated that Alphonso Taft might be the Republican Presidential nominee if there were a

---

[20] "A Catholic Organ on Judge Taft," New York Times, August 30, 1875.

[21] C. Williams, Life of Rutherford B. Hayes (Boston: Houghton Mifflin, 1914), 384.

[22] L. Jorgenson, The State and the Non-Public School, 1825-1925 (Colum-bia: U. of Missouri, 1987), 220.

deadlock at the convention, commending his "great ability, high character, intrepid honesty and rare aptitude for executive trusts."[23]

A later critic referred to him as "a judge of more respectability than ability."[24] Certainly his contributions to Grant's principal achievement, the defusing of the electoral crisis at the end of the administration, were not as significant as those of the dean of the Cabinet, Secretary of State Hamilton Fish.

In May 1872, he delivered a lecture at the University of Cincinnati. He rejected the proposition that public universities were of benefit only to the more fortunate classes: "Learning is not in its nature exclusive. When provided freely for everyone who is willing to endure the necessary self-denial and labour, it is the greatest and best leveller known, for its levelling is upward and never downward." He believed that was "far better for a boy to study with an understood plan or purpose before him, formed at least during his first year of college life."[25]

He campaigned vigorously for Grant in the 1872 campaign. He said that the Republicans had "destroyed slavery, root and branch [and] carried the Declaration of Independence into the Constitution, where it is today. Another four years of Republican rule might place the reconstructed States out of danger." The Democratic candidate, Horace Greeley "would not have the moral power and influence to restrain violence and enforce obedience to necessary measures in the reconstructed States. Grant saw clearly that not only civil but political rights had to be accorded to the coloured race or their liberty would prove a failure and the war against secession a failure."[26] In the event, not even Grant could enforce Reconstruc-

----

[23] "The Present Outlook from Ohio," New York Times, May 23, 1876.

[24] W. Hesseltine, Ulysses S. Grant, Politician (New York: Ungar, 1935), 396.

[25] AT, A Lecture on the University of Cincinnati, Its Aims, Needs, and Resources, May 1872, 39, in WHT, Papers, Reel 593.

[26] AT, Speech at Avondale, September 13, 1872, in WHT, Papers, Library of Congress, Reel 593.

tion. As a candidate for nation building, the South in 1865 bore little resemblance to post-World War II Germany and Japan, with their universal literacy and widespread private property ownership. If it was not quite today's Iraq, Vietnam, or Afghanistan, many of the later difficulties in reforming reluctant populations were fully operative.

Having served Grant for a year, he concluded that "I am satisfied that it was not chance or any use of superior military forces which gave him success, but a self-poised mind that combined facts into practical plans, with courage to carry them out without hesitation."[27]

As Secretary of War he directed bureau chiefs to reduce their own budgets. Unlike his predecessor William Belknap who had been impeached by the House of Representatives, he refused to appoint post merchants except on the recommendation of the officers at the post applied for. In 1864 he expressed to the newly appointed Chief Justice Chase the view that "to be Chief Justice is more than to be President, in my estimation," a view he transmitted to his son William Howard Taft,[28] but not to his grandson Robert, who declared that he had no interest in a judicial career.

Grant was under some duress when he appointed Taft. Grant's last Annual Message impressively conceded: "Mistakes have been made as all can see, and as I admit, but it seems to me oftener in the selections made of assistants ... in nearly every case selected without a personal acquaintance."[29]

---

[27] 27 Simon (ed.), The Papers of Ulysses S. Grant (Carbondale: Southern Illinois U., 2005), 182.

[28] Case Papers, Library of Congress, December 3, 1864, see 7 C. Fairman, History of the Supreme Court of the United States, Part 2 (New York: Macmillan, 1987), 70.

[29] 27 Simon (ed.), The Papers of Ulysses S. Grant (Carbondale: Southern Illinois U., 2005), 62.

"He was compelled to remake his cabinet under a gruelling fire from reformers and investigators; 'half its members were utterly inexperienced; several others discredited; one was even disgraced.'"[30]

The War Secretaryship was first offered to Senator Lot Morrill of Maine, who declined it, saying that he was "not in harmony with the personal surroundings of the President; he had a great distrust of Shepard and Babcock, the influences which he supposed shaped the President's course and had brought discredit on the country and administration."[31]

Grant had initially been reluctant to appoint Taft, saying that "[Taft] had been frequently suggested but he would not think of him," and asking "whether he had not been tainted by liberalness"; he was assured by Secretary Bristow that Taft "was the strongest kind of a hard money man."[32]

Taft's brief tenure of about ten months as Attorney General was not wholly uneventful; his most notable opinion was that the 20-year-old son of a naturalized citizen was entitled to an American passport even though he intended to return to the nation of his birth: "where a naturalized citizen applies for a passport with a view to travelling or residing abroad, though his intended destination may be in the country of his former nationality, his right to have the passport issued to him is just as obligatory upon the Department of the Government charged with this matter as if he were a native-born citizen intending to go to the same country."[33]

He also joined other Cabinet members in stating the conclusion that communications between the President and Cabinet

---

[30] A. Nevins (ed.), Hamilton Fish: The Inner History of the Grant Administration (New York: Dodd Mead, 1937), 811.

[31] 27 Simon (ed.), The Papers of Ulysses S. Grant (Carbondale: Southern Illinois U., 2005), 77.

[32] 27 Simon (ed.), The Papers of Ulysses S. Grant (Carbondale: Southern Illinois U., 2005), 75ff.

[33] 15 Opinions of the Attorney General of the United States 114, 117 (1876).

members were entitled to executive privilege against congressional subpoenas, a position not fully vindicated until the famous case involving the Nixon tapes a century later, and still viewed as dubious by critics of "the imperial presidency."[34]

Perhaps more important were the directions he issued to U.S. Marshals about the impending federal elections that resulted in the deadlock between Hayes and Samuel Tilden, the "Compromise of 1877" and the ultimate election of Rutherford Hayes as President. "In [federal] elections, the United States secure voters against whatever in general hinders or prevents them from a free exercise of the elective franchise, extending that care alike to the registration lists, the act of voting, and the personal freedom and security of the voter as well as against violence on account of any vote he may intend to give as against conspiracy because of any that he may already have given ... any person who by force violates those rights, breaks [the] peace and renders it your duty to arrest him and to suppress any riots incident thereto ... there can be no state law or state official in this country who has justification to oppose you in discharging your official duties under the laws of the United States."[35]

This declaration was criticized by the *New York World* and by Senator James Bayard of Delaware. A Virginia newspaper referred to "Taft's order, destroying the freedom of elections in the Southern states."[36]

Taft responded, "They are not to intimidate any voter. They are to prevent intimidation ... upon this call from the Governor of South Carolina, how else could the President act than as he did? If any man thinks that Gen. Grant will shrink from performance of a high duty because it is difficult or perilous, such a man does not

---

[34] 27 Simon (ed.), The Papers of Ulysses S. Grant (Carbondale: Southern Illinois U., 2005), 186-87.

[35] "The Southern Elections: Fair Elections Provided For," New York Times, September 5, 1876.

[36] Petersburg (Va.) Index Appeal, September 8, 1876.

comprehend the character of the President ... The facts are too plain to admit of doubt in the mind of any man who regards evidence."[37]

Later, on October 25, virtually the eve of the election, he delivered a two-hour-long speech in the Hayes interest at the Cooper Union in New York.[38]

Taft was, in fact, an intense partisan in the Hayes campaign. E.L. Godkin, the editor of *The Nation*, wrote: "the conduct of Chandler and Taft during the late campaign ought to be made illegal." Hamilton Fish noted that "the new Attorney General extended his extreme influence in the South, where he controlled a host of employees. [Fish] did not believe that the Cabinet should be made an auxiliary of the Republican National Committee."

Taft's intervention in South Carolina was limited to the restoration of order; President Grant, a lame duck, strove for impartiality in the 1876 disputed election, refused to re-install a Republican legislature in South Carolina by force of arms and likewise refused to militarily intervene in Louisiana.[39] In effect, Grant implemented the "Compromise of 1877," ending military reconstruction before Hayes did.

Secretary of State Hamilton Fish, the most distinguished member of the Grant Cabinet, wrote that "a better attitude might have been expected from Taft. This big, smooth-shaven jurist, so portly that chairs groaned underneath him, his broad brow speaking intellect and his tight-pressed lips determination, unfortunately represented the essence of conservatism ... he was a Republican of the hard-shell school and spending most of his life in the border

---

[37] New York Times, October 20, 1876.

[38] "The Rebel War Claims: Democratic Plans Discussed," New York Times, October 26, 1876.

[39] A. Nevins (ed.), Hamilton Fish: The Inner History of the Grant Administration (New York: Dodd Mead, 1937), 859; J. Carpenter, Ulysses S. Grant (New York: Twayne, 1970), 165, 167.

city of Cincinnati, he had learned to suspect and hate the Southern tempo."[40]

Fish was the author of Grant's impressive last message urging enactment of the legislation resolving the electoral crisis.[41] Alphonso Taft's greatest service to his country came when he was Attorney General when along with Representative J. Proctor Knott, a Kentucky Democrat who was Chairman of the House Judiciary Committee, he drafted the legislation enacted by Congress that created an Electoral Commission to resolve the disputed 1876 Presidential election.[42]

The legislation was acceptable to the Democrats because they thought that the tie-breaking seat on the Electoral Commission would be occupied by Supreme Court Justice David Davis, who had become a Democrat after having been Abraham Lincoln's law partner and campaign manager. When Davis was elected to the Senate by the Illinois legislature while the bill was pending, the decisive seat fell to Justice Joseph Bradley, a Republican, who ultimately cast the deciding vote for Hayes. Bradley's disinterestedness was later supported by Professor Charles Fairman of Harvard in his exhaustive volume on the Electoral Commission,[43] part of the Oliver Wendell Holmes Devise History of the Supreme Court of the United States, though it was not conceded by Democrats at the time.

Although popular legend has it that an agreement to forego forcible continuation of Reconstruction was the price of Hayes' election (the infamous "Compromise of 1877"), in fact Redemption had already taken place in all states save South Carolina and

---

[40] A. Nevins (ed.), Hamilton Fish: The Inner History of the Grant Administration (New York: Dodd Mead, 1937), 844.

[41] 28 Simon (ed.), The Papers of Ulysses S. Grant (Carbondale: Southern Illinois U., 2005), 143.

[42] M. Northrop, A Grave Crisis in American History, 62 Century Magazine 923 (1901).

[43] C. Fairman, Five Justices and the Electoral Commission of 1877 (New York: Macmillan, 2009).

Louisiana and the Grant administration refused to embrace further coercion in those states.

As Minister to Vienna, to which he was appointed by President Chester A. Arthur after having sought Berlin,[44] Taft pressed for relief from limitations on American meat exports. In Russia from 1884 to 1885 he upheld the rights of visiting American Jews to engage in commercial and professional enterprises from which Jews were barred by Czarist legislation. After his return to the United States, he spoke of the death of the liberal Prince Rudolph, who is generally held to have died in a suicide pact. "The Crown Prince was of a literary and philosophical bent and had written books of weight and value. He had been associated with the army in such a practical manner as to be held in especial respect and esteem in competent military circles. His somewhat liberal ideas were carried into military life and I remember that innovations suggested by the Prince and Archduke John were of such a radical nature as to meet very vigorous opposition from the veteran circles. Had he lived and become Emperor I can see no reason for thinking that his reign would have been a less successful one than that of his father. I think the stories of his immorality have been exaggerated, as doubtless have been those of an estrangement between himself and his wife. He appeared by no means a person afflicted with melancholia and I am loth to believe that he took his own life. I am inclined rather to think that he was assassinated."[45]

As to Russia, Alphonso found "Alexander III ... a man frank in manner, and of a very genial and democratic disposition ... I should say, on the whole, that Russia is improving and progressing. I cannot say as to the intelligence among the people. The great attention of the government is centered on the army, on military power rather than popular education. They have institutions for education

---

[44] 30 Simon (ed.), The Papers of Ulysses S. Grant (Carbondale: Southern Illinois U., 2005), 287.

[45] "The Dead Crown Prince: Ex-Minister Taft's Recollections of Him," New York Times, February 6, 1889.

of children of the better classes, but nothing like the advantages for the military."[46] Alexander III, something of an unsung hero, was a supporter of the Holy Alliance, the Congress of Europe, and the Conference System that followed it, which together kept the peace in Europe for nearly a century; his life showed that an autocrat could also be a responsible international actor and a good European.

In 1885, Alphonso reported to Secretary of State Frelinghuysen that "[n]o foreigner is allowed to reside in Russia without a permit of residence as well as a passport. The difficulty is that the government in granting permits and licenses discriminates against foreign Jews, according to certain laws in force in Odessa and other cities, and declines to grant permits of residence to them unless they are merchants of the first guild, paying annually 900 rubles for a license."[47]

He was active in 1880 in a movement to seek a third term for President Grant, an affiliation used against President Taft when the third term issue was raised against Theodore Roosevelt in 1912.[48]

In 1887, Taft professed to be unalarmed by the gains made by the Union Labour and Prohibition parties in Cincinnati: "It is a good thing for the country, as I look at it, to have these old parties stirred up and to some extent perplexed by these rising young political organizations. [The Labour party] can hardly ask for anything the people will be willing to vote for that the two other parties will not be willing to concede."[49] This was the voice of a true conservative.

---

[46] L. Leonard, *supra*.

[47] "Russian Hatred of Jews: The Disclosures of Executive Document 470," New York Times, November 9, 1890, quoting A. Taft to Frelinghuysen, January 17, 1885.

[48] "An Unfortunate Precedent," New York Times, May 19, 1912.

[49] "Not Afraid of Them: Ex-Minister Taft sees Good in the Labor and Prohibition Parties," New York Times, April 24, 1887.

In the year before his death, the *New York Times*, noting a dearth of Ohio Republicans qualified for high office, noted that "Judge Taft was too old to be considered."[50]

His son President William H. Taft told a meeting of black Ohio clergymen in 1908 that "he was there for the purpose of expressing his sympathy with the Negro race in its struggle for better things: 'A sympathy which I have had from the time when I was a small boy, for I inherited it from my father Alphonso Taft, than whom the coloured race never had a better friend.'"[51]

Alphonso died in 1891. As a statesman, he had the prejudices with respect to both religion and the sectional conflict of a man of his place and time. His son William Howard Taft later wrote: "As I study the injustice that the radical Republicans did to Andrew Johnson, I am humiliated as a Republican. My father was a just man but I thought he sympathized with those who voted to impeach Johnson. I think his feeling against Johnson growing out of the assassination of Lincoln threw into the extremists of the Republican party a power that led to reconstruction and seriously affected to its detriment our country."[52] Although he was involved briefly in large events, he owes his enduring influence to his instruction of his five sons as a parent and the example as such that he set for them.

---

[50] "The Plight in which Ohio Republicans Find Themselves," New York Times, December 23, 1890.

[51] "Taft Congratulates Hughes on Victory," New York Times, September 16, 1908.

[52] WHT to Charles Taft II November 1, 1925.

THE SECOND GENERATION

William Howard Taft and his two brothers and two half-brothers came to maturity when the dominance of the Republican Party was at flood tide. They were in the Gilded Age, but not of it; in varying ways all were reformers who sought to curb its abuses, and all shared a family commitment to hard work and academic study.

The dominant political questions of their time involved the curbing and channeling of the powers of large private aggregates, both corporations and unions. No single citizen played a larger role in this than William Howard Taft, whose early Ohio decisions first legitimized and then curbed the powers of labor unions, who during the Benjamin Harrison administration helped draft and initiate prosecutions under the Sherman Antitrust Act, who 15 years later as President launched an unprecedented campaign of antitrust prosecutions and a federal corporation tax, and who set in motion legislative initiatives ultimately leading to creation of the Federal Reserve System and the Income Tax amendment.

CHARLES TAFT SR. (1843-1929)

Charles Taft was William Howard Taft's half-brother, by Alphonso Taft's first wife, Fanny Phelps. Spurred to academic excellence by his father, he graduated from Andover, received a B.A. and M.A. from Yale, an LL.B from Columbia, and a J.U.D. from Heidelberg. He acquired a large fortune of $15 million from his father-in-law, David Sinton—a fortune that helped sustain his brother, William Howard Taft, and nephew, Robert Taft, in politics. William Howard Taft publicly stated to Theodore Roosevelt: "you and my brother Charlie made that possible." A statement that irritated Roosevelt. Charles Taft's estate on his death in December 1929 was appraised at more than $6 million. Anna Sinton's estate,

Sinton Home on Pike Street

Taft Family Home

on her death in 1931, was estimated at more than $50 million. "She is reputed to have more than trebled the fortune which [her father] bequeathed her."

Her father's will made it mandatory that Mrs. Taft and her husband should occupy the old Sinton homestead on Pike Street as long as they lived. The neighborhood, once the most exclusive in the city, gradually has given way to factories. On one side of the homestead is a loft building and on the other a large book bindery.[1]

---

[1] "Mrs. Charles Taft of Cincinnati Dies," New York Times, February 1, 1931.

He was defeated as a candidate for the U.S. House of Representatives in 1872, but was elected in 1891 to the Ohio House for a two-year term and was elected to the U.S. House of Representatives in 1895. It was said that "Charlie's [George B.] Cox-sponsored term in Congress was, to say the least, undistinguished." He had as publisher of the *Cincinnati Times-Star*, which he acquired in 1879, opposed the Cox machine, but "when in 1894 the politically ambitious Taft accepted the nomination for Congress from Cox's stubby hands, the *Times-Star* became the Mecca boss' fanatical supporter."[2]

Charles Taft Sr.

In 1876, he led a committee urging land assembly for a new courthouse in Cincinnati, which led to litigation re-establishing the federal government's right of eminent domain.[3]

Anna Sinton Taft

Speaker Thomas Reed, an unsuccessful candidate for the Republican Presidential nomination in 1900 as an anti-Imperialist, offered Charles Taft the second place on his ticket, which was declined. He was a Theodore Roosevelt presidential elector in 1904, and attended the Republican national conventions in 1900, 1908, and 1912. He considered running for the U.S. Senate in 1909 but withdrew from the contest in the Ohio legislature. Along with Theodore Roosevelt and Elihu Root, he urged the bringing of a criminal libel indictment under the Assimilative Crimes Act against a political adversary, an effort rejected by the U.S. Supreme Court in

---

[2] F. Russell, The Shadow of Blooming Grove, Warren Harding and His Times (New York: McGraw Hill, 1968), 119.

[3] Kohler v. U.S., 91 U.S. 367 (1876).

1911.[4] In 1889, he opposed relaxation of the Sunday laws, which he saw as "fostering debauchery, opening the stores, and pressing into service that day the working people." He decried "German Know-Nothingism," which he identified with Sunday saloons, crime, and the rise of radical labor,"[5] thus sharing some of the nativist prejudices of his father.

He was the successful proprietor of the *Cincinnati Times-Star*, which he ran on conservative principles, eschewing yellow journalism. He introduced the use of leased wire services. He also owned the Cubs baseball team, but was unsuccessful in an effort to buy the *New York World*, which was acquired by Joseph Pulitzer. He successfully purchased and developed the 80,000-acre Taft Ranch in Texas, which included the towns of Taft, Portland, and Sinton, Texas. He sold 30,000 acres on generous terms to his tenant farmers, realizing $1 million on the sale. President William H. Taft visited the town in 1909; in 1921 a huge auction was held attended by more than 5,000 people; the family corporation finally disposing of its remaining land in 1928. He was active in the affairs of the Dixie Terminal Company. His wife was Jean White Ingalls; he had two children, a daughter [Anna] Louise of Seattle, and a son Peter, who died in 1889 shortly after his graduation from Yale, where he was valedictorian. His widow left $2 million for the study of the humanities at the University of Cincinnati; she decried the modern "lack of emphasis on the value of thought, conduct, and character." At least some of the Tafts shared the early American emphasis on the benefits of classical studies; Jefferson had urged that the books from which primary school students were taught to read should inculcate the basic facts of Greek, Roman, English, and American history, to render citizens immune from the blandishments of demagogues. He codified the Ohio school laws, and was the major benefactor of the Cincinnati Institute of Fine Arts and the Cincinnati Symphony. His political

---

[4] U.S. v. Press Publishing, 219 U.S. 1 (1911).

[5] Z. Miller, Boss Cox's Cincinnati: Urban Politics in the Progressive Era (New York: Oxford, 1968), 54, 65.

influence rests not on his own career but on the influence of his newspaper and on his financial support of his half-brother Will.

LOUISE TAFT SEMPLE (1879-1961)

Charles Taft's daughter, Louise Taft Semple, married William T. Semple of Seattle, a Professor of Greek from 1920 to 1959. On her death, her bequest for the study of classics at the University of Cincinnati was the largest gift that it had received in its history. The university, an underappreciated institution, now has a classical library of 260,000 volumes that is the largest of any American university and a classics department with 13 full-time members.

PETER RAWSON TAFT (1846-1889)

Peter Rawson Taft was a second half-brother of William Howard Taft. He was valedictorian at Yale but later suffered a mental breakdown. He married Annie Matilda Hulbert; they had a son, Hulbert Taft Sr. (1877-1959), who is discussed below.

Peter Rawson Taft

HENRY WATERS TAFT (1859-1945)

Henry Taft, another son of Alphonso Taft, was born in 1859. After graduating from Yale, he received his legal training at the University of Cincinnati and Columbia. He practiced at the Cadwalader firm in New York (later Cadwalader, Wickersham and Taft, which still survives) throughout his entire career, which was briefly interrupted by his service as a Special Assistant to the U.S. Attorney General, where he conducted the early stages of the successful case against the Tobacco Trust and the first successful

Henry W. Taft

criminal prosecution under the Sherman Act, that against the Licorice Trust, in which the corporate defendants were convicted and the individual defendants were acquitted. He argued several notable cases on procedure during his time with the government, including *Hale v. Henkel,*[6] *McAlister v. Henkel,*[7] and *United States v. McAndrews and Forbes.*[8]

On returning to private practice, he was involved in other significant antitrust cases involving the United Fruit Company[9] and the New Haven Railroad, and argued eight other cases before the U.S. Supreme Court.[10]

He presided over the New York Selective Service Board during World War I and was a member of the New York Board of Education and the Board of the City College of New York. He was instrumental in the creation of some of New York's most famous high schools, as well as of a normal college, which became Hunter College. He was a Trustee of the New York Public Library from 1908 to 1915 and was President of the University Settlement fostered by James Speyer, a client, and his wife Ellin Prince Speyer. The University Settlement, with many branches, is today the largest settlement

---

[6] 201 U.S. 41 (1906).

[7] 201 U.S. 90 (1906).

[8] 149 Fed. 823 (1906).

[9] American Banana Co. v. United Fruit Co., 213 U.S. 347 (1909).

[10] Hunt v. New York Cotton Exchange, 205 U.S. 322 (1907); Babbitt v. Dutches, 216 U.S. 102 (1910); Long Sault Development v. Call, 242 U.S. 272 (1916); Alice State Bank v. Houston, 247 U.S. 240 (1918); Banco Mexicano v. Deutsche Bank, 263 U.S. 591 (1924); Moore v. New York Cotton Exchange, 270 U.S. 593 (1926); Taft v. Bowers, 278 U.S. 470 (1929); and Taft v. Helvering, 311 U.S. 195 (1940).

house for immigrants in the United States. He was ahead of his time in urging in 1920 that the work done by Legal Aid Societies in civil cases should become a public function.[11]

He unsuccessfully sought election to the New York State Assembly in 1882 and the New York Supreme [Trial] Court in 1898. He later declined an offer of appointment to that court and had already declined an offer of the Republican nomination for Governor of New York in 1894. This decision was founded on his wife's resistance to loss of income; at the time, he was earning $55,000 a year, the equivalent of more than $1 million now.[12] This familial devotion to comfort over power limited his direct influence, though his independence of judgment owed something to his divorce from the responsibilities of public office.

He was a delegate to the 1920 and 1924 Republican national conventions and served as President of the Association of the Bar of the City of New York. At various times, he also declined a federal district judgeship, a Republican nomination for Congress, and an offer of appointment as United States Attorney for the Southern District of New York. He published several volumes of papers and memoirs, a book on local government reform, and two books about Japan, in which, echoing Theodore Roosevelt, he urged giving Japan a free hand in China.[13]

In 1920 he urged: "[Japan's] population is growing at the rate of 600,000 a year and the most ordinary considerations of prudence require that she should protect her people against the evils of overcrowding her already densely populated islands … she seeks to obtain an economic foothold in Manchuria, Mongolia, Shantung

---

[11] New York Times, January 4, 1920.

[12] J. Anderson, William Howard Taft: An Intimate History (New York: Norton, 1981), 45.

[13] H. Taft, Japan and America: A Journey and a Political Survey (New York: Macmillan, 1932); Japan and the Far East Conference (New York: Macmillan, 1927); see also H. Taft, Our Relations with Japan (New York: Japan Society, 1920).

and perhaps Siberia, as a means of procuring raw materials that she will encourage her people to emigrate to those countries is not only probable but seemingly justifiable."[14]

He re-affirmed this view in 1932: "By the Lansing-Ischii correspondence we stated as a feature of our national policy that we 'recognize that territorial propinquity creates special relations between countries and consequently the Government of the United States recognizes that Japan has special interests in China, particularly in the part to which her possessions are contiguous.' And while this statement never amounted to more than an informal statement of administration policy and was finally merged in or eliminated or modified by more formal documents, it still embodies a principle the force of which the U.S. must always recognize and it is as important to Japan as the Monroe Doctrine is to this country."[15]

The Lansing-Ischii correspondence had been preceded by a memorandum of a conversation in 1905 between Secretary of War Taft and Japanese Prime Minister Katsura under the terms of which the United States agreed that a Japanese protectorate over Korea would stabilize the region and Japan disclaimed any interest in the Philippines.[16] This policy of the Theodore Roosevelt administration was eroded by President Taft's Secretary of State, Philander Knox, who embraced an "Open Door" for American railway interests in China, and was further eroded by Secretary of State Stimson's resistance to Japanese hegemony over Manchuria during the Hoover administration and by Secretary Cordell Hull and Assistant Secretary Dean Acheson's imposition of an oil embargo against Japan and demands for evacuation not only of China proper but of Manchuria as well before Pearl Harbor.

---

[14] H. Taft, Our Relations with Japan (New York: Japan Society, 1920), 24.

[15] H. Taft, Japan and America: A Journey and a Political Survey (New York: Macmillan, 1932), 362.

[16] http://web.archive.org/web/20120209012012/http://people.usd. edu/~sbucklin/primary/taftkatsura.htm T. Dennett, "President Roosevelt's Secret Pact with Japan," Current History, October 1924

In a collection of essays published in 1920, Henry Taft urged development of America's waterways; resistance to Bolshevism; and the enactment of a statute rendering conspiracy to overthrow the government a criminal offense, anticipating the Smith Act of 1940.[17]

A second collection of essays published in 1941[18] was notable for its chapters on women and Jewish lawyers at the New York Bar. It also contains a chapter memorably denouncing the "heart balm" actions for alienation of affections, criminal conversation, breach of promise of marriage, and seduction as tools of blackmail. Today, after being abolished by constitutional amendments in more than 30 states, they are now being revived as civil actions for sexual harassment, with similar results.

Taft's last collection of essays includes an unexplained one-page appendix in tribute to New York's Jewish population, concluding, "Out of the Jewish group there probably is being produced a greater proportion of educated men and women than out of any other group that may be classified on the basis of race or religion or nationality. It seems logical to conclude that through them the moral and intellectual tone of the community is elevated."[19] Published just after the fall of France and the Vichy and Nazi legislation disqualifying Jews as lawyers, this appears to have been Henry Taft's personal protest against the events of 1940.

His views on international relations corresponded to those of his brother, President Taft. He co-authored a book, *The Covenanter*,

---

[17] H. Taft, Occasional Papers and Addresses of an American Lawyer (New York: Macmillan, 1920).

[18] H. Taft, Legal Miscellanies: Six Decades of Change and Progress (New York: Macmillan, 1941). *See also* H. Taft, An Essay on Conversation (New York: Macmillan, 1927); H. Taft, Kindred Arts: Conversation and Public Speaking (New York: Macmillan, 1929); H. Taft, A Century and a Half at the New York Bar (New York: Privately Printed, 1938); H. Taft, Opinions, Literary and Otherwise (New York: Macmillan, 1934).

19 *Id.*, 211-12.

Horace, William Howard,
Charles, and Henry

with his brother and Harvard President A. Lawrence Lowell expressing the views of the supporters of the League to Enforce Peace with its faith in international arbitration. He was President of the Japan Society of New York from 1923 to 1928 and from 1934 to the outbreak of war in 1941. The Society was at its peak in the late 1920s, with 1,300 members, declining to 850 under pressure from the depression in 1933 and to 517 by October 1941 because of the strain in U.S.–Japanese relations. On December 8, 1941, he summarily severed his connection: "I hereby resign as President of the Japan Society and as a member of the Board of Directors, my resignation to take place at once."[20]

He did not live to see the post-war revival of the Society in 1952, under the auspices of John D. Rockefeller III and others. His wife, the former Julia Walbridge Smith, was a convert to Roman Catholicism. He died in 1945,[21] survived by two sons, Walbridge Taft and William H. Taft II; a daughter, Louise, had married George Snowden and died in 1926. He was a virtual prototype of a civic-minded New York lawyer, but was conspicuous and unusual in his receptivity to the rise of new groups at the Bar.

---

[20] Japan Society, Celebrating a Century, 1907-2007 (New York: Japan Society, 2007).

[21] See the obituary in the 1946 Association of the Bar of the City of New York Yearbook.

HORACE DUTTON TAFT (1861-1943)

Horace Taft, William Howard Taft's youngest brother, left us a volume of memoirs, *Memories and Opinions*, published in 1942.[22]

Horace Dutton Taft

He recalled his childhood: "My sun shone brighter if we brought home good reports." "My father had an intense prejudice against tobacco, and none of us partook of it; he had no such feeling in regard to wine and liquor." "None of [our] extracurricular activities were arranged for us. If a boy did his duty in the school, was honest, reasonably unselfish and held his own with the other boys, that was enough. We learned to swim, but not because anybody taught us. We had plenty of games, but they were not organized. No radio, no Victrola, no automobile, no movies … I wish my father had put me into the hands of a carpenter one summer."[23]

Horace referred to his father as having a "New England conscience." Echoing him, he declared: "Nobody has referred to a New York conscience or a Pennsylvania conscience."

His attitude toward the aftermath of the Civil War is today unfashionable: "it is a pity that they cannot in some way set up a memorial to those seven senators [who acquitted President Johnson] to indicate the kind of stuff of which the statesmen of a Republic should be made. [Johnson] was a thoroughly conscientious man, anxious to carry out the policy that Lincoln had undoubtedly had in his mind. He was clumsy, obstinate and had a kink in his mind in regard to the Constitution. History now deals very harshly with Grant as President, but not unjustly so. When my father was appointed to the Cabinet to take the place of the Secretary of War

---

[22] (New York: Macmillan, 1942).

[23] *Id.* 11-15.

who was retiring because of peculations, some newspapers thanked God that they had got an honest man in the Cabinet."[24]

Hayes he regarded as "a very conscientious man, right on all, or nearly all, of the main questions that came up." "My own feeling was, and is, that the North made a horrible mistake in the reconstruction and in conferring the ballot indiscriminately on the enfranchised slaves and that it must take the consequences and leave the South to work out its own problem. Interference from the North can only exacerbate the bitterness between races and hinder progress."

Unlike his siblings, in his early life he was a supporter of free trade and of Grover Cleveland.[25]

Writing of his brother William Howard's tenure in the Philippines, he observed: "In the various centres of American and English population in the Orient there gathered a goodly proportion of the scum of the earth and at the opening of a new era in the Philippines they naturally flocked to Manila."

Writing of 1912, he observed: "It was impossible for my brother to avoid choosing one side or the other though he agreed with neither … he had no use for the methods of big business as was often shown in his court decisions, conversations, prosecutions and laws proposed … he was only convinced of Roosevelt's vicious hostility when it was perfectly evident to everyone else. The Taft administration occupied all the ground that [Roosevelt] had occupied when President. [Roosevelt] was compelled to be much more radical … a man who did not know what fair play meant. [Taft] praised Aldrich because he agreed with his campaign for banking reform."

On the Taft School, which he founded, Horace observed: "The movies, the radio, the automobile make it more difficult for boys in any grade of society to lead the simple life and to avoid undue dissipation of their energies. The ideal system is that by which each boy is trained according to his ability and develops the best that is in

---

[24] *Id.* 27.

[25] J. Anderson, *supra*, 95.

Taft School

him." His father "panicked as if a great crime had been committed" when Horace decided to become a schoolmaster."[26] The school was established in 1893, with 5 masters and 30 boarders. The required curriculum included Latin, Math, English, History, and Science, with Greek, French, and German as elective courses. By 1930, the school had 323 students and 27 masters; and by 2018, 598 students and 129 faculty. Horace Taft retired from the headmastership in 1936. The school became co-educational in 1971. Horace Taft gave the school its motto: *Non ut sibi ministretur sed ut ministret* ("Not to be served but to serve."). On his retirement, *Time* magazine said, "In a profession studded with Grand Old Men [he] was the grandest of them all."[27] An honorary degree citation from Williams College referred to him as "headmaster of headmasters."

---

[26] C. Anthony, Nellie Taft: The Unconventional First Lady of the Ragtime Era (New York: Morrow, 2005), 65.

[27] Time, June 1935.

He had an aversion to teachers' colleges: "They have a strangle hold upon the public school system. Superintendents generally come from these institutions and the teacher who would seek promotion must follow the methods they approve. A normal school is an institution in which subnormal students are taught by abnormal teachers. No teacher can begin his career in a public school without taking a course which in the eyes of countless sensible men is largely a waste of time."[28]

He urged privileged graduates to give time to Boys' Clubs: "One night a week, one Sunday a month, one week a year, ten boys." "This democratic life of ours involves many things, among them cooperation, self-government, obedience to authority, the doing of much uninteresting drudgery and so forth. An education which combines these in proper proportion is what we should aim at." He quoted Goethe: "Everything that liberates the spirit without a corresponding growth in self-mastery is pernicious." "The further we move on to the Golden Age in which the people shall rule, the more vital becomes the necessity that the people should obey."[29]

He summarized his educational philosophy and that of his school: "In scholarship I am a perfect democrat in wishing that every boy should have a chance to show what is in him, but a perfect aristocrat in feeling that a boy who shows that he has the right stuff should have every opportunity for development and that all of our strength should not be expended on the 'duffer.'"[30]

In politics he was conservative but independent. "In 1941, he was among forty-five prominent Americans who signed a telegram to President Roosevelt upholding the foreign policy of the administration." Unlike his nephew Robert, he was an outspoken interventionist before World War II: "We, in the 'helping England'

---

[28] *Id.* 226.

[29] *Id.* 246.

[30] Quoted in I. Ross, *The Tafts: An American Family* (Cleveland: World Publishing, 1964), 275.

organization are carrying out the strongest propaganda we can … hatred of England defeated the League of Nations and the appeal to that hatred on the part of the opponents of the League was the most discreditable part of the isolationist agenda."[31] In his old age, five years after his retirement when he was 80, he flirted with the eugenic movement, his happily unpublished "Taft Plan for Human Betterment" being too much even for Margaret Sanger.[32]

He was vehemently critical of the Roosevelt administration's tolerant attitude toward the sit-down strikes in the automobile industry: "All the good our President has done, and I am frank to admit that he has done much good, has been overcome by the growing lawlessness and class-hatred in the last several months. A democratic people exist on obedience and reverence for the law. There is nothing else in a free country."[33] In this view, he was to be echoed by his nephew Robert.

A conservative in both education and politics, he shared the interests and values of his brothers.

WILLIAM HOWARD TAFT (1857-1930)

The Man

President William H. Taft was always a large man. In his youth, he was involved in one or two fistfights, which contributed to his self-confidence. In maturity, his ideal weight was said to be 250 pounds, though he frequently exceeded it, at one time in his presidency weighing nearly 400 pounds. There were numerous jests about this; on reporting to Elihu Root, then Secretary of War, that he had arrived in good shape at the governor's residence in the Philippines,

---

[31] New York Times, October 1, 1940.

[32] "Giving It the Old School Try: The Taft Plan for Human Betterment," in nyu.edu/projects/sanger/articles/taftplan/php, see HT to Sanger, May 8, 1941

[33] Obituary, New York Times, January 29, 1943.

William Howard Taft and Mother

he received in reply a telegram inquiring "how is the horse." Although the legend that he got stuck in his bathtub appears to have been false, there is a famous photograph showing a plurality of small boys disporting themselves in it; there is another photograph showing Taft mounted on a water buffalo, to the latter's disadvantage. At the 1912 Republican Convention, the pro-Taft Texas delegation "had a flagpole to which was attached a huge pair of trousers made of wool from Texas Angora goats, on it a placard with the inscription "As pants the hart for cooling streams, so Texas pants for Taft."[34]

When speaking at Yale after assuming his post there after retirement from the presidency, his hosts found that the chair provided for the speaker was not large enough for Taft. Thoughts turned to a portly furnace man who worked in a basement, but there was some consternation when his chair, when retrieved, proved to have a bull moose on each arm. On one of Taft's early visits to Panama, "Wallace, the engineer had had the forethought to have one large dining room chair taken to a blacksmith shop and thoroughly braced and bolted to bear the weight of the distinguished visitor, a courtesy that Taft particularly appreciated since as he told Wallace, it gave him a great feeling of security throughout his stay."[35] General Goethals, who succeeded to some of John Findley Wallace's functions after

---

[34] M. Teague (ed.), Mrs L: Conversations with Alice Roosevelt Longworth (London: Duckworth, 1987), 88.

[35] D. McCullough, The Path Between the Seas: The Creation of the Panama Canal, 1830-1914 (New York: Simon and Schuster, 1977), 446.

Taft regretfully fired Wallace, referred to Taft as "the only clean fat man he had ever known."[36]

Alice Longworth said: "Dear Mr. Taft! I can see him now, a great pink porpoise of a man, sitting in the back of an open touring car, with his hands on his rotund belly."[37] He once ruefully observed "it is possible that the deprivation of everything good to eat does affect a man's bubbling appreciation of life."[38]

Notwithstanding this, Alice conceded that as a dancer Taft was "very light on his feet."[39]

Of her de facto chaperone on a cruise to the Far East: "I never once saw him either cross or upset. He was always beaming and genial and friendly through all his official duties and the task of keeping harmony among his varied and somewhat temperamental armies of trippers." His lectures to her were "more in sorrow than in anger. I always felt I could 'get away with' whatever it was he objected to."[40] A plaint of his from time to time was 'Alice, I think I ought to know if you are engaged to Nick [Longworth],' to which my reply was 'More or less, Mr. Secretary, more or less.'"

On his appointment to the Supreme Court, the lean Justice Holmes speculated that Taft might not have the energy to keep up with the work, but Taft proved to be one of the most productive of justices.

Occasionally President Taft made impolitic remarks, notably, in 1912, "even a rat in a corner will fight" and "I have been a man of straw long enough" or his reference to the Payne-Aldrich tariff bill

---

[36] *Id.* 510.

[37] M. Teague (ed.), Mrs L: Conversations with Alice Roosevelt Longworth (London: Duckworth, 1987), 139.

[38] M. Gratke, In Sickness and in Health: Conception of Disease and Ability in Presidential Bodies," www.scholarship.claremount.edu 23828.

[39] M. Teague (ed.), Mrs L: Conversations with Alice Roosevelt Longworth (London: Duckworth, 1987), 87.

[40] M. Teague (ed.), Mrs L: Conversations with Alice Roosevelt Longworth (London: Duckworth, 1987), 69.

WHT in Philippines

as "the best bill the Republican party ever passed." He considered that Theodore Roosevelt's "power of concentrated statement is that of a genius." The Progressives, for him, were "a religious cult with a father at the head of it."

Similarly he said of William Jennings Bryan, his opponent in 1908: "When the history of this period is written, Bryan will stand out as one of the most remarkable men of our generation and one of the biggest political men of our country."[41]

"We have been treading on air and need to get back to the ground again."

---

[41]   1 A. Butt, Taft and Roosevelt: The Intimate Papers of Archie Butt (New York: Doubleday, 1930), 286.

Although frequently portrayed as a maladroit politician in reference to his own personal interests, he was actually a far-seeing and effective one as respects his great causes, the strengthening of the judiciary, the curbing of excesses by both business and labor, and resistance to socialism and collectivism. Although a man of peace, he was also a clear-sighted realist about international relations. Dean Acheson's tribute to Harry Truman fits him well: "he did not let his ego get between himself and his work."

As President, he was charged with "vacillation, irritability, a complete inability to lead," and credited with "an excellent judicial mind, an integrity which was never clouded, great talent as an administrator, a wide and broad sympathy for human problems." He was once taken to a Bowery flophouse, whose inmates he addressed in his characteristic fashion: "If there is one thought I would convey to you it would be to hope, or forget the difficulties, the disasters of the past and go ahead with the thought of the future and the big things it may have in store for you."[42]

The justices of the Supreme Court have historically been a contentious lot, sometimes unable to agree even on the text of farewell letters for their retiring brethren. Justice Owen Roberts never got such a letter, because of the emendations to the letter requested by Justices Black and Douglas. Justice Clarke's letter was not signed by Justice McReynolds. This renders even more remarkable the letter received by Taft on his retirement in 1930, drafted by Justice Holmes and signed by all the justices, including Brandeis and McReynolds:

> "We call you Chief Justice still—for we cannot give up the title by which we have known you all these later years and which you have made dear to us. We cannot let you leave us without trying to tell you how dear you have made it. You came to us with achievement in other fields and with the prestige of the illustrious place that you lately

---

[42] E. Morris, Theodore Rex (New York: Random House, 2001), 231.

held and you showed us in new form your voluminous capacity for getting work done. Your humor that smoothed the rough places, your golden heart that brought you love from every side and most of all from your brethren, whose tasks you have made happy and light. We grieve at your illness, but your spirit has given life and impulse that will abide whether you are with us or away."[43]

Even Felix Frankfurter, who had said many harsh things of him, conceded on his retirement: "He is a dear man—a true human."[44] Early in his life, he was described as "the honest greenhorn at the poker table." Speaker Joseph Cannon paid tribute to his occasional political maladritness: "If Taft were Pope, he'd want to appoint some Protestants to the College of Cardinals." Will Rogers at the time of his death observed: "It's great to be great but it's greater to be human. We are parting with three hundred pounds of solid charity to everybody and love and affection for all his fellow men." Taft was also said to have "the most infectious chuckle in the history of politics.. It reminded me of the cluck a whippoorwill gives a laugh to himself when he has been whistling with special vim and mischief."[45]

Youth

An account of President Taft's careers must start with remarks at a reunion of the Taft family in Uxbridge, Massachusetts, in 1874, where it was declared that "they have wasted none of the time or the money of the public by abuses requiring judicial investigations."[46]

---

[43] 280 U.S. v (1930).

[44] Frankfurter to Holmes, March 3, 1930, in R. Mennel and C. Compston (eds.), Holmes and Frankfurter: Their Correspondence 1912-34 (Hanover, NH: U. Press of New England, 1996), 249.

[45] S. Hess, "Big Bill Taft," 17 American Heritage No. 6 (1966)

[46] H. Pringle, William Howard Taft (New York: Farrar & Rinehart, 2 vols. 1939) (hereafter "Pringle").

Taft as a young man forswore support of Roscoe Conkling and James Blaine who "smell too much of rings." He was described by the Kansas editor William Allen White as an "Angel of Light—Lovely Character." Early in his political career, he was credited with the "sunny disposition of an innocent child." In a jury speech early in his career as a prosecutor, he declared: "We deny nothing to Mr. Campbell except integrity and we say that that is the essential, the indispensable quality of a member of the Bar."[47]

He regarded William McKinley whose reputation is now sought to be restored by Robert Merry[48] and Karl Rove[49] as a "timid statesman" of "demonstrate[d] incapacity."[50] Judge Learned Hand, one of McKinley's contemporaries, viewed him as "a pharisaical jellyfish."[51] The efforts to rehabilitate McKinley are of a piece with recent tributes to the depressed and indolent Calvin Coolidge, about whom his contemporary H.L. Mencken observed: "Not a word came out of him on the subject of Prohibition. Not once did he challenge the speculative lunacy that finally brought the nation to bankruptcy. And all he could be induced to do about the foreign debts was to hand the nuisance on to poor Hoover."[52]

Of many of the Americans in the Philippines, President Taft said, echoing his brother Horace, "they forgot family and home. They betrayed their government and became thieves, removed

---

[47] 1 Pringle 90.

[48] R. Merry, President McKinley: Architect of the American Century (New York: Simon and Schuster, 2017).

[49] K. Rove, The Triumph of William McKinley (New York: Simon and Schuster, 2015)

[50] 1 Pringle 150.

[51] L. Hand to Augustus Hand, November 6, 1898, in C. Jordan (ed.), Reason and Imagination: The Selected Correspondence of Learned Hand: 1897-1961 (New York: Oxford U., 2013), 6.

[52] H.L. Mencken, "The Coolidge Mystery," Baltimore Evening Sun, December 29, 1930, in M. Rodgers, The Impossible H.L. Mencken (New York: Doubleday, 1991), 414, 417.

from the restraints of home life, without their families and with a disposition to gamble or drink or lead a lewd life."[53]

Of Harding, before his election, he said, notwithstanding the nominating speech that Harding had given for him in 1912: "he falls so far below the standard of Presidents we like to form in our minds that it distresses me. Everything sounds cheap and makes a man of intelligent discrimination wince when he reads."[54]

He advised his son Charles, who was going to France during the Great War, to think often of his fiancée since this "strengthens a boy against temptations which crowd in on him in the Army," and added, "you will almost be raped unless you brace yourself."[55]

His conservatism could occasionally lead him astray in his judgments. He was seriously taken aback by the raffishness of the German Ambassador to the United States, Count Bernstorff, whose standing in Germany was later impaired by the famous "bathing beauty photograph," showing him simultaneously embracing two scantily clad young lovelies in bathing suits. "The President is not over-partial to the Germans, and he has no liking at all for Bernstorff, whom he thinks very much of a prig. He has never thought the same of him since he saw him playing golf with a lady in his shirt sleeves. He did not object so much [to the lack of a coat] as he did to the fact that he wore a pink shirt and red suspenders."[56]

Bernstorff, however, made heroic efforts to foster a negotiated peace during World War I, and after it drafted a proposed treaty for the German delegation at Versailles generally conceded to be far wiser than the Treaty as adopted, founded a Democratic Club in Berlin, led the German League of Nations Association and a Pro Palestina group fostering Zionism, sought to ban bombing of

---

[53] 1 Pringle 168.

[54] WHT to Gus Karger, August 22, 1920, Folder 65, Cincinnati Museum Centre, quoted in J. Lurie, *supra*, 190.

[55] 2 Pringle 905ff.

[56] 1 A. Butt, *Taft and Roosevelt: The Intimate Letters of Archie Butt* (New York: Doubleday, 1930), 267.

civilians as the German delegate to the Preparatory Disarmament Conference, and went into exile in Switzerland upon the accession to power of the Von Papen government in 1932, clearly understanding what lay ahead.[57]

Taft's brother Horace, headmaster of the Taft School, once told his brother: "if you get stuck, I can give you a place in the school—the chair of Christian Manhood."[58]

In his *Duties of Citizenship*, he urged young men to go into politics: "the wealthy young man has to struggle much more and has to exhibit a moral courage much greater than that of the poor man [because of the] temptation to lack of effort and idleness, dilettantism, pure pleasure. [He can offer] the beneficial influence of disinterested patriotism and attention to public affairs ... there is such a class in England which has done wonders for their politics and the high tone of their public men ... one who does not do so is violating his duty." "Character is formed by the practice of self-restraint and self-sacrifice, by overcoming obstacles ... of the sons of those who have luxurious homes and cherishing surroundings only the few who have force of character successfully to resist these enervating influences will be among the leaders of the next generation."[59]

Majorities and minorities, he said, must "exercise that self-restraint without which popular government is absolutely impossible ... must keep within the checks of the law and the Constitution if the Government is to be preserved." Further, "the first wave of popular will should not find immediate expression in legislation."[60]

---

[57] G. Liebmann, Diplomacy Between the Wars: Five Diplomats and the Shaping of the Modern World (London: I.B. Tauris, 2011), ch. 3.

[58] 1 Pringle 162.

[59] WHT, quoted in J. Patterson, Mr. Republican (New York: Houghton Mifflin, 1972), 14.

[60] "He who conquers himself," Fresno, October 10, 1909, in 3 D. Burton (ed.), Collected Works of William H. Taft 265 (Athens, OH: Ohio U. Press, 2004) (hereafter "W.H. Taft, Works").

One aspect of character for him was "real genuine desire to make everybody happy by the little things of life, which after all constitute nearly all there is in life."[61]

Taft's hostility to the materialist excesses of the Gilded Age was an inheritance from his father, who on departing Vermont forswore going into law practice in New York City because "the notorious selfishness and dishonesty of the great mass of men you find in New York is in my mind a serious objection to settling there."[62]

Taft considered that self-respecting people should aspire "to affect government instead of being dependent on it."[63]

He alluded to "the irresponsible position of power to which the Republican Party was elevated by the [Civil] War." In his eulogy of Grover Cleveland in 1909 he credited Cleveland with checking "the corruption and demoralization in the Republican Party which were a necessary result of continued power during the War and the decade succeeding it."[64]

Taft was a Unitarian in matters of religion: "I do not believe in the divinity of Christ."

A Unitarian minister later recalled that he was "a very enthusiastic member of the Unity Club as a young man, and once took the part of a fairy in a fairy play. Will must have weighed 175 pounds then and made a very plump fairy to be sure."[65]

As a young man, he turned down an offer of the presidency of Yale University in 1899, believing that his Unitarianism rendered him unacceptable to a university founded upon Christian principles. However, he recognized "the elevating influence that [religion] has had and always will have in the history of mankind." In the

---

[61] "A Soft Answer Turneth Away Wrath," Mormon Tabernacle, September 26, 1909, in 3 W.H. Taft, Works 206.

[62] 1 Pringle 8.

[63] 1 Pringle 43ff.

[64] "Grover Cleveland," March 18, 1909, in 3 W.H. Taft, Works 59.

[65] "Taft Once Unitarian Fairy," New York Times, August 4, 1908.

Philippines, he negotiated with the Vatican to purchase the large land-holdings of the friars,"[66] acquired in 1903 for $7,239,000. He was careful to make clear that this was a commercial negotiation not constituting recognition of the Vatican as a state. "It was essential that the religious orders should cease to be agricultural landlords."[67] In his experience, Catholics "quarrel among themselves, but like the Democratic Party, they stand together against outsiders.[68]

He insisted on not discussing religion in political campaigns: "to go into a discussion of creed I will not do whether I am defeated or not."[69] "I believe the Catholic Church to be one of the bulwarks against socialism and anarchy in this country and I welcome its presence here."[70]

He lamented the fact that "today it is not true that [the ministry] attracts the ablest young men and this, I think, is a distinct loss to our society."[71] He accumulated "one of the nation's premier collections of law books."[72]

Taft frequently spoke to Jewish audiences, decrying Czarist Russia's "present humiliating and degrading prohibition against any of our citizens wishing temporarily to sojourn in foreign countries because of race or religion."[73] He was ultimately to abrogate the 1832 treaty that permitted this.[74]

---

[66] 1 Pringle 45.

[67] W.H. Taft, "Duties of Citizenship," in 1 W.H. Taft, Works 70ff.

[68] 1 Pringle 222.

[69] 1 Pringle 374.

[70] 2 Pringle 830ff.

[71] "Learned Professions and Political Government," University of Pennsylvania, February 22, 1903, 2 W.H. Taft, Works 205.

[72] C. Anthony, Nellie Taft: The Unconventional First Lady of the Ragtime Era (New York: Morrow, 2005), 87.

[73] Inaugural Address, March 4, 1909.

[74] W. La Feber, The American Search for Opportunity, 1865-1913, 2 Cambridge History of American Foreign Relations, 232.

He reiterated this protest in his 1911 Annual Message.

In a speech in Charlotte in 1909, he noted that "in three gubernatorial campaigns, my father was defeated in Republican conventions on the ground of his decision in the Bible case."[75]

In his book on *Liberty Under Law*, he declared that "[e]very university should encourage its students to the worship of God. It is unfortunate that we cannot well unite religion and moral training in our public schools. Men may be moral and not be religious, but they are exceptions." This sentiment was later echoed by the British jurist Patrick Devlin: "Some people will do the right thing out of charity, but for the great mass of men faith and hope are necessary also."

Taft's assessment of his administration to his wife in the July preceding his anticipated defeat in the 1912 election testified to his lack of personal vaingloriousness:

> "There are other and better things than being exceedingly popular. Roosevelt was exceedingly popular and still is in many quarters for reasons that I should not like to have attributed to me. I have held the office of President once, and that is more than most have, so I am content to retire from it with the consciousness that I have done the best I could, and have accomplished a good deal in one way or another. I have strengthened the Supreme Bench, have given them a good deal of new and valuable legislation, have not interfered with business, have kept the peace and on the whole have led people to pursue their various occupations without interruption. It is a very humdrum uninteresting administration and does not attract the attention or enthusiasm of anybody, but after I am out I think that you and I can look back to some pleasure in having done something for the

---

[75] "Judicial Decisions as an Issue in Politics," McClure's, June 1909, in 3 W.H. Taft, Works 90ff.

benefit of the public."[76] He declared that "the negative virtue of having taken no step to interfere with the coming of prosperity and the comfort of the people is one that ought highly to commend an administration and the party responsible for it, as worthy of further continuance in office. The great bulk of our people are not emotional, undiscriminating, superficially minded, non-thinking, or hero-worshipping. They have the virtue of sober second thought."[77]

The young Walter Lippmann gave a less kind assessment in 1914:

> "Taft was the perfect routineer trying to run government as automatically as possible. His sincerity consisted in utter respect for form; he denied himself whatever leadership he was capable of, and outwardly at least he tried to 'balance' the government. His greatest passions seem to be purely administrative and legal. The people did not like it. They said it was dead. They were right. They had grown accustomed to a humanly liberating atmosphere in which formality was an instrument instead of an idol. They had seen the Roosevelt influence adding to the resources of life."
>
> "[Roosevelt's opponents] felt that along with obviously good things, this sudden national fertility might breed a monster—that a leadership like Roosevelt's might indeed prove dangerous, as giving birth may lead

---

[76] WHT to Helen Taft, July 22, 1912, in L. Gould (ed.), My Dearest Nellie: The Letters of William Howard Taft to Helen Herron Taft, 1909-1912 (Lawrence: U. Press of Kansas, 2011), 235.

[77] D. Goodwin, The Bully Pulpit: Theodore Roosevelt, William Howard Taft, and the Golden Age of Journalism (New York: Simon and Schuster, 2013), 722.

to death" "[Roosevelt] succeeded where Taft failed, in preventing that drought of invention which officialism brings."[78]

But Lippmann's words expressing lack of fear of "monsters" did not reflect the hardened sensibility that followed two world wars. Taft's fear of "monsters" was not misplaced.

Writing in 1939, in a review of Peter Drucker's *The End of Economic Man,*[79] Winston Churchill had a less kind reflection on the quest for heroism and heroic leaders:

> "The average man is no longer prepared to tolerate twin evils of war and unemployment. They have become demons which haunt him, and his last hope is that they may be exorcised through the miraculous intervention of a demi-god. Men seek refuge in them not because they believe in them but because anything is better than the present chaos … the real weakness of totalitarianism is that it offers the Heroic Man as an ideal in place of the Economic Man. From the individual's point of view it may all be very well to have something to die for, but it is impossible to build up a society on a basis of lives which are meant to be sacrificed. That way lies anarchy, and it is because the organization which the dictators offer stands in the last resort for nothing that it will eventually fail."[80]

The Tafts in a troubled era never lost their belief in bourgeois capitalism and liberal democracy, whose revival after World War II surprised even Drucker. But they were consistently far more aware

---

[78] W. Lippmann. A Preface to Politics (2d ed.) (Ann Arbor: U. Michigan, 1914, 1962), 24, 78.

[79] (New York: John Day, 1939).

[80] W. Churchill, Book Review of P. Drucker, The End of Economic Man, Times Literary Supplement, May 27, 1939, 206.

than most defenders of the old order of the need to reform it. They wanted no part of a "Revolution of Nihilism." William Howard Taft was an avuncular paternalist. His personality was eclipsed by the more colorful figures of Theodore Roosevelt and Woodrow Wilson, but unlike some later Republican conservatives like Warren Harding, Calvin Coolidge, and Thomas Dewey, he offered more than negation.

Labor Law

Taft played a seminal role in the development of American labor law. It has been said that Taft was "arguably the most important single judicial figure in the development of American labour law between the Civil War and the New Deal."[81] "Taft's conception of the appropriate sphere of collective bargaining as face to face dealing between masters and workers within a single enterprise or circumscribed group of enterprises within a local product market was one of the key elements in pre-New Deal labour law."[82]

At one point, while still on the Sixth Circuit, he lamented that "more [labor] injunctions fell to me than almost any other judge of the United States."[83]

He upheld the right to strike: "They have labor to sell. If they stand together, they are often able to [obtain] better prices."[84] Earlier, in 1889 he declared: "every man is entitled to bestow his labor ... what one workman may do, and many may combine to do, without giving the sufferer any right of action against those who cause his loss." But this did not confer the right to engage in secondary

---

[81] C. Tomlin, "Labour Law," in 3 S. Engerman and R. Gallman, The Cambridge Economic History of the United States (Cambridge: Cambridge U., 2000), 625, 657.

[82] Id. 658.

[83] 1 Pringle 102.

[84] 62 Fed. Rep. 803 (6th Cir. 1894).

boycotts: "the terrorizing of a community by threats of exclusive dealing in order to deprive one obnoxious member of means of sustenance will become both dangerous and oppressive."[85]

Taft consistently expressed hostility to the use of ex parte injunctions in labor disputes,[86] and was willing to totally prohibit them, which has not yet taken place. In 1909 in a message to Congress, he proposed limiting the duration of ex parte injunctions to seven days. His 1908 acceptance speech declared that labor injunctions "often so discourage men from continuing what is their lawful right."[87]

He also declared: "I would favor a provision allowing a defendant in contempt proceedings to challenge the judge issuing the injunction and to call for the designation of another judge."[88] This reform has taken place in the federal courts.

In his book on *The President and His Powers*, he took the view that the President cannot grant pardons for civil as distinct from criminal contempt. The President also cannot be compelled to send the army to enforce a court order.[89]

He rejected Samuel Gompers' proposition that an injury to an employer's business was not an injury to his property rights. The injunction, he said in his inaugural address, is "a most needful remedy available to all men for the protection of their business against unlawful invasion."[90] However, after World War I and his experience on the War Labor Board, he took the view that "[i]njunctions in labor troubles are merely the emergency brakes for rare use and in

---

[85] Moores Co. v. Bricklayers Union, 1889 Ohio Misc. Lexis 119, 10 Ohio Dec. Report 48 (1889).

[86] 1 Pringle 352.

[87] Quoted in F. Frankfurter and N. Greene, *supra*, 65-66, 80 n.129.

[88] "Labour and Capital," Cooper Institute, January 10, 1908, in 1 W.H. Taft, Works 178.

[89] 6 W.H. Taft, Works 91, 95.

[90] 1 W.H. Taft, Works 55.

case of sudden danger. Frequent application of them would shake to pieces the whole machine. They should be availed of only when the soviet policy of a selfish aggregation of men pushes society against the wall into a desperate situation."[91]

This view now informs the anti-injunction provisions of the Norris–La Guardia and Taft–Hartley Acts, effectively restricting labor injunctions to those sought by public authorities, as distinct from private litigants, in national emergencies.

In 1908, he observed that "united action [produces] greater promptness in the advance of wages than if it were left to the slower operation of natural laws."[92] In the same lecture he provided a declaration of the rights of labor notable in its time:

> "Men have the right to leave the employ or their employer in a body in order to impose on him as great an inconvenience as possible to induce him to come to their terms. They have the right in their labor unions to delegate to their leaders the power to say when to strike. They have the right in advance to accumulate by contribution from all members of the labor union a fund which shall enable them to live during the pendency of the strike. They have the right to use persuasion with all other laborers who are invited to take their place in order to convince them of the advantage to labor of united action.[93]

The gains to labor from unionization may be less than labor's partisans assume: "estimates have ranged widely but the general

---

[91] Editorial, "Labor Injunctions," November 20, 1919, in J. Vivian (ed.), William Howard Taft: Collected Editorials, 1917-1921 (Westport, CT: Praeger, 1990), hereafter "Editorials," 310.

[92] WHT, "Capital and Labour," Cooper Institute, January 10, 1908, in 1 W.H. Taft, Works 247ff.

[93] Id. 268.

conclusion has been that at the peak of its membership unions in most industries increased wages by only 5% above those of non-union workers. In some sectors however such as mining and the building trades, the union wage effect may have been as high as 20%."[94] Wage differentials between skilled and unskilled workers narrowed during World War II and its aftermath when unions were at their strongest. This has been attributed to sharply curtailed immigration after World War I, but the widening of wage differentials afterward may be due to union decline. "The wide wage structures in the U.S. makes it unique among industrialized countries. Those countries with strong nationwide unions have far more compressed wage structures and far more extensive social insurance … pension, sickness, and unemployment coverage to mention but three aspects of the welfare state that far exceed that in the U.S."[95]

The wage structure has come full circle to what it was more than a half century ago." Nonetheless "labor productivity continued to increase after 1960 when unionization was on the decline." Labor's gains were ascribed to "publicly provided education, particularly at the secondary level and … immigration restriction."[96] Current controversies over immigration across the Mexican border are in considerable part a reaction to more recent deterioration in the share of wages in gross national product, from 52% in 1970 to 43% in 2019.

---

[94] C. Goldin, "Labor Markets in the Twentieth Century," in 3 S. Engerman and R. Gallman, The Cambridge Economic History of the United States (Cambridge: Cambridge U., 2000).

[95] C. Goldin, "Labor Markets in the Twentieth Century," 3 S. Engerman and R. Gallman, The Cambridge Economic History of the United States (Cambridge: Cambridge U., 2000), 584.

[96] C. Goldin, "Labor Markets in the Twentieth Century," in 3 S. Engerman and R. Gallman, The Cambridge Economic History of the United States (Cambridge: Cambridge U., 2000), 554, 616.

In his acceptance speech to the Republican Convention in 1908, Taft declared that strikes did not offend the antitrust laws.[97]

In his inaugural address in 1909, he declared his view that "the secondary boycott is an instrument of tyranny and ought not to be made legitimate." He had declared in the *Phelan* case in 1894 while on the Sixth Circuit that "the starvation of a nation cannot be the lawful purpose of a combination … if there is any power in the army of the United States to run those trains, the trains will be run." His Second Annual Message as President reiterated his opposition to "[legalizing] that crude social instrument, the secondary boycott."[98]

In the same message, he called for an eight-hour law for government workers. His Annual Message in 1911 urged employers' liability and workmen's compensation laws for railroads, on the ground that they would foster uniformity, speed, and reduced counsel fees.[99]

Later in the same year, he called on unions to "recognize the difference between the highly skilled and very industrious workman and the one only less skilled and less industrious [allowing] greater reward for greater skill and greater industry." He commended American labor leaders for "set[ting] their faces like flint against the propagandism of socialistic principles."[100] The agenda of leaders like Samuel Gompers and William Green and in a later day George Meany and Lane Kirkland was that of a regulated capitalism, not of state management even of the health and education systems.

In a speech later in the year he declared: "If I were a working man, I would probably become a member of a trades union, if I gain admission."[101]

---

[97] 3 W.H. Taft, Works 14.

[98] 4 W.H. Taft, Works 40ff.

[99] 4 W.H. Taft, Works, 250.

[100] W.H. Taft, "Labour and the Writ of Injunction," Orchestra Hall, September 16, 1909, in 3 W.H. Taft, Works 150.

[101] W.H. Taft, "Amendment of the Interstate Commerce Law," September 20, 1909, in 3 W.H. Taft, Works 180ff.

In March 1913, he vetoed a bill to prohibit use of funds to prosecute labor unions for violation of the antitrust laws, decrying it as an effort to legalize the secondary boycott, and as "class legislation of the most vicious sort."[102]

In another case,[103] he upheld an injunction against mass picketing. In a third case, reversed by the U.S. Supreme Court, he invalidated a waiver of a right to bring suit for ordinary negligence;[104] his position was ultimately vindicated by a statute enacted in 1906 invalidating the Supreme Court decision.[105]

At an early date, he opposed secondary boycotts, on account of the "remote motive" of the boycotters. In 1894 he was outraged by the Pullman strike, in which the nation's railroad workers, led by Eugene Debs, launched a nationwide strike in support of a relatively small number of workers in George Pullman's company town. He declared it to be "the most outrageous strike in the history of this country." In a subsequent eulogy of President Cleveland in 1909, he commended the late President for "stopping what had really grown to the proportions of an insurrection."[106]

He was horrified by Debs' pronouncement "we will starve your babies, we will prevent your food coming to you by stopping these railroads."[107]

He was quoted as having said at the time: "it will be necessary for the military to kill some of the mob before the trouble can be stayed. They have only killed six … as yet. This is hardly enough to

---

[102]　4 W.H. Taft, Works 366. *See* W. Taft, The Antitrust Act and the Supreme Court (New York: Harper, 1914), 98-99.

[103]　54 Fed. Rep. 730 (6th Cir. 1893).

[104]　Voight v. Baltimore and Ohio Southwestern Ry., 79 Fed. Rep. 561 (6th Cir. 1897), reversed 176 U.S. 498 (1900).

[105]　D. Goodwin, The Bully Pulpit: Theodore Roosevelt, William Howard Taft, and the Golden Age of Journalism (New York: Simon and Schuster, 2013), 217.

[106]　3 W.H. Taft, Works 59.

[107]　W.H. Taft, The Antitrust Act and the Supreme Court (1914) in 5 W.H. Taft, Works 185.

make an impression." The statement is said to have been made on July 8, 1894.

Shortly thereafter, in a case arising from the Pullman dispute, he held a union officer in contempt for violating an injunction against a secondary boycott seeking "a paralysis of all national railway traffic of every kind throughout that vast territory traversed by Pullman cars."[108]

In more mundane cases, his record had been more sympathetic to labor interests. He did not dispute the right to strike for better wages,[109] or the right of unions to collect funds for, and to pay, strike benefits.[110] He declared void contracts obtained by employers that waived the right to sue for gross negligence.[111] Similarly, he would not allow an assumption of risk defense to be raised when an action was brought for breach of a statutory duty; "to enable [an employer] to nullify a penal statute is against public policy."[112] These and other cases led Judge Learned Hand to write of him in 1921 "when he was Circuit Judge he was professionally tiptop. I think his stuff was as good as we used to get in the ordinary line of work."[113]

As President, he supported employer liability statutes, the Safety Appliance Act, voluntary workmen's compensation, and creation of the Children's Bureau.[114] In 1914, he noted disapprovingly that at one point TR wanted to use the army to mine coal.[115]

---

[108] In re Whelan, 62 F. 803, 805 (1894).

[109] 1 Pringle 128.

[110] 1 Pringle 137.

[111] 1 Pringle 139.

[112] 1 Pringle 142, citing Narrator v. Cleveland Ry. Co., 96 F. 298 (6th Car. 1899).

[113] L. Hand to F. Frankfurter, July 27, 1921, in C. Jordan (ed.), Reason and Imagination: The Selected Correspondence of Learned Hand: 1897-1961 (New York: Oxford U., 2013), 113.

[114] 1 Pringle 602ff.

[115] W.H. Taft, The President and His Powers (1914) in 6 W.H. Taft, Works 109.

He at one point disparagingly described himself as "a man who had issued injunctions against labor unions almost by the bushel, who has sent at least ten or a dozen violent labor agitators to jail."[116]

In 1918, after having served as President, he was appointed to the War Labor Board by President Wilson. On visiting plants in the South, he exclaimed: "How can people live on such wages" He declared: "employers have certain duties social in their nature that are not defined and are not enforceable in law but exist just as family duties of care and affection exist."[117]

He opposed "yellow dog" contracts requiring workers not to join unions as a condition of employment. He was opposed both to coercion of union membership and discharge on account of it. He did not seek to bar "closed shops" that hired only union members. The Board provided equal pay for women, minimum wages to assure subsistence, and required waivers from employers and unions of the right to strike or lockout. A conciliation board went into action "after they have tried economic powers." Cost-plus contracts were allowed, which caused both management and unions to become "spoiled" during the war, leading to strife afterward. The Board wielded sanctions that included the seizure of plants and the barring of men from work in war industry.[118]

The Board made an important contribution to union organization. "Its well-meant activities resulted in an impetus to company unionism—employee representation plans. Employers soon recognized its usefulness as a substitute for unionism amenable to their control."[119]

The "works councils" thus established generally met on the employer's premises with an employer representative present, and

---

[116] Quoted in J. Lurie, William Howard Taft, The Travails of a Progressive Conservative (Cambridge: Cambridge U., 2012), 54.

[117] WHT, Editorials, *supra*. November 26, 1918, 124.

[118] 2 Pringle 916-26.

[119] 4 S. Perlman and P. Taft, History of Labour Legislation in the United States: Labour Movements (New York: Macmillan, 1935), 408.

generally did not attempt anything in the nature of industry-wide bargaining as distinct from modification of plant rules, though they were useful in allocating the pain resulting from the post-war deflation and serving as a "safety valve" for grievances. Elected department committees dealt with department management and the chairmen of these committees comprised the general plant committee. Membership in the American Federation of Labor (AFL) increased from 2.072 million workers in 1916 to 3.260 million workers in 1919. By 1933, as a result of the post-war recession and the first three years of the great depression, there were 1.146 million workers in "company unions" and only 240.8 thousand in conventional labor unions.[120]

Later, company unions were disfavored in the Wagner and Taft–Hartley Acts; in a much-publicized episode in the second decade of the twenty-first century, a new German-managed Volkswagen plant was located in a right-to-work state after management discovered that the plant, if located in Ohio, could not have a works council because of the statutory ban on company unions.

A Commission under the chairmanship of the noted labor arbitrator John Dunlop recommended their legalization during the Clinton administration. A TEAM Act endorsed by several Carter-era cabinet officers passed both houses but was vetoed by President Clinton at the behest of the United Auto Workers.

After the War, Taft decried union abuses: "an apparent willingness to accept benefits enforced through fear of lawlessness, a disposition to use duress to compel laborers to join unions, and efforts to limit output and to create a dead level of wages and thus wipe out the necessary and useful difference in the compensation of those who are industrious and willful and those who are lazy and do not strive to increase the product of the employer whom they serve."[121]

---

[120] Id. 341, 352.

[121] Editorial, November 26, 1918, 124.

He also vigorously opposed the Plumb Plan for tripartite management of the nation's railroads which he thought would result in "lazy, wasteful, indifferent management."[122]

In 1922 as Chief Justice, he joined an 8-1 decision in the *Drexel* case[123] invalidating a federal tax on child labor as beyond the taxing power, although he asserted that he disagreed with a prior decision in *Hammer v. Dagenhart* invalidating a federal child labor statute as beyond federal power under the Commerce clause. In fact, he had defended the decision when it was rendered.[124]

Felix Frankfurter defended the *Drexel* decision, saying that it involved "dishonest use of the taxing power ... It is appropriate not to forget the services which the Chief Justice, while President, rendered on behalf of child welfare."[125] Justices Holmes and Brandeis were with the majority in the *Drexel* case; only Justice Clarke dissented. In the *Tri-City* case Taft joined the Court in upholding a state law prohibiting "yellow dog" contracts and overruling the prior *Hitchman* case, in *Tri-City* he had becomingly recognized that "employees may make their combination extend beyond one shop."[126]

The Court enjoined mass picketing but not persuasion or picket signs; Justice Brandeis joined the opinion and Justice Clarke was the lone dissenter.[127]

The decision was praised for outlining what picketers were permitted to do: "one representative for each point of ingress and egress ... [a] right of observation, communication or persuasion

---

[122]   Editorial, August 9, 1919.

[123]   Bailey v. Drexel, 259 U.S. 20 (1921).

[124]   Editorial, "Child Labor Legislation," June 20, 1918, 69.

[125]   F. Frankfurter, "Child Labor and the Court," The New Republic, July 26, 1922.

[126]   *See* F. Frankfurter and N. Greene, The Labor Injunction (New York: Macmillan, 1930), 39.

[127]   American Steel Foundries v. Tri-City Central Trades Council, 257 U.S. 184 (1921).

[that] shall not be abusive, libelous or threatening … [picketers] shall not approach individuals together but singly … shall not obstruct by importunate following or dogging steps."[128] Of it, Justice Holmes wrote: "I was delighted at the labor decision of the Chief Justice yesterday and though of course there were details as to which I should go further, I was so content to get what we got that I didn't think it wise to say any qualifying words."[129] Taft's more liberal younger son Charley later referred to the opinion as upholding "pink-tea picketing."

In *Truax v. Corrigan*,[130] generally considered his most anti-labor decision, he was with a five-member majority invalidating a state law limiting the issuance of labor injunctions to cases of "irreparable injury." This reflected Taft's regard for the authority and jurisdiction of courts as much as his views on labor issues and his hostility to what he considered "class legislation"; the restriction on injunctions was limited to labor cases leading to its invalidation under the Equal Protection clause of the Fourteenth Amendment. A similar restriction on injunctions in Section 20 of the Clayton Act was distinguished on the basis that the Equal Protection clause did not restrict federal legislation, a distinction that also reflected Taft's nationalist view that the federal commerce power extended to labor issues, which generally were not matters for the states. The *Truax* decision was criticized by Felix Frankfurter on the basis that it "deals with abstractions and not with the work-a-day world, its men, and its struggles."[131]

The case later was severely limited by the Norris–La Guardia Act signed by President Hoover which virtually brought an end to the federal labor injunction and the attendant use of the Army to

---

[128]   F. Frankfurter and N. Greene, *supra*, 117-18.

[129]   Holmes to Frankfurter, December 6, 1921, in R. Mennel and C. Compston (eds.), Holmes and Frankfurter: Their Correspondence, 1912-34 (Hanover, NH: U. Press of New England, 1996), 132.

[130]   257 U.S. 312 (1921).

[131]   F. Frankfurter, "The Same Mr. Taft," New Republic, January 18, 1922.

support management except in cases involving serious violence. Taft did not live to see or pass on the statute, which had the benign effect of allowing the United States to enter World War II without its army being perceived as an enemy of the labor movement.

Taft joined the Court majority in the *United Leather Workers* case[132] protecting local unions from suits under the Sherman anti-trust law on the basis that interstate commerce was not involved, the conservative Justices Butler, Van Devanter, and McKenna dissenting. In *United Mine Workers v. Coronado*,[133] he reached a similar result, after first holding that the union was an entity amenable to suit. The international union was held not liable since no actual agency was shown, an important victory for unions. Felix Frankfurter defended the decision, holding local unions amenable to suit: "Complete immunity for all conduct is too dangerous an immunity to confer on any group."[134]

The case was the American equivalent of, and cited, the British *Taff Vale* decision.[135]

In the second *Coronado* case,[136] he affirmed a judgment against the local union, while absolving the international.[137] "In the *Coronado* coal mining cases, the Court treated proof of the suppression of competition as the crux of the matter, even though its purpose in doing so was merely to provide a device under which it could discourage organizational or intolerable strikes under the Act and at the same time avoid using the Act to suppress bargaining or tolerable strikes."[138]

---

[132]   United Leather Workers v. Herbert and Meisel, 265 U.S. 457 (1924).

[133]   259 U.S. 344 (1922).

[134]   P. Kurland (ed.), Felix Frankfurter on the Supreme Court (Cambridge, Mass.: Belknap Press, 1970), 97.

[135]   Taff Vale v. Amalgamated Society, [1901] A.C. 426.

[136]   Coronado v. United Mine Workers, 268 U.S. 295 (1925).

[137]   268 U.S. 295 (1925).

[138]   C. Gregory, Labor and the Law (2d ed. 1961), 216-17.

He decided the *Bedford Cut Stone* case, a mass picketing case, against the union, a reaffirmation of the boycott cases, leading Frankfurter and Greene to allege that the Court had nullified Sections 17, 18, and 19 of the Clayton Act: "the more things are legislatively changed, the more they remain the same."[139] "[T]he federal government was willing prior to 1933 to restrict the organizational activities of labor unions."[140]

However, in *Adkins v. Children's Hospital*,[141] he joined Justices Holmes and Brandeis in dissenting from a decision invalidating the District of Columbia minimum wage law. In his view, *Hammer v. Dagenhart*,[142] on which the Court relied, had been limited in its authority by an almost contemporary decision in *Bunting v. Oregon*,[143] upholding a statute regulating the hours of work of women. He saw no difference between regulations of hours and regulations of wages; one was the multiplier, the other the multiplicand. He emphatically declared that "it is not the function of this court to hold congressional acts invalid simply because they are passed to carry out economic views which the Court believes to be unwise or unsound." He declined to join Justice Holmes' opinion deriding the "liberty of contract" doctrine.

In *Howat v. Kansas*, a decision reminiscent of the later *United Mine Workers* case in 1947,[144] Taft affirmed a contempt judgment entered in a labor arbitration case: "an injunction must be obeyed, however erroneous the action of the court may be … until its decision is reversed for error."[145]

---

[139] F. Frankfurter and N. Greene, *supra*, 176.

[140] C. Gregory, *supra*, 222.

[141] 275 U.S. 418 (1927).

[142] 247 U.S. 251 (1918).

[143] 243 U.S. 426 (1917).

[144] 330 U.S. 258 (1947).

[145] 258 U.S. 181 (1922).

In *Pennsylvania Railway v. Labor Board,* he upheld the constitutionality of the Railway Labor Board, noting that it had at its disposal no sanctions save those supplied by public opinion.[146]

His nationalism had been reflected in his unsuccessful veto as President of the Webb–Kenyon Act allowing the states to burden interstate commerce in alcoholic beverages, in which he took the view that this "would seem to confer upon Congress the power to amend the Constitution by ignoring or striking out one of its most important provisions."[147]

Substantive Due Process

Chief Justice Taft upheld an anti-narcotics statute over the dissent of Justices McReynolds and Sutherland, saying that it does not "render such qualification or interference with the original state right an invasion of it because it may incidentally discourage some in the harmful use of the thing taxed."[148] In another narcotics case, *United States v. Balint,*[149] he held that scienter was not requisite: ignorance of fact is not a defense "where the emphasis of the statute is evidently upon achievement of some social betterment rather than the punishment of the crimes as in cases of mala in se." He later dissented from an opinion that a statute allowing punishment at hard labor required an indictment by a grand jury, being joined by Justices Brandeis and Holmes in saying that it defined a regulatory offense, not an infamous crime in the constitutional sense.[150] The Roberts Court has recently been more insistent on the need for knowledge or intention in criminal prosecutions, both "liberal" and

---

[146] 261 U.S. 72 (1922).

[147] 49 Congressional Record 4291-92, 62nd Congress, 2nd Session.

[148] Nigro v. United States 276 U.S. 332 (1928).

[149] 258 U.S. 250 (1922).

[150] United States v. Moreland, 258 U.S. 433 (1922).

"conservative" justices defining narrowly the categories of regulatory offenses in which they can be dispensed with.[151]

He found scienter in another narcotics case where a doctor had prescribed an unusually large number of pills; Justices Holmes, Brandeis, and McReynolds dissented.[152]

He joined in invalidating a state bridge inspection law as an interference with interstate commerce in *Lemke v. Farmers Grain*.[153] Justices Brandeis, Holmes, and Clarke dissented. He also upheld the authority of the Interstate Commerce Commission to regulate intrastate rates where necessary to protect interstate commerce.

He personally wrote few substantive due process opinions, *Truax v. Corrigan*, which principally rested on the Equal Protection clause, being the most notable of them. He joined, however, in a number of such opinions written by others, including *Tyson and Brothers v. Banton* involving an anti-ticket-scalping statute, characterized as a naked interference with the free market substituting rationing by queue for rationing by price, a decision that "has awakened the condemnation of a good many but it is right, that is the way the academicians and those who are not in favor of any constitution get even with us."[154] This called forth a memorable Holmes dissent: "the legislature may forbid any business [subject to just compensation] when it has a sufficient force of public opinion behind it." Rejecting Sutherland's effort to declare that the theatre ticket business was not "affected by a public interest," Holmes said: "We have not that respect for art that is one of the glories of France. But to many people, the superfluous is the necessary."

---

[151] Rehaif v. U.S. ____ U.S ____ (June 21, 2019) (7-2 decision).

[152] United States v. Behrman, 258 U.S. 420 (1922).

[153] 258 U.S. 50 (1922).

[154] WHT to Horace Taft, January 7, 1929, WHT Papers, Library of Congress, Series 3, Reel 207.

Taft joined other substantive due process opinions, including *Ribnik v. McBride*,[155] invalidating state regulation of employment agency fees; *Liggett Co. v. Baldridge*,[156] invalidating a state law prohibiting the corporate practice of pharmacy; *Quaker City Cab Co. v. Pennsylvania*,[157] invalidating a heavier tax on incorporated cab companies; and *Frost v. Railway Commission*,[158] invalidating a requirement that drivers of automobiles for hire obtain certificates of convenience and necessity. Justices Holmes, Brandeis, and McReynolds dissented, McReynolds declaring that "the States are now struggling with new and enormously difficult problems incident to the growth of automotive traffic," Taft also joined an opinion holding unconstitutional state licensing of steamer ticket sales agencies, over the dissent of Justices Holmes, Stone, and Brandeis,[159] and in *Weaver v. Palmer Bros.*[160] voted to invalidate a statute prohibiting the use of sterilized shoddy materials in bedding, Justices Holmes, Brandeis, and Stone dissenting. He joined a 5-to-4 opinion holding a tax on long-term as distinct from short-term mortgages to be discriminatory.[161]

On the other hand, there were limits to his willingness to concur in the invocation of substantive due process. In one of his earliest cases, he joined an unanimous opinion upholding a statute prohibiting the corporate operation of cotton gins,[162] and in *Euclid v. Ambler Realty Co.*[163] joined Justice Sutherland's opinion upholding

---

[155]   277 U.S. 350 (1927). Justices Holmes, Brandeis and Stone dissented.

[156]   278 U.S. 105 (1928). Justices Holmes and Brandeis dissented.

[157]   277 U.S. 389 (1928).

[158]   271 U.S. 577 (1925).

[159]   Di Santo v. Pennsylvania, 273 U.S. 34 (1927).

[160]   270 U.S. 402 (1926).

[161]   Louisville Gas Co. v. Coleman, 277 U.S. 32 (1928).

[162]   Crescent Oil Co. v. Mississippi, 257 U.S. 129 (1921).

[163]   272 U.S. 365 (1926).

the constitutionality of zoning laws, Justices Butler, Sanford, and McReynolds dissenting.

The activism of the Taft Court in its relation to state government economic regulations, though it rarely spoke through Taft, has fostered a caricatured view of its total influence; "Taft unwittingly painted for the nation a picture of the Court as a monolith of reaction asserting the beliefs of the late nineteenth century in a changed world."[164]

In fact, Taft and his Court were a good deal more friendly toward social legislation designed to protect labor than that designed to protect small business. Taft's hostility toward big business cartels in antitrust cases caused him to be unsympathetic to barriers to competition erected by state governments.

The Taft Court's adventures in substantive due process nonetheless left an unfortunate legacy. As the late Roger Cramton noted: "the Court destroyed the capacity of the States to deal with a substantial area of private economic relations at precisely the time when economic and technological developments were building great public pressure for the regulation of economic activities. Frustrated by the Supreme Court, the people increasingly turned to the federal government for the effective handling of economic affairs. When substantive due process was finally dethroned, the habit of looking to Washington on many matters had been firmly established."[165] These substantive due process decisions invalidating state small business legislation led to Learned Hand's conclusion, at the end of Taft's tenure on the Court, that "I have an affection for his nature, straight and loving and loyal, for his kindness and his power of fine indignation ... While his influence on the Court, its working

---

[164] G. White, The American Judicial Tradition (3d ed.) (New York: Oxford, 2007) 156.

[165] R. Cramton, "The Supreme Court and the Decline of State Power," 2 J. Law and Econ. 175 (1959).

and its personnel, was of the greatest use, he fortified it in its most dangerous tendencies."[166]

The "small business" decisions were in accord with Taft's economic preferences as disclosed by his militancy on antitrust issues. The Court's record on labor legislation was more mixed, though it almost invariably upheld social insurance schemes, and Taft never denied the right to strike and the right to engage at least in what was called "pink tea" picketing.

Perhaps the Court's least appreciated opinion of this period was rendered just before he ascended the bench: the unanimous opinion of Justice Day in *Green v. Frazier*[167] in 1920 warding off an attack on the taxes imposed to finance the program of the North Dakota Non-Partisan League, the closest approach to state socialism ever enacted in the United States, providing as it did for state-operated banks and grain elevators.[168] The little-known case was later cited in a case upholding challenged activities of the Tennessee Valley Authority.[169] After *Green v. Frazier*, it was clear that the road to peaceful social and economic change remained open in the United States.

Chief Justice Taft dealt with gift taxes in two cases. In *Schlesinger v. Wisconsin*,[170] he voted to uphold a presumption that gifts within six years of death were in contemplation of death; Justices Holmes, Brandeis, and Stone dissented. In *Blodgett v. Holden*,[171]

---

[166] L. Hand to F. Frankfurter, February 6, 1930, in C. Jordan (ed.), Reason and Imagination: The Selected Correspondence of Learned Hand: 1897-1961 (New York: Oxford U., 2013), 164-65.

[167] 253 U.S. 233 (1920).

[168] L. Frazier, "Gov. Frazier's Own Story of the Non Partisan League: North Dakota Executive, Twice Elected by Farmers in Anti-Capitalist Movement, Describes Benefits and Economies Derived from New Form of Government," New York Times, May 16, 1920, 112.

[169] Tennessee Electric Power v. T.V.A., 306 U.S. 118 (1939).

[170] 270 U.S. 230 (1928).

[171] 275 U.S. 142 (1928).

a case affirmed by an evenly divided court, he would have held the federal gift tax to be beyond the authorization of unapportioned taxes on income provided by the Income Tax Amendment; Justices Holmes, Brandeis, Stone, and Sanford prevailed in affirming the opinion of the lower court.

In *Block v. Hirsh*,[172] he dissented, along with Justices McReynolds, McKenna, and Van Devanter, from a decision upholding wartime rent controls. "War, unless it is fought for liberty, is the deadly enemy of liberty," they declared, invoking as a precedent the rejection of claims of military necessity in the post–Civil War case of *Ex Parte Milligan*. Justice Holmes rejoined: "we are not warranted in saying that legislation that has been resorted to for the same purpose all over the world is futile."

Although his court invoked substantive due process to invalidate a large number of state laws during his tenure as Chief Justice, Justice Brandeis' daughter, Elizabeth Brandeis, acknowledged in her contribution to John R. Commons' *History of Labor* that "[i]n the period from 1918 to 1932, the U.S. Supreme Court made 12 decisions involving provisions in employers' liability or workmen's compensation laws. All of these decisions sustained the provisions involved. Taken as a group they show a complete acceptance of the compensation principle and a readiness to permit even extreme application thereof."[173]

In *Wolff Packing Co. v. Court of Industrial Relations*,[174] he joined all the justices but Clarke in invalidating a Kansas compulsory arbitration statute, there being no emergency declared by the legislature justifying disregard of liberty of contract and the statute being without coherent standards of decision. Earlier, in a lecture at the Cooper Institute in 1908, he had observed: "it is a very serious ques-

---

[172] 256 U.S. 135 (1921).

[173] 3 E. Brandeis, History of Labour Legislation in the United States: Labour Legislation (New York: Macmillan, 1935), 691.

[174] 262 U.S. 522 (1923).

tion under our Constitution whether a decree of a tribunal under a compulsory arbitration law could be enforced against the sale of the labor. It would come very close to the violation of the Thirteenth Amendment."[175]

Taft took a dim view of debtor relief legislation in mortgage foreclosure cases, a project recently revived a century after he wrote. His words are still pertinent:

> "the [Kansas] legislature passed stay laws which introduced many delays in the legal procedure of the State for the collection of mortgages. The people of Kansas learned a lesson from the result of this legislation which has not been forgotten. Capital fled the State of Kansas as men flee from a contagious disease and business became as dead in Kansas as if it had no population at all. The flight that followed taught the statesmen of that State the utilitarian doctrine that honesty is the best policy and that laws that drove creditors out of a State and frightened away all capital helped neither those who owed money or those who did not owe money in the State. These so-called remedial laws were very soon repealed."[176]

As a Supreme Court Justice, he enforced a new law requiring a three-judge court to enjoin a rate order.[177] He rejected an attempt by a railroad to enjoin a regulatory board from publishing its decisions.[178] In a rare concurring opinion, he upheld an injunction against a publication because of a clear danger to the administration of justice.[179] He refused to enforce an arbitration recommendation

---

[175] WHT, "Labour and Capital," Cooper Institute, January 10, 1908, in 1 W.H. Taft, Works 247.

[176] 5 W.H. Taft, Works 200.

[177] Cumberland v. Louisiana P.S.C., 260 U.S. 212 (1922).

[178] Penn. Ry. Co. v. Richmond Labour Board, 261 U.S. 72 (1923).

[179] Craig v. Hechi, 263 U.S. 255 (1923).

by injunction.[180] He held that a summary contempt proceeding was appropriate only for contempts committed in the presence of the trial judge,[181] and also that evidence in mitigation of contempt cannot be excluded in a contempt proceeding, and that it is frequently the better practice for the offended judge to disqualify himself.[182]

Contempt proceedings, he recognized, in holding that the President's pardoning power extended to criminal contempts, "were not hedged about with all the safeguards provided in the bill of rights."[183] Taft took the view that "[t]he abolition of the jury in civil cases would relieve the public of a great burden of expense, would facilitate the hearing of all civil suits, and would not with proper appeal deprive any litigant."[184]

He also deplored the fact that "[i]n many states, judges are not permitted to comment on the facts at all [and are] required to submit written charges to the jury upon abstruse questions of law."[185]

Antitrust Law and the Curbing of Plutocracy

"The guaranty with respect to the right of property," Taft declared, "would be undermined by a movement toward socialism. This movement has gained force by the use of accumulated wealth and power in illegal ways and by duress to suppress competition and center financial control in a few hands."[186]

---

[180]   Pa. Ry. System v. Pa. Ry. Co., 267 U.S. 203 (1925).

[181]   Leake v. United States, 267 U.S. 517 (1925).

[182]   Cooke v. United States, 267 U.S. 517 (1925).

[183]   Ex Parte Grossman, 267 U.S. 87 (1925).

[184]   "Administration of the Criminal Law," Yale Law School, June 26, 2005, 1 W.H. Taft, Works 306.

[185]   "Our Judges Lack Power, Says Taft," New York Times, May 4, 1911.

[186]   1 Pringle 339.

Notwithstanding the ban on the income tax imposed by the Supreme Court in the *Pollock* case in 1895, he considered that "an income tax might be wise," and the constitutional amendment authorizing it was launched during his administration.[187]

However, "throughout his Presidency he maintained that the income tax ought to be preserved for times of crisis," because of "the small matters of self-incrimination, perjury, and due process that would come of government meddling into the affairs of individuals."[188] He favored publicity for corporate campaign contributions.[189]

In Taft's lectures on *The Duties of Citizenship* delivered at Yale following his presidency, he decried the "muckrakers" for exaggerating the abuses thought to exist in political and business life and for having lost their sense of proportion. He favored a gradual approach toward the liquidation of concentrations of wealth: "Neither at the common law or under the Constitution is the right of descent of property or of devising it an inalienable right if the Legislature sees fit to give a tendency toward the division of fortunes." An editorial on "The Socialist Impulse" in January 1918 observed that "[a]ccumulated wealth may be divided by means which would not be revolutionary or require a change in the Constitution. A limitation upon the testamentary power in the discretion of legislatures would in the course of ten years, or certainly in a generation, work a very material division of the great fortunes. Inheritance taxes, already heavy, are quite likely to be increased, and these, together with the graduated feature of the income tax, may shift the burden of government on to the wealthy in such a way as to moderate the enthusiasm for accumulation."[190]

---

[187] 1 Pringle 344. He favored publicity for corporate campaign contributions.

[188] M. Bromley, William Howard Taft and the First Motoring Presidency, 1909-13 (Jefferson, NC: McFarland, 2003), 151.

[189] 1 Pringle 362.

[190] Editorial, January 1918, in Editorials, 29-30.

He recognized that the heedless exploitation of natural resources had reached its limit: "We used to think that our farming and agricultural land was so extensive that we could never exhaust it. The truth is we are up against it now."[191] This made him a worthy successor to Theodore Roosevelt as a conservationist.

He thought that the Panic of 1907 had its origins in "the waste of capital in extravagance of living and by the Spanish war, the Boer war and in the Russo-Japanese war and in such catastrophes as Baltimore [fire] and San Francisco [earthquake]." In addition, the "revelations of irregularities shocked investors and made them withhold what little lendable capital remained available."[192]

In a talk to Republicans in Kansas City in February 1908, he declared, of the period prior to the Theodore Roosevelt administration, that "we were passing into a regime of an irresponsible plutocracy."[193]

As early as 1895, he had said that "[t]he mad rush for wealth, the fevered conditions of business and the opportunity of making sudden fortunes have taken the attention of the more intelligent people from politics and made them blind or callous to political abuses."[194]

In *Liberty Under Law* Taft urged that "with material progress, advance is possible in education and intelligence, in art, in morality and religion, in the spiritual. To such advances we must look for the antidote for the poison of crass materialism, of the selfish and cruel

---

[191] "Conservation "Alaska," Seattle and Tacoma, September 29 and October 1, 1909, in 3 W.H. Taft, Works, 260.

[192] "The Panic of 1907," Merchants' Association, Boston, December 30, 1907, in 1 W.H. Taft, Works 232.

[193] "Achievement of the Republican Party," Kansas City Young Men's Republican Club, February 10, 1908, in 1 W.H. Taft, Works 281.

[194] "Recent Criticism of the Federal Judiciary," American Bar Association, August 28, 1895, in 1 W.H. Taft, Works 306.

pursuit of wealth, of the ignoble lassitude of luxury and the evils of plutocracy."[195]

In his acceptance speech in 1908, he again alluded to the "dangers of plutocratic government, toward which we were fast tending."

William Howard Taft's opinion in the *Addyston Pipe* case,[196] while a judge of the United States Court of Appeals for the Sixth Circuit, is regarded by many as the foundational case under the Sherman Antitrust Act. His role in its history was even more fundamental and little remembered; while Solicitor General in the Benjamin Harrison administration, he is said to have played a role in its drafting, and he amended the complaint in one of the first cases under the Act to add an allegation of monopoly: "the coal mines owned by the defendant corporations include all those from which it is practicable or profitable to send coal for consumption to the Nashville market."[197]

Richard Scylla has written: "that pro-business Republican legislators endorsed (and even sponsored) such centralizing regulatory laws indicates that they were as much the product of business's frustration with arbitrary and conflicting state regulations as of consumer frustrations with big business."[198]

In the words of Robert Bork: "given the time at which it was written, *Addyston* must rank as one of the greatest, if not the greatest, antitrust opinions in the history of the law."[199] It rescued the

---

[195]   7 W.H. Taft, Works 9.

[196]   85 Fed. Rep. 271 (6th Cir. 1898). *See* H. Duffy, William Howard Taft (New York: Milton, Baulch, 1930).

[197]   United States v. Tellike Mountain Coal Co., 46 Fed. 432, 436 ©. C. M. D. Tenn., 1891), *see* Letwin, Law and Economic Policy in America: The Evolution of the Sherman Antitrust Act (Chicago: U. of Chicago, 1965), 101, citing U.S. Department of Justice, Instruction Book 5, 290.

[198]   R. Scylla, "Experimental Federalism, 1789-1914," in 2 S. Engelmann and R. Gillman, The Cambridge Economic History of the United States (Cambridge: Cambridge U., 2000), 483, 539.

[199]   R. Bork, The Antitrust Paradox (Glencoe, IL: Free Press, 1993), 26.

law from the state of impotence and confusion resulting from two earlier decisions. In the *Trans-Missouri* case, the Supreme Court had appeared to say that the law condemned all agreements restraining trade, however trivial and whether vertical or horizontal, an unworkable rule. As later said by Justice Brandeis in the *Chicago Board of Trade* case: "all contracts restrain. To bind, to restrain is their very essence." The opinion also escaped from the narrow definition of interstate commerce adopted in the Sugar Trust case, *United States v. E.C. Knight and Co.*, which held a monopolistic trust immune from prosecution on the theory that its individual member manufacturers were engaged in purely local activities. Taft's *Addyston Pipe* decision made clear that sales in interstate commerce by a local manufacturer were regulated by the Sherman Act, and that the law condemning contracts in restraint of trade did not condemn provisions "ancillary to a main contract with a different purpose and which the common law has for years furnished practical and definite legal rules for determining."[200]

For Taft, the "rule of reason" adopted in the *Standard Oil* case meant "ancillary" at common law. Of *Standard Oil*, he said: "It was a good opinion. It did not take exactly the line of distinction I have drawn but it certainly approximates it." One commentator noted that it did not repeat Taft's "attempt to define precisely what reasonable restraints were" nor did it echo Taft's vigorous "aversion to judges determining how much competition is in the public interest."[201]

Justice Harlan's dissent he viewed as "a nasty carping and demagogic opinion intended to furnish La Follette and his crowd as much pablum as possible." Taft's opinion, however, had virtues which the *Standard Oil* opinion did not. Taft's opinion purported to condemn all restraints except ancillary ones; the "rule of reason"

---

[200] W.H. Taft, The Antitrust Act and the Supreme Court (1914), in 5 W.H. Taft, Works 232.

[201] E. Kirkland, Industry Comes of Age: Business, Labor and Public Policy, 1860-97 (Chicago: Quadrangle, 1967), 322.

led to an efficiency calculus, protracted trials, and battles of economists. As the criminologist Hermann Mannheim later observed: "This tactical change of front … was bound to deprive the Act of most of its emotional appeal to the man in the street … There is little glamour in charges of 'restraint' and 'monopoly' as soon as they are diluted with the 'rule of reason' and the test of inefficiency."[202]

The thrust of the Sherman Act thus became what it remains: a ban on horizontal cartels, condemning restraints that raised prices whether these were righteous or wicked in purpose.[203] "The injunction works both ways," Taft declared, "and it is useful both in keeping lawless working men and lawless capitalists within the law."[204]

Taft was hostile both to business trusts and to industry-wide bargaining and secondary boycotts by labor unions: "Judge Taft believed that there was a 'fair market' that preserved production opportunities for all American businesses, that the Sherman Act rendered the federal government a guarantor of that structure (which was beyond the ability of the States to protect) and that business combinations and monopolies directly threatened that structure and with it, American democracy itself."[205]

Bork observed: "Despite their differences in verbalization, Taft's and Peckham's rules are obviously very similar. Taft's non-ancillary restraint is the same thing as Peckham's restraint of trade (or direct restraint)—a cartel agreement. Taft's ancillary restraint was the same thing as Peckham's non-direct restraint (or indirect restraint)—an agreement eliminating competition only incidentally to the accomplishment of some other purpose sought by

---

[202] H. Mannheim, Criminal Justice and Social Reconstruction (London: Kegan Paul, 1946), 168.

[203] 1 Pringle 658.

[204] W.H. Taft, "Railroads and the Courts," Orchestra Hall, Chicago, September 23, 1908, in 2 W.H. Taft, Works 90.

[205] W. Eskridge and J. Ferejohn, A Republic of Statutes: The New American Constitution (New Haven: Yale U., 2010), 129.

the parties."[206] As for section 2 of the Act, condemning monopolies, "When a combination necessarily effects a monopoly, it is no defense that the combiners do not intend a monopoly but when the result is not complete or controlling on monopoly, the intent is the important factor."[207]

While on the Ohio state court Taft had written a lengthy opinion on trade secret law, upholding trade secret protection against a defecting foreman: "the process does not seem to have been successfully reproduced because of the effective trade secret protection."[208]

Taft deplored the fact that under the Sherman Act, the "burden has been thrown on the courts," but was ready to assume that burden[209] although the 1912 Republican platform favored a statutory definition of specific acts constituting antitrust violations.[210]

His tolerance of indefiniteness was not unlimited; as a Supreme Court Justice he invalidated a state antitrust law allowing operations at a "reasonable profit" on the ground that there was "no fixed standard of guilt in an adjudication affecting the accused."[211]

In late 1911, he called on Congress to "describe and denounce methods of competition which are unfair … underselling at a price unprofitable … the making of exclusive contracts with customers under which they are required to give up association with other manufacturers … a purely negative statute like the antitrust law may well be supplemented by specific provisions for the building

---

[206] R. Bork, "The Rule of Reason and the Per Se Concept: Price Fixing and Market Division," 74 Yale L.J. 775, 779 (1965).

[207] W.H. Taft, "The Antitrust Act and the Supreme Court" (1914) in W.H. Taft, Works 185ff.

[208] Cincinnati Bell Foundry Co. v. Dodds, 1887 Ohio Misc. Lexis 181, 10 Ohio Dec. Rep. 84.

[209] 1 Pringle 342.

[210] 1 Pringle 823.

[211] Cline v. Frink Dairy, 274 U.S. 445 (1927).

up and regulation of national and foreign commerce."[212] Some such measures were included in the Clayton Act, enacted during the Wilson administration.

In justifying the antitrust campaign, Taft declared:

> "Did it not stop for all time the then powerful movement toward the control of all the railroads of the country in a single hand? When all energies are directed not toward reduction of the cost of production for the public benefit by a healthful competition but to new ways and means for making permanent in a few hands the absolute control of the conditions and prices prevailing in the whole field of industry, then individual enterprise and effort will be paralyzed and the spirit of commercial freedom will be dead." "[O]nly in the last three or four years has the heavy hand of the law been laid upon the great illegal combinations that have exercised such an absolute dominion over many of our industries … [Because of the] irresponsibility of control in the hands of the few who are not the real owners [antitrust] must be enforced unless we are to banish individualism from all business and reduce it to one common system of regulation or control of prices like that which now prevails with respect to public utilities."[213] "Every trust of any size that violates the statute will, before the end of this administration in 1913, be brought into court to meet and acquiesce in a degree of disintegration by which competition between its parts will be restored and preserved."[214]

---

[212]   W.H. Taft, "Antitrust Statute," December 5, 1911, in 4 W.H. Taft Works 159, 170.

[213]   W.H. Taft, "Antitrust Statute," December 5, 1911, in 4 W.H. Taft, Works 170, 172.

[214]   1 Pringle, *supra*, 668-69.

Taft "saw the Sherman Act as judicially sound and also as lay-ing the basis for an alternative to a state-controlled economy which he opposed on principle and would oppose politically, in public, as his break with Roosevelt became irrevocable. The Court's decisions permitted Sherman Act prosecutions against any and all of the great corporations, something that would appeal to 'radicals,' satisfy lib-erals and conservatives opposed to State direction of the economy by an administrative bureaucracy, and undercut Roosevelt—with-out threatening the large-corporate organization of the economy as such."[215]

Roosevelt's program for more regulatory agencies was largely opposed by Taft. For him, antitrust "prosecutions were necessary as an antidote to 'socialistic sentiments.'" "The way to meet [socialism] was by direct challenge and by fighting it out at the ballot-box."[216]

Taft sought "a non-statist accommodation of the law to the corporate reorganization of capitalism ... with the Rule of Reason decisions of 1911 and the legislation of 1914 ... the American peo-ple had settled [the trust question]."[217]

This campaign was not popular with the business commu-nity, Lee Higginson complaining that "[i]t is almost impossible to learn in Washington what a man may or may not do or what a cor-poration may or may not do." Taft's military aide, Colonel Archie Butt, said that Attorney General George Wickersham "has about as much political judgment as an ox."[218]

Theodore Roosevelt, though the initiator of the campaign, later expressed the view that "[i]t is preposterous to abandon all

---

[215] M. Sklar, The Corporate Reconstruction of American Capitalism, 1890-1916 (Cambridge: Cambridge U., 1988), 304.

[216] Id. 367.

[217] Id. 369.

[218] Quoted in M. Bromley, William Howard Taft and the First Motoring Presidency (Jefferson, NC: McFarland, 2003), 302.

that has been wrought in the application of the cooperative idea in business to return to the era of cut-throat competition."[219]

It was his antitrust militancy that led the left-wing historian Gabriel Kolko to observe: "only William Howard Taft tampered slightly with the orderly synthesis of big business needs and national reform that characterized the unity of politics and economics that some call 'progressivism' but which, more precisely, should be termed 'political capitalism.'"[220]

Taft did not deny the necessity or propriety of delegations of power to administrative agencies, today a subject of renewed controversy because of sweeping over-delegations by Congress, decried by the late political scientist Theodore Lowi in *The End of Liberalism*[221]: "the inevitable progress and exigencies of government and the utter inability of Congress to give the time and attention indispensable to the exercise of these powers in detail forced the modification of the rule [against delegation]."[222]

This insight was later shared by Edward Levi, who referred to the antitrust laws as "saving us from our ignorance through the negative value of filling up a void otherwise too inviting for more harmful regulatory schemes."[223] Taft's Attorney General George Wickersham had declared: "The people cannot permit the uncontrolled centralization of power in private hands. If it cannot be prevented in one way, it undoubtedly will be in another. I should greatly deprecate the tendency to appeal to the government to fix prices or to regulate and control by intimate details the affairs of great corpo-

---

[219] Quoted in A. Schlesinger, Crisis of the Old Order (Boston: Houghton Mifflin, 1957), 22.

[220] G. Kolko, Main Currents in Modern American History (New York: Harper, 1976), 15.

[221] T. Lowi, The End of Liberalism (New York: W.W. Norton, 1969).

[222] WHT, Proceedings of the Bar in Commemoration of Chief Justice White, 257 U.S. xxv-xxvi.

[223] E. Levi, Book Review of G. and R. Hale, Market Power: Size and Shape Under the Sherman Act, 26 U. Chi. L. Rev. 672 (1959).

rations or possibly to become the silent partner in every vast enterprise, yet this is substantially the condition of affairs in Germany, which has adopted the policy of encouraging consolidation but also assumes the supervision and control of all large combinations."

George Wickersham

However, Chief Justice Taft made clear on the Supreme Court, "the legislature to prevent a pure delegation of legislative power must enjoin creation of canons of procedure and certain rules of decision in performance of its function."[224] He would have required as a condition of valid delegation both the "standards" said to be unnecessary by the administrative law scholar Kenneth Culp Davis and the "safeguards" (principally notice and comment rulemaking) that Davis urged.

In his book *Liberty Under Law*, Taft declared of the situation at the turn of the century: "the politics of the country bid fair to pass into corporate control. The railroads then defied attempts to regulate them. Presidential campaigns were largely conducted on contributions from great corporations."[225]

At a time when the Income Tax decision, *Pollock v. Farmers' Loan*, barred a federal income tax, Taft was not opposed to an income tax but thought that it should come about by constitutional amendment, not overruling decision. He was prescient in noting that an income tax "puts a premium on perjury," while noting that other governments "impose the tax where possible on the source of income in the hands of those who are not ultimately

---

[224] Wichita Ry v. P. U.C., 260 U. S. 48 (1922).

[225] 7 W.H. Taft, Works 11.

to pay it,"[226] anticipating by 30 years the plan for tax withholding devised by Beardsley Ruml during World War II and supported by his son Robert. Taft sought other ways of controlling great concentrations of wealth. One of them was a corporate income tax, which he described as an excise tax on the privilege of using the corporate form,[227] "a long step toward that supervisory control of corporations which may prevent a further abuse of power."[228]

"The publicity feature of the law is the only thing that makes the law of any special value. For it is not going to be a great revenue-raising measure."[229] He also sought to curb corporate abuses by having the government accumulate and publish corporate tax returns (a proposal contained in his Second Annual Message in 1910) and other data,[230] and favored requiring larger corporations to be federally incorporated to this end.[231] The securities laws of the New Deal, to which Robert Taft was not opposed, accomplished this objective.

Such corporations, under his proposal in January 1910, reiterated in December 1911, would be restricted from mergers and stock watering and compelled to submit reports: "a means of changing the character, organization and extent of their business into one within the limits of law securing compliance with the antitrust statute."[232] While there are today stringent disclosure requirements, the restrictions on mergers that Congress sought to impose in the

---

[226] 3 W.H. Taft, "Amendment to Interstate Commerce Act," September 20, 1909, in 3 W.H. Taft, Works 201.

[227] 1 Pringle 435. *See* W.H. Taft, "Mecklenberg Declaration," Charlotte, May 20, 1909, in 3 W.H. Taft, Works 135.

[228] W.H. Taft, "Concerning Tax on the Net Income of Corporations," June 16, 2009, in 3 W.H. Taft, Works 135.

[229] 1 A. Butt, Taft and Roosevelt: The Intimate Letters of Archie Butt (New York: Doubleday, 1930), 263.

[230] 1 Pringle 512ff.

[231] 1 Pringle 660.

[232] 15 Messages and Papers of the Presidents 7441, 7449.

Celler–Kefauver Act and bank merger legislation have been largely vitiated by Supreme Court decisions exalting "consumer welfare" over concern about "private government."

Taft frequently had to declare that he did not propose to exempt large corporations from the Sherman Act. It was said that "he stood pat on the Court. This was not a popular position." On the advice of his Attorney General, George Wickersham, who referred to the dangers of a new mortmain that had over-expanded the wealth of medieval monasteries, the Rockefeller Foundation was denied a federal charter, though it ultimately was incorporated in the State of New York.[233] (The political influence of large foundations aggravated by the incestuous behavior of their staffs of "philanthropoids" have been little remarked upon, though a Congressional committee under the late Congressman B. Carroll Reece, later chairman of the Republican National Committee, slightly curbed their power through legislation (later somewhat diluted) requiring minimum annual distributions.). Later congressional impatience with huge non-profit accumulations was manifested in an endowment tax enacted during the Trump administration.

He sought a reduced tariff to foster competition and was not wholly unsuccessful in obtaining one.[234] He secured a new tariff law after urging "a revision downward and not a revision upward,"[235] an unusual achievement for a Republican administration, even though the compromises he made to obtain the Payne–Aldrich tariff became a major issue in the 1912 Presidential election. "I said to them that it was either the corporation tax or the income tax or no bill at all."[236] "It would be correct to say that the progressives, represented by TR, betrayed him. More of the Roosevelt program was

---

[233] 1 Pringle 662-63.

[234] 1 Pringle 728.

[235] W.H. Taft, Speech of Acceptance, Cincinnati, July 28, 1908 in 3 W.H. Taft, Works 32.

[236] 1 A. Butt, Taft and Roosevelt: The Intimate Letters of Archie Butt (New York: Doubleday, 1930), 130.

enacted in the Taft administration than in the Roosevelt administration. In retrospect, the Payne–Aldrich tariff ... was a slight revision, but in the right direction, downward."[237]

His military aide observed: "The idea of veto [of the Payne–
Aldrich bill] is abhorrent to him for the reason that the bill carries
with it a number of Philippine tariff reductions, dear to his heart, as
well as the corporation tax."[238]

He disputed Progressive criticism of it, pointing out that it was
the product of political necessity. Roosevelt had spoken in favor of
the lowering of tariffs, but had not seriously taken on this difficult
issue. His unwillingness to launch a demagogic campaign for lower
tariffs has been said to reflect the fact that "[u]nlike Roosevelt, Taft
did not despise the 'economic man' but understood him and sympathized with his aims."[239]

The new tariff left 1,150 items unchanged, while there were
654 decreases and 220 increases. Tariffs were reduced on goods valued at $4.951 billion and increased on goods (chiefly wool) valued
at $878 million.[240]

He referred to it as being the "best tariff bill that the Republican Party ever passed," and told his brother Horace that he had
therefore forsworn the chance to "make cheap popularity by [a]
veto."[241] "I would popularize myself with the masses with a declaration of hostilities toward Congress. I would greatly injure the party

---

[237] S. Morison, The Oxford History of the American People (New York: Oxford, 1965), 831-32.

[238] 1 A. Butt, Taft and Roosevelt: The Intimate Letters of Archie Butt (New York: Doubleday, 1930), 140.

[239] D. Burton, William Howard Taft: Confident Peacemaker (Philadelphia: St. Joseph's U. Press, 2004) 61.

[240] WHT, "The Tariff," September 17, 1909, in 3 W.H. Taft, Works 157.

[241] WHT to Horace Taft, June 27, 1910.

and possibly divide it in just such a way as Cleveland brought dissension and rancor to the Democratic party."[242]

"Those gentlemen will have to pay the piper in the end because I think the public will demand a revision of the cotton and woolen schedules in future Congresses, while the other schedules will remain untouched."[243]

He deprecated frequent amendments of tariffs: "The tariff is something upon which business depends. If you change it, you are certain to disturb the calculations of business men and to bring about financial disaster."[244] Taft, however, favored modest "scientific" tariffs founded on study of the differences in American and foreign costs: "Protection secures a high rate of wages [and] induces such improvements in the methods of manufacture, as to reduce greatly the price." As a Supreme Court Justice, Taft held that the delegation to the President of power to vary tariffs within specified limits was not improper.[245]

These views were to be shared by his son Robert. President Taft considered that an income tax "is undoubtedly a power the National Government ought to have. It might be indispensable to the nation's life in great crises."[246]

Taft, however, was violently opposed to government ownership, for three reasons: lack of efficiency, acquisition costs, and excessive power in the federal executive. "Socialism looks to a dead level of life, to an absence of all motives for material progress, to a stagnation in everything; it requires an official tyranny to carry out

---

[242] 1 A. Butt, Taft and Roosevelt: The Intimate Letters of Archie Butt (New York: Doubleday, 1930), 144.

[243] WHT to Nellie Taft, July 11, 2009, in L. Gould (ed.), My Dearest Nellie: The Letters of William Howard Taft to Helen Herron Taft, 1909-12 (Lawrence, KS: U. Press of Kansas, 2011), 31-32 (hereafter "Dearest Nellie").

[244] 1 W.H. Taft, Works 175.

[245] Hampton v. United States 276 U.S. 394 (1928).

[246] W.H. Taft, "Concerning Tax on the Net Income of Corporations," June 16, 2009, in 3 W.H. Taft, Works 134.

its system." Property was "the mainspring of action that has led men to labor, to save, to invent, to increase the production of all human comforts and reduce their cost." "To compel equality not only of opportunity but of condition and of property" would produce the "least labor, least effort, and least self-sacrifice."[247]

He was to reiterate that "the motive of gain is the only one which will be constant to induce industry, saving, invention and organization … Governments are not adapted to do business as are individuals prompted by their gain in economy and efficiency and should not be so burdened."[248]

Taft also favored curbing stock-watering through more stringent state "blue sky" laws: "state laws which should forbid the issue of stock (or bonds) by any corporation until after an examination by a state board of supervision … and a certificate that the assets justify it would do much."[249]

He considered that "efforts to divide fortunes and to reduce the motive for accumulating them are proper and statesmanlike. It is not safe for the body politic that the power arising from the management of enormous or swollen fortunes should be continued from generation to generation in the hands of a few. The law of primogeniture was abolished in states where it had been adopted merely for the purpose of securing a division of the land … they can adopt the French method which requires the division of a large part of a man's fortune between all his children and gives him absolute power with respect to only a fraction. This would secure a division in the second generation and a probable change for the better in respect to such fortunes. A federal graduated inheritance tax [would be] a useful means," "correct in principle and certain and easy of collection."[250]

---

[247] W.H. Taft, Popular Government (New Haven: Yale U., 1914) in 5 W.H. Taft, Works 61ff.

[248] W.H. Taft, Liberty Under Law (New Haven: Yale U. 1922), 9, 11ff.

[249] W.H. Taft, "Recent Criticism of the Federal Judiciary," American Bar Association, Detroit in 1 W.H. Taft, Works 305, August 28, 1895.

[250] Inaugural Address, March 4, 1908, in 3 W.H. Taft, Works 46.

The only later use of a federal inheritance rather than estate tax was brief, during the "Second New Deal" before World War II.

In breaking up large fortunes he sought "the gradual effect of a long course of legislation and not … measures having an immediate and radical effect."[251]

Such a tax "shall enable the State to share largely in the proceeds of such large accumulations of wealth that could hardly have been brought about save through its protection and its aid." He also urged that the rule against perpetuities be made "much more drastic";[252] by contrast, some states recently have eliminated it completely for certain trusts. In South Dakota alone, there are as of 2019 $355 billion in such trusts, a five-fold increase in 10 years.[253] In a later work, he acknowledged that "no State, however bitter against its own rich men, would wish to deprive itself of their residence and of their tax producing quality."[254]

While Theodore Roosevelt had initiated and mobilized public support for the "trust busting" campaign, it flowered under Taft. Roosevelt in his 7 years instituted 44 antitrust cases; Taft in 4 years brought 22 civil cases and 45 indictments. The number of civil antitrust cases instituted was 6 under Benjamin Harrison, 7 under Cleveland, and 3 under McKinley.[255]

Some of his decisions were controversial; he abstained from acting against the National City Bank and brought an action (ultimately unsuccessful) against the steel trust, which angered Roosevelt because it questioned a merger involving a Tennessee

---

[251] W.H. Taft, "Legislative Policies of the Present Administration," Columbus, OH, August 19, 1907, in 1 W.H. Taft, Works 313-15.

[252] W.H. Taft, "Amendment of Interstate Commerce Act," September 20, 1909, in 3 W.H. Taft, Works 203.

[253] O. Bullough, "The Great American Tax Haven: Why the Super-Rich Love South Dakota," The Guardian, November 14, 2019.

[254] W.H. Taft, Popular Government (1914) in 5 W.H. Taft, Works 100.

[255] W.H. Taft, "A Republican Congress and Administration and Their Work from 1904 to 1906," Boise, ID, November 3, 1906, in 1 W.H. Taft, Works.

company that he had agreed to in 1907 at the behest of investment bankers whose assistance he had sought in quelling the panic in that year and it repudiated Roosevelt's effort to distinguish between "good" and "bad" trusts.

Taft's ultimate breach with Theodore Roosevelt was prompted in no small measure by Roosevelt's famous Osawotomie speech with its promise of heavy handed and highly discretionary regulation of prices in the meat, oil, coal, and railroad industries and its declaration that the Executive was the steward of the public welfare and that "every man holds his property subject to the general right of the community to regulate its use."[256] It was this that "irritate[s] the sensitive points of the social consciousness," leading Justice Holmes to declare: "If I had a vote I should vote for Taft."[257] The journalist Arthur Krock observed that "TR's forcefulness was obnoxious to those who disagreed with him. He was disposed toward a feudal relationship with opponents. He aroused hostility and returned it with interest[, whereas] Taft [was] an affable and charming gentleman."[258] The Countess de Chambrun, a relative of TR, said that "William H. Taft, calm, learned, judicial, and judicious, whose traditions resembled those of America's great Presidents, appeared flat and uninteresting as compared with the dynamic energy of the rough rider."[259]

In his 1912 Acceptance Speech, Roosevelt had called for "complete power to regulate and control all the great industrial concerns engaged in interstate business—which practically means all of them in this country."[260]

---

[256] 1 Pringle 572.

[257] Holmes to Lewis Einstein, October 28, 1912, in J. Peabody (ed.), The Holmes–Einstein Letters (London: Macmillan, 1964), 73-74.

[258] A. Krock, Memoirs (London: Cassell, 1968), 105.

[259] Countess de Chambrun, Shadows Like Myself (New York: Scribner, 1936), 151.

[260] Theodore Roosevelt, "A Confession of Faith," in 17 TR, Works (New York: Scribner) 254ff, 279, 281, *see* L. Gould, Four Hats in the Ring: The 1912

At this point, Taft credited Roosevelt with "insincerity, self-ishness, monumental egotism and almost the insanity of megalomania ... He did a great deal in leading the crusade against the dangers of concentrated wealth. He has done very little in the way of constructive statesmanship.... I shall still have some opportunity to strike a blow for decent government and the better things and I mean to do it."[261] "He is not a real democrat. He has not the spirit that makes him bow to the will of the people."[262]

Roosevelt's approach to antitrust was both less radical and more discretionary than Taft's. The government should attack "not the mere fact of combination but the evils and wrongdoing which frequently accompany combination."[263]

Taft favored an amendment to the antitrust laws excluding the formation of labor unions from their scope; his proposal would have required actual intent to restrain trade, thus excluding labor.[264]

A labor-specific exclusion was forthcoming in the Clayton Act enacted by Congress during the Wilson administration, which, however, went past Taft's desire in other respects. He decried the proposal of Roosevelt's Progressive Party to allow the government to distinguish between "good" and "bad" trusts, finding this to be "shifting, vague and indeterminate."

Taft's Supreme Court decisions gave further force to the antitrust laws. In *Essgee Co. v. United States*[265] he held that discovery of corporate documents was not self-incrimination within the meaning of the Fifth Amendment, a decision indispensable to effective-

---

Election and the Birth of Modern American Politics (Lawrence: U. Press of Kansas, 2008), 51.

[261] 1 Pringle 794.

[262] 1 Pringle 894.

[263] T. Roosevelt, "The Trusts, the People, and the Square Deal," 99 Outlook 654 (1911); L. Gould, *supra*, 51.

[264] W.H. Taft, "Amendment to Interstate Commerce Law," September 20, 1909, in 3 W.H. Taft, Works 190ff.

[265] 262 U.S. 151 (1923).

ness of the law. Earlier, in 1895, he had despairingly observed: "The nature of corporate wrong is almost wholly beyond the reach of courts especially those of the United States. The corporate miners and sappers of public virtue do not work in the open, but under cover; their purposes are generally accomplished before they are known to exist, and the traces of their evil paths are destroyed and placed beyond the possibilities of legal proof."[266]

In *Maple Flooring Assn. v. United States*[267] he rejected, as in *Addyston Pipe*, a distinction between "good" and "bad" trusts, dissenting from a holding that the gathering of price information by a trade association was not an antitrust violation. Earlier, in the *American Column* case,[268] a not very different trade association program had been condemned, Taft writing for the majority and Holmes and Brandeis protesting that the Sherman Act "did not set itself against knowledge," Brandeis adding that such loose arrangements were an alternative to industrial consolidation.

A historian of antitrust has observed that "[Taft's] policy blend of moralism and market efficiency broke up true monopoly but encouraged increased managerial centralization identified with oligopoly. At the same time, federal and state prosecutors used the Court's per se rule making most anti-competitive behavior in and of itself unlawful to prevent cartelization, which often helped small business." "Louis Brandeis and others predicted that the American judiciary's refusal to apply the rule of reason to cartel practices would foster corporate consolidation and the demise of small firms."[269]

---

[266] "Recent Criticism of the Federal Judiciary," American Bar Association, Detroit, August 28, 1895, in 1 W.H. Taft, Works 306ff.

[267] 268 U.S. 563 (1925).

[268] American Column Co. v. United States, 257 U.S. 377 (1921).

[269] T. Fryer, "Business Law and American Economic History," in 2 S. Engerman and R. Gallman, The Cambridge Economic History of the United States (Cambridge: Cambridge U., 2000), 477.

In *F.T.C. v. Western Meat Coop* he joined a dissenting opinion of Justices Holmes, Brandeis, and Stone that would have upheld the Federal Trade Commission's authority to order the divestiture of stock, holding that section 7 of the Clayton Act applied to acts before the institution of suit. In *General Electric v. United States*[270] he held that the setting of resale prices was beyond a patentee's rights, unless it retained ownership of the goods in an agency arrangement. He upheld the FTC in prohibiting collective enforcement of resale price maintenance.[271]

He joined the majority opinion of Justice Stone in *United States v. Trenton Potteries*,[272] the foundational case declaring horizontal price fixing to be a per se violation of the antitrust laws; Justices Van Devanter, Sutherland, and Butler dissented. In *Federal Trade Commission v. Clare Co.*[273] he denied the right of a company to challenge an FTC investigation before the bringing of an enforcement action; Justice McReynolds was alone in dissent.

In 1912, he genuinely feared Roosevelt: "He has gone too far. He will either be a hopeless failure if elected or else destroy his own reputation by becoming a socialist, being swept there by force of circumstances just as the leaders of the French revolution were swept on and on, all their individual efforts failing to stem the tide until it had run itself out."[274] "[It] is important that opposition [to the Democrats] not be Rooseveltian and wildly radical."[275]

"We know what we are fighting for, and that is the maintenance of the Republican party as a useful instrument for political and governmental work in the future. We are more concerned in

---

[270] 272 U.S. 426 (1926).

[271] F.T.C. v. Beech Nut, 257 U.S. 44 (1922).

[272] 273 U.S. 406 (1927).

[273] 274 U.S. 160 (1927).

[274] D. Anderson, *supra*, 183, quoting 2 Butt, *supra* 846-47.

[275] Taft Papers, April 14, 1912.

keeping our party solid and maintaining party discipline than we are in winning the next election."[276] In this, he was entirely successful.

He was not unduly disturbed by the triumph of Wilson, declaring in 1910 an attitude resembling that of former Prime Minister Asquith when he gave his party's support to the installation of a Labour-led government in 1924: "Sooner or later the country will demand its dose of Bryanism or its equivalent and I am in favor of never again using such efforts as we did in the past to stay it. Educate the people if we can, but whatever the country thinks is right, whether it is right or wrong, it is right for it to have. Something has been radically wrong in our legislation in the past that such combinations have been formed under our laws and that we have to resort to all sorts of special legislation to counteract it. It may be that after all the opposition may have some remedy which we are unable or unwilling to try."[277]

In the same year, he observed, with some prescience: "There are no great figures on the English political stage or in Germany or Austria or any of the European countries. There is a pettiness about the immediate period which gives me some concern. I believe we are undergoing some change of which we are unmindful. It may be one of the periods which come frequently before some great epoch, the apparent stagnation which comes immediately before the crystallization of some great world thought or movement."[278]

His view of Roosevelt was shared by Speaker Cannon: "Roosevelt was a man of transcendent genius but if he had been followed by another President, a counterpart of himself, one as forceful and as daring, the system of free government would have ceased to exist

---

[276] WHT to Nellie Taft, July 14, 1912, in Dearest Nellie, *supra*, 206.

[277] 1 A. Butt, Taft and Roosevelt: The Intimate Letters of Archie Butt (New York: Doubleday, 1930), 273.

[278] *Id.* 331.

in the country. He was one of the few men I have ever met of whom I was afraid."[279]

It was said that "Taft hunted no grizzlies, assailed no San Juan Hills, took no Panama, broke with no political party, cried for no wars, explored no veldts, and searched for no Rivers of Doubt ... the habit of down-rightness is, in the last analysis, what makes Taft an appealing subject for a biographer."[280]

He was left, by his own description, with "the irreducible minimum of the Republican party that was left when Roosevelt got through with it and after Wilson drew from it the votes of those Republicans who feared Roosevelt."

The 1912 campaign began with Warren Harding's nominating speech for Taft at the Republican convention, employing the rather appalling alliterating style of rhetoric made familiar after Harding's election to the presidency in 1920: "Progress is not proclamation nor palaver. It is not pretence nor play on prejudice. It is not the perturbation of a people passion wrought nor a promise proposed. Progression is everlastingly lifting the standards that marks the end of the world's march yesterday and planting them on new and advanced heights today. Tested by such a standard, President Taft is the greatest progressive of the age."[281]

Taft ran a leisurely front-porch campaign in 1912, succeeding in his object—keeping Roosevelt out of office. He took the view that "a President who is a candidate for re-election should remain at home and leave it to the judgment of the electorate whether or not his record of achievement" deserves a second term.[282] It was

[279] E. Morris, Theodore Rex (New York: Random House, 2001), 232.

[280] J. Chamberlain, review of Pringle, William Howard Taft, New York Times, October 29, 1939.

[281] F. Russell, The Shadow of Blooming Grove (New York: McGraw Hill, 1968), 230.

[282] D. Goodwin, The Bully Pulpit: Theodore Roosevelt, William Howard Taft, and the Golden Age of Journalism (New York: Simon and Schuster, 2013), 724.

Taft and Wilson Inauguration 1913

said by a sympathetic historian that Taft in defeating Roosevelt for the Republican nomination in 1912 and reclaiming that party, "defined American politics for the rest of the century … He defined constitutional, popular government and defended it against one of the greatest assaults it has suffered in its short history … Taft kept his nation from the extremes of his age … he distilled the era of its extra-constitutional meanderings and prevented that dipsomaniac slide toward state control and the weakening of the courts and the Constitution that was among the lesser impulses of the progressive movement."[283] He himself took the view after defeating Roosevelt

---

[283] M. Bromley, William Howard Taft and the First Motoring Presidency, 1909-13 (Jefferson, NC: McFarland, 2003), 3.

at the convention that "we have won what there was to fight about, what follows is less important."[284] His program in 1912 was cautiously reformist: civil service reform, banking reform, the protective tariff, a Federal Trade Commission, ending corporate campaign contributions.[285]

His campaign, though low-key, was innovative in the use of new media: "other methods of advertising are coming into vogue—the use of billboards and election signs and the advertising panels of the streetcar is a logical outcome of the science of advertising and publicity that so many industrial concerns had occasion to make use of."[286]

He wrote a friend just after the election: "In my heart, I have long been making plans for my future."[287] Of his writings, it was said: "There is never any exhortation and still less is there any lightness of touch. There was in his make-up a strong streak of paternalism."[288]

Conservation

In his inaugural address, Taft declared a purpose to "sav[e] and restore our forests and [foster] great improvement of waterways." He favored "the deepening and control of the channel of a great river system like that of the Ohio or of the Mississippi" and took the

---

[284] D. Goodwin, The Bully Pulpit: Theodore Roosevelt, William Howard Taft, and the Golden Age of Journalism (New York: Simon and Schuster, 2013), 729.

[285] C. Anthony, Nellie Taft: The Unconventional First Lady of the Ragtime Era (New York: Morrow, 2005), 310ff.

[286] WHT in Minneapolis Journal, October 21, 1912, quoted in D. Goodwin, The Bully Pulpit: Theodore Roosevelt, William Howard Taft, and the Golden Age of Journalism (New York: Simon and Schuster, 2013).

[287] Taft to C.C. Clark, November 9, 1912.

[288] 1 W.H. Taft, Works 67ff.

view that "a permanent improvement should be treated as a distinct enterprise and paid for by the proceeds of bonds."[289]

"Taft . . . inaugurated a new policy of issuing no permits to build dams on navigable waters without a quid pro quo to the government. From this policy was to develop the Federal Power Commission and the present 'yardstick' extension of federal activity into the public utility field,"[290] exemplified by the Tennessee Valley Authority. However, under pressure from the environmental lobby, there has been a virtual moratorium on federal water projects, whether for land reclamation or power generation purposes, since the Carter administration.

The Ballinger–Pinchot controversy dominated the last half of the Taft administration. Gifford Pinchot was a crusading head of the Forest Service, impatient with legal niceties, who gave credit to accusations of irregularities made by a clerk named Louis Glavis. Secretary of the Interior Richard A. Ballinger did not credit these allegations. In the course of an elaborate congressional investigation in which Louis Brandeis represented those questioning administration policy, it was found that Ballinger with Taft's agreement had placed in the file of the case "a written statement [containing] such analysis and conclusions as he had given me, [filed] with the record and dated it prior to the date of [the] opinion, so as to show that [the] decision was fortified by his summary of the evidence." Twenty-five years later, Brandeis, with astonishing hyperbole, characterized this as "the worst act ever done by any President."[291]

Taft did not seek Ballinger's resignation, believing that Ballinger had acted from honest motives. His action was later defended

---

[289] Inaugural Address, March 4, 1909, in 3 W.H. Taft, Works, 47.

[290] M. Freedman, Roosevelt and Frankfurter: Their Correspondence: 1928-45 (London: Bodley Head, 1967), 306.

[291] L. Brandeis to Bernard Flexner, May 23, 1940, in 5 M. Urofsky and L. Levy (eds.), The Letters of Louis D. Brandeis (Albany: SUNY Press, 1978), 641.

Mr. and Mrs. William H. Taft

by Harold Ickes, President Franklin Roosevelt's Secretary of the Interior, who characterized Ballinger as an "American Dreyfus."[292]

He justified the replacement of James Garfield by Ballinger at the start of his administration: "Pinchot dominated Garfield."[293]

To his wife, Taft wrote that even Roosevelt believed that "Gifford Pinchot is a dear, but he is a lunatic, with an element of

---

[292] H. Ickes, "Not Guilty Richard A. Ballinger: An American Dreyfus," Saturday Evening Post 212, May 25, 1940.

[293] WHT to Gus Karger, March 12, 1910, Folder 4, Karger Correspondence, Cincinnati Museum.

hardness and narrowness in his temperament, and an extremist." "I can't for a moment permit that complete demoralization of discipline that follows the reposing of such power in the hands of a subordinate. The heads of the departments are the persons through whom I must act, and unless the bureau chiefs are subordinate to the heads, it makes efficient government impossible."[294]

In a speech in September 1909, Taft asserted that forest lands should be administered by the Forest Bureau, in the interest of "the preservation of the forests, the equalization of the water supply and their effect upon the climate." He noted that three-fourths of forests were private, and that only 3% of private forest lands were properly managed, as against 70% of public forest lands. He urged that forest lands be held by the Forest Bureau, that agricultural land be disposed of in accordance with the Homestead Laws, and that phosphate lands and sites good for water power be protected by legislation so that the public could share in their proceeds.[295]

Later in 1909, he noted that "[t]here isn't in reference to river construction or river navigation, that improvement that we ought to have had in the last forty years." He suggested the establishment of storage stations along navigable rivers.[296]

In his Second Annual Message in 1910, Taft sought more authority to reserve forest lands in the Western states, licensing of water power sites with rising royalties to the government, withdrawal from the Homestead Acts of oil, gas, and phosphate lands in the continental United States and coal lands in Alaska, and creation of a national park for "the greatest natural wonder of the country ... the Grand Canyon of the Colorado." He urged enhanced reforestation, noting that there were reforestation projects for only 15,000 acres of the 150 million acres in national forests. He opposed any

---

[294] WHT to Nellie Taft in Dearest Nellie, *supra* 73.

[295] WHT, "Conservation of Natural Resources," Spokane, September 28, 1909, in 3 W.H. Taft, Works 214.

[296] WHT, "Remarks to the Waterways Convention, New Orleans, October 30, 1909), in 3 W.H. Taft, Works 312.

federal financing of a new
Alaska railway, and urged
that any construction on
District of Columbia park-
land be prohibited without
express authority of Con-
gress. He urged the federal
acquisition of lands on the
Virginia side of the Potomac,
including Arlington Cem-
etery, Fort Myer, and the
Virginia palisades. In urging
development of Alaska coal
lands with royalties flow-
ing to the government, he

*William Howard Taft Establishes the
Tradition of Throwing Out
the First Pitch on April 14, 1910*

observed: "Real conservation involves wise non-wasteful use in the
present generation with every possible means of preservation for
succeeding generations." In urging the benefits of a reciprocal trade
treaty with Canada (ultimately approved by Congress and rejected
by the Canadian Parliament), he declared that it would "increase
the supply of our natural resources which, with the wastefulness of
children, we have exhausted."[297] Taft was alleged to have said that it
"would make Canada only an adjunct of the United States."[298]

Taft effectively carried out his declared conservation policies.
"By July 1910, 71,518,558 acres of coal lands had been withdrawn
[from the Homestead Act] in the United States and about 770,000
acres in Alaska. On July 3, Taft signed a bill authorizing 8,495,731
acres of water power, phosphate and petroleum lands, an area equal
to the states of New York, Pennsylvania and South Carolina ... these
withdrawals were the first to be legally authorized" and validated

---

[297] Second Annual Message, December 6, 1910, in 4 W.H. Taft, Works, 55,
58, 91, 121.

[298] W. La Feber, The American Search for Opportunity, 1865-1913, 2
Cambridge History of American Foreign Relations, 215.

Roosevelt's withdrawals.[299] "It seems that Pinchot went off half-cocked and that Ballinger was innocent of the charges. President Taft actually did as much or more than Roosevelt for conservation. He was the first to reserve federal lands where oil had been found [and] obtained from Congress the authority to reserve coal lands which Roosevelt had reserved without specific authority [and] purchased in 1911 ... great timbered tracts in the Appalachians."[300]

An additional $20 million was appropriated to complete reclamation projects.[301]

In his book *Popular Government*, published in 1914, Taft endorsed "enterprises national in their character, a plan for keeping the Mississippi within its banks to be contributed to by the States but to be executed under federal authority." Subsequent years, continuing to our own time, have seen a series of disastrous floods.

However, he vehemently declared:

"There is being agitated a plan to build good roads in all the States ... The interstate traffic is so largely taken care of by railroads and river and sea navigation. The evils of pork barrel bills in rivers and harbors appropriations and in public buildings bills will seem small and inconsiderable in the mad chase for a share in the good roads bill which the imaginations of many congressmen have already made into law."[302]

Taft, who was called "the first motoring President," nonetheless sponsored a modest but unsuccessful roads bill in his last year in the presidency, a version of which was enacted during the Wilson

---

[299] D. Anderson, *supra*, 134.

[300] S. Morison, The Oxford History of the American People (New York: Oxford, 1965), 833.

[301] P. Coletta, The Presidency of William Howard Taft (Topeka: U. Press of Kansas, 1973), 98.

[302] 4 W.H. Taft, Works 97-98.

General Taft Riding a Carabao

administration. "I admit that the general government has the power for the purpose of promoting interstate commerce to build national roads."[303] "I do not believe in involving the Federal treasury in a weight of obligation to build roads that the State ought to build."[304] A national highway program was enacted at the behest of the Eisenhower administration in 1956. Although devised according to a coherent plan and administered without too much reference to the pork barrel, it undermined both freight and passenger railroads to an extent later regretted and taken together with unenlightened land use policies had malign effects on American urban life,

<hr>

[303] American Motorist, January 12, 1912, quoted in M. Bromley, William Howard Taft and the First Motoring Presidency (Jefferson, NC: McFarland, 2003), 235.

[304] Taft to Hills, September 21, 1912, quoted in M. Bromley, William Howard Taft and the First Motoring Presidency (Jefferson, NC: McFarland, 2003), 235.

fostering formless suburbs without cultural centers and a separation of work and residence, "neighborhoods of strangers and juris-
dictions without traditions." There was nothing in America like the
British Prevention of Ribbon Development Acts of the late 1930s,
though the failures in land use legislation were partially redeemed
by two private innovations: residential community associations and
commercial "Edge Cities" with property assessment powers.

Civil Rights

After his retirement from the presidency, he was elected President of the American Bar Association in 1914, using his authority
to exclude progressive lawyers like Louis D. Brandeis and William
Draper Lewis from important committees.[305]

Taft was later influential in the preparation of Canons of Judicial Ethics, Canon 19 of which influenced his later behavior as a
Supreme Court justice: "a judge should not "yield to pride of opinion or value more highly his individual reputation than that of the
court to which he should be loyal—dissenting opinions should be
discouraged in courts of last resort [which should] use effort and
self-restraint to promote solidarity of conclusion and the consequent influence of judicial decision." The provision was supplanted
in 1972, to the Courts' loss.

Taft displayed a concern with the plight of blacks unusual in
his time, making more speeches to black audiences than any president until Lyndon Johnson, though the policies of his administration gave them little tangible assistance. It was said of him that "he
went further than would any president or presidential candidate
down to Franklin Roosevelt in seeking the political support of a
once-enslaved people." "He extended his hand and a good bit of his

---

[305]   L. Gould, *President to Chief Justice* (Topeka: U. Press of Kansas, 2014),
15.

heart to the three main under classes: blacks, Catholics, and Jews.[306] Perhaps Taft was not a good politician after all, but a kind man who saw himself as President of all the people."[307]

As Governor of the Philippines, he imposed no race bar, regularly entertaining Filipinos at his palace.[308]

He referred to Southern congressional districts as "rotten boroughs," and declared his personnel policy as follows:

> "I am not going to put into places of prominence in the South where the race feeling is strong Negroes whose appointment will only tend to increase that race feeling, but I shall look about and make appointments in the North and recognize the Negro as often as I can."[309]

While he "exercised a careful discretion not thereby to do more harm than good," he declared in his inaugural address that he tried not to be deceived by "the mere pretence of race feeling manufactured in the interest of individual political ambition." He appointed the first black federal judge, to the Municipal Court of the District of Columbia and the first black Assistant Attorney General, William H. Lewis, and refrained from appointing a judge who had upheld a Jim Crow law.[310]

Later, he wrote: "I am having difficulty in finding places for intelligent Negroes. The prejudice against them is so strong that it makes few places available, and yet I must do something for the race for they are entitled to recognition. Roosevelt has treated them so

---

[306] D. Burton, Preface, 3 W.H. Taft, Works.

[307] D. Burton, Preface to 2 W.H. Taft, Works 7.

[308] 1 Pringle 175.

[309] 1 Pringle 347, 390.

[310] M. Bromley, William Howard Taft and the First Motoring Presidency, 1909-13 (McFarland: Jefferson, NC, 2003), citing American Review of Reviews, March 1912, 271.

abominably that I feel more friendly to them than ever and anxious to help."[311]

He clashed with Roosevelt over Roosevelt's treatment of black servicemen in connection with a famous episode at Brownsville, Texas.[312] "He had annoyingly drawn Roosevelt's attention to a conflict in the testimony of the eyewitness who 'saw' black soldiers kill Frank Napus, and suggested that the Senate be informed ... these scruples were however kept confidential."[313]

Benno Schmidt later observed that "Taft was considerably more dubious about black rights than even Roosevelt, committed as he was to sectional reconciliation and to Republican inroads in the Solid South. 'Winning the South' was a favorite campaign address, the themes of which were that Southern whites were the black man's best friends and that the South need not fear Republican efforts to enforce 'social equality.'"

The reason for Taft's restrained attitude toward reform of the South went beyond party politics and found their fullest expression in a conversation with his military aide Archie Butt: "It is very necessary for the South and the national government to get very close together, and I am going to do all in my power to bring about a closer union, not so much for the South as for the federal government itself. I can look ahead fifteen, twenty, possibly fifty years, for in that time some very serious questions are coming up, problems which are as serious as the Civil War itself, and when they come up the federal government will demand the support of the South for the maintenance of Anglo-Saxon law as we have it in this country. The Southern people are our most homogeneous people and by nature the most conservative—not the conservatism which comes from wealth and the desire to protect that which it has, but

---

[311] L. Gould (ed.), *My Dearest Nellie: The Letters of William Howard Taft to Helen Hebron Taft, 1909-1912* (Lawrence: U. Press of Kansas, 2011), 265.

[312] "Roosevelt and Taft Said to Have Clashed," *New York Times*, November 21, 1906.

[313] E. Morris, *Theodore Rex* (New York: Random House, 2001), 482.

a conservatism which stands for precedents, for unwritten law, for association and for the preservation of the Constitution."[314]

According to his Archie Butt, an unreconstructed Southerner, Taft considered that "we must depend on some of the South to help us out to hold the country from absolute socialism."[315] It was, paradoxically, the "black and tan" delegations from Southern states with only nominal numbers of Republican voters that gave him the Republican nomination in 1912; they were also important to his son Robert at the Republican conventions in 1940, 1948, and 1952.

This prophecy could be said to have been redeemed with enactment of the Taft–Hartley Act. Archie Butt urged on Taft the harsher proposition that: "I believe the South is ready to break away from its losses just as soon as the Republicans prove by their works that they have thrown the Negro overboard."[316] This prophecy was realized in 1964 with the nomination of Barry Goldwater, an opponent of civil rights legislation. In a real sense, Taft was the originator of the Republicans' Southern Strategy, not rendered explicit until the Nixon administration.

In office, however, Taft's administration maintained the policy of prosecuting and investigating peonage. It pursued the Grandfather Clause cases but did not otherwise contest Jim Crow or make black appointments in the South. Rejecting a claim for clemency by a man convicted of peonage, Taft declared: "Fines are not effective against men of wealth. Imprisonment is necessary. [Clemency] would give real ground for the contention often heard that it is only the poorer criminals that are really punished."[317]

---

[314] 1 A. Butt, Taft and Roosevelt: The Intimate Letters of Archie Butt (New York: Doubleday, 1930), 111.

[315] 2 A. Butt, Taft and Roosevelt: The Intimate Letters of Archie Butt (New York: Doubleday, 1930), 479.

[316] 2 A. Butt, Taft and Roosevelt: The Intimate Letters of Archie Butt (New York: Doubleday, 1930), 512.

[317] D. Daniel, Shadow of Slavery (Urbana: U. of Illinois, 1990), 93, *see also* R. Logan, The Betrayal of the Negro (New York: Macmillan, 1964), 347.

In 1909, he came close to intervening in a Georgia Railroad strike in which the union pressured the railroad to discharge black workers: "I had practically issued the order to patrol the line from Atlanta to Augusta with federal troops and you know what that would mean in the South. But the law on the subject is so clear and my duty was so manifest that I should not have hesitated a minute had the strike not ended as it did."[318]

Taft vetoed a bill seeking to impose a literacy test on immigrants.[319]

"The class should be intelligent enough to know its own interests, should as a whole care enough to look after its interests." He noted that at the time of liberation from slavery, only 5% of Southern blacks were literate. He regarded the developing shift in the South from grammar to industrial education as a good thing. He defended educational and property qualifications for voting if they were impartially administered, taking the view that the Fifteenth Amendment "does not involve social equality" and that it was "not intended to give [the Negro] affirmative privileges as a member of his race." In his inaugural address, he observed that the Fifteenth Amendment "has not been generally observed ... It is clear to all that the domination of an ignorant irresponsible element can be prevented by constitutional laws which shall exclude from voting both Negroes and whites not having education or the other qualifications thought necessary for a proper electorate."[320] Of the Southerners, he charitably observed: "they cast about to make the

---

[318] 1 A. Butt, Taft and Roosevelt: The Intimate Letters of Archie Butt (New York: Doubleday, 1930), 110.

[319] 2 Pringle 623. He abhorred lynching, noting that when people are "assembled in a mob, they soon lose their conscience." W.H. Taft, Duties of Citizenship, in 1 W.H. Taft, Works.

[320] 3 W.H. Taft, Works 52.

law square with existing conditions by property and educational qualifications."[321]

It is not generally appreciated that today's restrictions on literacy tests derive from elaborate provisions in the Voting Rights Act of 1965 and not from the Constitution.

He took the view that "[e]verything which tends to send the immigrants west and south into rural life helps the country. Congestion in the City of New York does not make for the better condition of the migrant or increase his usefulness as a member of the community."[322]

He was, however, not a restrictionist in matters of immigration, unlike his son Robert, who came to political maturity at a time when there were more than 10 million Americans unemployed. The Taft administration was a time of record immigration and relatively full employment. In 1913, before the post-war recession and the recrudescence of nativism, Taft told a group in New Haven:

"Perhaps your industries require skilled labour and doubtless you have that skilled labour. I think this might prompt you to organize industrial schools to create a supply of this skilled labour. The Italians and Russian Jews have come here since my time. Often they are looked upon as undesirable. I want to testify that they make good citizens, as loyal in appreciating and benefiting the institutions of this country as many Americans who do not."[323]

---

[321] "Achievements of the Republican Party," Kansas City Young Men's Republican Club, February 10, 1908, W. Taft, Works 281.

[322] W.H. Taft, Second Annual Message, December 6, 1910, in 4 W.H. Taft, Works 64.

[323] T. Hicks, William Howard Taft: Yale Professor of Law and New Haven Citizen (New Haven: Yale U., 1945), 25.

Asked whether he would return to Cincinnati, he referred to his family's New England origins and said "New Haven is good enough for me." While there, he was "forceful in his insistence that 'the Green' remain undisturbed, for he deemed it the centre and symbol of the New Haven community."[324]

In the wake of World War I he was a supporter of the League of Nations Minority Treaties promoted by the Franco–British journalist and scholar Lucien Wolf. He had observed that "[i]t is not too much to say that people of the Jewish race have suffered more in this War, as non-combatants, than any other people, unless it be the Serbians or Armenians."[325]

In his book *Liberty Under Law* Taft acknowledged that "[t]he fifteenth amendment has been nullified in eleven Southern states so that at least a million colored voters do not vote."[326] "Both parties have wisely decided to let the election problem work itself out and to await the local solution that the results of fraud and violence at elections will compel."[327]

This smacks of overoptimism, but the demise of de jure voting discrimination worked by the Supreme Court decision in the *Grandfather Clause* cases was no small thing. As the historian Kenneth Stampp has observed: "Negroes were no longer denied equality by the plain language of the law, as they had been before radical reconstruction, but only by coercion, by subterfuge, by deceit, and by spurious legalisms … When, however, state-imposed discrimination was, in effect, an evasion of the supreme law of the land, the odds, in the long run, were on the side of the Negro."[328]

---

[324] D. Burton, Taft, Holmes and the 1920s Court (Teaneck, NJ: Fairleigh Dickinson U., 1998), 2.1

[325] 7 W.H. Taft, Works, "The League of Nations and Religious Liberty," 54.

[326] 7 W.H. Taft, Works, 7ff.

[327] "Recent Criticism of the Federal Judiciary," American Bar Association, Detroit, August 28, 1895, in 1 W.H. Taft, Works, 298-99.

[328] K. Stampp, The Era of Reconstruction, 1865-1877 (New York: Vintage, 1965) 215.

He decried "demonization of the entire race on account of a comparatively small criminal class that formed the dregs of the Southern population."[329] In a speech on "The Future of the Negro" to a black audience in the Allen Temple in Cincinnati on September 15, 1908, Taft noted the increase in literacy among blacks from 5% to 50% in the preceding 40 years. He observed that "Prejudice fades away most rapidly when there are pecuniary reasons for its disappearance." He declared: "I have not always thought that higher education among the Negroes should be encouraged but ... I am convinced I was in error." He urged the training of doctors, because many blacks "do not understand the laws of hygiene and when they are ill they are quite likely not to receive proper medical attention." Ministers were needed to advise "in respect to all the trying problems that must arise in their lives." There was a wide field for black lawyers, "not so wide as that of medicine or the ministry." He spoke of the need to hold to account officers of the law in connection with lynchings. "We still retain in our nature a great deal of the original animal ... the spirit of the mob seems to be a different spirit from that of the individuals making it up." Blacks "suffered the contemptuous insults of white men not at all his equal either in point of intelligence or devotion to duty.... he is not thereby released from the burden of responsibility that he must assume to win his way in the community by industry and thrift."[330]

In 1915, he condemned the failure of the authorities in East St. Louis, Illinois, to protect blacks against a white mob: blacks "had the constitutional right to enjoy the same protection extended by Illinois to all of its laboring men and women, white or black," and the authorities had shown "weakness, political cowardice, and utter inefficiency."[331]

---

[329] W.H. Taft, "Southern Democracy and Republican Principles," Lexington, KY, August 21, 1907, in 1 W.H. Taft, Works 245, 247.

[330] 1 W. H. Taft, Works 55ff.

[331] L. Gould, Chief Executive to Chief Justice (Lawrence: U. Press of Kansas, 2014), 91.

Later, in 1909, he spoke to a black congregation on "Hopeful Views of Negro Difficulties," noting that "your race is a musical race and an oratorical race, and I am neither musical nor oratorical … I would not have you for a moment abate the thought of the duty imposed on every one of you of making as much of the talent that the Lord gives you as you can."

To another black audience in Augusta, Georgia, in January 1909, he declared:

> "You must condemn your criminals with the same severity that you condemn white criminals. You are naturally suspicious when a man is condemned that there may be race prejudice entering into the condemnation. You cannot ask for justice on the one hand and then say you ought to be released from its enforcement on the other."[332]

After World War I, Taft took the view that "[p]robably the dearth of labor in the North and the increasing economic value of the Negroes to the South will stimulate migration as a defence against injustice and make it more effective."[333]

His reaction to race riots in Chicago in August 1919 resulting in 38 deaths was to urge leaders of both races in large cities to jointly take measures "to stop hysteria, to allay alarm, and to arrest loud-mouthed agitators and criminals before the trouble begins. Troops in impressive and overwhelming force must be summoned at once." This sensible recipe is not always followed, as in the disturbances in the author's native Baltimore in 2015.

On the Supreme Court Taft wrote two opinions, both involving the rights of Chinese. The opinions faced in different directions.

---

[332] "The Outlook of Negro Education," Haines Normal and Industrial School, Augusta, GA, January 19, 1909, in 2 W.H. Taft, Works 203.

[333] Editorial, "Racial Prejudice," June 2, 1919, Editorials at 220.

In *Gong Lum v. Rice*,[334] perhaps the high water mark of racial discrimination, a Chinese student was required to attend the local colored school, Taft, conceding that if there was no colored school in the neighborhood, a different question would be presented. The opinion was unanimous; it did not involve constitutional claims.

In *Yu Cong Eng v. Trinidad*,[335] Taft held invalid a prohibition on the keeping of business books in a foreign language, on the authority of *Meyer v. Nebraska*, a famous substantive due process opinion by Justice McReynolds in which Taft had joined, which scornfully declared: "Evidently the legislature has attempted intentionally to interfere with the calling of modern language teachers, with the opportunities of pupils to acquire knowledge and with the power of parents to control the education of their own." Taft saw the statute as a "mere excuse for an unjust discrimination or the oppression or spoliation of a particular class."

Taft also joined the later McReynolds substantive due process decision in *Pierce v. Society of Sisters*[336] with its explicit rejection of the educational ideals of Plato's *Republic* and ancient Sparta and its denial of "any general power of the State to standardize its children by forcing them to accept instruction from public teachers only. The child is not the mere creature of the State; those who nurture him and direct his destiny have the right, coupled with the high duty, to recognize and prepare him for additional obligations." He also joined in the application of the Fifth Amendment due process clause to extend *Pierce* to the Territory of Hawaii.[337]

Holmes and Sutherland dissented in *Meyer* but not in *Pierce*; even Learned Hand, along with Holmes the most stalwart opponent of substantive due process, had no problem with the result, as distinct from its reasoning.

---

334 275 U.S. 78 (1927).

335 271 U.S. 500 (1926).

336 268 U.S. 510 (1925).

337 Farrington v. Tokusbige, 273 U.S. 284 (1927).

In an age when a prominent liberal internationalist, Thomas Friedman of the *New York Times*, has held up as an ideal the abolition of private schools and mandatory education from the age of three,[338] it is useful to be reminded of an era in which some elements of individualist, as distinct from collectivist, liberalism commanded almost unanimous agreement. "Parents, as a rule, are fond of their children, and do not regard them merely as material for political schemes," Bertrand Russell wrote in 1929. "The State cannot be expected to have the same attitude."[339] Few of today's "liberals" recall that Article 26(3) of the Universal Declaration of Human Rights affirms that "[p]arents have a prior right to choose the kind of education that shall be given to their children."

Taft joined Justice Holmes' unanimous decision in *Nixon v. Herndon*,[340] the first of the modern voting rights cases, invalidating the "white primary." The opinion contains declarations later abandoned by the court in voting rights cases, with perhaps dubious results: "Color cannot be made the basis of a statutory classification ... the law in the States shall be the same for the black as for the white, that all persons whether colored or white shall stand equal before the laws of the State."

From the end of his presidency in 1912 to his death in 1930, he served as a member of the board, and from 1914 as chairman, of Hampton Institute, a college for Negroes emphasizing vocational training. He and Charles Eliot, the President of Harvard, commended it as a model for both blacks and whites, and went so far as to call it "the first major reform in American education in several hundred years." This view has continuing pertinence; if persisted in, it might have created a black middle class of small businessmen and artisans rather than the more bureaucratic and vulnerable black middle class later arising from affirmative action policies of

---

[338]   T. Friedman, "If I Ruled the World," Prospect, February 2017.

[339]   B. Russell, Marriage and Morals (New York: Liveright, 1929), 216-17.

[340]   273 U.S. 536 (1927).

large governmental and private organizations. The Institute offered courses in auto mechanics, forging and welding, brick masonry, plastering, electricity, cabinetmaking, upholstery, tailoring, dry cleaning, machine shop, plumbing and heating, sheet-metal and roofing, printing, and carpentry. Over time, its program changed to that of a conventional university. It awarded its first bachelor's degree in 1926 and now has schools of engineering, pharmacy, business education, journalism, nursing, liberal arts, and science. Its industrial program was criticized by some prominent black leaders, including W.E.B. Du Bois and John Hope, as "accommodating to white prejudice and supportive of racial discrimination," though Du Bois and Booker T. Washington, who organized Tuskegee Institute along similar lines, were later reconciled. It was the avowed purpose of Hampton to "fit the pupil for the life he is likely to lead." It offered, at the least, "access to a wider world," but became "a prime target for vitriolic condemnation by those who demanded quality education for black people and an end to white paternalism."[341]

Taft saw Hampton as "a source of profit, of peace, of law and order, and of general community happiness."[342]

Taft joined the Hampton board with the understanding that he would not be required to attend more than one meeting each year, a commitment that he kept. He felt that the school should shun controversy; when the Virginia legislature passed a Jim Crow law requiring segregation of all places of public assembly, he joined in counseling a course of evasion, not resistance: the school declared that access to all its assemblies was restricted to its students, faculty, and alumni and others asking to be put on a list of associates. He was not sympathetic to student protests and demonstrations, which were met with suspensions: "it is difficult to be patient with

---

[341] R. Engs, Educating the Disadvantaged and Disinherited (Nashville: U. Tennessee, 1999), 164, 167-68, see also D. Spivey, Schooling for the New Slavery: Black Industrial Education 1868-1915 (Westport, CT: Greenwood, 1978).

[342] WHT, The Influence of Hampton, Report of the Department of the Interior, Bureau of Education, Bulletin 23 (1923), 3-4, see D. Spivey, supra, 37.

such an exhibition, and they ought to be taught a lesson that we shall not be bothered again. It is a disposition to ape the absurdities of other institutions—public schools—in some cities where the children are influenced by the wild ideas of their parents in the matter of democratic control of the school by the children." He exchanged about 400 letters with the Institute's presidents, and was especially active in a fund drive in 1925 that matched a $3 million gift toward endowment. "Taft's intimate connection with, and great interest in, Hampton's whole program were partially responsible for several of the larger bequests which the school received from major philanthropists. His connection with national politicians most probably helped the school hold on to its land in the face of several federal encroachments and in turn he may have helped various Black people, recommended by Hampton's President, to get the government jobs they wanted. Taft's connection with Hampton Institute marked the high point in the school's involvement with the most important national political leaders. Almost every President from the time of Hampton's founding to Taft's administration visited the college, but none did so after Taft left office."[343]

In the 1912 campaign, Taft stated his position on women's suffrage: that it was up to the states. He noted that about a million women had already been enfranchised.[344]

During his years at Yale, Taft warned schoolgirls to acquire the means of self-support and not to rush blindly into handicapping marriages. While teaching at Yale, he deplored "the lack of erect bearing, the indifferent manners and slouchy dress among the students" as well as smoking, gum-chewing, and late-night dancing.[345] In *Liberty Under Law*, written after leaving office, Taft supported

---

[343] H. Young, "William Howard Taft and Hampton Institute," in K. Schall (ed.), Stony the Road: Chapters in the History of Hampton Institute (Charlottesville: U. Press of Virginia, 1977), 125, 136, 156, 157.

[344] 2 Pringle 823ff.

[345] L. Gould, Chief Executive to Chief Justice (Lawrence: U. Press of Kansas, 2014), 31.

women's suffrage by reason of "the spread of education and knowledge of public affairs among them, the increase of those who had
no male voters to act for them, and the pressure on them to earn a
separate livelihood."[346]

After departing from the presidency, Taft supplemented his
income on the lecture circuit, though without obtaining the extor-
tionate fees now prevalent, and enjoyed train travel in sleeping cars.

In 1919, he wrote: "I am inclined to think that modern progress
requires that women's influence be allowed to exert itself through
the ballot … Of course, it will dilute the electorate by introducing a
good deal of ignorance into it in greater proportion than now exists,
and the still greater element of inexperience."[347]

As a Supreme Court Justice, he rejected any contention that
the suffrage amendment extended beyond voting rights. In his dissent in *Adkins v. Children's Hospital*[348] from a decision invalidating a
minimum wage law for women, he declared:

> "The Nineteenth Amendment did not change the
> physical strength or limitations of women upon which
> the decision in *Muller v. Oregon* rests."

During World War I, he urged that "trained nurses in the
Army should have military rank and commissions. They are as
necessary in winning the war as the infantry and artillery … rank
counts much in enforcing order and discipline."[349]

He attributed Wilson's re-election in 1916 to "the emotional
votes of the women, the extreme speeches of Roosevelt and the
besotted comfort of the Western farmers."[350] Judge Learned Hand

---

[346] 7 W.H. Taft, Works 7.

[347] J. Lurie, *supra*, at 185, citing Taft-Karger Correspondence, Cincinnati
Museum Centre, Folder 48.

[348] 261 U.S. 525 (1923).

[349] Editorial, June 14, 1918.

[350] 2 Pringle 899.

was also to comment on Wilson's peculiar appeal to women: "He had, and I should say that it was his greatest failing, the gift of inspiring others, particularly women, with a sense of the loftiness of his moral principles. Men like Wilson are soothsayers, misleaders of the children of men." A British writer, Richard Law, similarly observed: "A phenomenon like Neville Chamberlain would have been inconceivable before [women's suffrage] in 1918."[351]

His most robust statement on the position of women was contained in a speech at a college in Mississippi in 1909:

> "I shall be glad that I shall not have any property to leave to my boys, of whom I have two; but for my daughter I am going to scrape together as much as I can give her and as good an education as I can so that she shall take in the lesson which I first sought to announce as the text of my discourse, that she marry only when she chooses to marry and not because of circumstances."
>
> "We have not opened all the avenues to livelihood which they are quite as well able to fill and, in a certain sense, better able to fill, than we are."
>
> "The great principle of popular government is that each class in the community, assuming it has intelligence enough to know its own interest, can be better trusted to look after that interest than any other class, however altruistic that class."

When Taft made his last will, his children were in their forties and safely married. With the exception of three bequests to employees, a $10,000 bequest to Yale, $7,500 to the Taft School, and $2,500 to All Souls Unitarian Church, his entire estate was left to his wife. Had she predeceased him, half the estate would have gone to his daughter and a quarter to each of his sons.

---

[351] J. Gottlieb, "Guilty Women," Foreign Policy and Appeasement in Inter-War Britain (Basingstoke, 2015), 173.

As a trial judge in Cincinnati, Taft was protective of the rights of witnesses, once declaring: "I will not have you humiliate this witness any further."

He was of the view that "the jury ought never to be abolished in an Anglo-Saxon country in criminal cases," though he defended the right of judges to summarize and comment on evidence as well the right of judges to set aside verdicts and manage trials to avoid prolixity.[352]

The instructions of the President to the Second Philippine Commission, drafted by Taft, provided for recognition of most of the Bill of Rights except for trial by jury and the right to bear arms. Taft's biographer concluded in 1939 that "[i]ts phrases stand up well, very well indeed, although 40 years have passed since it was drafted."[353]

He attached great importance to the writ of habeas corpus: "The common law stands for the utmost liberty of the individual and as a price of this liberty it imposes on the person enjoying it the burden of looking out for himself. At the common law, the prisoner or his friends has the practical remedy of the writ, which being of high privilege he may obtain for the asking of any judge, who runs the risk of incurring the heaviest penalty himself if he refuse."[354]

However, he regarded Lincoln's claim of a right to suspend habeas corpus in the civil war as "well founded."[355]

He was unhappy about some of the constitutional limitations on law enforcement. The defendant's right of allocution, derivative of the Sixth Amendment right of confrontation, prevented the prosecution from using depositions at trial; the Fourth Amendment limited discovery of corporate papers; some courts had held

---

[352] W. Taft, Duties of Citizenship, in 1 W.H. Taft, Works 27.

[353] 1 Pringle 184.

[354] W.H. Taft, "Administration of Criminal Law," Yale Law School, June 21, 2005, 1 W.H. Taft, Works 327.

[355] W. Taft, The President and His Powers (1914) in 5 W.H. Taft, Works 110.

that the right of jury trial precluded judges from commenting on evidence. He was also unhappy about the privilege against self-incrimination. He lauded the practice of the English courts of limiting the questions available on appeal in criminal cases.[356]

In his Annual Message in 1911, he endorsed American Bar Association bills codifying the harmless error rule and allowing special verdicts.[357]

Taft had a calm attitude toward anarchist bombings: "A man who bided his time and kept his counsel and had no confederates could work widespread destruction with impunity. But vicious purpose in human nature carries its own antidote in other qualities which usually accompany it. The plotter seeks others to aid, and gives the place of danger to the neophyte. Egotism and vanity are usual traits of men who conceive world reform through hatred and destruction of those they envy. They must talk. They must boast. They must have the praise of their followers and their sympathizers. The trail to their crimes is posted by the harangues of their orators."[358]

While on the Supreme Court, Taft delivered a number of important criminal law judgments. In *United States v. Lanza*,[359] he held that the double jeopardy clause was not violated by successive federal and state prosecutions, thus preventing either government from immunizing a defendant from further prosecution. "If a State were to punish … by small or nominal fines, the race of offenders to the courts of that state would not make for respect for the federal statute."[360] The decision was re-affirmed by a 7-2 majority in June 2019.[361]

---

[356] "Labour and the Writ of Injunction, Orchestra Hall, September 16, 2009, in 3 W.H. Taft, Works 140ff.

[357] 4 W.H. Taft, Works, 215.

[358] Editorial, "Coping with Bomb Throwers," June 14, 1919.

[359] 267 U.S. 87 (1925).

[360] *See also* Ponzi v. Fessenden, 258 U.S. 254 (1922).

[361] Gamble v. United States, ____ U.S. ____ (June 17, 2019).

He decided two important cases involving automobiles. In *Brooks v. United States*,[362] he upheld the Dyer Act, penalizing interstate transportation of stolen automobiles. In *Carroll v. United States*,[363] he held that an attenuated showing of probable cause would suffice to justify a search of an automobile. His Dyer Act decision was a strained and reluctant one: "Congress can prohibit the interstate spread of an evil thing, although it cannot prohibit the spread of something harmless in itself in order to suppress an evil which is properly the subject of state police regulation." In correspondence, Taft explained that a stolen car was "a canker. It attracts shady and disreputable individuals."[364]

He also held in *Hammerschmidt v. United States*[365] that anti-government propaganda could not be prosecuted under a statute penalizing fraud against the government and in *Ex Parte Grossman*[366] that the president can pardon a person convicted of criminal contempt of court.

In the famous free speech cases of his era, *Gitlow*, *Whitney*, and *Schwimmer*,[367] he voted with the government, not joining the Holmes and Brandeis concurrence in *Whitney* and dissents in *Gitlow* and *Schwimmer*. In the last case, Sanford also dissented. Underlying Taft's caution in free speech cases was a fear of crowds and demagogues and a belief in deliberative, representative government shared by Herbert Hoover, who had written in 1922: "The crowd only feels; it has no mind of its own which can plan. The crowd is credulous, it destroys, it consumes, it hates, and it dreams—but it

---

[362] 267 U.S. 432 (1925).

[363] 267 U.S. 132 (1925).

[364] Taft Papers, Library of Congress, Reel 614, pp. 6-7, Brooks v. United States, quoted in B. Cushman, "Inside the Taft Court," 2015 Supreme Court Review 345.

[365] 265 U.S. 182 (1924).

[366] 267 U.S. 87 (1925).

[367] Gitlow v. New York, 268 U.S. 652 (1925); Whitney v. California, 274 U.S. 357 (1927); United States v. Schwimmer, 279 U.S. 644 (1929).

never builds ... man in the mass does not think but only feels. The mob functions only in a world of emotion. The demagogue feeds on mob emotions and his leadership is the leadership of emotion, not of intellect and progress."[368] Free speech, for Taft, unlike many of today's "liberals," had as its purpose sustaining a political order, by giving minorities the wherewithal to fight again without violent revolution. He would have agreed with Learned Hand's declaration in the *Masses* case that "[o]ne may not counsel or advise others to violate the law as it stands. Words are not only the keys of persuasion but the triggers of action, and those which have no purport but to counsel violation of law cannot by any latitude of interpretation be a part of that public opinion which is the final source of government in a democratic state."[369] He would not have approved (nor would Hand) the later pronouncement of the Supreme Court in *Brandenberg v. Ohio*[370] that such speech was permissible unless lawless action was imminent and that no respect was due to existing political settlements: an exaltation of individual will over societal interests.

In *Moore v. Dempsey*,[371] the first case applying the Bill of Rights to state criminal procedure, Taft joined Justice Holmes' prevailing opinion; Justices McReynolds and Sutherland dissented.

In the hotly contested case of *Olmstead v. United States*,[372] he held that wiretapping did not violate the Fourth Amendment because it did not constitute a physical trespass. "Here we have evidence only of voluntary conversations secretly overheard," not a search of "material things." His brother Horace observed of him that "pitted against old unscrupulous criminal lawyers and before judges

---

[368] H. Hoover, American Individualism (New York: Doubleday. 1922), 24-25.

[369] Masses Publishing Co. v. Patten, 244 F. 535 (S.D.N.Y. 1917).

[370] 395 U.S. 444 (1969).

[371] 261 U.S. 86 (1924).

[372] 277 U.S. 438 (1928).

of mediocre ability and juries of less than mediocre intelligence, he acquired that strong conviction that lasted him all his life, that the American system of justice requires thorough reform in the selection of judges and juries and that in any criminal case in America the dice are heavily loaded in favor of the accused, I have no doubt that that was in his mind when the case of wire-tapping came up in Prohibition days when he was on the Supreme Court bench."[373]

The case is remembered for the Holmes and Brandeis dissents: "I think it a less evil that some criminals should escape than that the government should play an ignoble part." "The greatest dangers to liberty lurk in insidious encroachment by men of zeal, well-meaning but without understanding."

In 1921, reviewing a book on administration of the criminal law, he criticized the latitude given to peremptory challenges and the time spent on jury selection, evils later exacerbated by the Supreme Court opinion in *Batson v. Kentucky*, making each peremptory challenge the subject of litigation without reducing the number of challenges. He also deplored the excessive granting of postponements in cases where defendants were released on bail: "it is by delay that the criminals with money secure immunity." He also regretted state legislation impairing the right of judges to comment on and summarize evidence.[374]

In *United States v. Fruit Growers Express*,[375] he enunciated the principle that criminal statutes were to be narrowly interpreted. Other cases upheld a defendant's right to be present for all communications with a jury,[376] denied that a prisoner on death row had a right to serve a sentence for years prior to his execution ("the penitentiary is no sanctuary and life in it does not confer immunity

---

[373] H. Taft, Memories and Reflections (New York: Macmillan, 1942), 114.

[374] Editorial, "Crime in the U.S.," February 6, 1921, Editorials 532.

[375] 279 U.S. 363 (1929).

[376] Shields v. United States 273 U.S. 583 (1927).

from capital punishment provided by law"),[377] applied the "harmless error" rule,[378] and held that a court had no power to grant probation after a term of imprisonment had commenced.[379]

He also upheld a statute allowing automobiles associated with crimes to be forfeited to the government, a statute recently said to have been much abused.

Educational Issues

It was said of the Tafts that "they respected education in the New England tradition and claimed as much of it as they could."[380]

Alphonso Taft, a hard taskmaster, once declared "mediocrity will not do for Will."[381]

Governor Taft introduced free education under municipal auspices in the Philippines.[382]

For university students, education in his view was a mixed blessing. The tendency toward parlor socialism was due to the fact that "students ordinarily are much better able to master the main principles than their complicated variation or modification due to intervening causes. In their eyes, selfishness can never be enlightened." Nonetheless, "all college graduates poor as well as rich have time enough and energy enough and ought to have interest enough to attempt to make the politics of the neighborhood in which they live better."[383]

---

[377] Kelley v. Oregon, 273 U.S. 589 (1927).

[378] Sigurola v. United States, 275 U.S. 106 (1927).

[379] United States v. Murray, 275 U.S. 343 (1928).

[380] 1 Pringle 19.

[381] *Id.* 22. Alphonso took the view that "Manhood doesn't properly come until one is 30 years of age." *Id.* 458.

[382] *Id.* 184.

[383] "Duties of Citizenship" in 1 W.H. Taft, Works 14ff.

He told a group of black educators that one problem was "a desire for everybody to be a general ... You have got to make them better by treating each individual mind and soul."[384]

He identified a need for some form of federal assistance to education, at least in parts of the South:

> "We have always prided ourselves on our public schools, but we had a great shock to that pride when we examined the statistics of illiteracy revealed by the rigid examination of men drafted or enlisted into the army for the great war ... our teachers are not properly paid and therefore they are not properly prepared to teach ... the negroes and the foreign born greatly increase the numbers needing special attention. It is so great a work that the agency of the national government must be involved for help in some practical and ameliorating way in the states where illiteracy is more prevalent, funds are not available from state resources, and national assistance may be properly extended."[385]

His son Robert shared this view, securing federal aid to education legislation that passed the House but fell victim to a Senate filibuster.

In his last published editorial before his ascent to the Supreme Court, he called for a revival of classical education in Greek, Latin, and Mathematics, deploring "courses in new pedagogy of doubtful value." "The kindergarten method of training a child under the age of six has been extended to the education of youth. Under such an impulse the demoralizing wholesale college elective system was introduced, it is time for a wise reaction from radical and destructive pedagogical views." The older curriculum, in his view "stimulates

---

[384] 2 W.H. Taft, Works 185ff.

[385] "Liberty Under Law," in 7 W.H. Taft, Works 11ff.

close mental attention and enforces logical deduction and induction and synthesis and analysis."[386]

In his Second Annual Message in 1910, President Taft urged creation of a Bureau of Health, including all schools of medicine, as well as a heavy federal tax on the manufacture of phosphorous matches: "the diseases incident to this are frightful."[387]

Prohibition

Taft's attitude toward alcohol prohibition did not differ greatly from that of his father Alphonso Taft: "coercive and officious legislation."[388]

In *Duties of Citizenship*[389] Taft said it was "foolish to enact laws incapable of enforcement." "In cases where the sale of liquor cannot be prohibited in fact, it is far better to regulate and diminish the evil than attempt to stamp it out. The constant violation or neglect of any law leads to a demoralized view of all laws." He unsuccessfully vetoed the Webb–Kenyon Act, which expanded the ability of the states to enforce Prohibition, and later dissented from the Supreme Court decision upholding it.

His most extended statements on Prohibition came after he had retired from the presidency and had become Professor of Law at Yale. They took the form of letters to the *New Haven Journal-Courier* in 1918.

In the first of these, he declared:

"I am opposed to national prohibition ... because I think it is a mixing of the national government in a matter that should be one of local settlement. I think

---

[386] Editorial, "Study of the Classics," July 5, 1921, Editorials, 593.

[387] 4 W.H. Taft, Works, 48, 65.

[388] 1 Pringle 81ff.

[389] 1 W.H. Taft, Works.

sumptuary laws are matters for parochial adjustment. I think it will vest in the national government and those who administer it so great a power as to be dangerous in political matters ... except in local communities where the majority of citizens are in favor of the law, it will be violated ... and as such demoralize the enforcement of all laws ... I think it is most unwise to fasten upon the United States a prohibitory system under the excitement of the war which ... every sensible supporter of prohibition in the end will regret.... I don't drink myself at all, and I don't oppose prohibition on the ground that it limits the liberties of the people. I think that in the interest of the community and of the man who cannot resist the temptation to drink in excess ... other citizens in the community may be properly be asked and compelled to give up drinking, although that drinking may do them no injury. My objections to prohibition are as I have stated them above."[390]

Three months later, he elaborated on his views:

"The business of manufacturing alcohol, liquor and beer will go out of the hands of law-abiding members of the community, and will be transferred to the quasi-criminal class ... large numbers of federal officers will be needed for its enforcement. The central government now has very wide war powers. When peace comes, these must end, if the republic is to be preserved. If, however, a partisan political head of the internal revenue department, or of a separate department created for the purpose, shall always be able through federal detectives and policemen to reach into every hamlet, and every ward,

---

[390] New Haven Journal-Courier, June 8, 1918, in T. Hicks, William Howard Taft: Professor of Law and New Haven Citizen (New Haven: Yale U., 1943), 146.

and to every purlieu of a large city and use the leverage of an intermittently lax and strict enforcement of the law ... he will wield a sinister power, prospect of which should make anxious the friends of free constitutional government ... Elections will continuously turn on the rigid or languid execution of the liquor law ... The ever-present issue will prevent clear and clean cut popular decisions on the most important national questions ... Individual self-restraint, the influence of improved social standards and criticism, and the restrictions enforced by the employers of labor for industrial reasons have probably had more to do with moderating the evils of intoxication than statute law ... The regulation of the sale and use of intoxicating liquor should be retained by the States."[391]

His view that nationalizing what had been a local issue would disrupt rational discussion of economic and foreign policy questions was amply borne out by the effects of the later drug war, "gay rights," and abortion controversies.

When the Prohibition Amendment was ratified, he urged its serious enforcement especially against liquor stills but pointed out that it could be repealed after a decade if experience so warranted,[392] which in the event it was.

As a Supreme Court justice, he deemed it his duty to enforce prohibition. In *Samuels v. McCuddy*,[393] he held that there were no property right in an inventory of liquor.

---

[391] New Haven Journal-Courier, September 2, 1918, in T. Hicks, *supra*, 147.

[392] Editorial, "Enforce Prohibition," February 5, 1919, in Editorials, 172.

[393] 267 U.S. 188 (1925).

Banking and Commerce

Although orthodox in his economics, Taft believed that the currency system should be "not so arranged as to prevent its volume to be increased temporarily to counteract the sudden drain of money by hoarding in a panic."[394]

He opposed deposit insurance, but favored postal savings as a means of providing security for small depositors, and as President secured creation of a postal savings system.[395]

At the time, savings banks in 32 states accounted for only 1.6% of funds on deposit.[396]

Deposit insurance, he declared, "takes a man's money to pay another man's default and instead of strengthening our banking system will break it down by destroying the value of banking experience and character and capital and offering inducement to reckless and speculative bankers without character or capital."[397]

Four days later, he observed that "it is quite difficult for a bank examiner to discover the unwise recklessness and speculative loans."[398]

This prophecy was amply vindicated during the savings and loan crisis of the 1970s fostered by brokered deposits, the payment of excessively high interest rates to attract deposits, self-dealing, and improvident investment in commercial real estate. Postal Savings Banks, Taft said in the same speech, "would attract deposits in panics which could be re-deposited in banks." This was precisely what happened during the Great Depression. In his acceptance speech in July 2008, he had said that deposit insurance was impracticable

---

[394] 1 Pringle 342.

[395] 1 Pringle 370.

[396] 1 Pringle 515ff.

[397] "The Republican Party: What It Has Done," National League of Republican Clubs, Cincinnati, September 22, 1908, 2 W.H. Taft, Works 82-83.

[398] "Postal Savings Banks and the Guaranty of Bank Deposits," St. Paul, September 28, 1908. 2 W.H. Taft, Works 116.

without "a supervision so close as practically to create a government bank," essentially the regime that prevailed from 1933 until the 1960s, a period in which permitted bank and savings and loan investments were sharply restricted.

In defense of postal savings, he observed that "[w]e have passed beyond the time of what they call the laisser-faire school which believes that the Government ought to do nothing but run a police force." Citing the example of the transcontinental railways, he noted that the government "can stand the lack of an immediate return on capital."[399]

He noted that although he favored an elastic currency, tariff revision, and curbs on abuses of the labor injunction, "you will find me very much under suspicion by our friends in the West."[400]

He fostered discussions, including famous meetings at Jekyll Island, leading to proposals for a Reserve Association of America designed to "avoid the only real objection to a central bank, that of concentrating enormous fiscal power in a political head or a few money kings."[401]

In his 1911 Annual Message he favored "a reasonable representation of the Government in the management. Both the National system and the State system should be fairly recognized." In the wake of the Panic of 1907, speaking in Boston, he renewed a call for a more elastic currency, but, noting the existence of gold-backed currency, a government surplus and prosperous agriculture, declared: "a great conservative victory has been won and the coming of socialism has been stayed."[402]

In his Second Annual Message in December 1910, Taft supported legislation allowing American banks to establish branch

---

[399] "Postal Savings Banks," Milwaukee, September 17, 1909, in 3 W.H. Taft, Works 163.

[400] 1 Pringle 390ff.

[401] 2 Pringle 720.

[402] "The Panic of 1907," Merchants' Association, Boston, December 30, 1907, 1 W.H. Taft, Works 240.

banks abroad. Later, as a Supreme Court justice, he dissented from a decision, *First National Bank v. Missouri*, applying state laws prohibiting branch banking to national banks.

As a young man, Taft wrote: "the States' Rights principle is a constant quantity in the politics of the country so long as the Republic continues to exist as it ought."[403]

He decried "state socialism, an increase in the power of the central government—a long step away from the individualism which it is necessary to retain in order to make real progress."[404]

Taft conceded to the national government almost plenary powers over interstate commerce. As Alpheus Thomas Mason has observed: "In a series of major decisions he endorsed the sweeping construction of the commerce power that the Hughes court endorsed only after F.D.R.'s threat to pack it."[405]

In his book *The Presidency and Its Powers* (1914), he cautioned that "[a] centralized system of government in which the President and Congress regulated the doorsteps of the people of this country would break up the union in a short time." One commentator has characterized him as "a federalist who viewed state regulation suspiciously [and] championed the federal government."[406]

He took the view that the Income Tax amendment, even when supplemented by the war power, did not authorize taxation of state or municipal bonds or the salaries of state officers, largely prevailing on the first issue but not the second.[407]

As a Supreme Court justice, he upheld the federal Packers and Stockyards Act,[408] the Grain Futures Act over the dissent of Justices

---

[403] 1 Pringle 43.

[404] 1 Pringle 344.

[405] A. Mason, William Howard Taft: Chief Justice (London: Oldbourne, 1964), 302.

[406] F. Lee, in 7 W.H. Taft, Works, Preface.

[407] Editorial, October 18, 1918, in Editorials, 103.

[408] Stafford v. Wallace, 258 U.S. 495 (1922).

Sutherland and McReynolds,[409] and the federally compelled pooling of railroad revenues,[410] as well as a federal narcotics tax from whose validity Justices Sutherland, McReynolds, and Butler dissented.[411]

Justice Holmes wrote that Taft's opinion in *Stafford v. Wallace* was "fine. It has a sort of march, like the movement of interstate commerce it describes."[412]

He was also ungrudging in upholding state powers of taxation, declaring in one case: "Actual equality in taxation is unattainable. The theoretical operation of a tax is often very different from its practical incidence due to the weakness of human nature and anxiety to escape tax burdens … The Fourteenth Amendment was not intended and is not to be construed as having any such object as these stiff and unyielding requirements of equality in state constitutions."[413]

However, a state tax on oil storage tanks was held improper under the Commerce Clause over the dissent of Justices McReynolds and Sanford.[414]

Felix Frankfurter made the charge that "[b]etween 1920 and 1930 the Supreme Court invalidated more state legislation than in the fifty years preceding."[415] This, however, was a product of the greater fecundity of state legislatures, which in turn was a product

---

[409] Board of Trade v. Olson, 262 U.S. 1 (1923).

[410] Dayton Goose Creek Ry. v. ICC, 263 U.S. 456 (1924).

[411] Nino v. United States, 276 U.S. 332 (1928).

[412] Holmes to Frankfurter, May 4, 1922, in R. Mennel and C. Compston (eds.), Holmes and Frankfurter: Their Correspondence, 1912-34 (Hanover, NH: U. Press of New England, 1996), 140.

[413] Puget Sound Power v. King County, 264 U.S. 22 (1924). *See also* Chicago Great Western Ry. v. Kendall, 266 U.S. 94 (1924); Sonneborn Bros. v. Cureton, 262 U.S. 506 (1923).

[414] Carson Petroleum v. Vial, 219 U.S. 95 (1929).

[415] P. Kurland (ed.), Felix Frankfurter on the Supreme Court (Cambridge, Mass.: Belknap Press, 1970), 455, quoting a contribution by Frankfurter to the Encyclopaedia of the Social Sciences.

of the social conflicts resulting from the mass immigration preceding World War I.

In 1920, while still a Yale law professor, Taft declared that Wilson's Supreme Court nominees Brandeis and Clarke represented "a new school of constitutional construction which if allowed to prevail will greatly impair our fundamental law ... to weaken the protection it should afford against socialist raids upon property rights."[416]

His recognition of federal power in commerce clause cases led one scholar to observe, when the Wagner Act relating to labor unions was constitutionally vindicated in 1937,[417] that "It was a triumph of the first magnitude for the New Deal, and William Howard Taft had a part in it."[418]

It is at least arguable that had Taft still been Chief Justice in 1933-36 rather than Charles Evans Hughes that the cases involving the Agricultural Adjustment Administration, the National Recovery Administration, and the Guffey Coal Act[419] would have been decided differently at least as far as their Commerce Clause holdings were considered. More generous recognition of the federal commerce power might have avoided the Roosevelt administration's end run around these cases by using conditions on the states attached to taxing and spending legislation, the device used to sustain its unemployment compensation and later "civil rights" measures.[420]

---

[416] WHT, "Mr. Wilson and the Campaign," 10 Yale Review 1, 19-20 (1920).

[417] N.L.R.B. v. Jones and Laughlin, 307 U.S. 1 (1937).

[418] D. Burton, Taft, Holmes, and the 1920s Court (Teaneck, NJ: Fairleigh Dickinson U., 1998), 151.

[419] United States v. Butler, 297 U.S. 1 (1936); Schechter Poultry Co. v. United States, 295 U.S. 495 (1935); Carter v. Carter Coal Co., 298 U.S. 238 (1936).

[420] Carmichael v. Southern Coal Co., 301 U.S. 495 (1937); Steward Machine Co. v. Davis, 301 U.S. 548 (1937).

This technique, aggravated by the power to threaten withholding of all federal funds to states and institutions conferred by the mis-called Civil Rights Restoration Act,[421] has been used to destroy the authority of the states over such subjects as speed limits, drinking ages, and discipline of college students, and has only recently begun to be checked.[422] It is far more destructive of federalism and state authority than legislation under the Commerce Clause, is denied to the German federal government,[423] and is antithetical to a central purpose of the U.S. Constitution, which was to end the system of federal requisitions upon the states and federal coercion of them that obtained under the Articles of Confederation.

Taft curtailed federal criminal jurisdiction in a number of opinions. Removal of a case against a federal officer in the absence of official acts was held improper in *Maryland v. Soper*.[424] The federal taxing power could not be used to regulate futures trading or child labor.[425] The states could require insurers to reject applicants within 24 hours[426] and could regulate truck loads.[427]

The most federally oriented cases written by Taft were *Terral v. Burke*,[428] invalidating a compelled waiver of access to the federal courts; *Railroad Comm. v. Chicago, Burlington and Quincy*,[429]

---

[421] 102 Stat. 28 (1988), overruling a holding of Grove City College v. Bell, 465 U.S. 555 (1984).

[422] National Federation of Independent Business v. Sibelius, 567 U.S. 519 (2012).

[423] H. Uppendahl, "Intergovernmental Relations in the Federal Republic of Germany," in A. Norton (ed.), The Present and Future Role of Local Government in Great Britain and the Federal Republic of Germany (London: Anglo-German Foundation, 1985), 35-48.

[424] 270 U.S. 9 (1926).

[425] Hill v. Wallace, 259 U.S. 44 (1922); Bailey v. Drexel, 259 U.S. 20 (1921).

[426] National Union v. Wainberg, 260 U.S. 71 (1922).

[427] Morris v. Derby, 274 U.S. 135 (1927).

[428] 257 U.S. 529 (1922).

[429] 257 U.S. 563 (1922).

preempting state railroad rate making; *Champlain v. Brattleboro*,[430] holding an interstate shipment of logs immune from state taxation; and *First Natl. Bank v. Missouri*,[431] where Taft dissented from a decision upholding state restrictions on branch banking by national banks. In *Oregon Ry. v. Navigation Co.*,[432] Taft invalidated a state agricultural quarantine over the dissents of Justices McReynolds and Butler.

On Roosevelt, Taft said that he "ought more often to have admitted the legal way of reaching the same ends."[433] Taft tried to foster "maintenance and enforcement of reforms ... freedom from alarm on the part of those pursuing proper and progressive business methods."[434]

Taft as Chief Justice

He respected Justice Holmes but felt that he "lacks the experience of service in government that would keep him straight on constitutional questions."[435] Brandeis, he conceded, "thinks much of the court and is anxious to have it clear and consistent and strong."[436]

He regarded Brandeis as "a muckraker, an emotionalist for his own purposes, a Socialist ... who had certain high ideals in his imagination," an evaluation in part traceable to Brandeis' uncharitable imputations against him at the time of the Ballinger–Pinchot affair.[437]

---

[430] 260 U.S. 366 (1922).

[431] 263 U.S. 640 (1924).

[432] 270 U.S. 87 (1926).

[433] 1 Pringle 347.

[434] 1 Pringle 390ff.

[435] 2 Pringle 955ff.

[436] 2 Pringle 980.

[437] 2 Pringle 935ff.

Brandeis acknowledged that "things go happily in the conference room with Taft."[438]

In 1922, he was successful in getting Congress to enact legislation creating a Conference of Circuit Court Judges with authority to assign judges across circuit lines, Congress adding a requirement that the transfers have the consent of both the sending and receiving court. The Act also provided for 21 new federal judges and for collection of judicial statistics. In 1925, he succeeded in obtaining a statute eliminating the mandatory jurisdiction of the Supreme Court except in cases challenging state legislation on constitutional grounds. This proved to have large and unexpected effects, inconsistent with Taft's view that "courts are but conservators; they cannot effect great social or political change."[439]

The statute implemented the view he had earlier expressed about the appropriate scope of certiorari jurisdiction: "It is very important that we be consistent in not granting the writ of certiorari except in cases involving principles the settlement of which is of importance to the public as distinguished from that of the parties in cases where there is a real and embarrassing conflict of opinion and authority between the circuit courts of appeal."[440]

At one point he declared: "the federal judges of the South are a disgrace in any country, and I'll be damned if I put any man on the bench of whose character or ability there is the slightest doubt."[441]

Elsewhere, he observed that "[i]mpeachment of judges is becoming more common and I think that it is well that it is so."[442]

---

[438] A. Bickel (ed.), The Unpublished Opinions of Mr. Justice Brandeis (Cambridge: Belknap Press, 1957), 203.

[439] "Recent Criticism of the Federal Judiciary," American Bar Association, Detroit, August 28, 1895, in 1 W.H. Taft, Works 306.

[440] Layne and Bowler v. Western Well Works, 261 U.S. 387, 393 (1922).

[441] D. Anderson, *supra*, 168, quoting 1 A. Butt, Taft and Roosevelt: The Intimate Letters of Archie Butt (New York: Doubleday, 1930), 300-01, 356.

[442] L. Gould (ed.), My Dearest Nellie: The Letters of William Howard Taft to Helen Herron Taft, 1909-1912 (Lawrence: U. Press of Kansas, 2011), 233.

In August 1908, he proposed various federal court reforms. He favored simplified codes of procedure, being highly critical of the Field Code in New York. He felt that courts of first instance should render prompt oral decisions, and that in general, there should be only one appeal as of right. Better compensation was needed for judges of courts of limited jurisdiction. There should be arbitration of personal injury suits against public service corporations with damage caps like those in the workmen's compensation laws. Judges should have no interest in the fees of their courts. With tongue only slightly in cheek, he referred to a Philippine practice of withholding judges' salaries until a certificate was received attesting that the last 60 days' business was fully disposed of.[443]

While President, he looked for "[a]n honest man and a good lawyer, professional competency and standing, vigor and effectiveness, and conventional political considerations such as geographic distribution and party representation"[444] in making judicial appointments at all levels.

He took the view that "ordinary considerations of political partisanship have much less application to the appointment of judges than they do to other and temporary offices."[445]

In a speech in Pocatello, Idaho, in 1911, Taft declared: "I love judges and I love courts. They are my ideals, that typify on earth what we shall meet hereafter in heaven under a just God."[446]

As an opinion-writer, he has not secured the admiration of academics, though Judge Robert Bork gave him pride of place among judges when asked at the hearings on his abortive nomination for Supreme Court Justice about Justices he admired: "he used to work

---

[443] "The Federal Courts," Hot Springs, VA, August 6, 1908, 2 W.H. Taft, Works 7ff.

[444] A. Bickel, The Judiciary and Responsible Government, 1900-21 (New York: Macmillan, 1984), 7.

[445] "Mecklenburg Declaration," Charlotte, May 20, 1909, in 3 W.H. Taft, Works 88.

[446] New York Evening Post, October 6, 1911, quoted in 1 Pringle 264.

Taft and Supreme Court 1922

carefully with text, textual materials and historical materials to try to give a very balanced decision about constitutional matters."[447]

In August 1911 Taft vetoed a bill providing for statehood for Arizona and New Mexico because of a provision for recall of judges in the Arizona Constitution, condemning it as "pernicious in its effects, destructive of independence in the judiciary, likely to subject the rights of the individual to the possible tyranny of a popular majority, injurious to the cause of free government."[448]

"On the instant of an unpopular ruling," Taft cautioned, "while the spirit of protest has not had time to cool and even while an appeal may be pending from his ruling in which he might be sustained, he is to be hailed before the electorate as a tribunal, with no judicial hearing, evidence, or defence, and thrown out of office and disgraced for life because he has failed in a single decision it may

---

[447] New York Times, September 19, 1987.

[448] 47 Congressional Record, 62nd Congress, 1st Session 3964 (August 15, 1911).

be, to satisfy the popular clamor. Think of the enormous power for evil given to the sensational muckraking part of the press in rousing prejudice against a just judge by false charges and insinuations the effect of which in the short period of an election by recall it would be impossible for him to meet and offset. What kind of judgments might those on the unpopular side expect from courts whose judges must make their decisions under such legalized terrorism? ... a powerful lever for influencing judicial decisions and an opportunity for vengeance because of adverse ones." Roosevelt had declared in a speech at Columbus, Ohio, on February 21, 1912: "when a judge decides a constitutional question, when he decides what the people as a whole can or cannot do, the people should have the right to recall the decision if they think it wrong." This all-encompassing pronouncement included federal as well as state courts, and even constitutional rulings in criminal cases. The Progressive Party platform confined itself to a demand for recall of state court constitutional decisions.[449]

Taft's fervent insistence on the finality of judicial decisions, in the words of Senator Henry Cabot Lodge, "turns Taft from a man into a principle."[450]

"No man and no party in the country," Taft declared, "have done so much to destroy the confidence of the people in the justice of the courts and in the existence of any possible independent judiciary as have Roosevelt and the Progressive Party."[451]

"He has leaped far ahead of the most radical leaders of the Progressive party and his heart is not with them, but he deludes himself that he will be able to guide it and stem it when he gets in power. He can't do it. He has gone too far. He will either be a hopeless failure if elected or else destroy his own reputation by becoming a socialist,

---

[449] Gould, *supra*, 140.

[450] Gould, *supra*, 59.

[451] WHT, "The Future of the Republican Party," Saturday Evening Post, February 14, 1914.

being swept there by force of circumstances just as the leaders of the French Revolution were swept on and on, all their individual efforts failing to stem the tide until it had run itself out."[452]

His foredoomed but principled candidacy in 1912 led one biographer to declare that "[n]o man of better training, no man of more dauntless courage, of sounder common sense, or of higher and finer character has ever come to the Presidency than William Howard Taft."[453]

"Judicial recall. Judicial recall. The words themselves are so inconsistent that I hate to utter them," Taft declared.[454]

Arizona was admitted to the Union in 1912 after it removed the offending article from its proposed Constitution, following which it later restored it. Taft thought that periodic election of judges was a check less dangerous than recall since it involves "consideration of the work of a judge for a full term of years." Removal of a judge by legislative address, permitted by many state constitutions but rarely used, should involve a full hearing and be almost as elaborate as an impeachment trial.

In 1926, Taft sought an act that would give the Supreme Court the power to promulgate rules of procedure, which was not enacted until 1934 following his retirement from the Court.

In 1924, Taft was successful in blocking a bill by Senator Caraway that would have precluded federal judges from commenting on testimony.[455]

In 1925, a proposal by Taft for a new Supreme Court building was defeated in the Senate by a vote of 50 to 22, but was restored in a conference committee. A lot was purchased in 1928 and two representatives of the Court were placed on the building committee. In

---

[452] 2 A. Butt, Taft and Roosevelt, *supra*, 846.

[453] Gould, *supra*, 61.

[454] "Taft Denounces Recall of Judges," New York Times, January 21, 1912.

[455] A. Mason, William Howard Taft: Chief Justice (London: Oldbourne, 1984), 130.

1929, $9.7 million was appropriated; the building designed by Cass Gilbert was opened in 1932, the main speaker declaring that "this building is the result of [Taft's] intelligent persistence."

Taft successfully opposed a bill to establish federal police courts to enforce prohibition, fearing a loss in the prestige of the federal courts; the bill failed in 1926. Taft also opposed a bill to abolish diversity of citizenship jurisdiction in civil cases, asserting that it had helped secure capital for the development of the South and the West.

He did not welcome Wilson's appointment of Attorney General McReynolds to the Supreme Court: "McReynolds would not make a good nor a great judge. He is very narrow-minded and an intense partisan, full of the wind of rhetoric and of limited vision generally." [456]

Taft heavily influenced judicial appointments in the Harding and Coolidge administrations. He was instrumental in the appointments of Justices Sutherland, Butler, and Sanford; his support of Butler was in part due to his desire to increase from two to three the number of Democrats on the Court. His choices did not resemble his appointments when he was President when he was "much less ideologically committed than he was later to become, seeking still to occupy the middle ground in politics and not free of re-election worries." [457] He was frustrated, however, by Coolidge's accommodation of Senators in the appointment of district court judges and his reluctance to appoint Democrats. Occasionally, he used heavy weapons to have his way. He wrote to Coolidge in support of the nomination of Augustus Hand to the Second Circuit and recruited Harlan Fiske Stone, George Wickersham, and Charles Evans Hughes to do likewise. [458] He supported the appointment of

---

[456] WHT to Gus Karger, July 20, 1914, Folder 22, Cincinnati Museums Center, quoted in J. Lurie, *supra*, 179.

[457] A. Bickel, *The Judiciary and Responsible Government, 1900-21* (New York: Macmillan, 1985), 9.

[458] W. White, *A Puritan in Babylon* (New York: Macmillan, 1938), 348.

William H. Taft Swearing in Herbert Hoover 1929

Attorney General (and former Columbia law professor) Harlan Fiske Stone to the Court, but at the close of his career on the Court, when taken ill, he refused to resign until President Hoover promised to appoint Charles Evans Hughes rather than Stone as Chief Justice.

He was pleased by Coolidge's victory in the 1924 election: "This country is no country for radicalism. I think it is really the most conservative country in the world."[459] He wanted Coolidge to run again in 1928: "He is the strongest man we have and he is safe ... since Harding was nominated I have just lost confidence in my political judgment as to the nominations of either party," but upon Coolidge's refusal supported Hoover against old-guard opposition "[i]f the Republican party is to win in this election, it has got to put a candidate who does not smell in any way of the old Republican organization which ... in 1920 smeared the whole party."[460]

---

[459] 2 Pringle, *supra*, 968.

[460] W. White, A Puritan in Babylon (New York: Macmillan, 1938), 350, 375.

Although he viewed them as "progressives" he fostered the appointment of Learned Hand to the Second Circuit Court of Appeals in 1924 and of his cousin Augustus Hand to the same court in 1927.[461]

By the time he reached the Supreme Court, Alexander Bickel observed, Taft was "neither temperamentally nor in fundamental outlook was Taft really a progressive."[462]

In fairness to Taft, it should be observed that some historical events had intervened, including World War I, Wilson's temporary dictatorship, and the Bolshevik revolution. There is also a tendency to forget that there were Communist revolutions in Bavaria and Hungary, a Bolshevik invasion of Poland, a near-revolution in Norway in 1919, and left-wing insurrections in Minneapolis and Seattle, forgotten now but commemorated in two best-selling books, Eric Severeid's *Not So Wild a Dream*[463] and Jan Valtin's *Out of the Night*.[464]

The Harvard professor Mark De Wolfe Howe later charged Taft with a "crippling fear of change which so warped intelligence and sympathy that understanding and imagination were destroyed."[465] To such criticisms, his son Robert rejoined: citing "his firm conviction, perhaps the strongest of all the beliefs that moved him—that law enforcement, law and order, was the first essential of civilization. He believed that if respect and compliance with law was ever broken down, it would destroy all the benefits of civilization, including those of workmen as well as everyone else. This is the key to his violent feeling about the Pullman strike—also to his

---

[461] *See* Taft to Harlan Fiske Stone, August 1, 1924; Taft to Learned Hand, April 27, April 30, and May 25, 1927; Taft to Charles Evans Hughes, April 26, 1927, cited in A. Mason, *supra*, 182, 187.

[462] A. Bickel, The Judiciary and Responsible Government, 1900-21 (New York: Macmillan, 1985), 32.

[463] (New York: Knopf, 1946).

[464] (New York: Alliance, 1941).

[465] 53 Harvard Law Review 505 (1940).

violent feeling against the Wets."[466] The progressive William Allen White wrote of Taft: "He had no submerged political past. He was the same yesterday, today, and tomorrow, the honest profoundly convinced intellectual conservative, a statesman of charm who could meet his political foes at a punchbowl with graceful naivete and eviscerate them in the forum wearing the same dimples all the while."[467]

In his eight years on the Court, Taft wrote 30.25 opinions per term as against average production by justices of 20.25 opinions; Justice Van Debater averaged less than 10 opinions.

In his Second Annual Message in 1910 Taft noted: "Several of the Lord Chancellors of England and of its Chief Justices have left their lasting impress on the history of their country by their constructive ability in proposing and securing the passage of remedial legislation effecting law reforms. The purpose and chief usefulness of a Supreme Court is to expound the law and especially the fundamental law—the Constitution."

He regarded reform of procedure as a way of assuaging popular grievances about the power of courts. In his book *Popular Government* Taft declared: "The ultra reformers, the 'hair trigger' gentlemen pay little attention to the tedious detail of reforming procedure so as to reduce the cost of litigation and to speed final judgments." While President, he sought justices "young and vigorous enough to go into the questions of methods in equity cases and if possible revise the entire procedure of this country and put it more in line with that of Great Britain."[468]

Moreover, in the hands of wise judges, the Constitution was not inflexible: The Court is "willing to recognize progress, to treat the Constitution as elastic enough to permit a construction which will conform to the growth and necessities of the country, to view

---

[466]　RAT, Papers, August 31, 1939.

[467]　W. White, A Puritan in Babylon (New York: Macmillan, 1938), 285.

[468]　2 A. Butt, Taft and Roosevelt, *supra*, 439.

constitutional restrictions with reasonable regard to the changes that have taken place in our business and in our society. Great judges and great courts distinguish between the fundamental and the casual. They make the law to grow not by changing it but by adapting it ..."

Overruling opinions were to be avoided except to effectuate "a view entertained by most people and evidenced by expressions of popular will in the press, in the pulpit, in juridical writings, as well as by legislative action and popular elections. All of these evidences should cover a period long enough to have no doubt about the clarity of the opinion or its deliberate character."

Political Reform

Taft noted that spending cases do not come before the Supreme Court, a reference to the doctrine of *Frothngham v. Mellon,* since somewhat qualified in Establishment Clause cases.

Taft abhorred the direct primary, especially for judicial elections. "Under the convention system, men who were not candidates were nominated for the Bench, but now in no case can the office seek the man." He referred to "the disgraceful exhibitions of men campaigning for the place of State Supreme Court judge and asking votes on the ground that their decisions will have a particular class flavor ... Men ask to be made judges not because they are impartial, but because they are advocates; not because they are judicial but because they are partisan."[469]

Anticipating a later reform, he urged that the whole Senate not sit in impeachment trials, but delegate to a Committee the taking of testimony.

Pointing out that the receivers of banks were appointed by the Comptroller of the Currency, he urged that the same practice be adopted for other receivers, since their appointment by courts

---

[469] Popular Government, 5 W.H. Taft, Works 122.

"gives the court a meretricious power and cast upon it a duty that is quite likely to involve the court in controversies adding neither to its dignity nor its hold on the confidence of the public." This change was not brought about until 1984 with the creation of the United States Trustee system. He was also opposed to judicial appointment of supervisors of elections which "made the courts for the time being alien courts."[470]

He held the same view about judicial appointments of clerks of court.

He supported the three-judge court acts, since repealed except in reapportionment cases, as a device to limit the abuse of injunctions. It was found that the Acts in practical effect gave the injunction power not to three judges but to the Court of Appeals judge presiding over the court, who tended to over-awe the District judges because of the threat of reversals in other cases.

Taft hinted at his approval of an arrangement like the delaying powers of the British House of Lords as a substitute for judicial review. "A system in which we may have an enforced rest from legislation for two years is not bad … it affords an opportunity for digestion of legislation and for the detection of its defects." "When we consider how short a period a decade is in the life of a nation, a delay of two or three years is not only tolerable but ought to be necessary."

His convictions about the appropriate role of the judiciary were carried forward in a number of his Supreme Court opinions. In *Tumey v. Ohio*,[471] he invalidated an arrangement in which the trier of fact was compensated from court costs. In *Watchtower v. Paused*,[472] he required actual rather than constructive notice to support a lawsuit under a non-resident motorist statute. He had also held that an Article I court could be given rate-making functions,

---

[470]   The President and His Powers (1914), 58.

[471]   223 U.S. 510 (1927).

[472]   276 U.S. 13 (1928).

but that no appeal to an Article III court would lie with respect to the rate schedules.[473]

He is said to have delayed his departure from the Supreme Court, despite illness, until he was assured that Charles Evans Hughes, rather than Stone, would succeed him as Chief Justice: "Stone is not a leader and would have a good deal of difficulty in massing the Court," Taft wrote to his brother Charles in May 1929. "I don't think that there is anybody of the Court, except Stone, who would think that he is fitted for Chief Justice."[474]

When Stone finally became Chief Justice by appointment of President Roosevelt ten years later, the Court became notably more disputatious and Taft's prophecy was abundantly realized.

Taft was an opponent of the direct primary for judicial and minor offices.[475] He was in favor of almost all mechanisms to check "efforts to make the selection of candidates, the enactment of legislation and the decision of the courts to depend on momentary popular pressure."[476] In 1912, he declared: "The initiative, the referendum and the recall, together with a complete adoption of the direct primary and an entire destruction of the convention system are now made the sine qua non of a real reformer" in disregard of "the necessity for checks upon hasty popular action."[477]

---

[473] Keller v. Potomac Electric, 261 U.S. 428 (1923).

[474] WHT to Charles P. Taft, May 12, 1929, WHT Papers, Library of Congress, Reel 311.

[475] 2 Pringle 559.

[476] 2 Pringle 755.

[477] WHT, "The Sign of the Times," Address to Electrical Manufacturers Club, Hot Springs, VA, November 26, 1912; Address to the Republican Club of New York, February 12, 1912, quoted in S. Milkie, "Progressivism Then and Now," in S. Milkie and J. Miler, Progressivism and the New Democracy (Amherst: U. of Massachusetts, 1999), 12. See also T. Olson, "William Howard Taft," in J. Tarrant and L. Leo, Presidential Leadership: Rating the Best and Worst in the White House (New York: WS Books, 2004), 131ff; P. Rego, "William Howard Taft: The Constitutionalist as Critic of Progressivism," in L. Bailey and J. Miler, In Defence

He regarded the initiative and referendum as "the work of political cranks and directly contrary to the spirit of the Constitution"; the recall was "a hair trigger to the bottom of politics."[478]

Two political scientists have recently revived interest in Taft's views. Samuel Milkie has observed: "The faith that William Howard Taft expressed in limited government has given way to support for ambitious programmatic initiatives that are pursued through political methods that corrode political and governmental institutions," while Jerome Miler has stated that the "progressive" reforms "have transformed American parties from mass to elite organizations and shifted the party battle away from the electorate and toward the bureaucracy and the courts where it has become rhetorically less a reasoned discourse and more one of relentless negativism and personal attack."[479] However, in his Acceptance Speech in 1908, under some duress, Taft declared that he personally favored the direct election of Senators.[480]

In 1908 he said that he thought that an income tax consistent with the Constitution could be devised. "Nothing has ever injured the prestige of the Supreme Court more than that [income tax] decision."[481]

Roosevelt's loose language in 1912 about recall of judicial decisions appalled him, potentially encompassing as it did even acquittals in federal criminal cases. After Roosevelt explained that he proposed recall only of state court decisions invalidating state statutes, Taft observed: "My experience on the bench has taught me the value of words. One of the most unsafe things to do is to go further

---

of the Founders' Republic: Critics of Direct Democracy in the Progressive Era (New York: Bloomsbury, 2015), 83ff.

[478] New York Times, May 9, 2013, quoted in L. Gould, Chief Executive to Chief Justice (Topeka: U. Press of Kansas, 2014), 12.

[479] S. Milkie and J. Miler, *supra*, 11, 282.

[480] 4 W.H. Taft, Works 32.

[481] 1 A. Butt, Taft and Roosevelt: The Intimate Letters of Archie Butt (New York: Doubleday, 1930), 134.

than the facts … It seems to me that I am the only hope against radicalism and demagoguery."

Taft was an advocate of publicity for campaign contributions,[482] the merit system for civil servants, a single six-year term for the President (echoing Alexis De Tocqueville), and non-voting Senate seats for the Cabinet, a proposal approved by congressional committees in 1864 and 1881.[483]

On the single term he urged "six or seven years and ineligible thereafter," which would give the president "greater courage and independence in the discharge of his duties."[484]

As for the District of Columbia, he declared that "[President] Washington intended this to be a Federal city … I am opposed to the franchise in the District." However, he wanted municipal functions to be exercised by the City's appointed government, not by central government bureaus.[485] He was similarly opposed to territorial status, let alone statehood for Alaska. "It is agriculture … and attachment to the ground that makes a permanent population."[486]

Elsewhere, he observed of the Wilson administration's war cabinet: "Party association seems necessary to make a cabinet work harmoniously under our system. But the selection of some experienced and able Republicans for particular tasks would greatly strengthen the administration in its work."[487] This lesson was taken to heart by Franklin Roosevelt when he added Henry Stimson and Frank Knox to his cabinet on the eve of World War II.

---

[482] Speech of Acceptance, Cincinnati, July 28, 1909, in 3 W.H. Taft, Works 31.

[483] 2 Pringle 823ff.

[484] New York Times, October 13, 1915.

[485] "Government of the District of Columbia," D.C. Chamber of Commerce, May 8, 1909, 4 W.H. Taft, Works 65ff.

[486] "Alaska," Seattle and Tacoma, September 29 and October 1, 1909, in 3 W.H. Taft 220ff.

[487] Editorial, December 28, 1917, in Editorials.

In his Second Annual Message in 1910, Taft proposed the addition of parcel post to the rural free delivery postage system, and unsuccessfully urged a distinction in second-class mail rates between text and advertising portions of magazines: "this would relieve many useful magazines that are not circulated at a profit."

The same message contained prophetic and cautionary words about the cost of public pensions. Taft noted that the British plan for public employees was "virtually a contributory plan, with provision for refund of their theoretical contributions," not very different for a 401(k) plan in today's United States. The proposed non-contributory pension for federal workers was denounced by Taft:

> "a civil pension is bound to become an enormous, continuous and increasing tax on the public exchequer; it is demoralizing to the service since it makes difficult the dismissal of incompetent employees after they have partly earned their pension and it is disadvantageous to the main body of employees themselves since it is always taken into account in fixing salaries and only the few who survive and remain in the service until pensionable age receive the value of their deferred pay. The simplest and most independent solution of the problem for both the employee and the Government is a compulsory savings arrangement, the employee to set aside from his salary a sum sufficient with the help of a liberal rate of interest from the Government to purchase an adequate annuity for him on retirement, the accumulation to be indubitably his and claimable if he leaves the service before reaching the retirement age or by his heirs in case of his death."[488]

In his Annual Message in 1911, Taft asked for federal legislation aimed at narcotics and obscene publications. He unsuccessfully

---

[488]   4 W.H. Taft, Works 73-74.

sought to include collectors, postmasters, immigration commission-
ers, and marshals in the civil service, a project ultimately successful
except as to marshals, who are still outside it. Taft also observed
of civil servants that "one of the real objections to the permanent
tenure of the civil service is their tendency to associate in unions or
societies and to attempt a betterment of their terms of employment
using their political power as a body to enforce their demands ...
There is a danger of their controlling the legislature unduly through
united political action."[489] He would not have been enthusiastic
about the legalization of public employee unions later fostered by
the Kennedy administration.

A message on economy and efficiency in January 1912 proposed the first federal budget, a reform adopted after Taft's term,
together with approved methods of copying, elimination of required
endorsements on "buck slips" and of requirements of notarization
of accounts, consolidation of offices, standardization of reports, and
use of proper lighting methods.[490]

Later, Taft opposed nationalization of the telegraph system as
part of the postal service:

> "I do not think that it is in accord with the best
> public policy thus greatly to increase the body of public
> servants."[491]

He favored Progressive proposals for a short ballot and reduction of state and local elective offices but opposed the initiative and
referendum, saying that the multiplication of contests "will tire
[voters] into such an indifference as still further to remove control
of public affairs to a minority."[492]

---

[489] WHT to Nellie Taft, August 15, 1912, in Dearest Nellie, *supra*, 271.

[490] 4 W.H. Taft, Works 249.

[491] 4 W.H. Taft, Works 324.

[492] Acceptance Speech, 1912, D. Anderson, *supra*, 195.

"Examine the record in referendum states and you will find that the total vote on legislative referenda varies from 75% to 25% of the votes cast for candidates at the same election."[493]

In his book *Popular Government* published in 1914, Taft opposed compulsory voting, noting that it produced blank ballots in Switzerland. Constitutional amendments should require a majority of those voting in the election, not those voting on the amendment. He advocated short ballots and opposed direct democracy devices.[494] He made an exception for local referenda, "making the going into effect of the law depend upon the question whether it can be really enforced … the referendum left to the option of the legislature will be so infrequent as not to endanger the representative system."[495]

The long ballot, he said, produced "fatigue, confused mind, tired eyes, and a disgusted feeling … [as well as] the exaltation of cranks and the wearying of the electorate of their political duties."[496]

He quoted Lord Acton on the objections to direct democracy, Acton first having praised "the safeguards which in the deliberations of a single memorable year, [America] had set up against the power of its own sovereign people."

"[The Athenians] wanted to be bound by no laws that were not of their own making. In this way the emancipated people of Athens became a tyrant; and their government, the pioneer of European freedom, ruined their city by attempting to make war by debate in the market-place. Like the French Republic, they put their unsuccessful commanders to death. They treated their dependencies with such injustice that they lost their maritime empire. They plundered the rich until the rich conspired with the public enemy and they crowned their guilt by the martyrdom of Socrates."

---

[493] W. Taft, Popular Government (New Haven: Yale U., 1914), 44-47.

[494] 5 W.H. Taft, Works 39.

[495] 5 W.H. Taft, Works 42.

[496] 5 W.H. Taft, Works 45, 48.

Taft becomingly conceded that the Guaranty clause of the Constitution did not invalidate the initiative or referendum, a question decided by Justice Holmes when he was on the Supreme Judicial Court of Massachusetts. The purposes sought to be served by the recall could be served by allowing the governor to remove a public officer after a hearing (a procedure, adopted in New York State, later employed by Governor Franklin D. Roosevelt to remove Mayor Jimmy Walker of New York City).

Taft was vehement in his denunciation of the malign effects of the direct primary, and the unsatisfactory nature of recent major-party presidential candidates gives his views great resonance. "A convention system will take the more moderate man whose name will appeal to the independent voter, a primary election in 1860 would certainly have nominated Seward, not Lincoln, in 1876 would have nominated Blaine, not Hayes ... [The primary benefits] men of wealth and of activity and of little modesty ... without real qualifications for office." He condemned "[e]xtremists [who] would hurry us into a condition which could find no parallel except in the French Revolution or in that bubbling anarchy that once character-ized the South American Republics ... not progressives ... they are political emotionalists or neurotics."[497]

In his *Liberty under Law*, Taft observed: "Certainly we are not a pure democracy governing by direct action and the great men who framed our fundamental law did not intend that we should be ... [The general primary] has made impossible as a candidate for elec-tive office everyone who is not the choice of the machine or is not independently wealthy." He suggested informal extra-legal conven-tions to winnow candidates and advise the electorate, predicting "they do not dare [to repeal the primary] lest their opponents make political capital of it." At conventions "no one but loyal members of a

---

[497] Quoted in Gould, *supra* at 55.

party should have a voice." He vigorously condemned the California laws allowing cross-filing of candidates in both parties' primaries.[498]

He proposed to give cabinet members non-voting seats in Congress with the right to introduce bills and to speak or be questioned about any issue arising in the Congress, an effort to adopt some of the features of the British cabinet system,[499] a proposal approved by Congressional committees in 1864 and 1881.

Taken in all, there is no reason to doubt the just verdict of Charles and Mary Beard on his administration: "Compared measure by measure with Theodore Roosevelt's regime, President Taft's administration, though less spectacular, could be correctly characterized as on the whole more 'progressive.'"[500]

Imperialism

William Howard Taft has been criticized as the Governor General who presided over the sanguinary later stages of the suppression of the Philippine insurrection.[501] His testimony about what was involved had the merit of candor: "that cruelties have been inflicted, that people have been shot when they ought not to have been, that there have been individual instances of water cure, that torture which I believe involves pouring water down the throat so the man swells and gets the impression he is going to be suffocated and then tells what he knows … all these things are true."[502] He was not, however, an enthusiast for acquisition of the Philippines. "I was

---

[498] Editorial,"The General Primary," September 17, 1918, in Editorials, 89.

[499] D. Anderson, *supra*, 151.

[500] C. and M. Beard, The Beards' Basic History of the United States (New York: Doubleday, 1946), 386-87

[501] J. Bradley, Imperial Cruise (Boston: Back Bay, 2010).

[502] Quoted in H. Graff, American Imperialism and the Philippine Insurrection: Testimony of the Times, Selections from Congressional Hearings (Boston: Little Brown, 1969), 92.

very much opposed to taking them." It involved "assumption of a burden by us contrary to our traditions and at a time when we had quite enough to do at home."[503]

Just how far removed his attitudes were from those of the typical imperialist is revealed by his statement that "I find it hard, myself, to subscribe to the Monroe Doctrine." He characterized the sponsor of the Spanish–American War, William Randolph Hearst, as "a dealer in filth … this hideous product of yellow journalism, this immoral monstrosity."[504]

It was said of Taft as Governor General that "massive, patient, capable, radiating goodwill, he had both charmed and reassured the enemy whom he embraced collectively as 'our little brown brother' … Taft had succeeded so well in the Philippines as diplomat and executive that his conversion to imperialism passed almost unnoticed. Only recipients of his classified dispatches understood how deeply he despised the people he governed."[505]

Taft characterized Filipino politicians as "liars," crediting them with both "politeness" and "insincerity"; he viewed gambling as a national vice of the Filipinos. He noted that they were quick to reject any implication of inferiority:[506] "the greatest liars it has ever been my misfortune to meet," "ambitious as Satan and quite as unscrupulous," inferior to "the most ignorant negro." "Utterly unfit," "they need the training of fifty or a hundred years before they shall ever realize what Anglo-Saxon liberty is."[507]

On being appointed to a commission to govern the Philippines, he immediately recommended that five Filipinos be added to

---

[503] Pringle, 160.

[504] Pringle, 319.

[505] E. Morris, Theodore Rex (New York: Random House, 2001), 102.

[506] Pringle, 173-74.

[507] Quoted in O. Alfonso, Theodore Roosevelt and the Philippines (Manila: U. of Philippines, 1970), 44-46.

it, so as to give them a near majority; in the event, only three were added.[508]

As a Commissioner, he rejected claims of exclusive military authority: "large parts of the territory would become free of hostilities and it would greatly aid the Army in subduing the remainder if object lessons in the benefits of American civil government could be offered."[509] "We have promised them civil government, and a government in which there is a power which may make arbitrary arrests without being subject to a legal inquiry hardly deserves the name of civil."[510]

He favored use of transportation to Guam as punishment: "transportation to that island has terrors for the natives that are not exceeded by those of the death penalty."[511]

His regime was guided by the decision of the Supreme Court of the United States in the *Insular Cases*, holding that all the provisions of the U.S. Constitution were not automatically applicable to the newly acquired overseas territories, a decision later reiterated by him in holding that there was no jury trial in Puerto Rico in the case of *Balzac v. Puerto Rico*: "incorporation [of American law] is not assumed without express declaration of an implication so strong as to exclude any other view."[512]

Of this decision, Professor Owen Fiss observed: "interests could be satisfied in many different ways, some of which would pose fewer legal problems than the formal maintenance of 'colonies.' By 1905, the real question was not whether the Constitution would

---

[508] Pringle, 199ff.

[509] WHT to Adnan Chaffee, October 13, 1901, Root Papers, Library of Congress, 3-4.

[510] *See* B. Linn, *The Philippine War, 1898-1902* (Lawrence: U. Press of Kansas, 2000).

[511] WHT to Root, September 21, 1900.

[512] 258 U.S. 298 (1922).

follow the flag, but whether it would follow the United Fruit Company. Everyone knew the answer to that question."[513]

Later he joined Justices Holmes and Brandeis in dissent in an effort to apply civil law to save an action in Panama that would otherwise have been time-barred.[514]

Little or no consideration was initially given to the possibility of organizing the new possessions as territorial governments and admitting them as states, the mode of practice followed on the American continent under Jefferson's Northwest Land Ordinance and its progeny. Among them, only Hawaii eventually became an American state.

Taft arrived in Manila in June 1900. A general amnesty had just been declared and Taft's promise of civil government led the leader of the insurrection, Emilio Aguinaldo, to come down from the hills and sign an oath of allegiance in the spring of 1901.[515] By July of 1901, the insurrection had been localized, though an ambush of American troops on the Island of Samur and atrocities committed by them in reprisal resulted in investigations and protests in the United States.[516] Forty-eight American troops had been massacred; the reprisals took the lives of 759 Filipinos.

Taft was instrumental in securing a 25% tariff concession for the Philippines and a ban on Chinese labor. Under Taft's presidency, a provisional government was set up for two years in Cuba involving 6,600 troops at 27 posts, and American troops were withdrawn in 1909;[517] the infamous Platt Amendment of 1915, making

---

[513] O. Fiss, Troubled Beginnings of the Modern State (New York: Macmillan, 1993), 252.

[514] Panama Railway v. Rock, 266 U.S. 209 (1924).

[515] D. Burton, Taft, Wilson and World Order (Teaneck, NJ: Fairleigh Dickinson U., 2003), 34.

[516] N. Miller, Benevolent Assimilation: The American Conquest of the Philippines, 1899-1903 (New Haven: Yale U., 1987), 82.

[517] 1 Pringle 310.

Cuba a virtual American protectorate, was the work of the Wilson administration.

Taft was conscious of the fragility of the pro-capitalist Diaz regime in Mexico,[518] declaring: "I can only hope and pray that his demise does not come until I am out of office," a prayer and prophecy that was gratified. Later, he was to observe of Mexico: "we cannot make the qualifications of Sunday school superintendents square with the necessities of the situation where anarchy prevails."[519]

While Taft voiced commitment to the preservation of American economic interests, it has been said that he "nonetheless transcended the pattern set by the political origins of his administration in two ways. Taft believed in a strict interpretation of the Constitutional prerogatives of the President and accepted far more than did Roosevelt or Wilson the restraints on presidential action imposed by a traditional view of America's role in the world. These beliefs led him to refrain from using force against Mexico without the consent of Congress. Taft's beliefs also led him to emphasize neutrality toward Mexico and abstention from involvement in Mexico's internal affairs."[520]

Of the Wilson administration's handling of Mexico, he observed: "Could anything be more botched than this Mexican business … They have made their trouble in Mexico and they might have avoided it."[521]

His guiding premises in governing the Philippines were avowedly paternalistic. He was not afflicted with the liberal guilt of E.M. Forster and the inter-war critics of imperialism, nor did he subscribe to any theories about the "noble savage." The "poor and ignorant are easily influenced by the educated of their own race";

---

[518] 1 Pringle 435ff.

[519] 1 Pringle 865.

[520] P. Hales, *Revolution and Intervention: The Diplomacy of Taft and Wilson with Mexico, 1910-17* (Cambridge: MIT Press, 1970), 4.

[521] WHT to Charles Hills, July 28, 1913.

the educated "are in favor of an oligarchy ... there would be inter-
necine warfare and chaos." "One must feed a man's belly before he
develops his mind or gives him political rights."[522]

But he was no admirer of British colonial policy. British
"opium policy has not been controlled by the highest or purest
motives ... it can hardly be said that she has given great time to the
improvement of the individual among her tropical peoples." He saw
the Filipinos, who were mainly Christian as a result of the efforts
of Spanish missionaries, as "far more subject to Western influence
than the Mohammedan or the Buddhists, both of whom regard the
Christian religion with contempt." He promoted education; at the
end of his two years as governor 25% of Filipino youth of school
age were in school receiving instruction in the English language, as
against a nominal number under the Spanish dispensation. Church-
state problems were addressed by allowing religious instruction in
the schools for one hour and a half three times a week, but only
to pupils whose parents had given written consent. Teachers were
precluded from "teaching or criticizing the doctrine of any church,
religious sect, or denomination."[523]

The remittances of Filipino nurses and special education
teachers from the United States remain the largest single source of
foreign exchange for the Philippines.

Taft, unlike many British colonialists, resolutely opposed any
color bar in official dealings (although, unlike Sir Gerald Templer
in 1950s Malaya, he did not seek to root it out in private clubs). His
wife declared: "we insisted on complete racial equality. We made it
a rule from the beginning that neither politics nor race would influence our hospitality in any way."[524]

---

[522] 2 Pringle 46.

[523] R. Escalate, The Bearer of Pax Americana: The Philippine Career of
William Howard Taft (Manila: New Day, 2007), 102.

[524] C. Anthony, Nellie Taft: The Unconventional First Lady of the Ragtime
Era (New York: Morrow, 2005), 148. See P. Kramer, The Blood of Government:

This recognition of the Brotherhood of Man was not popular with the Army, a ditty of the time reading:

"They say I've got brown brothers here
But still I draw the line
He may be a brother of Big Bill Taft
But he ain't no brother of mine"

He was not a great optimist about progress in the Philippines, which during his term was afflicted not only with the insurrection but with a rinderpest disease that killed most of its work animals and several typhoons. He had to combat "the idea that labor is degrading or an evidence of slavery ... idleness, savagery, cruelty and torpor ... have thus far retarded the races born under the equatorial sun." His conclusion was that "we must have them for a generation or two generations or perhaps even three."[525]

This was so even though he recognized that "the exercise of power without danger of criticism produces an irresponsibility in a public officer which, even if his motives are pure, tends to negligence in some cases and arbitrary action in others."[526] Nonetheless, he was prepared to continue with "the white man's burden" notwithstanding the original error in assuming it: "we are living in an age when the intervention of a strange nation in the affairs of a people unable to maintain a government of law and order to assist the latter to better government becomes a national duty and works for the progress of the world."[527]

His pessimism about the prospects of a stable democracy in the Philippines proved justified, and he identified the reason for it:

Race, Empire, the United States and the Philippines (Chapel Hill: U. of North Carolina, 2006).

[525] 2 Pringle 50.

[526] 2 Pringle 53.

[527] 2 Pringle 177.

"two generations of over-concentration on sugar makes a society in which there are wealthy landowners holding very large estates with valuable and expensive plants and a large population of unskilled labor. In such a community there is no farming or middle class tending to build up a conservative self-respecting community capable of self-government."[528]

Taft proposed high limitations on plantation size where the government disposed of land: 20,000 acres for sugar lands, 5,000 acres for other lands. Congress imposed a lower 2,024 acre limit.[529]

He was accused of creating an oligarchy by co-opting and making local leaders of leaders of the rebellion. He thought that growth of the educational system would offset the effects of this. Instead, many graduates were absorbed in the oligarchy. His commitment to localism had a paradoxical effect. In Louis Halle's words: "The anti-imperialists would have been right except for one thing. Once we had pacified the Philippines by brute force, we applied ourselves to the task of governing them in the spirit of our own institutions. Instead of our imperialism altering the character of our institutions, our institutions altered the character of our imperialism."[530]

As for Philippine statehood, he shared the view of Elihu Root, who preceded him as Secretary of War: "Statehood for Filipinos would add another serious problem to the one we have already. The Negroes are a cancer in our body politic, a source of constant difficulty, and we wish to avoid developing another such problem."[531]

---

[528] Speech of Acceptance, Cincinnati, July 28, 1908, in 3 W.H. Taft, Works 28.

[529] Escalante, *supra*, 193.

[530] L. Halle, "Looking Backward," in A. Campbell, Expansion and Imperialism (New York: Harper, 1970), 169.

[531] Quoted in T. Smith, America's Mission (Princeton: Princeton U., 1995), 44.

Taft pointed out that "only about 3% of the Filipinos vote and only 5% of the people are said to read the public press. [Independence would] subject the great mass of these people to the dominance of an oligarchical and probably exploiting minority."

In addition, conditions favored neither the introduction of jury trial because of the low literacy level nor the right to bear arms.[532] Taft pointed out that there was originally 80% illiteracy. "We are endeavoring to evolve a homogeneous people, fit to determine, when the time arrives, their own destiny. We are seeking to arouse a national spirit, and not, as under the older colonial theory, to suppress such a spirit. Freed from American control, the integrating forces of a common education and a common language will cease; sanitary progress is bound to be arrested."[533] He took credit for municipal elections, subject to literacy tests, election of provincial governors, and the presence of three Filipinos among the eight members of the governing commission.[534]

His strategy for pacification involved appointing former rebels as leaders of local governments. "Taft promoted devolution to (1) elected local officials and (2) indirectly elected provincial governors. A Manila-based party was given ample patronage opportunities." In 1908, he himself wrote of "the organization of a Philippine oligarchy or aristocracy competent to administer government and then turn the Islands over to it."[535]

"By cultivating the upper crust, he strengthened the wealthy families that had originally emerged during the Spanish colonial era, and many still hold sway."[536]

---

[532] Escalante, *supra*, 188.

[533] 4 W.H. Taft, Works 327.

[534] The Republican Party: What It Has Done (Cincinnati: National League of Republican Clubs, 1908).

[535] P. Hutchcroft. Autonomy in the American Philippines, 1900-13, 59 J. Asian Studies No. 2, (2000), 279.

[536] S. Karnow, In Our Image (London, Century, 1990), 127.

By 1904, as Theodore Roosevelt's chief surrogate in the 1904 election campaign, he was able to report that: "The Object of War has been accomplished. Tranquility and good order prevail in the Islands. The number of white troops in the Islands has been reduced from 75,000 to 15,000,"[537] He considered that establishment of a native constabulary was essential to pacification.[538]

As president, he was to defend federal appointment of a majority in the Puerto Rican upper house against claims for an elective assembly.[539]

In Panama, he applauded the federal creation of "a large complete and well-trained organization with full police powers, exercising utmost care." He effectively supervised construction of the Panama Canal from his appointment as Secretary of War in May 1904 until his retirement from the presidency in March 1913.[540] "The Panama Canal was built under three Presidents, not one— Roosevelt, Taft, and Wilson—and in fact, of the three, it was really Taft who gave the project the most time and personal attention. It was Taft who fired Wallace and found John Stevens, Taft who first spotted Goethals. When Taft replaced Roosevelt in the White House in 1909, the canal was only about half finished. Taft made five trips to Panama as Secretary of War and he visited twice again during the time he was President."[541]

During TR's administration, he had been given responsibility for the Canal as Secretary of War because of his department's experience with rivers and harbors and military roads. He recommended

---

[537] WHT, Address delivered before the Chamber of Commerce of the State of New York (New York, 1904), quoted in D. Brody, Visualizing American Empire (Chicago: U. of Chicago, 2010).

[538] Escalante, *supra*, 129.

[539] Second Annual Message, December 6, 1910, in 4 W.H. Taft, Works.

[540] D. Andrews, William Howard Taft: A Conservative's Conception of the Presidency (Ithaca: Cornell U., 1968), 18.

[541] D. McCullough, The Path Between the Seas: The Creation of the Panama Canal, 1830-1914 (New York: Simon and Schuster, 1977), 512.

reducing the size of the Panama Canal Commission from seven members to three, duty free entry into the Canal Zone of Panamanian goods, and uniform postal rates. He advised Roosevelt that an American naval demonstration was essential to secure the Canal against Colombia, because the Panamanian army was "not much larger than an army on an opera stage." When he discharged Wallace as Canal director, he refused to bargain with him: "for mere lucre, you change your position overnight. In my view, a duty is an entirety and is not fulfilled unless it is wholly fulfilled."[542]

Like a good lawyer, he maintained the fiction of Panamanian sovereignty over the Canal Zone. "I agree that to the Anglo-Saxon mind a titular sovereignty is a 'barren ideality' but to the Spanish or Latin mind—poetic and sentimental—enjoying the intellectual refinements and dwelling much on names and forms—it is by no means unimportant."[543]

Later, in assuring Canadians that the United States had no plans for territorial acquisition following upon a reciprocal trade treaty, he declared: "we have taken over heavy duties and obligations the weight of which ought to destroy any temptation to further acquisition of territory."[544]

In 1906 he had presided over an intervention in Cuba, concluding that "Cuba is no more fitted for self-government than the Philippines" and that "since he had little faith in the development of a sound ruling class, Taft had little faith in the development of Cuba itself."[545] In an address at the University of Havana, Taft declared his premise about such a ruling class: "The rights of property are the motivation for accumulation, next to the right of liberty is the basis for all modern successful civilization and until you have the

---

[542] Id. 379, 408, 457.

[543] Quoted in S. Morison, The Oxford History of the American People (New York: Oxford, 1965), 825.

[544] 4 W.H. Taft, Works, 123.

[545] R. Minger, "William Howard Taft and Cuba," in A. Campbell, Expansion and Imperialism (New York: Harper, 1970), 119, 121.

community of political influence and control which is effected by the conservative influences of property and property ownership, successful self-government is impossible."[546]

"Taft established himself as the temporary executive of a Cuban administration, 'conforming as far as may be to the Constitution of Cuba' and operating under the Cuban flag."[547] In his 1911 Annual Message, speaking of Cuba, he declared: "I seriously doubt whether I have such authority [to intervene] in any circumstances, and if I had I would not exercise it without express congressional approval. Proper solution of the present difficulties would be annexation if we consulted the interests of the Cuban people, but the circumstances are such that the United States cannot take this course now, though in the future it may have to do so." He sought specific statutory authority to govern the Canal Zone: "the control ought to approximate a military government: orders of the President, issued through the War Department."

His policy in Puerto Rico endures: "I believe the demand for citizenship is just and that it is amply earned by sustained loyalty on the part of the inhabitants of the island … the demand must be entirely disassociated from any thought of statehood … the fullest possible allowance of legal and fiscal self-government." His opposition to Puerto Rican statehood was later shared by the diplomat George Kennan. Both denied that a political culture "with its origins in English soil" in Justice Frankfurter's words, had an infinite capacity for absorption, a fear also shared by Alexis De Tocqueville in his writings in the 1840s.[548] A revisionist critic of American Caribbean policy acknowledged his "superb legal mind," crediting him with "a love for the law and the respect for property, precedent, compromise, peaceful settlement, and the power of money that are

---

[546] D. Burton, Taft, Holmes and the 1920s Court (Teaneck, NJ: Fairleigh Dickinson U., 1998), 76.

[547] E. Morris, Theodore Rex (New York: Random House, 2001), 461.

[548] A. Craitu (ed.), Tocqueville on America After 1840: Letters and Other Writings (Cambridge: Cambridge U., 2009).

common to many lawyers," but charged that Taft's so-called "dollar diplomacy" in the Western Hemisphere and China "developed not orderly societies but nationalist revolutions."[549] It was said that "[u]nlike McKinley and Roosevelt, he cared little about managing news releases, saw few reporters, withheld information, and took the position that the public had little right to be informed."[550]

He opposed Roosevelt's use of executive agreements rather than treaties in his dealings with the Dominican Republic.[551]

Later, he defended the landing of U.S. troops in Nicaragua "because it was done at the request and with the consent of the lawful authorities.[552]

In 1914, he warned, unsuccessfully, against intervention in Mexico lest it involve "a tedious war against guerrillas in a trackless country which will arouse no high patriotic spirit and … will leave us still a problem full of difficulty and danger."[553]

After the War, he again cautioned against extravagant demands for American rule over Mexico, entailing "granting the ballot to the adults of a population of 15,000,000, 80% of whom are entirely illiterate and none of whom speak English."[554]

Although Taft pursued "dollar diplomacy" to nurture and protect American commercial interests in Central America and the Caribbean, this approach did not take primacy in his dealings with Mexico. It has been said that "Taft's policy toward Mexico deserves

---

[549] W. La Feber, The American Search for Opportunity, 1865-1913, 2 Cambridge History of American Foreign Relations 210.

[550] W. La Feber, The American Search for Opportunity, 1865-1913, 2 Cambridge History of American Foreign Relations 205.

[551] D. Andrews, *supra*, 21.

[552] W.H. Taft, The President and His Powers (1914), in 5 W.H. Taft, Works 75.

[553] W.H. Taft, The United States and Peace (1914), in 5 W.H. Taft, Works 121ff.

[554] WHT, Editorials, *supra*, December 6, 1919, 317.

recognition as a great act of presidential statesmanship and self-restraint in the use of national power."[555]

When the Diaz government was in process of being overthrown, Taft ordered a show of force on the Mexican border. He pledged himself to consultation with Congress before departing from a policy of non-intervention. Unlike Woodrow Wilson, he considered that "when dealing with a country like Mexico, one cannot allow ethical considerations to influence one in respect to a State policy when the time has been reached making the only thing worthy of consideration to be the capacity of the man at the head of things to introduce law and order."[556]

Taft was willing to curb the military. As president, he directed the closing of unneeded Navy yards, noting that the United States had twice as many Navy yards as Britain, though only half its fleet.[557]

He also urged in 1910 that "[t]he general plan for an army of the United States at peace should be that of a skeleton organization with an excess of trained officers and thus capable of rapid enlargement by enlistments, to be supplemented in emergency by the national militia and a volunteer force." He sought to reform military pensions, which were not for those who "from a mere mercenary motive seek to obtain some legal relation with an old veteran tottering on the brink of the grave." In his annual message in 1911, he defended the existing bureau system of the army established in 1901.[558]

He recommended creation of a Council of National Defence to unify the armed services, an idea not taken up again until 40 years had passed. He affirmed the proposition, repudiated in our time, that the National Guard "could not be employed as a national force

---

[555] D. Anderson, *supra*, 265.

[556] WHT to Gus Karger, July 22, 1913, Cincinnati Museum Center.

[557] Second Annual Message, 4 W.H. Taft, Works 46.

[558] 4 W.H. Taft, Works 214.

beyond the limits of the United States in a foreign expedition."[559] (The Seventh Regiment of New York had refused to go to Cuba.)

In the Philippines, Taft concluded that "[t]he Army is not well adapted to the administration of civil government" and that "fancied danger of an uprising … is always held up by military men as a bogey."[560] He remarked on "the indifference with which the military treat claims for the use of property by individuals."[561] He felt that "[a] standing army should be looked upon with suspicion and reduced to the lowest number."[562]

In a book published in 1914. *The President and His Powers*, Taft asserted that "the president determines the movements of the army and navy in war … [and] can order the army and navy where he will," and also that an appropriation to the president's contingency fund was not a military appropriation subject to a two-year constitutional limit.[563]

In a newspaper column in praise of the late Theodore Roosevelt published in 1919, he displayed an enthusiasm for universal military training that was not to be shared by his son Robert:

> "universal military training of the Swiss type may well be instituted in this country both as insurance against unjust aggression and as a proper preparation for a contribution to the world's police forces as the United States may be called upon to make. Incidentally, it will constitute an important factor in the education of our youth in the duties of life."[564]

---

[559] 5 W.H. Taft, Works 149.

[560] 1 Pringle 185-86.

[561] 1 Pringle 213.

[562] "The Army of the United States," Board of Trade, Columbus, OH, April 2, 1908, in 1 W.H. Taft, Works 134.

[563] 6 W.H. Taft, Works 97ff.

[564] 7 W.H. Taft, Works 183.

He elsewhere referred to "universal military training to teach the youth of the nation the ways of health, the uprightness of self-respect and the discipline of obedience."[565]

He praised the World War I draft boards and non-commissioned officers: "In a republic, the military man who equitably selects and transfers the civilian into a willing soldier performs the fundamental and indispensable function of making the potential capacity of a free democracy into actual military strength."[566]

He regarded the Great War as "a cataclysm ... a retrograde step in Christian civilization,"[567] the loss to the conqueror would be "only less, if indeed it be less, than the loss to the conquered.... The King or Emperor who begins a war puts at stake the stability and integrity of his dynasty." He delivered cautionary words that resonate in our time: "It is a great deal more important in cases like this to allay public excitement than to give passionate expression to a sense of wrong. A demand for war that cannot survive the passion of the first days of public indignation and will not endure the test of delay is one that should not be yielded to."[568]

He had applied this test in his policy toward Mexico, of which it was said that "the restraints on Taft's action arose from the calm and patient manner in which he implemented his principles rather than from the principles themselves."[569]

In writing of the delay in American entry into World War I, he observed: "The absence of hot passionate action on our part, our long-suffering patience with German truculence and murder have

---

[565] Editorial, February 21, 1918, in Editorials, 38.

[566] Editorial, December 27, 1918, in Editorials, 143.

[567] 2 Pringle 871.

[568] 1 Pringle 877-78.

[569] P. Hales, Revolution and Intervention: The Diplomacy of Taft and Wilson with Mexico, 1910-17 (Cambridge: MIT Press, 1970), 261.

tended to solidify our people in this war,"[570] an observation similar to that in Churchill's notable eulogy of Neville Chamberlain.

Taft made strenuous efforts to secure a reciprocal trade agreement with Canada; the treaty was ratified by the Senate during his term in office but rejected by the Canadian Parliament due to fear that it would lead to the loss of Canada's independence or her exclusion from imperial preference arrangements with Britain.[571] Taft's enthusiasm for the Canadian treaty was founded on his view that "the real reason for the increase in prices in the things that go to make up the food of our inhabitants is the fact that all the good land has been or is being rapidly taken up."[572] His qualification of the post–Lincoln Republican belief in protectionism was thus a reaction to the closing of the frontier, also the impulse for the American imperialism that he initially resisted in the Philippines but at least partially embraced in the Caribbean.

Unlike Theodore Roosevelt, Taft believed in arbitration treaties, identifying as the greatest disappointment of his presidency his failure to secure ratification of treaties with Britain and France.[573]

The Great War and Its Aftermath

After the outbreak of the Great War, Taft criticized the British blockade of Belgium. He regarded Lodge and Roosevelt as warmongers.[574]

In the period prior to Versailles, Taft was the leader of an organization called the League to Enforce Peace, which had a four-point program. Its preamble declared premises similar to those of

---

[570] Editorial, "National Unity," August 4, 1918.

[571] 1 Pringle 583-602.

[572] "Conservation of Natural Resources," Spokane, September 28, 1909, 3 W.H. Taft, Works 260.

[573] 1 Pringle, 738-55.

[574] 2 Pringle 872-73.

Franklin Roosevelt, with his forgotten Five Policemen: "Always peace has been made and kept, when made and kept at all, by the superior power of superior numbers acting in unity for the common good ... the time has come to devise and to create a working union of sovereign nations to establish peace among themselves and to guarantee it by all known and available sanctions at their command."[575]

Of this organization, Alice Roosevelt Longworth was to observe: "We felt that my father had advocated the idea of the League of Nations in his Nobel Prize acceptance speech. And then Taft had come up with his League to Enforce Peace and we had squabbled about that. We didn't like other people's Leagues muscling in on our own."[576]

Theodore Roosevelt's vision of world order was not dissimilar, though it more explicitly relied on spheres of influence for the "policemen": "The association of nations [Theodore Roosevelt] had in mind—briefly outlined in his Nobel Peace Prize speech of 1910—was to be endowed with international police powers. To be efficient at all, it ought to be organized as an armed league restricted to the main 'civilized' nations, each being entrusted with the supervision of a given region of the globe, so as to be in a position to back world peace by force if necessary."[577]

The Taft organization's program was:

"First, all justiciable questions arising between the signatory powers, not settled by negotiation shall, subject to the limitations of treaties, be submitted to a judicial

---

[575] D. Burton, Taft, Wilson and World Order (Teaneck, NJ: Fairleigh Dickinson U., 2003), 68, 128-29.

[576] M. Teague (ed.), Mrs L: Conversations with Alice Roosevelt Longworth (London: Duckworth, 1987).

[577] S. Ricard, "Anti-Wilsonian Internationalism: Theodore Roosevelt in the Kansas City Star," in D. Rossini, From Theodore Roosevelt to FDR: Internationalism and Isolationism in American Foreign Policy (Staffordshire: Keele U., 1995), 40.

tribunal for hearing and judgment, both upon the merits and upon any issue as to its jurisdiction of the question.

Second, all other questions arising between the signatories and not settled by negotiation shall be submitted to a council of conciliation for hearing, consideration and recommendation.

Third, the signatory powers shall jointly use forthwith both their economic and military forces against any one of their number that goes to war or commits acts of hostility against another of the signatories before any question arising shall be submitted as provided in the foregoing.

Fourth, conferences between the signatory powers shall be held from time to time to formulate and codify rules of international law which unless some signatory shall signify its dissent within a specified period, shall thereafter govern in the decisions of the Judicial Tribunal mentioned in Article 1."

Taft believed that U.S. Supreme Court decisions in matters arising between the U.S. states would help in defining which controversies were justiciable.

At the end of the War, he urged "continuance of this existing league of great powers to protect the new republics of Europe."[578]

The British, French, and Italians in fact staged a series of conferences to deal with new problems in the years after the War; the most fruitful from Taft's perspective was a conference at Spa to which the new Polish government appealed for help against a Bolshevik invasion, resulting in 1922 in the dispatch of an Anglo-French military mission including several hundred French officers that helped turn the tide in what the British Ambassador to Germany, Lord D'Abernon, called one of the "Twenty-One Decisive Battles of the World."

---

[578] Editorial, December 30, 1918, in Editorials, 145.

At the end of the War, he urged more decisive action against the Bolsheviks. "No matter how the [Wilson] administration tries to hide it, it is action against the Bolsheviks. They did not want to intervene in Russia lest they alienate this gang of robbers and cutthroats ... now we are sending 25,000 men where we really need 100,000 all on the theory that we can send a smaller force and not be responsible for military intervention as if we sent a large force. [It] reminds me of the plea of a girl who had an illegitimate baby, who sought an excuse of her offense by saying it was such a little one."[579]

In June 1918, he urged that "[i]n international matters, a definite policy and prompt action usually bring results. Looking for something to turn up ends in doing nothing until it is too late to do anything."[580]

In September 1918, he again urged a force of 200,000 men, thinking that Wilson was then committed to intervention.[581] In December 1918, he declared: "I know what we ought to have done. We ought to have sent 200,000 men in there originally and with additional forces from our Allies we could have stamped out Bolshevism. When a man says he will encumber the earth and that the only way to have happiness on earth is to kill you—the only way you can deal with him is to kill him."[582] He had a profound fear of Bolshevism: "By virtue of blatant lying the utter failure of Bolshevist rule to bring comfort or contentment to the masses of the people has been concealed somewhat from the discontented elsewhere, but it will out." As for Bolshevism in the United States: "It is noisy here. It needs watching. It should be restrained."[583]

---

[579] 2 Pringle 910.

[580] Editorial, June 6, 1918, "Watchful Waiting Won't Save Russia."

[581] Editorial, "Our Task in Russia," August 22, 1918, Editorials, 84.

[582] "A League of Nations Our National Policy," December 6, 1918, in 7 W.H. Taft, Works 144.

[583] W.H. Taft, Liberty Under Law, in 7 W.H. Taft, Works 7ff.

Too much has been made, however, of one of his letters written in 1929 shortly before his death: "I am older and slower and more confused. However, as long as things continue as they are, and I am able to answer to my place, I must stay on the Court to prevent the Bolsheviks from getting control."[584]

He believed that the League of Nations should have an adjudicatory function: "court before sheriff." It should use economic as well as military force. Domestic disputes should be excluded from its jurisdiction (as was later done in Article 23 of the U.N. Charter), as should immigration and tariff questions. An agreed limitation of armaments should be reviewed every decade. "I do not believe that the plan of common disarmament is a practical plan."[585]

Harding was "talking too much allowing himself to say things about the League that are unnecessary."[586]

He supported ratification of the Treaty of Versailles, with its League, with or without reservations, going so far as to appear with President Wilson at a pro-League rally at the Metropolitan Opera House in New York on March 4, 1919.[587] He took the view that "[i]t was impossible for us to maintain the theory of isolation that did not in fact exist. It will be equally impossible for us to keep out of another European War."[588]

He took a dim view of many of the Senators of the period, referring to the "vicious narrowness" of Reed; the "explosive ignorance" of Poindexter; the "ponderous Websterian language and lack of stamina" of Borah; the "vanity" of Lodge; the "selfishness, laziness, narrow lawyer-like acuteness" of Knox; the "emptiness and sly partisanship" of Hale; and the "utter nothingness" of Fall.[589]

---

[584] 2 Pringle 963, 967.

[585] W. Taft, Popular Government in 5 W.H. Taft, Works,150ff.

[586] 2 Pringle 926ff.

[587] D. Burton, Taft, Wilson and World Order, *supra*, 112ff.

[588] *Id.* 121.

[589] WHT to Gus Karger, February 22, 1919.

He "disagreed with [Wilson] on issues of substance, such as the self-determination of nations."[590]

"Lines of race and of language are not always so clearly drawn that convenient and compact states may be established with them. The world compact must itself contain the machinery for settlement of inevitable disputes."[591]

Nonetheless, he would have voted for the League Covenant both as submitted and with reservations. Immediately after the Republican victory in the 1918 Congressional elections, he prophetically warned that "[i]n the settlement of the Treaty of Paris between the United States and Spain after the Spanish–American War, President McKinley facilitated the acquiescence of the Senate by appointing on his commission to settle the terms of the treaty Republican and Democratic members of the Foreign Relations Committee of the Senate.[592]

He also vainly warned Wilson that "he will have to leave Europe before the text of the treaty is hammered out ... In such matters, the President has neither the time, the taste, nor the experience to make his presence of the same great value as in the launching of the congress."[593]

His acceptance speech in 1908 included a denunciation of Russian anti-Semitism: "distinctions are made in respect to the treatment of our citizens based on considerations repugnant to our government and civilization."[594] This referred to a treaty negotiated by Ambassador James Buchanan before the Civil War that confined Jews revisiting Russia to the Pale of Settlement. The speech also contained a plea "to place in the hands of the Federal Executive the means of enforcing the treaty rights of aliens," as did his

---

[590] F. Gerrity, Preface to 7 W.H. Taft, Papers xi.

[591] "Obligations of Victory," November 9, 1918, in 7 W.H. Taft Works.

[592] Editorial, "A Republican Congress," November 7, 1918, 114.

[593] Editorial, November 20, 1918.

[594] 4 W.H. Taft, Works 30.

Second Annual Message in 1910.[595] More than a century later, this has not happened; observance of treaties giving foreigners the right of access to their consuls is still at the discretion of the States.[596]

After the failure of the Senate to ratify the Treaty and League, Taft pressed for American adherence to the World Court. The Senate finally agreed in 1929 to three protocols allowing limited participation, subject to two reservations: (1) notwithstanding its non-membership in the League, the United States would have a vote in the selection of judges (2) the United States would not be subject to the compulsory jurisdiction of the Court in any case unless two-thirds of the Senate approved. He upheld the principle of secret senate debates on treaties: "Senators should not be limited in their opportunity to speak freely of the motives of other nations and their characters as members of the family of nations before entering into proposed contracts with them."[597]

Taft urged that Allied troops not stop on the Armistice line but proceed to Berlin: "If the Prussian military caste retains its power to control the militarist foreign policy of Germany after the War, peace will not be permanent … as long as the present military caste controls the German military and foreign policy, peace will be impossible." This prophecy was delivered in September 1917, Taft analogizing the situation as regarded Germany with the American Civil War: "Either slavery or disunion lost or won."[598]

In November 1917 he thought that "Germany is halted, but she is not whipped, and we have to send an army of 5,000,000 instead of 2,000,000 to win this war." "We need not insist on a republican form of government like ours. A constitutional monarchy would meet the requirements … [but] they will look for a scapegoat and their

---

[595] 4 W.H. Taft, Works 19.

[596] 4 W.H. Taft, Works 49. *See* Medillin v. Texas, 552 U.S. 491 (2008).

[597] Editorials, "Secret Diplomacy in the Senate," November 1 and 8, 1917.

[598] "The Menace of a Premature Peace," Montreal, September 26, 1917, in 7 W.H. Taft, Works.

violent reaction will drive the Hohenzollern dynasty from power." In October 1918 he declared: "Unconditional surrender is what we must have, and we must pay the price."[599]

In October 1918, he expressed fear that an armistice would lead to "an interminable discussion of what [Wilson's] Fourteen Points mean or include ... Surrounding Prince Max [of Baden] and at his back will be the Kaiser, Hindenburg, Ludendorff, and the Crown Prince ... [Prince Max] says he will consent only to 'an honorable peace.'"[600]

He was not at all optimistic about the successor states: "The old powerful empires were much more likely to maintain peace than are these numerous new governments, left to themselves. Unless we exercise the power of the father over these new children of ours, they will prove unruly and bring about the very war that we are trying to prevent by creating them."[601]

He supported the minority treaties later required by the League: "We shall be derelict in our duty if we do not require as part of the fundamental law in these new republics that the Jews shall have as great religious freedom as they have in the United States."[602]

"The Central European rulers earned what has come to them because they plotted to fasten upon the world the tyranny of military control ... Russian autocracy, abominably unjust ... Yet in the ruins of these empires we have lost the equilibrium of obedience to law."[603]

---

[599] Editorial, October 3, 1918, Editorials, 94.

[600] October 8, 1918, in 7 W.H. Taft, Works.

[601] "The League: Why and How," Philadelphia Ledger, December 17, 1918, in 7 W.H. Taft, Works 172.

[602] "League of Nations and Religious Liberty," Philadelphia Ledger, December 30, 1918.

[603] W.H. Taft, Liberty Under Law in 7 W.H. Taft, Works 7ff.

He decried the Landsdowne letter "of an old and sick states-man of reactionary traditions."[604]

"From now on," he accurately prophesied, "we are likely to be more concerned with the violent reaction from one-man autocracy to the despotism of the mob."[605]

Brest-Litovsk in his view "seeks to satisfy new national aspira-tions of Finland and the Ukraine under circumstances which will put them under German and Austrian influence and make them a constant menace to the peace of Europe." As to Ukraine at least, this lesson has not yet been learned by the United States.[606]

He held to the British view of Wilson's demand for "freedom of the seas." "So far as freedom of the seas in time of peace is concerned, where the British flag floats, there is and has always been freedom of the seas."[607]

The Far East

Taft viewed the possibility of Japanese domination of China with complacency, perceiving a threat to the United States only if Japanese aspirations were directed to the open sea.[608]

In his view, "war between Japan and the United States would be a crime against modern civilization. It would be as wicked as it would be insane."[609]

Consistently with this view, he declared in his Second Annual Message in 1910 that he regarded the Japanese annexation of Korea

---

[604] Editorial, December 3, 1917, Editorials, 11-12.

[605] Editorial, "The End of Monarchy," November 11, 1918, Editorials 118.

[606] Editorial, February 28, 1918, Editorials, 39.

[607] "Disarmament and Freedom of the Seas," December 11, 1918, in 7 W.H. Taft, Works 147ff.

[608] 1 Pringle 287.

[609] 1 Pringle 176.

as the "final step in a process of control of the ancient empire by her powerful neighbor that has been in progress for several years past."

In his inaugural address he saw clouds on the horizon in the Far East, alluding to "the international controversies that are likely to arise in the Orient growing out of the question of the Open Door [in China] and other issues." Against a background of civil disturbances in the Western states, he sought to ameliorate friction with Japan over immigration. He was pessimistic about "Asiatic immigrants who cannot be amalgamated with our population," urging "mutual concessions between self-respecting governments. We must take every precaution to prevent, or failing that, to punish, outbursts of race feeling among our people."[610]

He was warned by Theodore Roosevelt: "our vital interest is to keep the Japanese out of our country and at the same time to preserve the good will of Japan. The vital interest of the Japanese on the other hand is in Manchuria and Korea. It is therefore probably our interest not to take any steps which will give the Japanese cause to feel that we are hostile to them or a menace to their interests. The 'Open Door' policy in China was an excellent thing and will I hope be a good thing in the future for us as it can be maintained by general diplomatic agreement, but as has now been proved by the whole history of Manchuria, both under Russia and under Japan, the 'open door' policy as a matter of fact completely disappears as soon as a powerful nation determines to disregard it and is willing to run the risk of war rather than forego its intention. Now on the other hand, whereas our interests in Manchuria are really unimportant and not such that the American people would be content to run the slightest risk of collision about them, our interest is in keeping the Japanese out of our own country."[611]

---

[610] Inaugural Address, March 4, 1909, in 3 W.H. Taft, Works 48ff.

[611] Roosevelt to Taft, December 22, 1910, in 2 E. Morrison, Letters of Theodore Roosevelt 189-90. He also told British Foreign Minister Grey that Japan should be encouraged to go into Manchuria, and that any interference with

Japanese Foreign Minister Komura frankly avowed in the Diet on February 1, 1910, that the Japanese government intended in the future to direct emigration to Manchuria and Korea.[612]

Under Secretary of State Knox the United States in disregard of such warnings made several efforts to enlarge its influence in North China in connection with railroad financings, which collapsed by the close of the Taft administration in the face of Japanese and British resistance, leading Henry Adams to observe that "Knox has managed to get his head punched in China."[613]

In a letter to Taft dated December 22, 1910,[614] Theodore Roosevelt had warned:

> "I utterly disbelieve in the policy of bluff, in national and international no less than in private affairs, or in any violation of the old frontier maxim, "Never draw unless you mean to shoot." I do not believe in our taking any position anywhere unless we can make good; and as regards Manchuria, if the Japanese choose to follow a course of conduct to which we are adverse, we cannot stop it unless we are prepared to go to war, and a successful war about Manchuria would require a fleet as good as that of England, plus an army as good as that of Germany."

As a sympathetic biographer of Taft observed: "As the protégé of Theodore Roosevelt, Taft should have known better than to have

---

her national expansion would bring trouble on the American-Canadian Pacific Coast. Grey to Bryce, January 20, 1911 in Bryce Papers 122 n.37.

[612] O'Brien to Knox, February 10, 1910, Department of State, 893.77/792.

[613] W. and M. Scholes, The Foreign Policy of the Taft Administration (Columbia: U. of Missouri Press, 1970), 211.

[614] W. and M. Scholes, The Foreign Policy of the Taft Administration (Columbia: U. of Missouri Press, 1970), 211.

challenged Japan and Russia in their own back yard, but his 'experts' in the [State] department did not discourage him."[615]

"[H]e slowly, hesitantly began divorcing U.S. policy from the legitimacy his predecessors had given to Japan's sphere of influence."[616]

Conclusion

In summing up William Howard Taft's career, in 1936 the editors of the *Dictionary of American Biography* charged him with "vacillation, irritability, a complete inability to lead," while crediting him with "an excellent judicial mind, an integrity that was never clouded, great talent as an administrator [and] wide and broad sympathy for human problems." "His fatal error was his belief that the Republican party could be continued in power without giving ground to its more liberal wing."[617]

By 2013 the record looked different. Nicholas Lemann wrote: "The real trustbuster was Taft … Taft was also far more aggressive than Roosevelt in taking on protective tariffs … Taft's economic positions seem more liberal to us."[618]

Knowing what we now do about "regulatory capture," the "New Nationalism" and "Modern [corporate] Republicanism" have lost much of their appeal, and Taft's concern with the limitation of corporate and union power and with the separation of powers and rule of law within government has gained greater currency.

---

[615] D. Anderson, *supra*, 250.

[616] G. Kolko, Main Currents in Modern American History (New York: Harper, 1976), 59-60.

[617] 9 D. Malone (ed.), Dictionary of American Biography 269 (New York: Scribner, 1936).

[618] N. Lemann, "Progress's Pilgrims," New Yorker, November 18, 2013.

Taft's most emphatic statement on the separation of powers came in his 71-page opinion in *Myers v. United States*,[619] holding that removal of a postmaster confirmed by the Senate did not require consent of the Senate, because of "the paralysis to which a partisan Senate and Congress could subject the executive arm ... To hold otherwise would make it impossible for the President in case of political or other differences with the Senate to take care that the laws are faithfully executed." Justices Holmes, McReynolds, and Brandeis dissented, Justice Holmes on the ground that Congress' right to create the office encompassed its right to destroy it, and Justice Brandeis in a lengthy opinion famously asserting that the Constitution was enacted "not to promote efficiency but to preclude the exercise of arbitrary power ... the people must look to representative assemblies for the protection of their liberties." Taft's opinion was circumscribed so as to preserve Congress' power to circumscribe the removal of officials appointed not by the President but by the heads of departments, a limitation Taft and others thought necessary to preserve the independence of the civil service.[620]

In the later case of *Humphreys' Executor v. United States*,[621] decided in 1935, Brandeis' view prevailed as to quasi-judicial members of federal administrative agencies, as distinct from executive appointees generally. It is important to note that Taft joined in the later opinion of Justice Van Devanter, for a unanimous court, in upholding Congress' power of investigation in *McGrain v. Daugherty*,[622] including its power to attach and incarcerate contumacious witnesses without the need for the powers of a court.

Although seemingly maladroit as an electoral politician, he thought about institutions and played for the long term. Succeeding

---

[619] 272 U.S. 52 (1926).

[620] R. Post, "Taft's Epochal Opinion in Myers v. U.S.," 45 Journal of Supreme Court History 167 (2020).

[621] 295 U.S. 602 (1935).

[622] 223 U.S. 134 (1927).

Roosevelt, he "tr[ied] to accomplish just as much without any noise." He successfully defended the judicial branch against TR's assaults; strengthened it by seeking the Judiciary Act of 1925; sought budget legislation enacted ten years after he left office; sought a Tariff Board to reduce congressional logrolling, a short-lived reform also enacted after he left office; and carefully nurtured a Republican alliance with the South, which he reluctantly saw as a necessary bulwark against collectivism. He backed Booker T. Washington's program of industrial education and small-scale entrepreneurship for blacks, which while in New Haven he urged also upon Italian and Jewish immigrant groups, a cause submerged, for better or worse, by W.E.B. Du Bois' claims for higher education and more Marxist analysis of the predicament of blacks. While Theodore Roosevelt had scandalized the South by having Washington to lunch at the White House on one occasion, Taft saw him and his successor, Dr. Moton, on many occasions. Taft once surprised his wife by calling her from the railroad station in Cincinnati to tell her he was bringing home a luncheon guest, who proved to be one of his former black servants.

In 1912, just before leaving the presidency, he was instrumental in organizing the U.S. Chamber of Commerce, which he saw as a necessary counterweight to the rising power of labor unions: "We want your assistance in carrying on the government in reference to those matters that affect the business and the business welfare of the country, and we do not wish to limit your discretion in that matter. We wish that your advice should be as free and unrestricted as possible, but we need your assistance and we ask for it."[623]

It was said of Taft that he was "as aggressive in the pursuit of his agenda in the judicial realm as Theodore Roosevelt was in the Presidential."[624] His ability to mobilize the Supreme Court and his strengthening of its control over its docket preserved it as an important institution. As Professor Donald Anderson has

---

[623] WHT Address, April 22, 1912, *see* www.uschamber.com/timeline.

[624] R. Anderson, "Building National Consensus: The Career of William Howard Taft," 68 U. Cincinnati L. Rev. 323 (2000).

observed: "What if the Court confronting FDR in 1937 had been characterized by scores of highly controversial 5-4 decisions, a proliferation of concurring and vitriolic dissenting opinions, a greater degree of incivility among the justices, too many plurality opinions and too few majority opinions, stare decisis ignored whenever expedient, opinions liberally laced with revisionist 'scissors and paste' history, the vicious politicization of the appointment process, and a dumbing-down of the Court through the appointment of 'stealth' justices with little distinction except the virtue of indistinction and confirmability—all contributing to a growing public perception of the Court as a highly politicized institution unworthy of popular respect. It is difficult to imagine that FDR would have behaved as cautiously and deferentially toward such a Court or that public opposition to his Court-packing plan would have been as severe … To the extent that the modern Court has diverged from the Taft model of judicial behavior, it threatens to become an institution of national disunity and dishonor, undermining our shared values and national sense of community, and raises serious questions about the long term legitimacy of judicial review, the rule of law, and of constitutional democracy itself."[625]

HELEN HERRON TAFT (1861-1943)

Helen Taft, William Howard Taft's wife, had known him since she was 18 years old, and joined him in an amateur theatrical group. She is generally credited with urging him on to the presidency, deferring the quiet life on courts that he would have preferred. She was considered bold in riding in the inaugural parade with her husband. Her earnestness was famously satirized by Theodore Roosevelt's rambunctious daughter, Alice Roosevelt Longworth: "I have perfected what I called Mrs. Taft's hippopotamus face and was able

---

[625] D. Anderson, Building National Consensus: The Career of William Howard Taft, 68 U. Cin. L. Rev. 323, 355-56 (2000).

to put it on just as we were going
through the [White House] gates
and say 'This, darlings, is what
is coming after you.'"[626] In the
White House, where she began
serving food at White House
receptions,[627] she entertained so
energetically that she was felled
by a stroke, from which she grad-

Helen Taft

ually recovered during the rest of her husband's presidency, which
denied him the benefit of her usually good political advice.

She was not universally admired. Of her, Alice Longworth
wrote: "She was a woman full of gentility and she quickly became
very possessive of the White House. She had the idea of having liv-
eried men at the front door and things like that. And she took to
driving in state around the Potomac to listen to the band. I think
her personality had a good deal to do with the breakup of Taft's
friendship with my father. There was an abrasive quality there."[628]
Her successful opposition to the appointment of TR's son-in-law
Nicholas Longworth as Minister to China did not aid TR's relationship with Taft.[629]

She "liked to smoke, drink beer, and play cards for money."[630]
She was a leader in the creation of the Cincinnati Symphony. When

[626] M. Teague (ed.), Mrs L: Conversations with Alice Roosevelt Longworth
(London: Duckworth, 1987), 140.

[627] M. Teague (ed.), Mrs L: Conversations with Alice Roosevelt Longworth
(London: Duckworth, 1987), 66.

[628] M. Teague (ed.), Mrs L: Conversations with Alice Roosevelt Longworth
(London: Duckworth, 1987), 140.

[629] C. Anthony, Nellie Taft: The Unconventional First Lady of the Ragtime
Era (New York: Morrow, 2005), 250ff.

[630] D. Goodwin, The Bully Pulpit: Theodore Roosevelt, William Howard
Taft, and the Golden Age of Journalism (New York: Simon and Schuster, 2013), 5.

Alice Longworth, RAT, and Martha Taft

her husband was in the Philippines, she led agitation for preservation of the walls of the City of Manila.[631]

Her memoirs, published in 1914,[632] disclose her drive and sharp intelligence. The Germans of Cincinnati, in her view "made for a more liberal Sunday, … brought the study of German into the public schools; and … developed a strong taste for good music." Her father had been a law partner of President Hayes. She regarded her father-in-law, Alphonso Taft, as "'gentle' beyond anything I ever knew. He was a man of tremendous firmness of purpose and just as set in his views as anyone well could be, but he was one of the most lovable men that ever lived because he had a wide tolerance and a strangely 'understanding sympathy' for everybody."

When her husband went on the Bench at an early age, "he seemed to me suddenly to take on a maturity and sedateness quite

---

[631] D. Goodwin, The Bully Pulpit: Theodore Roosevelt, William Howard Taft, and the Golden Age of Journalism (New York: Simon and Schuster, 2013), 220. 271.

[632] H. Taft, Recollections of Full Years (New York: Dodd, Mead, 1914).

out of keeping with his actual years and I dreaded to see him settled for good in the judiciary and missing all the youthful enthusiasm and exhilarating difficulties which more general contact of the world would have given him." "Mr. Taft was strongly opposed to taking the Philippines. He was not an anti-imperialist in the sense that he believed the Constitution required us to keep the boundaries of the United States within their continental limits, but he thought the Antipodes rather a far stretch for the controlling hand and he thought the taking of the Philippines would only add to our problems and responsibilities without increasing in any way the effectiveness and usefulness of our government." When offered the governorship, he "at once saw that it would be years before the Philippine problem would begin to solve itself. So he resigned from the Bench; the hardest thing he ever did."[633]

On arrival in the Philippines, she related, his "rickshaw man has enlisted the services of at least half the population of the village to help him in attaining the crest of the hill." The anti-imperialists, in her view, failed to recognize that "'independence' meant nothing more nor less than the merciless exploitation of the many by the few and the establishment of worse conditions than any the people had ever known." Her husband believed that upon the election of McKinley, the rebels "must be given an opportunity to come in and if they do not come in a short time, they ought to be deported from the country and sent to Guam." "My husband is supposed to be the author of the phrase 'our little brown brothers' and perhaps he is. It did not meet the approval of the army, and the soldiers used to have a song which they sung with great gusto and frequency and which ended with the conciliating sentiment: 'He may be a brother of William H. Taft, but he ain't no friend of mine.'"[634]

"Taxation, civil service, provincial and municipal organization, currency and finance, police, harbor improvements, roads and

---

[633] Id. 2, 6, 18, 22, 30, 32, 34.

[634] Id. 58, 69, 83, 89, 111, 125.

railways, customs, postal service, education, health, public lands, an honest judiciary and revision of the code of laws; these were some of the vital problems, but underlying them all was the immediate necessity for the establishment of tranquility and confidence." She related that on her visit to Rome where her husband negotiated with Pope Leo X over the friars' lands, the Pope "asked Bob what he expected to be when he grew up and my self-confident son replied that he intended to be Chief Justice of the Supreme Court. I suppose that he had heard the Chief Justiceship talked about by his father until he thought it the only worthy ambition for a self-respecting citizen to entertain."[635]

She was a determined woman, of formidable mien, not the "hippopotamus" depicted by Alice Roosevelt, but also a woman whose influence was not especially due to the feminine graces.

---

[635] *Id.* 129, 132, 248.

THE THIRD GENERATION

The third generation of the Taft dynasty no longer had the luxury of making their careers during a long period of Republican ascendancy. They functioned in a harsher political climate, and responded in different ways: Hulbert, in a posture of total intransigence; Robert and Helen, by expertly fighting a rear-guard action tempering the new collectivist values; and Charles by entering into accommodations with the New Deal without abandoning his conservative political sympathies.

Their task was the curbing of aggregates of public rather than private power. They resisted price and wage controls, proposals for the conscription of labor, delegations to the Executive of war-making power, creation of new federal agencies, and erosion of the power of courts, while voicing suspicion of supra-national groupings and foreign alliances.

HULBERT TAFT SR. (1877-1959)

Hulbert Taft Sr., son of Charles Taft, was the long-time publisher of the *Cincinnati Times-Star* and founder of the Taft Broadcasting Company. He became the editor in 1908 and served as Chairman until 1958. In 1929, he had a much-publicized interview with Benito Mussolini, followed by one with Leon Trotsky. He was described by the journalist John Gunther as the most conservative man he had met in the United States. On his death, an obituary observed: "The Old Guard might die, but it will never surrender." His king-making editorials had much to do with the survival of Cincinnati as one of the few large cities in the United States that regularly voted Republican in his time, the Republicans controlling the mayoralty for 40 of the 57 years from 1914 to 1971, though he deviated from this allegiance in the cause of family solidarity

Hulbert Taft Sr.

to support Charles Taft Jr.'s non-partisan Charter Movement in local politics.[1] His newspaper was one of the few not to lay off personnel during the Depression, when he shared in across-the-board pay cuts, declaring "we will all manage to earn our bread and butter." Among his causes were smoke abatement, Ohio River purification, school construction, and retail trade expansion. "His endorsement was considered tantamount to election." He once declared that despite his Republicanism, "I found a good many agreeable Democrats in Cincinnati," one of them was John J. Gilligan, later Governor of Ohio, who he repeatedly endorsed. The young Potter Stewart, later a Justice of the Supreme Court, in his youth was one of his reporters. He unsuccessfully tried to acquire the *Cincinnati Enquirer* in 1952; the *Times-Star* was sold to the Scripps-Howard chain in 1958, by which time it was losing $1 million a year; he was the only dissenter on the board. On his death in 1958, the *Enquirer* referred to him as "a newspaperman of the old school—a man of lively opinion and stout loyalty, a good friend and a foe able to test anyone's mettle."[2]

Hulbert Taft had two sons, Hulbert Taft Jr. (1907-1967) and David G. Taft (1916-1962), both of whom were also active in the affairs of Taft Broadcasting; and two daughters, Katherine Taft Benedict (1909-2001) and Margaret Taft Tytus (1913-2008), a horsewoman and licensed pilot, who was active in the preservation of Ohio Indian artifacts and in support of classical studies.

---

[1] R. McKay, "The Rapid Rise and Fractious Fall of Taft Broadcasting," *Cincinnati Magazine*, July 1987.

[2] "Hail and Farewell," *Cincinnati Enquirer*, July 24, 1958; "Death Signs Last '30' for Hulbert Taft, Sr., 81," *Cincinnati Enquirer*, January 20, 1959, p. 1; J. Hunter, "The Way We Were: Hulbert Taft's Missing Editorial," *Cincinnati Magazine*, December 1, 1984, p. 57.

ROBERT A. TAFT (1889-1953)

Personality and Values

Robert A. Taft, older son of President William Howard Taft, did well in Greek and Latin, but never learned to speak a foreign language. He was admonished by his father to put studies first, and not to be distracted by athletics. He was an enthusiastic debater, but was not ready on his feet. He did not excel in essay contests, but graduated from all his schools at the top of his class. He felt that college students in politics "may even arouse the sort of opposition which always greets a tactless missionary,"[3] a lesson not learned by today's student demonstrators, who at the least can be credited with electing Ronald Reagan as Governor of California and Richard Nixon as President of the United States, and whose efforts in 1968 at Yale were later disparaged by one of his descendants, John T. Taft. His father had not joined in many of the more advanced "free speech" opinions beloved of today's liberals, and on any fair view it was the discipline of the civil rights movement that brought it success, aided by the abstention of its most noted leaders from inflammatory rhetoric. The Vietnam student demonstrations, by outraging a "silent majority," did more to extend the Vietnam War than to end it; it was elite opinion that did that, though Taft, as his record on labor issues showed, was aware of the importance of providing legal outlets for discontent.

Advising his brother Charlie several years after graduating from Yale, Robert Taft observed: "It seems to me that I took elementary courses in so many things that I never got advanced in anything; now I believe I would like to have something that I really know about, preferably English literature ... never touch a modern language, which are stupid and useless."[4] The Tafts nonetheless were

---

[3] J. Patterson, *Mr. Republican: A Biography of Robert A. Taft* (New York: Houghton Mifflin, 1972), 38.

[4] Patterson 42.

Robert A. Taft Learning the Budget

believers in traditional liberal education in history and literature, disciplines that some deride as non-utilitarian. They are the study of how human beings behave in fact, not the study of how they ought to behave according to the fanatical economists of left and right.

One of his professors regarded him as "[v]ery bright, but too practical a mind." Arriving at Harvard, he said: "I do not intend to go into athletics or to be a social lion or to do missionary work or to be interviewed." He was "decidedly cool to all those outside his inner circle and to anyone he believed was wasting his time." Later, it was said that "his interests outside politics were narrow. [He was] one of the hardest-working senators of any, ever … uncomfortable with such traditional political activities as working a crowd, wearing fraternal regalia, kissing babies, or flattering local worthies."[5] His immediate aspirations were modest: "I don't see why you can't take part in politics and in every campaign and convention and the like and not hold office, at least until you have established enough of a law practice so you can go back and make money enough to live

---

5   RAT, in Encyclopedia.com.

on."[6] Accordingly, on the advice of his father, he declined a Supreme Court clerkship with Mr. Justice Holmes, which almost certainly would have altered his outlook considerably, and went back to Cincinnati, his father more wisely having warned him that much talent got lost in New York law offices and that it was an advantage to start practice in a community where he was known.

His view was that "the only way to get ahead was to try hard and keep on trying." In the end, he furnished "a remarkable exception to the rule that sons of great men seldom display the elements of greatness,"[7] though Harry Truman took the view that "the son is elected because people remember the outstanding character of the father."[8]

His academic application may have contributed to the occasional dourness of his personality. The Tafts were driven by the family tradition of academic excellence; Alphonso's son Peter Rawson Taft died shortly after his graduation from Yale as valedictorian. The Taft emphasis on intense study did not usually have the fatal results of Theodore Roosevelt's stress on military valor, one Roosevelt son dying in war; a second a suicide; and a third dying of a heart attack after landing in the first wave of troops at Utah Beach while in his fifties.[9]

As a Senator, he frequently took impolitic positions. He opposed the nomination of David Lilienthal to the Atomic Energy Commission, viewing him as "secretive and ambitious," leading one of his allies to say: "There goes the scientists' vote, the Jewish vote in New York and a big chunk of the independent vote." He had a dry wit. He also observed: "Children are relatively inexpensive until they become self-supporting."[10]

---

[6] Patterson 51.

[7] Patterson 168.

[8] Patterson 274.

[9] W. Mann, The Wars of the Roosevelts (New York: Harper, 2016).

[10] Patterson 344, 347.

Taft "ate well, slept well, lived without pose, never became melancholy." His response to a meat shortage was unpopular: "Eat less meat and eat less extravagantly." He regarded Thomas E. Dewey as the "Boy Orator of the Platitude." In the eyes of Harold Ickes, Taft in 1944 was "Babe Ruth," and the Republicans "sent in a batboy with the bases full and only one run needed." He had, according to William S. White, "a certain feeling of noblesse oblige to all who served him, however poorly."[11]

It was observed that "it was absolutely essential in the Taft family of his earlier years to do things for oneself—and still is in that family." But, it was said, "life never prepared him for a perception of the thin margin on which most of his fellow men must operate." He regarded Congress as "'safer' in constitutional matters, and primarily because of the Senate." New Dealers, he thought, "had discovered the art of perpetual emotion."[12]

He was described as "the only elevated Western politician, apart from Churchill, who never used a ghost-writer."[13] "It is only in the Senate that modern conditions still give hospitality to the political individualist."[14] His personality, it was said, "was seriously flawed by pedantry, by stiffness, and by occasional bull-handedness."[15] "When he speaks out, he says what he thinks at the time …, his duty as a citizen and a legislator prevails over such considerations as that of being the Republican majority leader."[16]

"The Taft Republican," it was said, "believes in stability, in order, in solvency as one of the highest of ends, in moving very slowly and

---

[11] White, *supra*, 9.

[12] White 48.

[13] White 204.

[14] White 198.

[15] R. Rovere, What Course for the Powerful Mr. Taft," New York Times Magazine, March 23, 1953.

[16] A. Krock, "Taft and the Policy of the Free Hand," New York Times, May 29, 1953.

changing almost never. He believes very much in tradition." "The Taft Republican party," it was said after his death, "is disembodied without him ... really lies buried on Indian Hill outside Cincinnati."[17] "People knew him less and less. They thought that because there was one fixed constant in him—his institutional concern for the Republican Party—his ideas and notions were fixed."[18] "He was a highly individualistic man who thought in a highly institutional way."[19]

He was eulogized by his former chief Herbert Hoover as "more nearly the irreplaceable man in American public life than any we have had in three generations."[20] Elsewhere, Hoover said of him: "He became in the Senate a bulwark against those forces of reaction that would tear the U.S. into sects and cults of warring theorists. He brought to the social problems of his country a trained and political mind."

In lauding Hoover to the Chicago Yale Club in 1920, he expressed his own methods and values: "He met objections by conference, persuasion and fair dealing with opposing interests. He reduces a question first to its simplest terms. He approaches it from the widest possible point of view and works out the fundamental principles on which the solution must be based. He acquires a complete knowledge of his subject by consulting experts and by extensive reading. He will be in fact a leader of public opinion and not its reflection."[21] Hoover, he said, again echoing his own experience: "belongs to that class of rock-bottom Americans who become more intensely American the more they see of foreign countries."[22]

---

[17] White 20, 282.

[18] White 27.

[19] White 279.

[20] White 269.

[21] Chicago Yale Club, April 5, 1920, 1 C. Wunderlin (ed.), Papers of Robert A. Taft (Kent, OH: Kent State U., 2001) (hereafter "R. Taft, Works"), 230ff.

[22] RAT to Curtis Lindley, April 14, 1920. 1 R. Taft, Works 232.

At the 1920 Republican convention, "Bob Taft was one of the fixtures of the Hoover room. He was, he announced, for Hoover 'first, last, and always.'"[23] In early 1929, he declined Hoover's offer to appoint him an Assistant Attorney General. Hoover, in fact, had been his mentor as much as his father. He served in Hoover's Food Administration and relief efforts during and after World War I, corresponded with him throughout his lifetime, and referred to him as "the Chief." He shared Hoover's abhorrence of the British blockade of neutrals during the War and of Germany afterward, and his views on domestic policy bore a striking resemblance to those expressed in Hoover's 72-page tract, *American Individualism*.[24]

"We shall safeguard to every individual an equality of opportunity to take that position in the community to which his intelligence, character, ability and ambition entitle him ... while he in turn must stand up to the emery wheel of competition." He shared Hoover's abhorrence of collectivism and interest-group politics. Hoover declared in 1922, with a vehemence equaled at the time among intellectuals only by Bertrand Russell's *Practice and Theory of Bolshevism*[25] that "socialism in a nation-wide application has now proved itself with rivers of blood and inconceivable misery to be an economic and spiritual fallacy and has wrecked itself finally upon the rocks of destroyed production and moral degeneracy."[26]

"If warring interests ... dominate legislators and intimidate public officials, [o]ur Government will then drift into the hands of timorous mediocraties dominated by groups until we shall become a syndicalist nation on a gigantic scale."[27]

---

[23] F. Russell, The Shadow of Blooming Grove (New York: McGraw Hill, 1968), 357.

[24] (New York: Doubleday, 1922), 9.

[25] (London: Allen and Unwin, 1920).

[26] H. Hoover, American Individualism (New York: Doubleday, 1922), 36.

[27] Id. 43.

But like his father, he also shared Hoover's conviction that concentrations of wealth must be curbed: "The domination by arbitrary individual ownership is disappearing because the works of today are steadily growing more and more beyond the resources of any one individual, and steadily taxation will reduce relatively excessive individual accumulations."[28]

He was the embodiment of what the Yale Law Professor Charles Reich at a later time was to call "Consciousness One." Reich's statist Consciousness Two met its end in 1989; his Consciousness Three, with its ethic of self-indulgence, is with us still, the cause of many political conflicts and discontents.

Taft was of a personally tolerant disposition, saying of a Farmer-Labor spokesman and the Communist Earl Browder that they "uttered the wildest sentiments in the most agreeable way and were both quite attractive."[29]

Taft in his youth was said to resemble "a chemistry professor, a small-town bank president, possibly a Sunday school superintendent." When his former partner John Hollister, then a Congressman, offered to press for a widow's pension for Helen Taft, Robert Taft responded: "unless a matter of this sort is a matter of course established in the cases of Mrs. Wilson and Mrs. Roosevelt, we do not desire to press it in any way."

In his largely extemporaneous speech to the Gridiron Club in 1939, which was generally judged to have been a fiasco, he observed: "I came down to Washington prepared to meet a raging New Deal lion and instead I find a rather sleepy and confused lion enjoying an overdose of social and political security and a heavy meal of grilled millionaire." He did not make himself popular with his doubtless well-taken observation that "not one of [the journalists] seems to be interested with interpreting the country to Washington."[30]

---

[28] *Id.* 39.

[29] Patterson 150ff.

[30] Gridiron Club, April 15, 1939, 2 R. Taft, Works 23.

He warned his son Robert against entering a large law firm in New York, as he had been warned by his own father, urging him to be sure that "you don't get into a rut as so many lawyers do in New York."[31]

In 1948, when it was rumored that Truman might appoint him to the Supreme Court, he told a columnist that "I have never been interested in a judicial position."[32]

In 1950, he tendered to a friend advice on how young people should launch their careers, also echoing his father's advice: "They ought to choose a profession or business, and usually choose it in their home where their children are well known. The trouble with our diplomatic corps is that most of them don't know what America is about. Bureaucratic jobs in Washington don't lead anywhere. I take a young man into my office every two years to do my legal work but he has to be a law school graduate and I don't encourage him to stay more than two years."[33]

In 1943, Taft was an advocate of drastically increased taxation during wartime: "I am all in favour of taxing the rich up to the limit. I believe that those with incomes in the past of $100,000 or more must look forward to living on not more than half the amount they have formerly enjoyed."[34]

In a speech to the Wayne County Medical Society in 1946, Taft declared: "Several years ago at Mackinac I had the privilege of serving on a committee with Governors Dewey and Bricker. We wrote into our resolutions at that time that it was the function of government to prevent hardship and suffering and secured the adoption of that declaration over the opposition of those who took the nineteenth-century view that such prevention was impossible.

---

[31] RAT to RAT Jr., September 6, 1945.

[32] RAT to Walter Winchell, June 28, 1948, 3 R. Taft, Works 457.

[33] RAT to Elsie Wilson, May 1950, in 4 R. Taft, Works 150ff.

[34] Patterson 256.

Today it can be done ... because of the tremendous productivity of a system of free enterprise."[35]

In 1952, he was unhappy because "I didn't like the fact that we have so many big businessmen in the cabinet."[36]

Taft "dressed plainly and drove his own car, travelled in day coaches, and held sycophants at arm's length."[37] In 1946, his car was an 11-year-old Buick.[38]

He was famous for an episode in Georgetown when he attended a party at which the other official guests had arrived in chauffeured limousines. "Senator Taft's car" the doorman bellowed on his departure from the building. "It's a good car," Taft observed to him, "but it doesn't come when it is called." In April 1948, the liberal columnist Richard Rovere referred to him as "shy, quiet, and deferential," while being "the ablest figure in American politics today, and in many ways the man with the firmest integrity and independence of mind ... informed intelligence and massive sincerity of purpose make him seem, alongside the *papier mache* statesmen of the period, almost a figure of granite."[39]

He was credited by Joseph and Stewart Alsop, who disagreed with him on most foreign policy issues, as possessing "unfailing strength of character, good sportsmanship, and an odd attractive kind of impersonal common sense."[40]

He was described by John Gunther with being "about as magnetic as a lead nail."[41]

---

[35] Wayne County Medical Society, October 3, 1946, 3 R. Taft, Works 210.

[36] Patterson 328ff.

[37] Patterson 203.

[38] Patterson 337.

[39] R. Rovere, "Taft: Is This the Best We've Got?," 196 Harper's 289 (April 1948).

[40] Patterson 418.

[41] J. Gunther, Inside U.S.A. (London: Hamish Hamilton, 1947), 456.

Taft took the view that "people can adhere to sound principle without stirring up class hatred if they will admit the good faith of their opponents, avoid personalities and try to project in clear and calm language the reasons for their own faith … Peace on earth depends not on surrender but on meeting opposition in a spirit of tolerance, sympathy, and good humor."[42]

In 1933, while still in Ohio, he observed that "it is improper for the Republican party to receive money from [utility companies] when they will be called upon shortly after election to determine gas and electric rates."[43] In a Memorial Address at Arlington Cemetery on May 30, 1939, he cautioned an audience of veterans that "[p]atriotism is not confined solely to those who bear arms for their country."[44] He decried personal attacks: "I believe progress can be made best by a direct discussion of the issues without personal attacks."[45] "The Communist procedure has always been to knock down anyone who has become an effective opponent of their ideology, hoping that it will deter all others from active opposition to their plans."[46] Rule 13 of the fashionable later writer Saul Alinsky's *Rules for Radicals* was "Pick the target, freeze it, personalize it, and polarize it."[47]

Describing the influence of his father, he observed: "Most of my political philosophy was derived from [WHT] and I never read any of his opinions or speeches that I do not wonder at his clear-sighted analysis of governmental problems. My father loved people and was one of the most tolerant men I know. He had no prejudice against any man or woman in any walk of life except, I think, when they drank too much."[48]

---

[42]   Radio Address, December 25, 1938, 1 R. Taft, Works 602.

[43]   RAT to William J. Howard, October 23, 1933, 1 R. Taft, Works 455.

[44]   2 R. Taft, Works 37.

[45]   RAT to Marjorie Shannon, October 10, 1946, 3 R. Taft, Works 213.

[46]   Radio Broadcast on CIO-PAC, October 26, 1946, 3 R. Taft, Works 217.

[47]   S. Alinsky, Rules for Radicals (New York: Random House, 1971), 130.

[48]   RAT to John Graves, January 20, 1947, in 3 R. Taft, Works 241.

A speech in 1948 to the Inland Press Association declared many of his premises:

> "We want a better people, people of a strong char-acter—God-fearing, industrious, self-reliant, honorable and intelligent. [There] must be such a standard, even for the poorest, that happiness and character is possible. Americans have not been the most orderly people in the world. Mass action has been permitted to nullify law in many cases. It is perhaps our greatest fault, exhibited in black markets, bootlegging, labor violence. And, in an extreme form, lynching. The New Deal advocates of a totalitarian state found that their first job must be to dis-credit both Congress and the courts.
>
> No child should suffer for the sins or the misfor-tunes or the inadequacies of his father [but] financial aid is likely to destroy the incentive of those other than the children who receive the assistance, usually the least able and energetic of the entire population. But certainly the government must not destroy the incentive of other workers by providing a higher standard for non-workers than for those who earn their own way."[49]

This proposition was later held to be legitimate by the Supreme Court in the case of *Dandridge v. Williams*,[50] sustaining family maxi-mums on welfare grants and argued by the present writer.

Apropos of Colonel Robert McCormick of the *Chicago Tri-bune*, he wrote a friend: "I hope that you got the Colonel off safely to Europe, where I trust he won't start a war with the British."[51]

Although he had many differences with Harold Ickes, the most outspoken interventionist among the New Dealers, there

---

[49] Inland Daily Press Association, February 10, 1948, 3 R. Taft, Works 385.

[50] 397 U.S. 471 (1970).

[51] RAT to Walter Trohan, July 1, 1948, quoted in R. Divine, *supra.*

was a relationship of mutual respect. Taft was a pallbearer at Ickes' funeral.[52]

It was said of him that "[i]ssues determined his Senate associations; personalities were all but irrelevant"; he displayed "a luminous candor of purpose."[53]

His wife, Martha, was described as "a born campaigner, quick, practical, witty and extroverted." Her finest hour came in the 1938 campaign when, facing a hostile audience of coal miners who had just heard a speech about the humble origins of Taft's opponent, she responded: "My husband is not a simple man. He did not start from humble beginnings. My husband is a very brilliant man. He had a fine education at Yale. He has been trained well for his job … Isn't that what you prefer when you pick leaders to work for you?"[54]

She was also noted for her jabs at the Truman administration: "To err is Truman." "Delirium Trumans." She had studied at the Sorbonne, was a co-founder of the American–Israel Society, and, unlike her husband, was a thoroughgoing pacifist before World War II. Her father, Lloyd Bowers, a Cincinnatian, had been President Taft's Solicitor General and would almost certainly have been named by him to the Supreme Court had he not died at an early age. Of Bowers, Justice Holmes wrote: "I know of no one whom I so want to see on our Bench as much as I did the late Solicitor General."[55]

In 1922, while in the Ohio legislature, Taft, echoing his grandfather, opposed a bill sponsored by the Ku Klux Klan that would have mandated the reading of verses of Scripture in the public schools, declaring that in the Bible "religion overshadows all else." The journalist John Gunther, no partisan of Taft, observed that

---

[52] RAT to Jane Ickes, February 26, 1952, 4 R. Taft, Works 357.

[53] W. White, *supra*, 200.

[54] I. Ross, *supra*, 350, 376.

[55] Holmes to Sr Frederick Pollock, September 24, 1910, in 1 M. Howe (ed.), Holmes–Pollock Letters (Cambridge: Harvard U., 1961), 169-70.

"This Klan episode, largely forgotten now, would be well worth recounting in detail."[56]

He also supported an anti-Klan bill requiring secret organizations to file their membership lists with the state. At the time, the Klan claimed to have 400,000 members in Ohio, 14 chapters in Taft's Hamilton County, and had elected Mayors in Akron, Portsmouth, and Youngstown,[57] as well as governors in Indiana and Oregon and a majority of the California legislature. It had been a veto group at the 1920 and 1924 Democratic conventions, the first of which nominated Franklin Roosevelt as Vice President and the second of which heard his memorable "Happy Warrior" speech on behalf of Al Smith and condemned the Klan by only a fraction of one vote. This history explains much of Roosevelt's later failure to relieve the plight of Jewish refugees for fear of political repercussions.

In 1928, as the Chairman of the Hoover campaign in Ohio, he decried the nativist and anti-Catholic speeches of the Assistant Attorney General for prohibition enforcement, Mabel Walker Willebrandt: "I feel that if Mr. Hoover is defeated at all, it will be because of Mrs. Willebrandt's speeches and the trend given to the campaign thereby, and if that occurs, her speeches certainly will become historic."[58]

Zionism

As early as 1918 Robert Taft upheld the Balfour Declaration and the cause of Jewish colonization in Palestine.[59] However, in 1939 he opposed a proposal to admit 20,000 Jewish refugee children outside of normal immigration quotas at a time when there were millions of unemployed in the United States: "no substantial

---

[56] J. Gunther, Inside U.S.A. (London: Hamish Hamilton, 1947), 456.

[57] Patterson 96-101.

[58] RAT to Walter Newton, September 27, 1928, 1 R. Taft, Works 350ff.

[59] RAT to Edward Baker, November 1, 1938, 1 R. Taft, Works 593.

part of the refugee problem can be solved by immigration into any country because there are potentially a million and a half refugees and no country is willing to receive more than a few. The only practical method of dealing with them seems to be some plan for colonization in Asia or Africa. The plan of admitting 20,000 children and separating them from their parents does not seem desirable to me. It imposes a hardship that may be greater in many cases [than] if these children remain with their families. It inevitably suggests a reunion and a request for admission of the children's families at a later time."[60]

In 1944, he told a Zionist organization that "'National Home' clearly implies the Jewish people who desire to come to that home shall not be excluded by law."[61]

He initially voiced opposition to federal aid to parochial schools, but ultimately favored leaving the matter to the states. In 1945, he observed: "I doubt if we should give government money to a school which teaches a particular religion. It seems to me that our Constitution is set up on the theory of a complete separation of State and Church and that it is wise to maintain this."[62]

In 1947, he supported pressure on Britain to admit 100,000 Jews to Palestine.[63]

In 1948, he corresponded with Theodore Roosevelt's son Archibald Roosevelt, who had urged him to avoid "meddling into other peoples' business to the detriment of ourselves and others." Taft observed: "At the height of the war I think it would have been easy for the British and ourselves to establish a small Jewish state which would take care of the Jews being forced out of Central Europe. At the time I don't believe the Arabs could have made any

---

[60] RAT to Dorothy Fulton, June 28, 1939, 2 R. Taft, Works 52.

[61] American Palestine Committee, March 9, 1944, 2 R. Taft, Works 531.

[62] RAT to Edward Hoban, November 5, 1945, 3 R. Taft, Works 93, also RAT to Edward Freiling, January 18, 1946, 3 R. Taft, Works 121.

[63] RAT to Edward Newman, April 8, 1947, 3 R. Taft, Works 269.

effective protest. If the State had been set up properly and wisely, I believe it would have been a *fait accompli* at the end of the war. Under present circumstances … it presents an extremely difficult problem and I don't know whether the present [partition] plan can possibly be carried through or not."[64]

At the time of the recognition of Israel by the United States, Taft presciently advised that "[w]e should insist on the original partition plan."[65]

His support of Zionism may have been decisive in his narrow election victory in 1944.[66] While supporting Israel, he was influenced by Rabbi Abba Hillel Silver's view that "large scale immigration into the U.S. would ease pressure on the British and American governments and might deprive the Jewish state of a large number of settlers," a view that is thought by some to have contributed to the deaths of a million Hungarian and Romanian Jews who might have been saved by greater efforts at rescue during the later stages of World War II.[67] He was said to have "created a contest in which Truman felt the need to campaign for the Jewish vote." In June 1950, he urged that Jerusalem be partitioned between Israel and Jordan.[68] He considered that Israel "has taken a very expensive job off our hands and therefore they are entitled to turn to us for assistance and reimbursement in the tremendous task they have undertaken for the entire world."[69]

In his last published statement, written on his deathbed and delivered for him by his son Robert Taft Jr., Taft told the National Association of Christians and Jews: "[Israel] undertook to relieve

---

[64] RAT to Archibald Roosevelt, January 7, 1948, in 3 R. Taft, Works 379.

[65] Recognition of Israel, October 26, 1948, 3 R. Taft, Works 468.

[66] Recognition of Israel, October 26, 1948, 3 R. Taft, Works 468.

[67] D. Wyman, The Abandonment of the Jews (New York: Pantheon, 1984), 157-77, 327-30.

[68] RAT to Mrs. A.M. Goldish, June 1, 1950, 4 R. Taft, Works 163.

[69] "Taft Urges End to Near East Split," New York Times, March 9, 1953.

the world of the problem of resettling a large number of Jewish refugees, for which the world had proposed no better solution.... Because of that [1948] war, partly through the intolerance of their own leaders, 900,000 refugees left the Jewish section of Palestine. If this National Conference gets into the international field, it can do nothing better than to try to solve this question by resettlement, either within or without Israel. Plans have been made but little progress has been achieved. Tolerance in which you believe and I believe must extend to these Arab refugees, no matter what the cause of their distress. There seems to be no peaceful solution in the Near East until this refugee problem is settled."[70]

Early in his career in the Ohio Senate, Taft lent his support to a number of causes favored by organized labor, including a constitutional amendment prohibiting child labor,[71] a bill requiring labeling of convict-made goods, and a minimum wage for women.[72] He favored a ban on "yellow dog" contracts, but declared: "My inclination is very much opposed to any system which provides for the payment of money to men for doing nothing."[73] During the early years of the Depression, he took the view that it was important to "increase the share of the wage and salary earner."[74] He supported minimum wage regulation, but not regulation of working hours.[75] "Hour regulation to spread work in the long run does employees no good."[76] He was hostile to professional strike-breakers and labor spies.[77]

---

[70] National Association of Christians and Jews, May 26, 1953, 4 R. Taft, Works 480.

[71] RAT to Haas Brothers, November 13, 1924, 1 R. Taft, Works 295.

[72] Patterson 70ff.

[73] Patterson 135.

[74] Patterson 145ff.

[75] Patterson 174.

[76] "Address to the Friends of the Library of Cuyahoga County," November 16, 1939, 2 R. Taft, Works 91.

[77] Patterson 185ff.

He criticized a mediation report prepared by his brother Charles on legal grounds: "The report seemed to me unfair in suggesting the signing of a contract before a vote was taken instead of pursuing the proper course under the Wagner Act.[78]

In general, he felt that "[n]ew conditions had developed to which the American system of political and economic freedom did not sufficiently adjust itself ... because we were slow to act, because confidence was at a low ebb, the ideology of the new despotisms spread to this country and was embraced consciously or unconsciously by many people ... planned economy, collective production, and price-fixing was the instrument that had kept Europe poor."[79]

In 1939, he stressed that "labor unions have always been held legal by the U.S. Supreme Court."[80] "The Republican Party was the friend of labor in putting through the restriction of immigration whereas the New Dealers today are extremely doubtful whether they want to continue the strict policy of immigration restriction which the Republican Party inaugurated. As for myself, I voted for the Child Labor Amendment and minimum wage laws for women and workmen's compensation laws and the law outlawing yellow dog contracts before Congressman Smith got into politics at all."[81]

In the U.S. Senate, he supported the Case Bill, which banned secondary boycotts, and provided for the co-administration of welfare funds, a mediation board, and a 60-day cooling off period before strikes. Congress failed to override a Presidential veto.[82]

During the war, a statute allowed the administration to seize strike-bound plants, but only after Taft added amendments barring

---

[78] RAT to Horace Taft, July 6, 1937, 1 R. Taft, Works 541.

[79] "Taft Hits Trend to 'Middle Ages,'" New York Times, February 28, 1940.

[80] T. Smith and R. Taft, Foundations of Democracy: A Series of Debates (New York: Knopf, 1939) (hereafter "Smith and Taft") 9.

[81] Id. 175.

[82] Patterson 305.

the requisitioning of machinery and equipment or seizure of privately owned firearms.[83]

In 1942, he responded with vehemence to a suggestion from Colby Chester that the Republicans portray themselves as the party of the middle class, a scruple not shared by today's Democrats: "I thoroughly disapprove the idea of openly appealing to the middle class. I cannot imagine any greater mistake than to appeal to any class as such. We may not be able to get a majority of labor or of the lowest income groups but in order to win, we must get a fair proportion." Three months later he wrote the columnist George Sokolsky: "The whole thing is typical of people like Chester, Girdler, Trippe and other Willkie supporters. It is really an argument tending toward Fascism. The idea is to seize power by adopting every principle of demagoguery, and then use it to tie government and big business together."[84]

Taft sponsored three amendments to the Employment Act of 1946 which established the Council of Economic Advisors. One established a goal of a balanced budget over a period of years. A second required that self-employment in agriculture, commerce, industry, and the professions be counted as employment in making policy. A third required that outlays made to gain full employment be weighed against other national needs, such as those for defense.[85]

The Act thus rejected permanent deficit spending, as well as guaranteed employment and "any notion that the President was the nation's economic arbiter."[86]

---

[83] RAT to Merwin Hart, July 22, 1940, 2 R. Taft, Works 276, *see* 55 Stat. Part I 742 (1942).

[84] RAT to Colby Chester, August 12, 1942, 2 R. Taft, Works 372; RAT to George Sokolsky, January 25, 1943, 2 R. Taft, Works 425.

[85] A. McClure, The Truman Administration and the Problems of Post-War Labour (Teaneck, NJ: Fairleigh Dickinson U., 1969), 194.

[86] F. Burd, *supra*, 200.

As amended, the legislation read as follows:

"The Congress hereby declares that it is the continuing policy and responsibility of the Federal government
to use all practicable means consistent with its needs and
obligations and other essential considerations of national
policy, with the assistance and cooperation of industry, agriculture, labor, and State and local governments,
to coordinate and utilize all its plans, functions and
resources for the purpose of creating and maintaining,
in a manner calculated, to foster and promote free competitive enterprise and the general welfare, conditions
under which there will be afforded useful employment
opportunities, including self-employment, for those able,
willing and seeking to work, and to promote maximum
employment, production, and purchasing power."[87]

Taft successfully opposed a Temporary Disputes Settlement
bill sponsored by the Truman administration that had passed the
House and that authorized the drafting of strikers, saying that it
"violates every principle of American jurisprudence." His unaccus-
tomed allies in the fight were William Green of the AFL (American
Federation of Labor) and Philip Murray of the CIO (Congress of
Industrial Organizations).[88]

His most notable legislative achievement was the Taft–Hartley
Act, passed over President Truman's veto in 1947 by a vote of 68 to
25, with only three Republicans (Langer, Malone, and Morse) dissenting. The Act was passed at a time when 3 to 6 million man-days
per month were lost to strikes. President Truman had in some measure paved the way with proposals of his own seeking compulsory

---

[87] B. Bernstein and A. Matusow, The Truman Administration: A Docu-
mentary History (New York: Harper, 1966), 47.

[88] A. McClure, The Truman Administration and the Problems of Post-
War Labour (Teaneck, NJ: Fairleigh Dickinson U., 1969), 154-55.

arbitration, anathema to Taft (and also to Justice Brandeis), and bans on jurisdictional strikes and secondary boycotts. In responding to the veto message, Taft declared: "Corporations have long been required to file reports, both with State and local authorities. Why not unions? ... Everybody else in the United States is subject to harassment by lawsuits. Why not unions? We have simply provided that unions are subject to the same general laws or agency as any other corporation or citizen in determining their liability for the acts of the agents."[89] The Act has provided "an effective check on union growth in the Sun Belt."[90]

Taft permitted two liberal Republicans, Irving Ives and Wayne Morse, to remain on the Labor committee in the Senate. "I felt that the Dewey side had a right to a seat there."[91]

Many of his proposals were rejected in committee and restored after floor debate, the exception being his proposed restraints on industry-wide bargaining. "All members of the Committee stated publicly that the bill that resulted, even with the minority report, represented a genuine committee effort. All members agreed that a fair and conscionable compromise, the mark of a true legislative product, resulted."[92]

Under the bill, foremen were outside the union organizing provisions, jurisdictional strikes, mass picketing and secondary boycotts were banned, and unions were made liable for damages. The closed shop was banned, and there was a provision (later removed with Taft's acquiescence) for votes on strikes. With respect to the ban on secondary boycotts, dear to Taft's heart and that of his father,

---

[89] Congressional Record, 80th Congress, First Session, A3043-4, quoted in B. Bernstein and A. Matusow, *supra*, 128-31.

[90] H. Brogan, The Penguin History of the United States (Harmondsworth: Penguin, 2d ed. 1999), 595.

[91] W. White, *supra*, 71.

[92] H. Millis and E. Brown, From the Wagner Act to Taft-Hartley (Chicago: U. of Chicago, 1950), 376.

Taft said that the Committee "never succeeded in having anyone tell us any difference between different kinds of secondary boycott."[93]

As to foremen, Taft declared: "where foremen were unionized, the accident rate doubled and discipline vanished."[94]

Earlier, Taft had written: "I do not oppose Stassen's suggestion that elections be held before strikes can be called … but I have no real hope that any election will change the usual result."[95]

There was no ban on industry-wide bargaining, though one had been sought by the House of Representatives. The act banned coercion of workers by unions. The act permitted actions for damages but not injunctions for secondary boycotts and jurisdictional strikes. There was a ban on union contributions in federal elections and a ban on federal employee strikes, and provision for the filing of non-communist affidavits by unions.[96]

Under the Act, replaced strikers could not vote in union elections or strike votes and there was a ban on boycotts of subcontractors.[97] States under section 14(b) of the Act were allowed to ban the union shop. This corresponded to the view expressed by his father in 1910: "I put above everything, the right of every man to labor as he will, to earn the wages that he will and, if he choose, to stay out of labor organizations, that is the standpoint that the President of the United States must occupy in dealing equality to every citizen of the United States."[98]

There was a provision for injunctions at the instance of the government but not of private parties against "national emergency

---

[93] H. Millis and E. Brown, From the Wagner Act to Taft-Hartley (Chicago: U. of Chicago, 1950).

[94] H. Millis and E. Brown, From the Wagner Act to Taft-Hartley (Chicago: U. of Chicago, 1950).

[95] 466 RAT to Ezra Frye, February 17, 1947, in 3 R. Taft, Works 244.

[96] C. Gregory, Labor and the Law (2d ed.) (New York: Norton, 1961), 437.

[97] W. White, *supra*, 71.

[98] "Taft's Labor Views Told to Trainmen; President Says He Believes in Unions, But Also in Right to Stay Out of Them," New York Times, April 4, 1910.

strikes." Taft pointed out that this was "limited to strikes involving substantially an entire industry and threatening the public health or safety … in view of the temporary character of the injunction, we did not think it necessary to provide for seizure."[99]

"We have done nothing to outlaw strikes for basic wages, hours, and working conditions after proper opportunities for mediation."[100]

Taft made clear that there were "omitted … those proposals made by employers to destroy the unions … total abolition of welfare funds, complete regulation of internal affairs of unions, compulsory arbitrations, repeal of the Wagner Act."[101] The Wagner Act in his view was enacted "in order that the employees of a single employer might act as one in dealing with the one employer."[102] He was opposed to denying strikers protection under the Act: "A democratic government cannot prohibit strikes and remain democratic."[103]

Taft "distinguished between measures designed to assist cooperative organizations and measures proposing that government regulate agriculture and labour and industry."[104]

Taft was of the view that the Act was needed because "the power is all on the side of the labor leaders except perhaps as to the very largest companies in the United States. The labor leaders have acquired a great power which inevitably has been abused." Its critics urged that some of its supporters "wished to weaken the power of all labor organizations in the economic and [political scene," and condemned its alleged "weakening of all unions, its weakening of restraints on employers who still seek to avoid a democratic system

---

[99] RAT to Leland Gordon, April 25, 1947, in 3 R. Taft, Works 275.

[100] H. Millis and E. Brown, From the Wagner Act to Taft-Hartley (Chicago: U. of Chicago, 1950), 576.

[101] Statement on Labour, May 5, 1947, 3 R. Taft, Works 281.

[102] W. White, *supra*, 76.

[103] Patterson 302.

[104] Smith and Taft 268.

of labor relations, its interference with collective bargaining, its encouragement of litigation rather than of solving problems at the bargaining table."

The decline of private-sector unions lends force to this charge, though it was largely due to the impact of international trade and movement to a more decentralized service economy. The lack of any employee organizations in many large companies, Wal-Mart being an example, does make it as to them, "unlikely that the masses of people will receive that training in discussion, patience, tolerance and acceptance of majority decision necessary for the development of a stable and efficient representative government."[105] This is in part due to the failure to raise fine levels for unfair labor practices to accommodate inflation, and in part because of the stringent interpretation of the Wagner Act restrictions on so-called "company unions."

He was said to be "reaching for the jugular vein of [New Deal] power ... [His] only major legislative accomplishment that was genuinely popular."[106]

The House bill, a one-sided document, had been drafted by the National Association of Manufacturers; the Senate bill was acclaimed as "the finest example of Taft on facts." Taft had opposed proposals for regulation of the internal affairs of unions (forthcoming 15 years later under the Landrum–Griffin Act), anti-featherbedding regulations, and regulations of mass picketing.[107]

During the debate, Taft declared of his principal adversary: "I won't leave the floor when [Claude] Pepper is speaking. Fellow's able; very able; very good mind."[108]

---

[105] H. Millis and E. Brown, From the Wagner Act to Taft-Hartley (Chicago: U. of Chicago, 1950), 676.

[106] W. White, *supra*, 75-79.

[107] F. Burd, *supra*, 237-38.

[108] W. White, *supra*, 72.

The restriction on federal employee strikes was not in Taft's Senate bill but was added in the conference committee. It provided for immediate discharge, forfeiture of civil service and a three-year ban on federal employment, and was enforced during the air traffic controllers' strike early in the Reagan administration. The provision relating to national emergency strikes does not apply to railroad workers covered by the Railway Labor Act. Taft observed: "It does not seem to me that a sixty-day delay in a matter affecting the safety and health of the entire nation is any substantial modification of the right to strike."[109]

Taft sponsored an unsuccessful provision that would have limited unions to employees of a single employer and would have preclude international unions from coercing local unions. He allowed voluntary contributions to union Political Action Committees. Taft was concerned about nationwide bargaining, but "would not like to disturb this relationship without further study. Carried to extremes, it certainly carries the same threat of monopoly as an association of employers."[110]

On the other hand, he stressed that "the existence of company unions, financed by employers and therefore inevitably controlled by the employers was one of the evils the Act sought to remove."[111]

This provision during the Clinton administration was expansively interpreted by a pro-union National Labor Relations Board (NLRB), giving rise to a proposed Teamwork for Employees and Managers Act inspired by recommendations of all but one member of the Dunlop Commission (Commission on the Future of Worker-Management Relationships) appointed by President Clinton to legalize employee participation programs and works councils on the European pattern. The Commission included several former Secretaries of Labor in Democratic administrations. The Commission

---

[109] RAT to Henry La Cossett III, May 7, 1947, in 3 R. Taft, Works 282.

[110] RAT to De Witt Emery, June 10, 1947, 3 R. Taft, Works 388.

[111] Smith and Taft 186.

recommended that the prohibition on company unions be amended to make clear that it was not contravened by "discussi[on of] inter-related issues of working conditions and of how to share the gains" where these were incidental to an employee participation program's discussion of production, quality, safety and health, training, and voluntary dispute resolution issues.[112]

The bill passed both houses, but was successfully vetoed by President Clinton at the behest of union leaders.[113]

Union membership in manufacturing industries fell from 7.8 million, 38.9% of the manufacturing work force in 1973, to 3.3 million, 19.3% of the manufacturing workforce in 1998.[114] Following the unions' success in snuffing out the threat of the TEAM Act, union membership in manufacturing fell to 1.4 million in 2016, 9.6% of the manufacturing workforce.[115]

Taft was concerned about laxity of enforcement with regard to rules allowing employers to hire apprentices and beginners on special terms.[116]

Summarizing, Taft said that "[o]ur changes were based on existing decisions and their purpose is clear. I don't think it will require a great many court decisions to interpret it. About one half the provisions of the law were intended to protect the rights of individual workmen, either against employer or labor union leader."[117]

In Taft's view, the preferential union shop, a "limited type of compulsory membership contract, is a complete answer to the 'free

---

[112] Commission on the Future of Worker-Management Relationships, Report (Washington: GPO, 1994), 24.

[113] L. Troy, Twilight of the Old Unionism (Armonk, NY: M.E. Sharpe, 2004).

[114] L. Troy, Twilight of the Old Unionism (Armonk, NY: M.E. Sharpe, 2004).

[115] Bureau of Labor Statistics, Union Members: 2016, www.bls.gov/newsrelease/pdf/union2/pdf (January 26, 2017).

[116] RAT to Lawrence Shumer, June 17, 1947, 3 R. Taft, Works 293.

[117] RAT to Robley Stevens, July 15, 1947, 3 R. Taft, Works 303.

rider' argument so often advanced to support the need for a closed shop."[118]

Taft made clear that the Act "does not restore in any way the power of an individual employer to secure a court injunction, the power which was effectively taken away from him by the Norris–La Guardia Act. The only result of not filing a non-communist affidavit is to abolish the union's privilege to avail itself of the Wagner Act."[119]

The provisions banning union campaign contributions were evaded by the creation of Political Action Committees. The ban on closed shops was ineffective in maritime unions and the building trades. "I am not so certain that we can oppose a closed shop that has existed in many industries for many years."[120]

The ban on strikes before expiration of contracts was avoided through contract provisions authorizing them. Taft opposed a provision that would have increased the antitrust liability of unions.[121]

Section 14(b) proved to be the most important provision of the statute, fostering the migration of industry to non-union states in the South. Union membership rose from 14 million in 1947 to 17.5 million in 1957, partly due to increased public employee unionism, and the number of strikes dropped by half in the first two years of the Act, but following enactment of the Trade Expansion Act of 1962, the pressure of international and interstate competition fostered a sharp decline in private-sector union membership, which continues. By 2014, it was said that "[i]n labor politics, the 'right to work' codified by the Taft–Hartley Act has seriously constrained the right to bargain collectively established by the National Labor Relations [Wagner] Act." The decline of private-sector unions was

---

[118] C. Tomlins, "Labour Law," in 3 S. Engerman and R. Gallman, The Cambridge Economic History of the United States (Cambridge: Cambridge U., 2000), 687, 688.

[119] "Statement on Taft-Hartley," September 12, 1947, 3 R. Taft, Works 307.

[120] RAT to Stanley Martin, January 23, 1940, in 2 R. Taft, Works 115.

[121] F. Burd, *supra*, 239.

also due to "job insecurity caused by increased global competition, contingent and part-time work, short-term contracts, and volatile and frequent shifts in consumer demand requiring flexible management practices ... [Unions were] geographically, economically and politically confined in a minority of States in the North and Far West."[122]

The Act in total was characterized as "the only major change in New Deal legislation to pass Congress and one of the few important bills ever to be devised and passed wholly without the assistance of any executive department."[123]

"The Taft bill was a remarkable achievement. It testified to the extraordinary political skill of its sponsor. Taft had only a slim Republican majority in a Senate that reflected more urban and liberal views than did the House. [H]e had to keep the Senate bill unencumbered by restrictive House provisions ... to override a possible veto."[124]

Another commentator noted that Taft's perspective was not that commonly represented. He declared that "the solution of employer–employee relationships rests on a sound system of collective bargaining. It means the Wagner Act should be retained." His object was "to keep the great economic groups out of government and in the private sphere leaving the government smaller and more judicial."[125]

For him, there was to be no American equivalent of the "Beer and Sandwiches at Number 10 [Downing Street]" that gave rise to over-manning, labor strife, and economic stagnation in Great Britain. "Senator Taft was not the legislative ogre that he was later represented as by both organized labor and Truman in the 1948 election

---

[122] J. Jenkins and S. Milkus, The Politics of Major Policy Reform in Post-War America (Cambridge: Cambridge U., 2014), 9, 108, 121.

[123] Patterson 366.

[124] S. Hartmann, Truman and the 80th Congress (Columbia: U. of Missouri, 1970), 86.

[125] F. Burd, supra, 239-64.

campaign. Taft's handling of the committee displayed an objectivity in his approach to the problem of postwar labor relations for which he was seldom given credit by later observers."[126]

Because he regarded unions as legitimate and upheld the process of collective bargaining, he almost certainly would have sought to adjust upward the fine levels for unfair labor practices by management, the erosion of which by inflation has rendered nugatory the rights of workers to organize conferred by the Wagner Act. It was said that "Truman and his successors used the law effectively to enhance the results of collective bargaining and to maintain a reasonable level of industrial peace."[127]

The Act "re-accommodated federal policy to core values of managerial prerogative [and] furthered the tendency toward fragmentation of bargaining units by inviting the severance of skilled and professional groups, by requiring the separate organization of certain kinds of employees (notably security personnel) and otherwise by generally limiting the NLRB's discretion to find large-scale units." "Wildcat strikes, sit-downs, slowdowns were now expressly outlawed. Containment of unions was epitomized in the bans on closed shops, the authorization of more sweeping bans in state legislation, the new unfair practices, the legitimation of employer campaigns against unionization of their workforces, introduction of the decertification election and authorization of voting by replacement workers in decertification elections."[128]

In late 1949, Taft prepared but did not sponsor amendments to restrict nationwide bargaining. In March 1950, he issued a statement on the coal strike criticizing the delayed use of Taft–Hartley,

[126] A. McClure, The Truman Administration and the Problems of Post-War Labour (Teaneck, NJ: Fairleigh Dickinson U., 1969), 171-72.

[127] D. McCoy, The Presidency of Harry S. Truman (Lawrence: U. Press of Kansas, 1984), 99.

[128] C. Tomlins, "Labour Law," in 3 S. Engerman and R. Gallman, The Cambridge Economic History of the United States (Cambridge: Cambridge U., 2000), 687, 688.

stating that the government's position on the contempt issue was weak, and urging new legislation limiting nationwide bargaining, while opposing compulsory arbitration.[129]

In July 1950, he issued a statement on unemployment in the coal industry, urging a tariff on imported crude oil[130] that would have served the nation well in the 1970s and after. In 1951, he acquiesced in a minor amendment eliminating elections on whether to have a union shop after a bargaining agent has been recognized. These "impose a heavy burden on the [National Labor Relations] Board and have almost always resulted in a favorable vote." The amendment allowed a vote on demand of 30% of the workers. Taft elsewhere noted that 87% of strike votes supported the union position.[131]

In 1953, he condemned President Dwight D. Eisenhower's short-lived appointment of Martin Durkin of the Plumbers' Union as Secretary of Labor as "an effort to fool the American people into supposing that appeasement of labor leaders was either possible or desirable."[132]

Taft's law partner, John Hollister, who was a Congressman in 1932, sought his advice about whether he should indulge his inclination to oppose the Norris–La Guardia Act, which virtually ended the ability of the federal courts to issue labor injunctions of the sort William Howard Taft had issued in *Truax v. Corrigan*. Taft's reply was vintage Taft: "My own experience is that the only thing to do is to vote in accordance with a reasoned opinion. You are merely objecting to the unreasonable extent of the prohibition against court action which may at times be necessary, and that you are

---

[129] March 8, 1950, 4 R. Taft, Works 138.

[130] "Views on Unemployment in Coal and Other Industries," July 1, 1950, 4 R. Taft, Works 174.

[131] "Statement on Bill Amending the National Labour Relations Act, July 30, 1951, 4 R. Taft, Works 304; *see also* RAT to Kent Low, August 17, 1951, in 4 R. Taft, Works 311.

[132] W. White, *supra*, 209.

quite willing to go along with a disapproval of the 'yellow dog' contract and the abuse of the injunction which has undoubtedly taken
place in some cases."

Taft's unwillingness to see the law abused is illustrated by
another incident involving the investment banker Lewis Strauss, a
friend of Taft from his Paris days. In 1925 Taft wrote to Strauss:
"You ask whether I would be interested in bringing a suit for a
shareholder of the Columbia Broadcasting System to enjoin the
company from permitting any speaker to make statements subver-
sive of the Constitution. I do not quite see any legal basis for such
a suit, and while I do not insist in winning in all cases, I do like to
feel that I have at least one leg to stand on. I think, therefore, I had
better decline."[133]

Domestic Issues

Early in his career, Robert Taft declared his opposition to
monopolies, secondary boycotts, and stock speculation, and his
support of "scientific" tariffs.[134] During World War I, he worked for
Herbert Hoover's Food Administration and shared Hoover's belief
in voluntary price controls in wartime and the view that selfishness made peacetime price controls unworkable.[135] During World
War II, he voted for the Office of Price Administration (OPA) legislation, but wanted its use confined to basic farm commodities.[136]

In endorsing Hoover for President in 1928, Taft declared:
"He has strongly supported the protective tariff and the policy of
restricting immigration so that the American standard of living
may not be impaired. He has strongly opposed the cancellation of

---

[133] Taft to Lewis Strauss, July 22, 1935, in 1 R. Taft, Works 491.

[134] Patterson 43ff.

[135] Patterson 70.

[136] Patterson 240ff.

the foreign debts—he opposes the price fixing and equalization features of the McNary–Haugen bill."[137]

Taft was indubitably a protectionist, and the protection of manufacturing industry (and consequent partial impoverishment of the South) had been Republican party policy since the inauguration of President Lincoln. He advocated "scientific" tariffs based on costs of production: "I believe in the protection principle. I see no reason why our farmers, manufacturers, workmen and minerals should not be protected against depreciated currencies, starvation wages, and foreign subsidy. Executive tariff making under definite standards is a better method [than legislation]. Secretary Hull is a pronounced free trader and Congress has imposed no standard to guide his actions."[138]

In the Roosevelt and Truman administrations, under the influence of four Southerners—Secretaries of State Hull and Byrnes, Secretary of the Treasury Vinson, and Undersecretary of State Will Clayton—the South had its revenge: a policy of free trade and currency convertibility, continuing to this day, was adopted, not to the benefit of most Northern manufacturing industries.

In a wide-ranging speech to the Warren, Ohio, Chamber of Commerce in 1935, Taft called for "restoration of the antitrust laws to full force and effect," in the wake of the National Recovery Administration (NRA).[139]

In answering a questionnaire from Professor William Z. Ripley in 1937, Taft said that while he saw no practical problems with the court decisions under Ohio corporation law, "it gives too much power to majority stockholders and the management of corporations."

[137] RAT to Clifford Ward, May 1, 1928, 1 R. Taft, Works 339.

[138] Address to the National Republican Club, New York Times, March 3, 1940.

[139] Speech to Warren Chamber of Commerce, April 9, 1935, 1 R. Taft, Works 481.

In a letter in 1940, writing about the Miller-Tydings Fair Trade Law providing for resale price maintenance, whose enactment he had initially opposed, Taft said: "I might change my mind [on fair trade] because all these things are a matter of degree. There is one practice, for instance, of which I certainly disapprove, and that is the sale of goods below cost as a leader."[140] He again condemned sales below cost in an address in Boston in 1944.[141]

His views on taxation were stated in an address at the William McKinley centennial in 1943: "There should no longer be double taxation on the stockholders of corporations and no longer any preference to investors in municipal bonds. There is no capital gains tax at all in England."[142] Double taxation was subsequently curbed but not eliminated by enactment of legislation giving capital gains treatment to "qualified dividends."

At the beginning of the war, he urged that the normal rate of personal income tax be increased from 4% to 10%, and that both federal and municipal bond interest be taxed. He opposed increased business taxation: "Taxes on business are passed on to the people, but they tend to discourage business activity."[143] "Many small businesses had slight investment capital ... profits represent the savings which are effected by ability, ingenuity, and persistence."[144]

His overriding fear, at the root of his so-called isolationism, was that "[n]othing is so destructive of forms of democratic government as war. The so-called mobilization of wealth carried out in a New Deal spirit, might well result in the socialization of all property. I doubt whether we would ever again see real operation of private enterprise or real local self-government in the United

---

[140] RAT to Victor Keys, April 23, 1940, 2 R. Taft, Works 134.

[141] Boston City Club, January 14, 1944, 2 R. Taft, Works 517.

[142] January 7, 1943, 2 R. Taft, Works 406.

[143] New York Times, December 14, 1940.

[144] "Senators Oppose 6% Profit Plan," New York Times, September 27, 1941.

States. We would be likely to find ourselves with an absolutely arbitrary government in Washington and a plebiscite every four years to determine who should control it,"[145] not a bad description of the American polity under the administrations of Clinton, the junior Bush, Obama, and Trump.

In 1944, he alluded to America's 6 million farmers and 2 million small businessmen, denounced sales below cost as a marketing tactic, favored elimination of information returns for nonprofit organizations and declared: "If this country becomes a country of big business we are not a great deal better off than if we socialize the entire nation and let the government run business."[146] He would not have been a celebrant of the growth of Amazon and Wal-Mart.

He shared his father's views about inheritance taxation: "The policies of inheritance taxation are rapidly cutting down on large fortunes and I think that in America there is plenty of evidence that the old maxim still prevails 'from shirtsleeves to shirtsleeves in three generations."[147] "There were too many people rich beyond their deserts. I thoroughly approve of the New Deal measures to prevent fraud and sharp practices through the sale of securities which was one of the principal methods of acquiring undeserved wealth."[148] What he would have thought about the massive commissions paid to hedge fund managers by state and local pension funds can well be imagined.

In April 1935, Taft declared:

"I have a good deal of sympathy with Mr. Tugwell's proposal that the government buy up and plant in trees as much marginal land as they can possibly afford and which the owners are willing to sell, thereby eliminating

[145] RAT, "Our Foreign Policy," 6 Vital Speeches 348 (March 1940), Address to the National Republican Club, New York Times, March 3, 1940.

[146] Boston City Club, January 14, 1944, 2 R. Taft, Works 517.

[147] Smith and Taft, supra, 19.

[148] Smith and Taft, supra, 266.

producers who can never attain a decent standard of living under any system. It may be that the government should experiment with a government control of the coal or oil industry, or both. Here also we have an excessive supply of a natural resource which the owners desire to cash in on immediately."[149]

Taft endorsed "refinancing of farm debts, acquisition of marginal land, cooperative bargaining," and also stated that "formation of labor unions and farm cooperatives should be encouraged."[150]

In his debates with Congressman Smith in 1939, he returned to this theme: "the government should buy or lease a great deal of the marginal land and take much of it out of immediate production by the planting of trees which in time will allow the U.S. to produce more of its paper and pulp." He urged "a reasonable subsidy in the form of benefits for soil conservation."[151]

He later urged appointment of an Assistant Secretary of State for Fisheries.[152] At present, there is a Deputy Assistant Secretary for fisheries under an Assistant Secretary for environment and fisheries.

Taft consistently favored subsidies for soil conservation purposes.[153] "Mr. Wallace's high prices discourage the international trade which Mr. Hull is trying to promote. I favor the reclamation of lands, but not the Wallace policies."[154] "In general, I think subsidies should be limited to soil conservation payments and payments

---

[149] Speech to Warren Chamber of Commerce, April 9, 1935, 1 R. Taft, Works 481.

[150] RAT to George Chandler, November 20, 1935, in 1 R. Taft, Works 494.

[151] Smith and Taft, *supra*, 222.

[152] RAT to George Marshall, January 20, 1948, in 3 R. Taft, Works 382.

[153] T. Smith and R. Taft, Foundations of Democracy (New York: Knopf, 1939); Boston Republican Club, December 12, 1939, in 2 R. Taft, Works 95ff.

[154] Boston Republican Club, December 12, 1939, in 2 R. Taft, Works 95ff.

to encourage the production of crops which can be produced in this country but which are still imported."[155]

He told a sympathetic Republican: "We can get away with repeal of loan policies, parity payments and limitations of production ... the farmer still is at a great disadvantage as compared to the city workman with a job, and ... some constructive effort must be made to correct that disadvantage."[156] He initially opposed parity payments. He favored some price controls on farm commodities in wartime conditions.

He opposed the Brennan Plan for income supports.[157] This reflected his vision of himself as a Manchester liberal, not a conservative, and also influenced his equivocation in relation to the "fair trade" laws. Whether a society in which family farms and retail businesses were greatly diminished and heavily dominated by Archer-Daniels-Midland, Cargill, Wal-Mart, and Amazon really corresponded to his social ideals may be doubted, but he was well behind temperate free market economists like Wilhelm Ropke, Henry Simons, Joseph Schumpeter, and even Friedrich Hayek in recognizing and seeking to temper the social costs of untrammeled capitalism.

He supported tax incentives for farm cooperatives, analogizing them to labor unions. He voted to cut down farm subsidies throughout his career. It was said of him that "the Midwestern Republicans, of whom he was in so many ways the personification, lost control of and touch with Taft on the single point where they were themselves more relatively liberal—that is, in the area of farm subsidies. Taft on this issue merged with the little group of extreme right-wing Eastern Republicans, who were as powerful in the House of Representatives as they were powerless in the country."[158]

---

[155] RAT to Harold Jones, February 13, 1940, in 2 R. Taft, Works 119.

[156] RAT to Ralph Golland, April 8, 1940, 2 R. Taft, Works 129.

[157] Patterson 429ff.

[158] W. White, The Taft Story (New York: Harper, 1954), 62.

In 1939, he admitted to Walter Lippmann that "I know less about agriculture than most of the other important matters before Congress and the country."[159]

As a young man, Taft supported anti-lynching bills and opposed the influence of the Ku Klux Klan in the Ohio legislature of the 1920s.[160] He "always insisted on a Negro nominee for the Legislature and for City Council."[161] In a radio address on the Constitution in 1938, he declared, with more than slight exaggeration, that "The Supreme Court has been the bulwark of independent religion. It has been the bulwark under which the colored race has preserved its freedom and made such extraordinary progress in 75 years."[162] In a letter to the NAACP leader Walter White written in 1938, Taft declared that he would vote for cloture on anti-lynching legislation and favored extension of social security to domestic and agricultural workers, and was opposed to differentials in the minimum wage law. He avoided declaring himself on the issue presented by discriminatory labor unions.[163]

In a commencement speech at Howard University in 1939, he noted that "Colored people have not taken their proportionate place as businessmen and they may well devote their attention to operating more of the stores that serve their people." "You can only do it by your own efforts. The function of government is largely negative and defensive. There is still an economic discrimination that we must do our utmost to reduce. No one else has suffered as much from the scourge of unemployment." He denounced lynching and the recent exclusion of the singer Marian Anderson from Constitution Hall, and concluded with an exhortation to education, quoting

---

[159]   RAT to Walter Lippmann, May 30, 1939, in 2 R. Taft, Works 37.

[160]   Patterson 174.

[161]   Patterson 205ff.

[162]   Radio Address on the Constitution, 1 R. Taft, Works 584.

[163]   RAT to Walter White, October 31, 1938, in 1 R. Taft, Works 592.

Lord Brougham: "Education makes a people easy to lead, but diffi-cult to drive; easy to govern, but difficult to enslave."[164]

Three months later, he told leaders of the African Methodist Episcopal Church that: "If we ever get to socialism in the U.S., a race which represents only 10% of the total population is going to get the worst jobs in the most undesirable industries." He cautioned against over-reliance on Works Progress Administration (WPA) work pro-grams with dead-end jobs: "a kind of economic servitude akin to serfdom."[165] Throughout his Senate career, he favored anti-lynching legislation and the abolition of poll taxes. In 1944, he expressed his support for the quasi-voluntary Fair Employment Practices Com-mittee (FEPC) that then existed, as well as for abolition of the poll tax, and opposed federal aid to education (a position that he later modified).[166]

In February 1945, he drafted and introduced Senate Bill 459, which would have created a federal FEPC with investigatory pow-ers and the power to create local commissions.[167] He opposed a compulsory FEPC, the burning civil rights issue in the immediate post-war period, but voted to break the filibusters against it,[168] and in June 1945 issued a statement decrying such a filibuster.[169]

In opposing the Truman administration's bill, he noted that it contained no rules of evidence, that under it, anyone could bring suit; the result would be employment quotas. "Race and religion will enter into every [employment] decision [and] will create more bad racial and religious feeling than any other method which can

---

[164]   Address at Howard University, March 2, 1939, 2 R. Taft, Works 12.

[165]   Address to the African Methodist Episcopal Church, Washington, DC, June 22, 1939, in Congressional Record, 84th Congress, App. 3096.

[166]   RAT to Janet Marks, September 26, 1944, in 2 R. Taft, Works 587.

[167]   Statement on FEPC Bill, February 5, 1945, in 3 R. Taft, Works 17.

[168]   Patterson 300ff.; RAT to Sidney Thompson, April 5, 1947, 3 R. Taft, Works 268.

[169]   Statement on FEPC, June 29, 1945, 3 R. Taft, Works 58.

be pursued." Later in 1945, he observed: "I doubt if we can out-bid Mrs. Roosevelt. Just at present the Negroes will be satisfied with nothing but the FEPC bill. This is something which violates any possible party philosophy we might adopt."[170] "I am not in favor of bringing a federal bureau into every office to pass on the complaints of individuals regarding their treatment by their employer."[171] This position was later echoed by Senator Everett Dirksen, who successfully amended the bill which became the Civil Rights Act of 1964 by requiring the exhaustion of state remedies in employment discrimination cases.

In a statement to the Negro press of Ohio in 1944, he explained his opposition to a federal ballot for servicemen, but stressed that no poll tax would be required of them when they used state ballots.[172] In late 1946, he wrote: "We probably will propose a constitutional amendment [on poll tax]."[173] He also indicated that "if the evidence supports the allegations [of fraud directed against black voters], I shall vote against seating Senator [Theodore] Bilbo." The Bilbo controversy was mooted by Bilbo's death. A later Supreme Court opinion confirmed Taft's view that a Constitutional amendment was necessary to abolish the poll tax in state elections.

He did not press hard for enactment of the civil rights legislation that he personally favored, declaring of the lame-duck session in 1948 "The Congress had forty pledges to perform on, and there is no reason to pick out that one [civil rights] more than any of the others."[174] As with his father, his benevolent attitude toward blacks was subordinated to the necessity of maintaining a coalition with Southerners to preserve limited government. He declared that "for

---

[170] RAT to Charles Hilles, 3 R. Taft, Works 46.

[171] RAT to Mrs. Lowell Hobart, August 10, 1950, in 4 R. Taft, Works 183.

[172] Statement to the Negro press of Ohio, April 14, 1944, 2 R. Taft, Works 545.

[173] RAT to Robert Snowden, December 27, 1946, 3 R. Taft, Works 234.

[174] W. White, *supra*, 121.

some reason the Dewey–Eisenhower group … never had any interest in the South because it interferes with their idea that we should
appease the minorities of the North."[175]

"Taft essentially campaigned for delegates and popular support in the South by casting issues like the FEPC essentially as race-
based extensions of the federal bureaucracy."[176] In the same year, he
assured A. Philip Randolph that "I am in favor of an unequivocal
anti-segregation amendment" to any bill providing for Universal
Military Training, a concept which Taft opposed.[177]

Anticipating later voting rights legislation, he declared in 1948
at a Republican rally in Nashville that "I can see good reasons why
the federal government should interest itself, within the limits of
the Constitution, in the matter of the election of federal officers and
the protection of constitutional rights."[178] He declared his position
on cloture to the NAACP's Walter White in early 1949: "[I favor]
a fair amount of debate on public issues and sufficient time for the
public to be informed of what is being done. Two thirds is perhaps
more than is necessary. I have always voted for closure … when I
feel that adequate time has been given." Later, he explained "I have
always said that I would vote for cloture on any bill after adequate
debate had been had. After all, we have a system based on majority
rule. If the minority undertakes to prevent action by the majority
beyond proper limitations, we are likely to find Congress completely
discredited."[179] The required majority for cloture was ultimately

---

[175] D. Reinhard, The Republican Right Since 1945 (Lexington, KY:
U. Press of Kentucky, 1983), 98, citing RAT to R. Snowmen, RAT Papers, Library
of Congress, Box 1206.

[176] M. Bowen, The Roots of Modern Conservatism (Chapel Hill, NC:
U.N.C. 2011), 63.

[177] RAT to A. Philip Randolph, February 5, 1948, in 3 R. Taft, Works 384.

[178] Republican Rally, Nashville, October 11, 1948, in 3 R. Taft, Works 459.

[179] RAT to Harry McCall, January 30, 1946, in RAT Papers, Library of
Congress, Box 874, Folder "Full Employment Bill."

reduced to three-fifths of those voting.[180] The subsequent replacement of rare "speaking filibusters" with commonplace non-speaking filibusters following the failure of premature cloture votes would have appalled Taft. It has indeed prevented majority rule as to most issues and has brought Congress into disrepute.

Responding to criticism by White, he later observed: "Mr. White's complete prejudice is shown by the fact that he has never said a word against segregated schools in the District of Columbia and the failure of the Democratic administration to abolish them during a period of 20 years of complete control of the government."[181] During his 1952 campaign for the presidency, Taft told the same correspondent that "if elected ... I will appoint a Colored man as one of the secretaries at the White House ... so that Colored people may feel they have a definite line of approach to me."[182]

Taft was the only major political figure in any branch of government to keep his head in the controversy over the relocation of American citizens of Japanese descent after Pearl Harbor. "In the Congress, the only audible dissent from the internment policy was in the Senate, where only Robert A. Taft of Ohio objected,"[183] the legislation being carried by voice vote in both Houses. The Supreme Court unanimously upheld the restrictions in the *Hirabayashi* case.[184] Dissenting Roosevelt administration figures like Attorney General Francis Biddle did not speak out in public.

Senator Taft on the floor of the Senate referred to the authorizing statute as the "sloppiest criminal law I have ever read or seen

---

[180] RAT to Walter White, January 20, 1949, in 4 R. Taft, Works 9.

[181] RAT to John Peag, December 29, 1951, 4 R. Taft, Works 320ff.

[182] RAT to John Peag, May 14, 1952, in 4 R. Taft, Works 375.

[183] C. Black, FDR: Champion of Freedom (Washington: Public Affairs, 2005), 723. All the justices of the Supreme Court joined in upholding the exclusion orders in the *Hirabayashi* case (320 U.S. 81) in June 1943, although in December 1944 Justices Jackson, Roberts, and Murphy dissented in the *Koramatsu* case (323 U.S. 214).

[184] Hirabayashi v. United States, 320 U.S. 81 (1943).

anywhere. I certainly think the Senate should not pass it. I do not want to object because the purpose of it is understood … The bill does not say who should prescribe the restrictions. It does not say how anyone shall know that the restrictions are applicable to that particular zone. It does not appear that there is any authority given to anyone to prescribe any restriction. I have no doubt an act of that kind would be enforced in wartime. I have no doubt that in peacetime no one could be convicted under it because the court would find that it was so indefinite and so uncertain that it could not be enforced under the Constitution."[185]

In 1950, Taft voted against an interstate compact to set up a segregated medical school.[186] In 1951, commenting on a report on discrimination by the black Nobel prize–winner Ralph Bunche, Taft observed: "I certainly agree with all that Mr. Bunche says, except as to some of the methods he proposes to accomplish the elimination of discrimination. This can be accomplished to some extent by law, but in other respects only by a steady process of education."[187] He declared, and appeared to believe: "I see no reason to think that inequality of intellect or ability is based on racial origin."[188] He considered that Earl Warren, the author of the *Brown v. Board of Education* decision, "represents all the New Deal principles," and in 1951 Taft did not object to school segregation "as long as states provide equal educational facilities."[189]

In 1939, he contributed a short chapter on anti-Semitism to a book on the subject; his statements were not platitudinous: The prejudice against Jews, he said, derives from the fact that they are "peculiarly intellectual and have enjoyed by reason of their ability

---

[185] Congressional Record, March 19, 1942, 2726.

[186] RAT to Joseph Fulton, January 24, 1950, 4 R. Taft, Works 128ff.

[187] RAT to A. Frank, July 23, 1951, 4 R. Taft, Works 302.

[188] Patterson 330; RAT to L.H. Foster, March 18, 1947, in 3 R. Taft, Works 263.

[189] 4 R. Taft, Works 510.

and industry a greater average success … [they] give away a larger portion of their income" and are "artists and patrons of music, art, and science." "Spain has never fully recovered [from their expulsion]. The driving of the Jew from Germany is going to do Germany itself much more harm than it is doing even to the unfortunate victims of that policy today."

At Versailles, he observed: "An attempt was made to separate each nation from every other nation and give each nation a complete freedom from political control by men of other nationalities. It would have been better to recognize the common economic interest of people living near each other. It is not clear that [races] should be mixed or that they ever will be. If we once create distinctions [based on race] we may still have a rule of the majority for a while, but it is not a rule of the whole people.… the deliberate stimulation of race or religious prejudice threatens the foundation of the Republic. We can at least make intolerance unpopular among our own friends."[190]

In 1946, Taft opposed the proposed Equal Rights Amendment to the Constitution: "I cannot find that there is any real discrimination against women, and it might well be that the amendment would nullify a good deal of legislation passed to give some special protection to women workers."[191] In 1951, he wrote that he "favor[ed] the ERA although I am very doubtful about the necessity for its adoption. Under the circumstances, I do not feel like pressing the matter."[192]

---

[190] R. Taft, "Laying Ghosts of Ignorance," in S. McCall, For the Honor of the Nation: Patriotism of the American Jew Hailed by Christian Historians (New York: Plymouth Editions, 1939), also in Congressional Record, 76th Congress, App.3276.

[191] RAT to Katherine Fitzgerald, May 23, 1946, in 3 R. Taft, Works 152.

[192] RAT to Helen Reinheimer, May 1951, 4 R. Taft, Works 280ff.

The McCarthy Era

Senator Taft felt, as it turned out with reason, that there had been substantial Communist penetration of some of the New Deal agencies (most consequentially in the Treasury Department). He therefore said "on net results, I think [McCarthy] has done the country a real service,"[193] a conclusion that many later historians hold against him. One of the more even-handed evaluations of the post-war "red scare," Ted Morgan's *Reds*, concluded otherwise, but only because the much-maligned House Un-American Activities Committee under Martin Dies and the Truman loyalty-security program had already removed most of the Communists from government.[194]

Some of Taft's statements were more extravagant: "[McCarthy was] a fighting Marine who risked his life to preserve the liberties of the United States. The greatest Kremlin asset in our history has been the pro-Communist group in the State Department who surrendered to every demand of Russia at Yalta and Potsdam and who promoted at every opportunity the Communist cause in China until today Communism threatens to take over all of Asia."[195]

Taft's insensitivity to the plight of McCarthy's victims was due to his view that political actors, which nearly all of them were, needed thick skins: "McCarthy has been reckless in his statements... [T]hey are absolutely nothing to the attacks that have been made on me by the left-wing groups and the labor bosses during the last eight years."[196] "[A]ssume the innocence of all the persons mentioned in the State Department ... whether Senator McCarthy has legal evidence, whether he has understated or overstated his case, is of lesser importance. The question is whether the Communist influence in

---

[193] RAT to Benjamin Hubbell Jr., August 17, 1951, 4 R. Taft, Works 312.

[194] T. Morgan, Reds: McCarthyism in Twentieth Century America (New York: Random House, 2004).

[195] Quoted in Leffler, *supra*, 344.

[196] RAT to Jerome Preston, July 27, 1951, 4 R. Taft, Works 301.

the State Department still exists."[197] It was said of Taft that "[l]ike John C. Calhoun a century earlier, Taft proved far from unwilling to restrain his more extreme followers."[198]

This led Alistair Cooke to observe: "to an alien who had come from a libertarian country ... liberty is not in our time a markedly American passion. Equality is the watchword; equality of privilege in prosperity, and equality of care in hard times. In the Senate especially there was an alarmed minority ready to make political hay by blurring distinction between an old sympathizer and an old spy. [The trouble with the exploitation of the issue of domestic Communism] was that it brought back into favor the odious trade of the public informer. It gave the FBI an unparalleled power of inquiry into private lives that ... could open up for generations of mischief-makers an official wholesale house of blackmail. It tended to make conformity sheepish and to limit by intimidation what no Western society worth the name can safely limit: the curiosity and idealism of the young. It helped therefore to usher in a period when a high premium would be put on the chameleon and the politically neutral slob."[199]

This was written 70 years before the emotional repulsion of an FBI director from both major party presidential candidates convulsed the politics of the nation and gave rise to not wholly unjustified allegations about an American "deep state."

The Truman administration responded by creating the Federal Loyalty-Security Program, elaborated by Eisenhower, which Truman later characterized as his worst mistake, and which the lawyer Lloyd Garrison later said resulted in "the building up of a large establishment of secret police, the creation of a new profession

---

[197]   Quoted in E. Goldman, *supra*, at 215.

[198]   R. Divine, The Illusion of Neutrality (Chicago: U. of Chicago, 1962), 26.

[199]   A. Cooke, Generation on Trial (New York: Knopf, 1950), 17-18, 39-40.

of security officer with vested interests in perpetuating the existing regimes."[200]

The journalist Richard Rovere wrote that "Taft knew that McCarthy was dangerous, and though he had nothing but scorn for William Jenner and Harold Velde, he knew that they were men of modest abilities and he felt he had engineered a brilliant coup by bottling McCarthy up in Government Operations ... he himself had never thought that Communists represented half as serious a menace as the Left liberals and welfare statists."[201]

Budget and Taxation

While in the Ohio legislature, Taft favored financing of public works on a "pay as you go" basis, was opposed to bonds to cover budget deficits, and urged increased taxing power for cities and a 55% supermajority requirement for bond referenda.[202]

He believed that "practical necessity allowed temporary deficit spending although fiscal responsibility justified state-dictated restrictions on the financial independence of local governments."[203]

He opposed "tinkering with capitalism and playing around with deficit spending." He disliked New Deal monetary policy, or the lack of it, but initially supported the National Recovery Administration minimum wage provisions, old age pensions, and unemployment insurance. He sold bonds to buy stocks, anticipating inflation, but his overall view was that "there is very little the Government

---

[200] L. Garrison, "Some Observations on the Loyalty-Security Program," 23 U. Chi. L. Rev. 1 (1955).

[201] R. Rovere, Senator Joe McCarthy (New York: World, 1960), 188.

[202] Patterson 95ff.

[203] F. Burd, Robert A. Taft and the American Understanding of Politics (Chicago: University of Chicago, Thesis T 17276, 1969), 19.

can do to really modify the tremendous economic forces involved in a world-wide business depression."[204]

His most considered view on the sources of the depression was set out in a series of notes he composed in August 1933. In these, he ascribed it to:

> "excessive loans abroad
> excessive investments in capital improvements beyond
>   real need
> fictitious values of securities
> tariff wars
> overproduction stimulated by new tariffs, cartels, com-
>   modity speculation
> limitation of credit or currency
> over-expansion of debt—foreign loans, some installment
>   selling, securities at unsound values."

He ascribed the crash to "[d]ecrease in purchasing power, slowing down of circulation. We got ahead in everything except perhaps houses which cost too much. We had so much we loaned it on unsound terms abroad. More money must go into directly consumable goods and the only way to do that is to increase the share of the wage and salary earner … a violent readjustment produced by war was bound to reduce purchasing power in some places and stimulate production elsewhere. Effect of this postponed by international loans, and all came together cumulatively when the bubble once broke and unsoundness of such loans was demonstrated."[205]

He disapproved of price-fixing as a remedy, except for oil and coal, but was not opposed to sound public works. In November

---

[204] Patterson 151, *see* RAT to Robert Lucas, May 17, 1933, 1 R. Taft, Works 444.

[205] Notes on the Great Depression, August 25, 1933, 1 R. Taft, Works 449.

1929, he supported an effort to get President Hoover to pressure the Federal Reserve Board to inflate the currency.[206]

It is now generally agreed that the 1929 crash was perpetuated and extended by the deflationary monetary policy of the Federal Reserve.[207]

In a wide-ranging speech to the Warren Chamber of Commerce in 1935, he defended the Securities Exchange Act as well as the Reconstruction Finance Corporation, the Home Owners Loan Corporation, and the Farm Loan boards (the last three were all Hoover administration initiatives). He was opposed to federal control of securities issuances, deeming state blue sky laws sufficient. However, "I see no objection to control of principles of banking credit by the federal government instead of by the Federal Reserve banks. Those who administer the system are going to require high courage and extraordinary brains ... Would the wisest men in 1927, 1928, and 1929 have taken the necessary steps for the tightening of credit in every field?"[208]

By November 1935, he thought that regulation of banks and securities issuers had gone too far: bank regulators may be "infected by the general psychology of the entire nation." "Today there is no real capital market."[209] In 1939, he declared: "no one has invested either time or money in new enterprises in the last five years."[210]

As for the Public Utility Holding Company Act: "If there is stock watering it can be prevented by control of securities as in the case of railroads." He favored "[s]tabilization of world currencies on

---

[206] RAT to George Harrison, November 21, 1929, 1 R. Taft, Works 365ff.

[207] *E.g.,* M. Friedman and A. Schwartz, The Great Contraction, 1929-33 (Princeton: Princeton U., 2008).

[208] Warren Chamber of Commerce, April 9, 1935, 1 R. Taft, Works 481.

[209] Patterson 256.

[210] New York Times, February 12, 1939.

a reasonable basis and a return to the gold standard which is the only practical basis of such wage stabilization."[211]

In a letter to his former Yale professor Irving Fisher in 1936 he noted: "I have read most of your books and I believe you will simply have to put me down among the unregenerate. I have the highest regard for your views and your very clear presentation of them and the mere fact that I differ with those views does not in any way lessen the regard I have for you."[212]

In 1936, he told his brother Charles Taft, who agreed, that he regarded Hoover's effort to blame the 1933 bank panic on Roosevelt as "extreme."[213]

"Free trade," he observed, "is a beautiful theory and probably means a greater average prosperity for the entire world, but it seems obvious to me that it seems to level standards of living so that while the Chinese may be benefitted, the American standard is reduced. There is a time perhaps when we could have relied on our own mechanical ability but that day has gone by."[214]

In decrying economic imperialism, he declared: "It is said that foreign investment will make for peace. I don't think history shows anything of the kind." Moreover, "aggressive U.S. investment in the Third World … would eventually necessitate tight control of political and economic developments in those nations."[215] He decried intervention in the domestic affairs of other states: "force should not be called for against any internal domestic policy, except rearmament in excess of a quota imposed or agreed to. Interference in domestic policies, even such matters as tariffs or the treatment of minorities, would be more likely to make war than to prevent it."

---

[211] RAT to George Chandler, November 20, 1935, in 1 R. Taft, Works 493.

[212] RAT to Irving Fisher, May 8, 1936, in 1 R. Taft, Works 516.

[213] RAT to CT, July 30, 1936; CT to RAT, July 28, 1936, in 1 R. Taft, Works 523.

[214] RAT to Vincent Starzinger, March 29, 1940, 2 R. Taft, Works 127.

[215] RAT to Vincent Starzinger, March 29, 1940, 2 R. Taft, Works 127.

This fear of trade agreements, though unfashionable, was not misplaced. The brutal fact is that because of the failure of the American educational system to improve productivity of the work force, the United States has been increasingly uncompetitive in manufacturing, and even in the more sophisticated service industries that are the mainstays of the British economy, the generality of its workers have found their relative position deteriorating. Of the British loan after World War II he said, "we insisted on sterling being made convertible with dollars. We have created the impression that we are desirous of forcing American control over the free world, and particularly imposing the Hull–Clayton theory of free trade."[216] He complained that "[n]o man in Congress was consulted as to possible alternatives as to what might be approved, neither any Republican nor any Democrat."[217]

Robert Taft was no Anglophile; he had never forgotten what he had seen as a young man of the consequences of the continuance of the British blockade in 1919; like H.L. Mencken, he tended to take the view that the British had brought their subsequent troubles on themselves, not least by their obtuseness at Versailles.

His general views on taxation were set forth in 1934: "I do not particularly approve of a general sales tax except as an emergency and supplemental tax. Unquestionably an income tax is a fairer tax but it must be remembered that the federal government has practically pre-empted the income tax field ... there is a difference between earned and unearned income. It has always seemed to me that this difference is justified when you consider that the years during which a man may receive any substantial salary are very limited."[218] Notwithstanding recent additional taxes on investment

---

[216] H. Berger, "Senator Robert A. Taft Dissents from Military Escalation," in J. Paterson, Cold War Critics (Chicago: Quadrangle, 1971), 167ff.

[217] RAT, "The British Loan," Vital Speeches XII, June 5, 1946, 501-02.

[218] RAT to George White, December 7, 1934, 1 R. Taft, Works 476.

income included in the Affordable Care Act, high levels of federal and state payroll taxation still disadvantage wage earners.

In 1935, he observed: "There seems to be no rhyme or reason in a distribution of wealth through deliberate inflation—lack of confidence as to future monetary recovery has interfered with recovery. Granting that in times of depression a reasonable increase in the public debt may be justified, it is an insidious danger which has led to inflation, repudiation and dictatorship in other countries and may do so here. There is certainly something to be said for the policy of getting reforms when you can get them, and the days of the 1929 boom were not days in which the people were interested in improving the system."[219]

"The federal unemployment insurance bill does not seem to me to be particularly open to criticism and I do not believe that it will be held unconstitutional. [It] incentivises employers to get away from the seasonal feature as much as possible."[220] This feature of the Act was largely due to the influence of Louis Brandeis.

Explaining his restrictionist attitude toward immigration, he said: "I do not think that anything is more responsible for our present condition than the unrestricted immigration before the world war which provided cheap labor for the steel mills and the mines."[221] He would not have shared the enthusiasm for "open borders" of the "liberals" of our time, nor former Vice President Gore's vision of a substantially border-free NAFTA pact. The views of Congresswoman Barbara Jordan's commission on immigration, thrown in the ashcan by the Clinton administration, would have been close to his own.[222]

---

[219] Warren Chamber of Commerce, April 9, 1935, 1 R. Taft, Works 481.

[220] RAT to George Candle, November 20, 1935, in 1 R. Taft, Works 494.

[221] RAT to Dorothy Fulton, June 28, 1939, in 2 R. Taft, Works 52.

[222] U.S. Commission on Immigration Reform, Final Report (Washington: GPO, 1997).

He did not believe in the reality of a social security reserve fund: "an entire nation cannot build up a reserve. Under any system they will have to raise the money by taxation at approximately the time it is to be paid out."[223] Recent exhaustion of the theoretical reserve fund shows that he was right.

In 1939, he opposed the Export-Import Bank on the basis that "it is unsound to stimulate exports by granting loans which will not be paid … the false stimulation given in the twenties accentuated the unemployment of the depression."[224] Later he said: "If we definitely stabilize the American dollar, we will make it the single standard of all world trade."[225]

He was an exponent of increased taxation, including a sales tax with exemptions for food, during the war. "Every person should pay at least ten percent of his income." He favored selective, not general, price controls, no controls at the retail level, a review board, no arbitrary freeze, and no use of prewar profits as a measure of allowable prices.[226]

He sought with success to abolish the National Youth Administration, the National Resources Planning Board, and presidential authority over the currency. He unsuccessfully opposed the Bretton Woods Agreement, the World Bank, and the International Monetary Fund. He feared large-scale foreign defaults like those in Germany, South America, and elsewhere that helped precipitate the depression. In 1946 he accurately forecasted that "[t]here has been so much money saved and there are so many unsatisfied demands that I look for reasonably full employment for five years after the war." He opposed renewal of the reciprocal trade agreements act

---

[223] Boston Republican Club, December 12, 1939, 2 R. Taft, Works 97ff.

[224] Statement on the Export-Import Bank, July 21, 1939, in 2 R. Taft, Works 58.

[225] Boston Republican Club, December 12, 1939, in 2 R. Taft, Works 95ff.

[226] Patterson 257.

on the basis that it was an improper delegation of power to the executive.[227]

In late 1945, he urged termination of war powers, repeal of the excess profits tax, a labor conciliation board, a prohibition of strikes during the life of labor contracts, a balanced budget and relief, health and housing appropriations for lower income groups only, with local administration.[228]

His position on health programs was "I am absolutely opposed to the Federal Government furnishing aid without a means test except to the extent of inspection in the public schools."[229]

In 1947, he supported a tax cut bill on "supply side" grounds, and noted that "American industry was being successfully presented in many quarters as the great victor in the war."[230] This was passed over President Truman's veto in 1948, as was an act curbing public assistance payments ordered by the courts

In 1948, he noted that "[i]nflation has arisen First from the huge government deficit during the War Second from the increase in bank credit Third from the increase in housing credit [and] Finally excessive purchasing power due to price restraints not accompanied by wage restraints."[231]

In 1950, he endorsed consumer credit controls.[232] These have completely disappeared, as have the constraints on grant of consumer credit once imposed by the state usury laws, held to have been preempted by a century-old law in the *Marquette National Bank*[233]

---

[227] Radio Address, August 7, 1945, 3 R. Taft, Works 66.

[228] Ohio Federation of Women's Republican Organizations, October 19, 1945, 3 R. Taft, Works 83.

[229] RAT to Samuel Ridings, August 2, 1946, in RAT, Papers, Library of Congress, Box 874, Folder "Health 1946."

[230] White 67.

[231] RAT to Minor Tuttle, July 31, 1948, 3 R. Taft, Works.

[232] Statement, Controls Bill, August 11, 1950, 4 R. Taft, Works 183.

[233] Marquette National Bank v. First of Omaha, 439 U.S. 299 (1978).

case in 1978. Similarly, the federalization of student loan administration carried out by the Obama administration has eliminated any underwriting of student loans, thereby enhancing the likelihood of loan defaults.

He derided the Truman administration: "Promise everyone everything and hope to back it up with government money."[234] In 1951, in his book *A Foreign Policy for Americans* in the wake of the outbreak of the Korean War, he supported a continuation of controls, a corporation tax increase and deficit spending for defense.[235] In the famous Morningside Heights agreement exacted from presidential candidate Eisenhower in 1952 he sought and obtained commitments to reduce expenses, avoid further socialization, respect state and local prerogatives, and retain the basic principles of the Taft–Hartley Act: "It was all in writing and it was all Taft."[236]

Taft's views on the appropriate contours of the criminal justice system were expressed in a letter to the Chairman of the National Commission on Law Enforcement at a time when the FBI was in relative infancy: "A national police organization might have to be set up interested not only in the enforcement of national laws but in the coordination of the activities of all local police. It should include some sort of bureau of criminal identification ... While of course the local police cannot be subjected to a national police."[237]

Later, in the wake of the Supreme Court decision in *Palko v. Connecticut*, making most of the Bill of Rights binding against the states, he expressed the view that "in their zeal to protect rights, the courts have given too much effect to the so-called due process clause."[238] While in the Ohio legislature, he opposed as an intrusion on civil liberties a prohibition enforcement bill allowing searches of

[234] White 96.

[235] Patterson 504.

[236] White 189.

[237] RAT to George Wickersham, June 12, 1929, 1 R. Taft, Works 363.

[238] Smith and Taft, *supra*, 27.

private homes; he later, when up for re-election, promised to pre-serve the status quo on prohibition.[239] It was said that his "father in his drinking days had a very strong head for alcohol; the son did not, and knew it."[240] President Taft had a strong prejudice against those who drank to excess, a vice from which his descendants were notably free.

In 1928, Taft observed of Al Smith: "I am willing to grant his courage, but a policy dictated by a complete misconception of the ideas of the South and West cannot be wise … for the single reason that Smith was wet the intelligentsia chose to scoff at Hoover's position and his speeches."[241] In a letter in April 1932, he urged that any constitutional amendment modifying prohibition be submitted to state conventions rather than legislatures, the course that was ultimately followed. "The vote on delegates at large would give in effect a popular referendum."[242] In July 1932, he was furnishing Ogden Mills, Hoover's Secretary of the Treasury, with drafts of prohibition repeal amendments.[243]

Education

Although Taft's meeting with Eisenhower at Morningside Heights after the Republican convention in 1952 is generally viewed as pulling Eisenhower rightward, Taft was actually to the left of Eisenhower on some health and education issues. Taft earlier had made it clear that he would not fire a Communist from a college faculty unless he taught communism. "Private universities have always been the protectors of free thinking of all kinds," a tradition carried on by Yale's President A. Whitney Griswold in the 1950s

---

[239] Patterson 92, 99.

[240] White 37.

[241] RAT to WHT, November 9, 1928, 1 R. Taft, Works 354.

[242] RAT to Wallace Brown, April 19, 1932, 1 R. Taft, Works 431.

[243] RAT to Ogden Mills, July 2, 1932, 1 R. Taft, Works 435.

when Taft was on the Yale Board.[244] In addition, although communists could and should be excluded from federal service, "we cannot make it a crime to be a Communist or to teach Communism."[245] In 1948, he decried "a new Democratic plan to subsidize universities and dominate the thinking of the teachers."[246] "The [congressional] committees shouldn't have the power to fire professors. That's up to the trustees."[247] In 1953, he qualified this view slightly, saying he would fire a communist from government service if he "is teaching Communist principles or is a member of the party subscribing to its rules of discipline."[248]

During the Depression, Taft opposed a tuition increase by the Taft School.[249] In 1943, he opposed bills providing for general federal aid to education.[250] The schemes he devised contemplated that poorer districts levying a prescribed tax for education would get federal grants to bring them, not to equality, but to a minimum decent standard. States would be allowed to handle the divisive issue of aid to parochial schools in accordance with their own laws. "If there is one thing I fear more than others, it is that of taking away from the States and local governments the power to determine their own education policies. Hitler's success in Germany was obtained by his control of the education of the youth, and I don't propose to have any such power vested in a Washington bureau."[251]

---

[244] Patterson 595.

[245] Patterson 445.

[246] "The Case Against President Truman," Saturday Evening Post, 1948, in RAT Papers, Library of Congress, Box 736.

[247] New York Times, March 7, 1953.

[248] RAT to Ethan Judd, April 22, 1953, 4 R. Taft, Works 474.

[249] Patterson 167.

[250] Patterson 240ff. Later, he came to favor "a floor under essential things to give all a minimum standard of living and all children an opportunity to get a start in life," 270ff.

[251] RAT to W.H. Albers, November 1, 1946, RAT Papers, Library of Congress, Box 872, Folder "Education 1946."

Under his proposal "[n]o money goes to the wealthier states. No other state gets any money unless it spends more of its own money for education than the national expenditure compared to wealth."[252]

As a member of the Yale Board, Taft had a skeptical attitude toward some of the University's more pretentious activities: "Why should Yale have all these collections? What good are they? I don't know what you do with dinosaurs, but somebody has to dust then, don't they? And that costs money"[253]

Taft, like all the Tafts, had great respect for learning, once observing "I think if an attorney has not $10 to pay for the use of the Circuit Court Library for life, he has no place as a member of the Bar of the District Court."[254] Elsewhere, he asserted that "[t]he giving up of the local control of libraries would be a step in the direction of less freedom and less democracy."[255] In a Letter on Education in 1943, he asserted that "[a]ny further weakening of local self-government will make it impossible to continue in this country a democratic form of government."[256]

Opposing the grant of an honorary degree to Soviet Ambassador Maxim Litvinov during World War II, Taft observed, after discussing Litvinov's somewhat disreputable early career, "the mere fact that Russia is our ally in arms and a victim of Hitler's aggression hardly justifies a great American university in granting a degree to its leaders who have no other qualification. The granting of a degree does not seem to be justified by outstanding mental or educational qualifications."[257]

---

[252] RAT to Edmund Lincoln, May 30, 1946, RAT Papers, Library of Congress, Box 872, Folder "Education."

[253] Patterson 344.

[254] RAT to John W. Peck, October 4, 1933, 1 R. Taft, Works 454.

[255] Address to the Friends of the Library of Cuyahoga County, November 16, 1939, 2 R. Taft, Works 91. *See also* RAT to Carl Vitz, July 30, 1946, 3 R. Taft, Works 165, opposing federal aid to libraries.

[256] Letter on Education, October 14, 1943, 2 R. Taft, Works 497 n.3.

[257] RAT to Charles Seymour, April 15, 1942, 2 R. Taft, Works 350ff.

In a Memorial Day speech at Arlington in 1939, Taft reflected on the strengths of the United States, one of them being that "with universal free education there has been no boy or girl born in the United States who has not had the opportunity to rise to the top of his or her line of activity."[258]

By 1945, Taft had altered his position on federal aid to education, a shift partly founded on political pressure from more ambitious Democratic administration proposals and partly founded on recognition of the gross disparities in income between Northern, particularly Northeastern, states and the states of the Deep South. In 1945, the per capita income of the richest state, Connecticut, was about five times that of the poorest state, Mississippi. (Today, in part by reason of industrial migration following the Taft–Hartley Act, the ratio is less than two to one.) Within the Southern states, the segregated black schools were victimized; in Louisiana, per capita expenditures on the white schools was four times as large as that in the black schools. Taft was unfairly stigmatized by one historian, who alleged that "by loading the aid to education bill with civil rights amendments, Senator Taft each year managed to provoke enough Southern senators into voting against it to turn the tide."[259]

For Taft, aid to the Southern black schools was the only good reason to have an aid to education bill.

In the course of a denunciation of socialized medicine in 1946, Taft noted the somewhat different situation of the public schools: "A primary education must be compulsory for every boy and girl in the nation and education through private schools cannot begin to do the job and never has attempted to do it ... In most states the

---

[258] Memorial Day Address, Arlington, VA, May 30, 1939, 2 R. Taft, Works 29.

[259] G. Perrett, Days of Sadness, Years of Triumph: The American People, 1939-1945 (New York: Penguin, 1974), 371.

system has been separated from political government as it could not be under the present administration of the federal government."[260]

The subsequent course of federal aid to education, with its mandates relating to such things as faculty desegregation, school discipline and the contents of school lunches makes Taft's point. Taft also pointed out that "state systems of taxation were set up originally to take care of education, judicial systems and essential city services like the police and fire." In 1939, he declared: "Surely it is better that those interested in education be compelled to sell the latest theory to the people of each district."[261] In 1947, he cautioned the American Association of School Administrators that "[w]hen a federal system develops faults, and it always does, these faults extend throughout the whole country on a universal scale."[262]

A bill co-sponsored by Taft and Democratic Senators Lister Hill of Alabama and Elbert Thomas of Utah, providing for $8 billion in federal aid for state education over 25 years passed the Senate on April 1, 1947, by a vote of 58 to 22. It was essentially a revenue-sharing bill with stringent safeguards against federal interference and no enforcement bureaucracies. Racially biased spending was banned, but there was no requirement of school desegregation.[263]

Taft declared: "I was largely instrumental in defeating a federal aid to education bill in the fall of 1943. I will say that I changed my mind ... because of the way wealth is distributed in the United States."[264] His attitude toward education was summed up by a friendly biographer, William S. White: "He thought that

---

[260] Speech to Wayne County Medical Society, October 3, 1946, 3 R. Taft, Works 210.

[261] Smith and Taft 103.

[262] Address to the American Association of School Administrators, March 6, 1947, in 3 R. Taft, Works 252.

[263] M. Brown, The Roots of Modern Conservatism: Dewey, Taft, and the Battle for the Soul of the Republican Party (Chapel Hill: U. of North Carolina, 2011), 52-53.

[264] 94 Congressional Record, 80th Congress, 2nd Session, 3291, 3350.

men should be on their own, but that children should not, in any sense. They were entitled, not as a matter of privilege but as a matter of right, to a decent roof, decent meals, decent medical care and a decent place in which to go to school. The rest, as they grew older, was up to them."[265]

He did not go so far as Henry Cabot Lodge Jr. and Margaret Chase Smith in a "Declaration of Republican Principles" circulated in 1950: "in our industrial society in which men and women are dependent for their livelihood upon economic factors wholly beyond their control, the Right to Life becomes largely an economic matter, giving rise to certain rights which can be implemented only by providing protection from economic hazards against which the individual cannot hope adequately to insure himself. These hazards include unemployment, old age, accident, ill health, disabilities, etc."[266]

Although a political scientist has urged that Senate Republicans generally became more liberal in the 15 years of Taft's tenure, it is difficult to make this case as to Taft himself. A study rates Republican and conservative Democratic Senators on a scale in which 1.0 is most liberal and 3.0 as least supportive of the Roosevelt and Truman administrations. Taft's overall rating was 2.64 in domestic affairs and 2.67 in foreign affairs, and fluctuated little over time. He was never firmly aligned with the most conservative Republicans like Senators Kenneth Wherry, Bourke Hickenlooper, Charles Wayland Brooks, Albert Hawkes, and Owen Brewster. Over time, the Republicans in the Senate became more internationalist and less conservative, resulting in a challenge to Taft's leadership after the Republican defeat in the 1948 elections, in which he prevailed over Henry Cabot Lodge Jr. by a vote of 28 to 14.

---

[265] W. White, *supra*, 50.

[266] J. Malsberger, From Obstruction to Moderation: The Transformation of Senate Conservatism, 1938-52 (Selinsgrove: Susquehanna U. 2000), quoting Leverett Saltonstall Papers, Massachusetts Historical Society, 1950 General Correspondence.

In 1947, Taft made his own contribution to education by agreeing to take two law clerks into his office each year, in imitation of Supreme Court practice.[267]

In 1947, a Taft-supported bill providing a 24 member board to insulate the National Science Foundation from politics was vetoed by President Truman.[268]

In 1952, Taft reluctantly supported a program of federal aid for medical schools[269]

Health and Welfare

In late 1931, Taft wrote a letter to the editor to the *Cincinnati Enquirer*, endorsing a $7.5 million bond issue, defeated at the polls in that depression year. In it, he observed: "The neglect of the penal and welfare institutions of the State of Ohio is generally recognized throughout the State and was forcibly brought to the attention of the entire State by the disastrous fire [killing 335 convicts] at the penitentiary in 1930. The State hospitals for the insane are badly overcrowded and only recently this condition resulted in a serious typhoid epidemic at the Cleveland State Hospital ... the institutions have been neglected because they have only been allotted the funds which remain after the other demands have been taken care of." Taft went on to refer to "the criminal neglect with which [the State] has long treated its helpless wards."

In 1943, Taft declared: "we should study the extension of federal aid to health and medical care without bossing the job or socializing medicine."[270] In 1945, he endorsed federal aid to hospital

---

[267] RAT to Wesley Sturges, June 11, 1947, 3 R. Taft Works 288.

[268] Address to Los Angeles County Republicans, September 16, 1947, 3 R. Taft Works 310.

[269] RAT to Chase Mellon Jr., January 1, 1952, 4 R. Taft, Works 338.

[270] Address to Ohio Federation of Women's Republican Organization, May 7, 1943, in 2 R. Taft, Works 432.

construction in the form of the Hill–Burton bill, co-sponsored by his Ohio Republican colleague Harold Burton, later a Justice of the Supreme Court. The Act provided for $75 million a year for five years.

In October 1946, he denounced the Truman administration's Wagner–Murray–Dingell bill, his speech bearing the title "Federal Compulsory Health Insurance is Not Insurance but Socialization of Medicine." He characterized it as "a plan for government administration of all medical care … Some people run to the doctor when they have the slightest thing the matter with them. Others have a feeling that except in serious matters it is a waste of time to see a doctor at all. Probably the wise man is between the extremes.… [The plan] undoubtedly will increase the total work to be done by doctors, which has the effect of decreasing the quality of service.… If we are going to give medical care free to all people, why not provide them with free transportation, free food, free housing and clothing all at the expense of the taxpayer.… above all I deplore the federalization of medicine.… That has not even been done in education."[271]

Some of his proposals in the same speech for alternative approaches to the improvement of health still resonate: "Providing of medical care for individuals is only one of the measures that have an effect on health. Probably more has been done and can be done by preventive measures and the extension of public health work in the elimination of disease and epidemics … Nearly all of our cities have general hospitals. Many localities have public health doctors. All doctors do a large amount of charity work. [He suggested] subsidizing of doctors where medical practice will not support a decent livelihood … public health work should be expanded substantially and supplemented by a more complete inspection of the health of schoolchildren in all public and private schools at the expense of the State. Legislation should be adopted for federal aid in the removal of pollution from interstate rivers." He favored federal grants to the

---

[271] Speech to Wayne County Medical Society, October 3, 1946, 3 R. Taft, Works, 210.

states for health clinics and for insurance premiums for the bottom 20% to 25% of the income distribution.[272]

Federal water pollution legislation was not adopted for another 15 years, school health inspections remain inadequate, and instead of subsidizing general practitioners in poorer areas reliance has been placed on mass production clinics and "medicaid mills."

"[The issue is] whether we are going to turn over our destiny to a bureaucracy of self-styled experts." Taft derided the relevance of the Selective Service statistics used to demonstrate the need for a federal program: since a large part of them "resulted from congenital defects, mental deficiencies or other causes which would not have been affected by more medical care."

Taft unsuccessfully sponsored the Taft–Ball–Smith bill for a medical inspection service for schoolchildren. He asserted that means-tested inability to pay (as with Medicaid, ultimately sponsored by two conservative Democrats, Robert Kerr and Wilbur Mills) was the only justification for free medical service. "The amount of income in these days of income tax deduction and social security is usually a definite ascertainable figure." "We should preserve the freedom of 75% of the population to choose their own medical care and I think we should preserve the freedom of the medical profession."[273] It has been said that "[i]n rejecting Truman's program, the Congress and the nation implicitly endorsed private medicine and individual responsibility. However, since bi-partisan support was not given to the Taft proposal, a comprehensive local program for the needy was not encouraged."[274]

He thought that Truman's plan involved "a principle of taxation, not of insurance," rendering doctors "responsible to the Government which pays them and not to their patients who do not."[275]

---

[272] F. Burd, *supra*, 175.

[273] F. Burd, *supra*, 179.

[274] F. Burd, *supra*, 180.

[275] New York Times, October 8, 1946, 26.

In a letter in 1949, he lamented the fact that "public health units cover about one-third of the country. Health inspection for school children covers much less than half the schools in the country."[276] In 1953, he explained to a correspondent: "I regard the furnishing of examination services for children, and perhaps some forms of treatment, as more public health work than socialized medicine."[277]

Housing

While in Ohio, he supported efforts to shorten the foreclosure period for tax sales of real estate. His arguments retain their cogency: "It is a very doubtful kindness to permit [a homeowner] to go on until his entire investment in his home is wiped out. It is better for him to recognize the situation, dispose of his house, and live on a scale more commensurate with his means. Certainly the State should not be in the business of financing improvident construction."[278] This lesson was lost on later sponsors of the Community Investment Act leading to sub-prime mortgages and the 2008 worldwide recession.

He supported federal home loan programs: "I believe in many respects the government can stimulate private industry particularly in the building field where reasonable contribution might be made by the government to any individual who has saved money and is willing to put his savings into a new home for himself."[279]

The Federal Housing Administration (FHA) "allowed almost the only real stimulus to business that the present administration has provided."[280] He supported President Truman's reorganization

---

[276] RAT to Harry Carr, December 22, 1949, 4 R. Taft, Works 115.

[277] RAT to Michael Burnham, April 1, 1953, 4 R. Taft, Works 468.

[278] RAT to George White, July 7, 1931, 1 R. Taft, Works 404.

[279] Radio Address on Unemployment, February 10, 1938, 1 R. Taft, Works 578.

[280] Smith and Taft, *supra*, 231.

and consolidation of housing agencies in 1947; only 11 of the 43 Senate Republicans did so.[281] In 1939, he observed: "private industry is able to supply housing which would rent at the same rates per month if the tenant could receive a subsidy of $200 per year per house. There should be a certain amount of government housing on a rental basis."[282] True to this limited commitment to public housing, Taft became a successful co-sponsor of the Wagner–Ellender–Taft bill, providing for creation of 1.25 million rental units a year for 10 years, leading a chronicler to proclaim: "Mr. Republican Turns Socialist."[283] Herbert Hoover was shocked by Taft's support of the bill.[284]

The bill consolidated separate organizations into a National Housing Authority, expanded the lending authority of Federal Home Loan Banks, allocated funds for both public and private construction, and authorized the sale to municipalities of temporary wartime housing to be converted into low-income units.[285] "Much of this housing was too cheaply constructed, and little attention was given to making the environment of the housing projects attractive or to helping the inhabitants to make the most of their new houses."[286] American housing authorities, as Taft suggested, have paid little heed to the admonition of the British Edwardian-era housing reformer Octavia Hill: "before reforming the houses, it is first necessary to reform the people in them."

He was opposed to giving tenants rent vouchers, for fear of creating a new entitlement: "If we attempt to give rent certificates,

---

[281] F. Burd, *supra*, 140.

[282] Statement on the Housing Bill, June 6, 1939, 2 R. Taft, Works 43.

[283] R. Davies, "Mr. Republican Turns Socialist," 73 Ohio History (Summer 1964), 135.

[284] 2 G. Best, Herbert Hoover: The Post-Presidential Years, 1933-64 (Stanford: Hoover Institution, 1983), 331.

[285] M. Bowen, *supra*, 52.

[286] D. McCoy, The Presidency of Harry S. Truman (Lawrence, KS: U. Press of Kansas, 1984), 172.

it will have to be a universal plan." He also feared that they would lead to more federal regulation, and thought that they would not stimulate necessary housing construction.[287] When rent certificates were introduced by Secretary of Housing Carla Hills during the Nixon administration, they were means-tested and far from universal.[288] Vouchers, in his view, do not get rid of slums or prevent new slums.[289]

He was opposed to a guaranty program for prefabricated houses: it "would permit favoritism now, and a shifting of materials from established methods of construction to something which at best is experimental." He was frustrated by the opposition to public housing: "the real estate board people have been extremely unreasonable as well as the so-called Home Builders' Association, which is made up of small housing contractors … [P]ublic housing really is not needed in the newer cities and most of the opposition arises there."[290]

The Taft–Ellender–Wagner bill was finally passed in March 1950; earlier versions had been gutted by Senator Joseph McCarthy's opposition to public housing and advocacy of prefabricated homes. The results of the Act were disappointing: "Only 156,000 units were started under it by 1952 and only 356,000 units had been built by 1964. Public housing was decidedly a mixed blessing."[291] Taft had contemplated the construction of 810,000 units. He was not worried about the effect on work incentives of the means-tested

---

[287] F. Burd, *supra*, 140ff.

[288] Address to Ohio Home Builders' Association, December 14, 1945, 3 R. Taft, Works 99.

[289] Address to Ohio Federation of Women's Republican Organizations, October 19, 1945, 3 R. Taft, Works 83.

[290] RAT to Morris McLean, November 29, 1947, in 3 R. Taft, Works 335.

[291] D. McCoy, The Presidency of Harry S. Truman (Lawrence, U. Press of Kansas, 1984), 172.

beneficiaries: "to those in the lowest income class it is not dangerous because little of the energy or incentive is found there in any
event."[292]

In 1947, he already took alarm at excessive liberality in federal
mortgage guaranty programs, which produced a spectacular crash
in 2008: "[The] increase in mortgages [was] deliberately stimulated
by government guarantees amounting to from 90% to 100% of the
cost; the program cannot be abandoned but it could be placed on a
sounder basis."[293]

Speaking to the Mortgage Bankers' Association in 1949, he
observed that there was "[v]ery low construction in the thirties
and inadequate construction during the war. If we could reduce
the cost of housing so that perhaps 75% of all families could afford
a new home, we could eliminate slums much more quickly at the
bottom … it is not intended to deal with transients or helpless individuals. The most helpless group will have to be taken care of in
public institutions." Taft did not foresee that because of the false
promise of federal 'community treatment' in the 1960s, there would
come a time when 90% of the beds in state public institutions no
longer existed; their former occupants provided most of the visi-
ble evidence of homelessness used to support demands for housing
programs.[294]

Early in his career in Ohio, Taft favored abolition of the
smaller townships and school districts, while endorsing the creation
of county planning commissions.[295] He was asked to comment on

---

[292] F. Burd, *supra*, 150.

[293] Address to St. Andrews Society of Philadelphia, December 1, 1947, 3
R. Taft, Works 339.

[294] Address to the Mortgage Bankers' Association, January 25, 1949, 4
R. Taft, Works 14.

[295] Patterson 560ff.

the Social Unit experiment involving maternal health centers in Cincinnati, and responded with characteristic open-mindedness:

> "I believe that one principal reason for failure is that Mr. and Mrs. Phillips are Socialists who do not hesitate to express their opinion. Not very much has been accomplished in developing community spirit and self-government. The health work is continuing and doing a great deal of good. The organization work is not worth the money spent. I doubt whether it is fair either to condemn the Unit as a failure or praise its success until 4 or 5 years' actual trial. I should like to see the work continued but of course it should not be continued by funds obtained on any statement of facts except what has actually occurred. I doubt whether it can succeed but I do not think that final failure is proved."[296]

The pioneer American social worker Mary Ellen Richmond made similar comments: "Your unit is to be babies and not milk; your aim is education and not super-imposed service ... You know and I know that insofar as relief tends to become complete or partial support for the able-bodied, it is no remedy. I should expect you to lay far less emphasis upon the centralization of social effort than you now do ... The passion for uniformity and order may easily land your experiment where others have landed. Freedom is the breath of life in social work as in education."[297]

He successfully sponsored a property tax reform in the Ohio legislature: "Only by a lower rate on personal property will it be possible to collect any more money from personal property. You cannot induce people to hold bonds or high grade stocks and pay

---

[296] RAT to Julian Barnes, April 14, 1920, 1 R. Taft, Works 232, *see* P. Mooney, The Organic City, 1880-1920 (Lexington: U. Press of Kentucky, 1987).

[297] Mary Ellen Richmond to Wilbur Phillips, July 29, 1915 (Mary Ellen Richmond Papers, Columbia University).

approximately half the income in taxes. Intangible property is so liquid that it very quickly disappears from the State."[298] This lesson has been lost on today's advocates of wealth taxes.

He also sponsored legislation limiting bonds to permanent improvements and requiring 60% voter approval for bond issues.[299]

He considered that "[t]he Home Rule provisions contained in Article 18 of the [Ohio] Constitution are an unqualified success … eliminat[ing] a great deal of friction in the state legislature."[300]

He laid the foundation for the growth of state income taxation by successfully urging the Hoover administration to make federal income tax returns available to Ohio to assist in its enforcement of its Intangible Property Tax, in all but name a tax on investment income. He told Arthur Ballantine, a Treasury official, that "[t]he Supreme Court has more and more hedged the States about in their constitutional powers of taxation until real estate has come to be almost the only source of reliance. The result is that more and more demands are made on the federal treasury, largely because they are able to reach wealth and business, while the states are so seriously hampered. The present demand for federal employment relief has only one real justification, that is the weakness of the state tax powers."[301]

He also wrote to President Hoover, his former Chief in Paris, "the federal government has a direct interest. If it is once admitted that the only government that can tax intangible wealth is the federal government, there will be the best of arguments for insisting that the federal government be called upon to appropriate money for unemployment relief and for every other public project in which it is felt that the wealthy ought to bear some part of the tax. It is only

---

[298]   RAT to J.W. Grant, March 15, 1926, 1 R. Taft, Works 317.

[299]   RAT to Thaddeus Brown, August 8, 1923, 1 R. Taft, Works 279.

[300]   RAT to William Chatfield, April 13, 1931, 1 R. Taft, Works 398.

[301]   RAT to Arthur Ballantine, January 11, 1932.

when that tax is measured by income that the federal income tax figures have some relation to the local tax."[302]

Treasury Department Order 4332 and Executive Order 5824 authorized Ohio to inspect federal income tax returns. Taft noted: "I regard the power to inspect federal income tax returns as essential to any enforcement of the state tax. Information which we can secure within the state is necessarily partial."[303]

In 1934, he opposed proposals to centralize Ohio's school system: "Every individual district is different; the people in each district desire different classes of service, and the attempt to turn over the whole business to the state seems to me utterly wrong."[304]

He was to say of the New Dealers that "[m]ost of them would be willing to abolish the States and turn over all local government to federal control. All of them favour the delegation of legislative power to the President and seem to forget that this was the first step in the growth of autocracy in Germany and Italy."[305] Assessing the NRA and AAA (Agricultural Adjustment Administration), he observed: "Their originators seem to feel that same preference for their most unfortunate products which a mother is said to feel for an idiot child." Their only defensible features were "the abolition of child labor and the establishment of minimum wage scales which might be done independently."[306] Later, he noted the regressive nature of New Deal taxation, continuing to this day: "When the New Deal wants real money, it turns to payroll taxes and processing taxes."[307]

[302] RAT to Herbert Hoover, February 27, 1932, 1 R. Taft, Works 420.

[303] RAT to Anthony Kraus, April 4, 1932, 1 R. Taft, Works 428.

[304] RAT to Carleton Darquist, July 13, 1934, 1 R. Taft, Works 479.

[305] W. White, *supra*, 44.

[306] Warren Chamber of Commerce, April 9, 1935, 1 R. Taft, Works 481.

[307] New Hampshire Republican Women's Club, April 30, 1936, 1 R. Taft, Works 505.

He urged turning back relief administrations to local communities with federal assistance. He also favored institutionalized sharing, on what is now the German and French models, of income and sales taxes: "The tax system could be greatly improved if there were a coordinated system agreed to by the federal government and the states. It is unreasonable, for instance, to have income taxes levied by both the federal government and the state. The state is not equipped to collect income taxes or intangible taxes adequately. It might well be agreed that all income taxes be collected by the federal government and a proportion turned over to the states. It might be much easier for the federal government to levy sales taxes at the source, and give each state a proportion based on the purchases in that state."[308]

In 1942, anticipating a later reform creating Subchapter S Corporations, he told Herbert Hoover, "I have talked to the Treasury about the proposal that small corporations be allowed to make returns as partnerships, but I haven't made any progress."[309]

He did not opposing tax withholding at source: "I believe myself that the Republicans are making a mistake in making a party issue of the Ruml plan."[310] In 1952 at his famous Morningside Heights meeting with Eisenhower, he secured a pledge that the normal federal role would be one of "advice, research, and assistance to the States, the local communities, and the people."[311] He was noted for opposition to "enlargement of federal popular power at the expense of the concept of states' rights and perquisites. If one sought to identify above all others the Man of the Resistance, one would have to settle upon Taft."[312]

---

[308] RAT to Edythe Cowie, December 28, 1936, 1 R. Taft, Works 531

[309] RAT to Herbert Hoover, September 1, 1942, 2 R. Taft, Works 365; RAT Papers, Library of Congress, Box 1286, Folder "Hoover 1941-48."

[310] RAT to Edward Lincoln, March 31, 1943, 2 R. Taft, Works 420.

[311] Id. 193.

[312] Id. 196.

In 1938, he observed that the New Dealers "have made big steps toward abolishing state and local home rule."[313] In 1939, warning against the consequences of war, Taft said: "I doubt whether, after another war, we would ever see real local self-government in the United States again or real operation of private enterprise ..."[314]

His viewpoint was later appreciated by David Halberstam, one of the leading journalistic critics of the Vietnam War: he was "uneasy with the coming of America the superpower and its growing obsession with anti-Communism. In his speeches, he systematically downplayed the Soviet military threat and he often scolded the administration for inflated rhetoric about the Communist danger, which he said was provocative to the Russians. He feared the dynamism of the Cold War would turn America into the policeman of the world, transforming it from a democracy to an imperial power, a role, he believed, for which we were ill-suited."[315] "Modern war," Taft also said, "is nothing but horror and mechanical destruction. It leaves the victor as exhausted as the vanquished." "Other people simply do not like to be dominated and we would be in the same position of suppressing rebellion by force in which the British found themselves during the 19th century."[316]

In general, he favored "[a] complete social welfare program retaining the system of incentive and the relative position of men according to their deserts while reducing the too-wide difference now existing."[317]

In decrying the proposed federalization of medical care in 1946, Taft pointed out that "[i]n his own City Council or State House, [a citizen] can make himself heard by appearing personally. He can write letters to the newspapers. In Washington, he can't

---

[313] Tippacanoe Club, January 29, 1938, 1 R. Taft, Works 554.

[314] Neutrality Act Revision, September 6, 1939, 2 R. Taft, Works 69.

[315] D. Halberstam, The Fifties (New York: Villard Books, 1993), 57.

[316] Id. 207.

[317] William McKinley Centennial, January 7, 1943, 2 R. Taft, Works 406.

even find the bureau or the man supposed to handle his problems. One of the principal services which congressmen perform is to save their constituents two or three days tramping through marble corridors ... Administration by states and local governments is genuinely democratic. Administration by Washington boards and bureaus is tyrannical."[318] In 1947, he observed: "the attitude of most federal bureaus generally comes to be that the people are too dumb to understand. The little clique which controls the bureau believes completely in its infallibility."[319]

Speaking of his proposal for limited federal aid to the poorest school districts in 1947, Taft said:

> "The federal government is authorized to levy taxes to provide for the general welfare of the United States and under that constitutional grant has the right to dispense money to the states and local districts for purposes not within the constitutional power of the United States to control or regulate. States in general have a limited power of taxation. They cannot raise their taxes above those of other states or their citizens and industries would drift into those other states. If we can reduce the federal interference to a matter of audit, we may hope to maintain local independence. We must also restrain the inclination of Congress. Thus [if] an amendment may require that no money shall be used for education which teaches socialism ... we are embarked on a course likely to lead to complete federal control. This bill is a state-aid bill and the state should be authorized to use the federal funds for the same purpose for which it uses its own state funds. As

---

[318] Speech to Wayne County Medical Society, October 3, 1946, 3 R. Taft, Works 202

[319] To Yale Alumni, February 22, 1947, 3 R. Taft, Works 247ff.

they approach the national average the necessity for aid from the national government will become less."[320]

Later, he succeeded in passing a tax reduction bill over President Truman's veto which lowered levies on transportation, luxuries, and capital gains, exempted a portion of stock dividend income, and enlarged depreciation allowances.

He opposed renewal of the Reciprocal Trade Agreements Act.

In 1948, he urged that "We ... put in people who believe in the autonomy of state and local government, people who do not seek power in their own right for their own particular ideology."[321]

Legal Issues

While in the Ohio legislature, Taft supported nonpartisan judicial elections. In 1922, he endorsed the federal declaratory judgments act and federal jurisdiction over violations of the treaty rights of aliens.[322] He regarded Franklin Roosevelt's court-packing plan as "an end of the Constitution and of judicial independence."[323] He lauded the Constitution in a radio address: "All over the world we have seen how easy it is for a temporary majority of the people to turn over all the powers of government to a dictator and how difficult it is to recover those powers once they are delegated. [The Constitution] is our bulwark today against both Fascism and Communism and against the bitter conflict between them which is destroying Spain and threatens to destroy Europe."[324]

---

[320] American Association of School Administrators, March 6, 1947, 3 R. Taft, Works 252.

[321] Steubenville High School, April 23, 1948, 3 R. Taft, Works 423.

[322] RAT to Richard Ernst, March 8, 1922, in 1 R. Taft, Works 265.

[323] RAT to Alfred Whitman, March 4, 1937, 1 R. Taft, Works 536.

[324] Radio Address on the Constitution, September 17, 1938, 1 R. Taft, Works 584.

In 1944, he criticized the Roosevelt administration's sedition trial of right-wing organizations, which collapsed.[325] He condemned the Nuremberg trial as a "miscarriage of justice." In 1950, he expressed the view that "[t]he Administrative Procedure Act is not nearly strong enough. It was written by a committee of which Mr. Dean Acheson was chairman and controlled substantially by the New Dealers." (This was a slight exaggeration, because the Act as passed represented a compromise between the Commission bill and one sponsored by the American Bar Association, which contributed the new concept of notice-and-comment rule-making.) He urged that every statute conferring regulatory powers "define clearly the extent to which administrative bodies may go."[326] Taft's dislike of the "substantial evidence" rule presuming correctness of administrative judgments was shared by some former New Dealers, including Judge Thurman Arnold.

In 1951, during the era of the Kefauver hearings, he urged that "the right to question a witness does not extend to having his voice recorded for the public or himself televised. It seems to me to subject a witness to an utterly unfair ordeal and to interfere seriously with his ability to answer accurately the questions that are asked him."[327]

While in the Ohio legislature, Taft, as previously shown, supported compelled publication of the membership lists of secret organizations.[328]

He favored selection of candidates by party conventions, not direct primaries: "No convention should nominate a candidate who has never been engaged in a political campaign before."[329]

---

[325] Patterson 256.

[326] RAT to W. E. Bradford, December 16, 1950, 4 R. Taft, Works 225.

[327] RAT to Will Robinson, August 28, 1951, 4 R. Taft, Works 315.

[328] Patterson 97.

[329] Patterson 234.

"The weakness of any reform movement," he observed early in his career, "is, though it succeed once or twice, a machine which is continuous is such a powerful means of getting out the vote in a city that it is almost certain to prevail in the long run ... bad as the machine may be, it is bound to do negative good in preventing radical changes into which any reform movement is apt to slide."[330]

In 1944, he vehemently opposed a federal ballot for soldiers, fearing a "khaki election" on the British 1919 model. He inserted a Section V guaranteeing against political propaganda. He strongly supported party organization: "Any softening in the harsh naturally ordained friction between leadership and opposition would be mortally dangerous to the whole health of the American political system."[331] As Senate majority leader, he would not permit the majority to bring up a bill unannounced.[332] In 1926, he condemned the direct primary in terms that have continuing resonance: "the worst influence today in state and national politics is the statewide direct primary. The quality of candidates and officials has steadily deteriorated since it was initiated. No man except one who has no business or one who is very rich can afford to enter a campaign. The direct primary has made impossible the existence of a State Party organization and the result is that no State Party in recent years has initiated or carried through any important policy of state government."[333]

The reason for his dedication to party regularity was summarized by Wilson Carey McWilliams: "the regular organization helped relieve candidates who were decent and honorable of any

---

[330] RAT to Martha Bowers, September 29, 1913, 1 R. Taft, Works 12.

[331] White 146.

[332] White 252.

[333] RAT to A. Anderson, July 24, 1926, in 1 R. Taft, Works 319; RAT to A.E. Anderson, July 24, 1926, 1 R. Taft Works 319.

need to engage in demagogy cant or vulgarity by assuming those burdens itself."[334]

He was equally opposed to the scheme of proportional representation fostered by the Charter element (of which his brother Charles was a member) for the Cincinnati City Council: "I am afraid I have not sufficient time to enter into any general discussion of the proportional representation system. The theory seems to me to be exactly wrong, that of the representation of separate minority groups instead of a representation of majorities."[335]

Further, "[proportional representation] emphasizes class distinction and is fundamentally opposed to the American system of representative government. It seems to me that it is bound to promote the election of the most radical representative of each class, instead of requiring that class to put forward a representative who will be satisfactory to at least a majority of the whole people."[336] The creation of "voting rights" districts to increase black representation in Congress illustrates the correctness of this observation.

"In order to keep two parties alive in the State or Nation, there must be an extension of the party system into local affairs, In view of my brother's activity in the matter, I should prefer not to have my views made public."[337]

He defended a new zoning ordinance: "Once in a while an industry is unable to locate exactly where it desires to go but I have yet to see any serious inconvenience resulting from this within the city limits, certainly nothing to argue with the tremendous protection given those who have bought property of a definite character expecting it to continue as such."[338] This respect for the vested rights

---

[334] W. McWilliams, Book Review of J. Patterson, Mr. Republican, New York Times Book Review, November 19, 1972, 1.

[335] RAT to Alden Kumler, December 23, 1927, 1 R. Taft, Works 333.

[336] RAT to Stuart Lewis, May 2, 1928, 1 R. Taft, Works 334 n.2.

[337] RAT to Henry Barnham, June 22, 1932, 1 R. Taft, Works 434.

[338] RAT to Leonard Smith Jr., February 28, 1931, 1 R. Taft, Works 396.

of home owners is a reproach to "fair housing" proposals advocating nondiscrimination against welfare recipients by private landlords.

He observed that "statutory tax limitations can accomplish economy in state and local government. They are wholly ineffective in limiting bond issues and should therefore be confined to current operating expenses. The proper way to limit taxes for debt purposes is a limitation of the debt-incurring power itself. I am very much opposed to incorporating any limit in the Constitution."[339]

In his view, "the Chairman of the Republican National Committee should not be a policymaker and probably the less he says himself, the better."[340]

"Isolationism"

Europe, in Taft's view, was a place where "minorities are a perpetual source of friction."[341]

In a letter to his father from Paris on January 5, 1919, he observed: "there must be a limit to the German power to pay and it must be about 20 billions, plus colonies ... certainly there ought not be a perpetual tribute. The extent to which commerce and private business have been wiped out can hardly be realized. If we don't sell our goods on credit we won't sell them at all and the financial break in the U.S. will be very serious. I am in favor of lifting the blockade of food now—no one pretends that the war is not won and its object was to win the war ... nothing is accomplished by starving Germany but Bolshevism [but] inertia is very strong."

On March 30, he again wrote his father to observe: "I am afraid that we will have to occupy Germany. I don't believe the present government can accept the peace they will be offered without falling ... it is not impossible that the whole of Central Europe will

---

[339] RAT to Henry Taft, November 23, 1933, 1 R. Taft, Works 456.

[340] RAT to Horace Taft, December 28, 1940, 2 R. Taft, Works 212.

[341] Patterson 198ff.

fall into Bolshevist hands if things do not change quickly. The armistice should have required the complete disarmament of Germany as of Austria. I understand that [General Tasker] Bliss urged this but [Marshal Ferdinand] Foch was afraid the Germans would not accept—no military purpose was served by the blockade ... All the army are so anxious to get home that it is doubtful whether you could get anyone to occupy Russia now even if it ought to be done."

The image of him as a reflexive isolationist is belied by the fact that he was one of seven Senate Republicans to vote to relax the Neutrality Act to allow "cash and carry" sales of munitions. "An arms embargo discriminates against weak and peaceful nations which have not increased their own munitions plants."[342]

In doing so, he parted company with William Borah, Henry Ford, Herbert Hoover, Gerald Nye, Charles Lindbergh, and Robert La Follette. One historian observed that "Senator Robert Taft to the horror of conservative-isolationist purists accustomed to considering him one of themselves demanded the Neutrality Act be thrown out and war materials be offered to anyone who wanted to buy—for cash, of course."[343]

When the Roosevelt administration's Jesse Jones asserted that "Britain is a good risk for a loan," Taft responded "Nonsense."[344]

Although the post-war British loan was fully repaid, Britain's Lend-Lease debt, as Taft had foreseen, was settled for pennies on the dollar. His attitude toward the post-war British loan was "I am still doubtful. The arguments for it seem to me almost entirely fallacious, but on the other hand I don't like to be responsible for

---

[342] Statement on Neutrality Act Revision, September 6, 1939 in 2 R. Taft, Works 69.

[343] G. Perrett, Days of Sadness, Years of Triumph: The American People, 1939-1945 (New York: Penguin, 1974), 23.

[344] Id. 65.

breaking up an alliance between the two English-speaking countries if that would be the result."[345]

He opposed the deal in which the United States exchanged destroyers for bases in British possessions. He opposed Lend-Lease: "we certainly don't want the same gum back," but would have supported $2 billion in cash loans to Britain, Canada, and Greece. In May 1940, he observed: "there is no disagreement on the necessity for preparedness. We pray for the escape of the British and French armies in France, abandoned by their [Belgian] ally. We can't have battleships and still go on adding dams and parks and post-offices. There is no recognition of the fact that preparedness is a deadly serious business which can only be accomplished through sacrifice. I think we must defend the United States by defending Canada, the Caribbean Sea and Northern South America, that is our natural line of defense."[346]

Six days earlier he had said, "[w]e certainly could not afford to let Hitler obtain a foothold anywhere on or near North America, Central America, or the northern part of South America; we should go to war, if necessary, to prevent such a happening."[347] Yet the Latin American division of the State Department has been a step-child and the economics and politics of Cuba, Central America, and Venezuela were allowed to fester as though the fate of these nations and the possibility of massive refugee flows from them was not a vital interest of the United States.

In February 1941, he observed with only partial prescience that "[a]n invasion of the United States by the German army is as fantastic as would be the invasion of Germany … by an American army and as unlikely to be undertaken."[348]

---

[345] Taft to Dr. H.H. Bene, February 20, 1946, RAT Papers, Library of Congress, Box 872, Folder "Demobilization 1946."

[346] Radio Address, May 29, 1940, in 2 R. Taft, Works 145.

[347] "Taft for Defensive War," New York Times, May 23, 1940.

[348] Quoted in J. Gunther, Inside U.S.A. (New York: Harper, 1949), 434.

He urged "establishing our defense lines based on the Atlantic and Pacific oceans … airspace has made it more difficult, not easier, to transport an army across an ocean and that conquest must still be by a land army."[349]

In June 1941, he was quoted as saying that "the victory of communism in the world would be far more dangerous to the United States than the victory of fascism" though "from the point of view of ideology, there is no choice [between them]."[350] Communism "is a greater danger to the United States because it is a false philosophy that appeals to many men. Fascism is a false philosophy that appeals to very few indeed." "There is a good deal more danger of the infiltration of totalitarian ideas from the New Deal circle in Washington than there ever will be from any activities of … the Nazi bund."[351]

"No war on behalf of a democratic country can possibly be successful unless it has the overwhelming support of the people, in whom and for whom that country has always been governed."[352]

A month later, he declined to exclude the possibility of a separate peace with Germany: "Any American must welcome the closest cooperation between England and Russia. But whether it is wise for England to bind herself not to make peace unless Russia consents is perhaps doubtful."[353]

He was always uncomfortable with the Russian alliance, and particularly with the rhetoric used in its support: "[Democracy] threatens to be a fetish without real meaning. If we let a name, a political slogan, direct our whole American policy without

---

[349] Quoted in C. Dueck, Hard Line: The Republican Party and U.S. Foreign Policy Since World War II (Princeton: Princeton U., 2010), 43.

[350] Decktterson 246, see "Taft Warns U.S. On Aiding Russia," New York Times, June 26, 1941.

[351] RAT to George F. Stanley, September 8, 1944, RAT Papers, Library of Congress, Box 31

[352] Radio Address, June 25, 1941, 2 R. Taft, Works 255ff.

[353] New York Times, July 14, 1941.

considering the purpose of that slogan, we are not going long to remain a democracy ourselves."[354]

One may contrast Lady Diana Cooper's advice to her son in the same month: "People hate Russians because they are Communists and have done atrocious things to their own people and would like to convert us all to their highly unsuccessful ways, but I prefer Russians so infinitely to Huns and fear their creed so much less than Naziism that I have no swallowing gulping trouble over fighting on their side. Communism at least has an idealistic aim—all men equal, no nations, no money, all races are brothers, share your cow with your neighbor because it belongs to the State, etc. I hope America will take it all right. They have a big Communist bogey which they maybe have more cause to have than us. We have none. A handful of rich people think the Nazis respect the positioned rich and that the Communists don't and they particularly want to hold on to their money. Never be caught by people who argue about Russia being worse than Germany—just consider if they are rich or poor."[355]

Taft took the view that "if peace is once restored, we could trade as well with Germany as with England." Germany was not a menace "particularly after the Russians had entered the war against the Germans."[356]

"A supposed hostility to Japan, a totalitarian nation, does not prevent Japan from being one of our best customers."[357]

In December 1940, his somewhat exaggerated view of airpower was reflected in his view that "nothing will end this war except an overwhelming delivery of airplanes from this country to

---

[354] "Assails War Alignments," New York Times, June 30, 1941.

[355] D. Cooper, Darling Monster: The Letters of Lady Diana Cooper to Her Son John Julius Norwich, entry for June 25, 1941 (New York: Overlook, 2014), 128-29.

[356] Quoted in W. White, The Taft Story (New York: Harper, 1954) 151, 152.

[357] RAT, "Aid to Britain Short of War," March 1, 1941, RAT Papers, Library of Congress, Box 1256.

England."[358] In January 1941, he took the view that "even the collapse of England is to be preferred to participation for the rest of our lives in European wars." A sympathetic critic observed: "Because Germany sapped itself on the icy plains of the Soviet Union, he could always argue plausibly that England would have survived without American intervention. And because a more neutral American policy on the Atlantic might have appeased the Nazis ... he could also maintain that Hitler might have pursued a policy of peaceful coexistence with America until the difficulties of holding on to extensive territorial acquisitions overwhelmed his successors and restored the old balance of power."[359]

Later he said, "I think I am willing to admit maybe I was wrong."

His equanimity about the possible collapse of Britain is the principal cloud over his historical reputation. His military estimate—that Britain could hold out without massive American aid—may have been correct, though the Battle of the Atlantic was a close-run thing. As late as January 1946, he told a correspondent "the time is coming when I think I can analyze the situation more clearly to show that we would be much better off if we had not entered the war."[360]

Similarly, he was almost certainly right that Germany could not invade the United States; as A.J.P. Taylor and others have pointed out, Germany did not have the high seas fleet in 1940 that she had in 1914. But what Taft underrated was the almost certain moral effects of Britain's fall on the United States. Already in 1940-41, many Americans were accommodating themselves to Nazi views and Nazi methods. Anne Morrow Lindbergh's *The*

---

[358] RAT to Horace Taft, December 28, 1949, 2 R. Taft, Works 212.

[359] Patterson 248-49.

[360] RAT to Dr. Francis Patton, January 23, 1946, in RAT Papers, Library of Congress, Box 874, Folder "Foreign Policy 1946."

Wave of the Future[361] was the most notorious example of this, but there were other more subtle adaptations: Peter Drucker's call for non-economic hierarchies in *The End of Economic Man*;[362] Thurman Arnold's emulation of Nazi propaganda methods in *The Folklore of Capitalism*;[363] the imitation of Nazi thuggery by the "storm troopers" of Father Coughlin's Christian Front in New York City; and, most significantly, the vision of the future world vouchsafed in James Burnham's *The Managerial Revolution*.[364]

Burnham's book reads seriously badly now: "The basis of the economic structure of managerial society is governmental (state) ownership and control of the major instruments of production … Why should the managers and their bureaucratic military allies accept a return that would thrust them back into the servant quarters?" Burnham held the view, akin to that of today's neo-conservatives, that war or preparation for war was a natural and perpetual state: "all economies are war economies … [W]ar is a normal and integral part of all human societies. When not fighting, they have been recovering from a previous fight and simultaneously getting ready for the next one." For Burnham, there are no concerts or balances of power, no Holy Alliances. The dynamism of Germany was attested to, for him, by the youth of its leaders; "the hopelessness of the position of the British capitalists has been shown … by the fact that they have absolutely no peace plans ('war aims')." For Burnham, Isaiah Berlin's "negative liberties," though instinctively upheld by the British and given voice by Churchill and by Roosevelt were not "war aims," nor was the Beveridge Report. He did not envision a Europe of national states rebuilt by old men: Winston Churchill, Clement Attlee, Charles De Gaulle, Leon Blum, Alcide De Gasperi, Carlo Sforza, Konrad Adenauer.

---

[361] (New York: Harcourt Brace, 1940).

[362] (New York: John Day, 1939).

[363] (New Haven: Yale U., 1937).

[364] (New York: John Day, 1941).

In February 1941 Taft opposed Lend-Lease but supported $2 billion in credits for Britain. Hitler "could hardly set out for America with the flower of the German Army and leave a smoldering volcano behind him. If we maintain a strong navy and air force, no nation will ever attack us across the ocean. War cannot impose on other peoples forms of government they do not want. War will never spread freedom of speech or of religion, freedom from want or freedom from fear, anywhere in the world."[365]

On Lend-Lease, he thought "it certainly authorizes him to take us into the midst of the war ... before we get through with that war, the rights of private property in the U.S. will be to a large extent destroyed."[366]

His list of objections to Lend-Lease were that the "[b]ill does not require financial resources to be exhausted ... includes our army and navy and permits them to be given away ... does not limit our aid to goods produced in the U.S. ... opens our ports to the British navy, always considered an act of war, authorizes the President to give anything away without repayment, confuses our already confused defense program and subordinates it to that of England, authorizes this gift and aid to any country including Germany ... an unbridled delegation of legislative authority and blank check appropriation [which] authorizes the President to make war on any nation in the world if he wishes to do so."[367]

Lend-Lease was described as "legislation for war giving the President unlimited, unprecedented and unpredictable powers," whereas Taft's loan bill "enables purchases in direct accordance with their needs."[368]

---

[365] "Aid for Britain Short of War," February 26, 1941, in 2 R. Taft, Works 226.

[366] RAT to Jane Ingalls, March 3, 1941, 2 R. Taft, Works 232.

[367] RAT Papers, Box 862, Folder "Lend Lease Bill, 1941."

[368] New York Times, February 26, 1941.

A month later, however, he voted for $7 billion in lend-lease aid for Britain, which passed the Senate by a vote of 67 to 9, the hard-core opponents being Senators D. Worth Clark of Idaho, Champ Clark of Missouri, Burton Wheeler, Hugh Butler, Gerald Nye, Henrik Shipstead, John Thomas of Idaho, and Robert La Follette, with Hiram Johnson and Alexander Wiley paired against.[369]

In May 1941, he thought that the British could defend themselves and by bombing Germany gain a more satisfactory peace, "but that is very different from crushing Hitler," which would involve "maintaining a police force perpetually in Germany and throughout Europe … a navy to attack across an ocean must be twice as large as the defending force."[370]

In April 1942, he conceded that "without our actual entrance into the war, Britain would probably have had to make a peace which would have amounted to a German victory."[371]

In October 1941, he took the view that repeal of the Neutrality Act would be an authorization of an undeclared naval war by allowing the arming of merchant vessels; the Senate voted for repeal 50-37.[372]

On the day after Pearl Harbor, he was told by Herbert Hoover that a European offensive would not be possible until 1945, would take two years, and involve two million casualties.[373]

As late as February 1948, he reaffirmed the view that "the story of our relations with Britain and Poland, the story of our relations

---

[369] New York Times, March 25, 1941.

[370] Radio Address, May 17, 1941, in 2 R. Taft, Works 242.

[371] RAT to Thomas Bowers, April 3, 1942, 2 R. Taft Works 343.

[372] G. Matthews, "Robert A. Taft, The Constitution, and American Foreign Policy, 1939-53," 17 J. Contemporary History 507 (1982).

[373] Statement on Neutrality Act, October 12, 1941, 2 R. Taft, Works 291; Hoover to RAT, December 8, 1941, R. Taft, Works 302 n.1

with Japan lend strong support to the idea that war was not completely distasteful to those who guided our national destiny."[374]

During the war, he joined others in criticizing the Morgenthau Plan, which "prolonged the war and made the Germans fight more bitterly." In September 1946, he criticized occupation policy: "we have fooled ourselves in the belief that by refusing to restore local freedom in Germany, Austria and Japan we could teach democratic principles by force. We have given countenance to the vengeful and impractical Morgenthau Plan while pretending to disown it."[375]

He urged President Truman to reconsider the "unconditional surrender" policy toward Japan. In 1948, he observed: "The policy of unconditional surrender left no one with whom we could even begin to negotiate and no possibility of setting up such a state, a vacuum in Europe into which Russia has been able to move." He blamed the implementation of the Morgenthau Plan in 1945-47 for the destruction of what would otherwise have been a market for Great Britain. He was unimpressed with the danger that Russia might have made a separate peace with Germany: "they would have to fight anyway to preserve the Russian national existence."[376]

In May 1943, he said, "I am unable to understand the mentality of those who criticize the deal with Darlan or the arrangements with Spain or any other step that will save American lives."[377]

Taft said of Lend-Lease that it "seems to contemplate an Anglo-American alliance perpetually running the world,"[378] a prospect he did not find attractive.[379]

---

[374] Lincoln Club of Denver, February 14, 1948, 3 R. Taft, Works 391.

[375] Ohio Republican Convention, September 11, 1946, 3 R. Taft, Works 171.

[376] Economic Club of Detroit, February 23, 1948, 3 R. Taft, Works 402.

[377] Address at Grove City College, May 22, 1943.

[378] Quoted in C. Dueck, Hard Line: The Republican Party and U.S. Foreign Policy Since World War II (Princeton: Princeton U., 2010), 63.

[379] Patterson 245ff.

In the late 1930s, Taft contemplated without complaint what he called "necessary socialist measures in Puerto Rico," reflecting his recognition of the dismal conditions there.[380] In 1943, he urged food relief for Puerto Rico and the regularization of shipments to it.[381] In a letter in April 1946, he urged autonomy for Puerto Rico except in the military and diplomatic field, and preferential entry for sugar into the American market. "Complete independence without tariff protection would nearly bring about starvation."[382] In 1947, in another letter, he observed: "highly educated nations do not increase in population as rapidly as those that are completely ignorant ... [There is] no remedy whatever [for Puerto Rico] except emigration and a general increase in the level of education."[383] He said that there "isn't the slightest evidence that we could make a success of our American raj [in Puerto Rico] where we have been for 45 years without relieving poverty or improving anyone's condition." While president, William Howard Taft, curbed autonomy on the premise that "we have gone somewhat too far in the extension of political power to them for their own good."[384] The recent Puerto Rican fiscal crisis gives force to this observation.

Subsequent history confirms this view; the island has especially high crime rates and underwent a debt crisis in 2016. Although the Roosevelt and Truman administrations, influenced by such New Dealers as Rexford Guy Tugwell, Harold Ickes, and Abe Fortas, took measures to aid Puerto Rico following the Ponce Massacre in 1934, the tax concessions to the pharmaceutical industry they had extended were subsequently withdrawn during the Reagan administration. During the Nixon, Ford, and Carter administrations,

---

[380] Patterson 260ff.

[381] New York Times, February 18 and 20, 1943.

[382] To John Taylor, April 17, 1946, 3 R. Taft, Works 135ff.

[383] 3 R. Taft, Works 255.

[384] Quoted in W. La Feber, The American Search for Opportunity, 1865-1913, 2 Cambridge History of American Foreign Relations 210.

mainland food stamp (1971, 1974, and 1977) and minimum wage (1974) rules were extended to Puerto Rico, with disastrous results.[385]

Taft's basic attitude toward a possible American imperium was stated in a speech in 1943 to the American Bar Association:

> "It was only after expiration of the naval treaties that our foreign policy became bankrupt ... the Philippines were regarded as indefensible and were to be made independent shortly. Potential power over other nations, however benevolent its purpose, leads inevitably to imperialism. We are so strongly democratic that we don't approve of ruthlessness even when necessary for success. We permit our colonial problems to be determined by domestic policies. We don't really want to boss other peoples, and so we don't do it well."[386]

Isaiah Berlin made similar observations about the last days of the British and French empires, ruthlessness having become unsustainable.

His proposition was that "other people simply do not like to be dominated." In a famous statement, he denied "[t]he manifest destiny of America to confer the benefits of the New Deal on every Hottentot."[387] In a speech in 1944, Taft criticized plans for the restoration of colonialism in Hong Kong and the Dutch East Indies.[388]

Taft regarded the proposals for Universal Military Training as proposals for a standing army, abhorrent to the framers of

---

[385] A. Castillo-Freeman and R. Freeman, "When the Minimum Wage Really Bites," in G. Borjas and R. Freeman (eds.), Immigration and the Workforce (Chicago: U. of Chicago, 1992), ch. 6.

[386] 2 R. Taft, Works 450ff.

[387] Patterson 289.

[388] "What Foreign Policy Will Promote Peace," June 8, 1944, 2 R. Taft, Works 552.

the Constitution, who feared a national police.[389] In July 1940, he opposed the Roosevelt administration's unsuccessful bill: "It may be necessary some day to have compulsory military training for all boys. But certainly not for girls. Some of the present ideas sound more like a glorified W.P.A. than any real training with military discipline."[390]

His wife, Martha Taft, was an ardent pacifist and a supporter of the Nye Committee.[391]

Throughout his career, in the words of William S. White, he displayed "a greater than average politician's distrust of the military."[392] In 1939, he observed in a Memorial Day speech that "we know that the romance has disappeared from modern warfare. The war to preserve democracy seems to have resulted in a tremendous increase in dictatorships.[393]

On April 14, 1940, Taft opposed draft legislation "because in my opinion no necessity exists requiring such tragic action."[394]

In 1943, during the war, he declared: "we must keep out of the internal affairs of other nations and we must learn to treat with tolerance conditions and ideologies which we may not understand ... there are dictatorships with which we cannot interfere. Any effort to impose democracy on the entire world would be impossible, and far more likely to cause war than to prevent it."[395]

---

[389] Patterson 70.

[390] "Taft Joins Fight on Training Bill; Declares Nation Should First Try a Voluntary System," New York Times, July 28, 1940.

[391] Patterson 200.

[392] W. White, *supra*, 46.

[393] Memorial Day Address, Arlington, VA, May 30, 1939, 2 R. Taft, Works 29.

[394] J. Gunther, Inside U.S.A. (New York: Harper, 1948), 434.

[395] Memorial Day Address, Arlington, Va., May 30, 1939, 2 R. Taft, Works 29.

"The Army has many advantages, a clean and regular life without great responsibility, an attraction in the very discipline and order which appeals to some men and offends others very greatly."[396] He maintained this attitude after the war, writing in 1948, "I do object to the continuation of the draft at all. I believe the Army should have started immediately after V-J day to build up a peacetime Army on a volunteer basis and not simply cut down on the size of the wartime Army."[397] More vehemently, he told Joseph Alsop, "I think that the conscription of men into the Army in peacetime is contrary to every principle of liberty and only justified by the need of preserving the nation. I believe we should occupy Germany or any part of it which may be necessary in order to prevent the building up of armament capable of being used in war."[398] The draft, in Taft's view, "cruelly cuts into a young man's career, deprives him of his freedom of choice, leaves him behind in the competitive struggle with his fellows, and turns society into a garrison state."[399]

In June 1940, Taft voted for increased military appropriations, but was one of five senators to oppose an excess profits tax.[400]

He voted against the confirmation of Henry Stimson as Secretary of War, in part because of Stimson's resistance while in the Hoover administration to Japanese ambitions in Manchuria, and against the draft, favoring instead higher military salaries to attract volunteers,[401] a policy later adopted by the Nixon administration.

---

[396] Quoted in F. Burd, *supra*, 269.

[397] RAT to Mrs. Robert Brookhaven, March 3, 1948, in RAT Papers, Library of Congress, Box 872, Folder "Demobilization 1946."

[398] RAT to Joseph Alsop, September 22, 1946, in RAT Papers, Library of Congress, Box 872, Folder "Draft 1946."

[399] Speech to Senate, August 14, 1940; RAT Papers, Library of Congress, Box 1255.

[400] Patterson 220.

[401] Patterson 240ff.

Notwithstanding this, he thought that "a profession of militarists ... leads inevitably to imperialism."[402]

In June 1940, after the fall of France, he declared: "I don't agree that there is any such crisis as justifies our giving the President authority to call out a large army. There is really no reason why Congress should adjourn. Congress has the legislative duty of determining the size of the army and also declaring war should that be necessary."[403]

At a rally in October 1940 he declared, somewhat prematurely: "The day of great conscript armies is over because they cannot stand against a smaller force trained to the accuracy of a machine."[404]

In May 1941 during the desperate hours of the Battle of the Atlantic, he declared in opposing Lend-Lease: "I am tired of those editors and statesmen who look on war as a game to be played with 130 million pawns. Convoys mean shooting, and shooting means war."[405] "As Taft had predicted, it was only a short time before the law led to an informal shooting war in the Atlantic."[406] "If [the president] can send troops to Iceland ... he can certainly send troops to Ireland ... to Scotland or England ... to Portugal."[407] "I detest every utterance of Mr. Hitler and every action of the German government in the last eight years, but we have no right to engage 130 million people in war, or send their sons or our own to war, except on

---

[402] Patterson 290ff.

[403] RAT to Frank Johnson, June 1940, in 2 R. Taft, Works 155.

[404] Milwaukee Rally, October 2, 1940, in 2 R. Taft, Works 179.

[405] Address, May 27, 1941, 2 R. Taft, Works 242.

[406] M. Radosh, Prophets on the Right: Profiles of Conservative Critics of American Globalism (New York: Simon and Schuster, 1975), 125.

[407] M. Radosh, Prophets on the Right: Profiles of Conservative Critics of American Globalism (New York: Simon and Schuster, 1975), 128.

the ground of their own interest."[408] "A nation is not an individual. It should not be moved by the same motives which properly inspire an individual. What may be brave and chivalrous for an individual to undertake may be completely selfish for a nation or a nation's leaders."[409]

Statements such as these led Isaiah Berlin to later state, apropos of the 1952 presidential campaign: "In a way, I preferred Taft [to Eisenhower] who was an honest, dry, narrow man. Still I suppose he would have led America to the same sort of disaster as Neville Chamberlain led England to, and he much resembled him."[410] Samuel Morison's conclusion about 1952 was that Taft "much more deserved to be President, for Taft had integrity, a deep knowledge of the governmental structure and political courage. As in the case of Henry Clay, courage lost Taft the nomination; he had made too many enemies, notably the labor union leaders, owing to the Taft-Hartley Act."[411]

As to 1940, this seems an accurate estimate, since a Taft presidency might have meant the fall of Britain. As for 1948, Judge Learned Hand prophesized: "If Taft were to get it, we should in the end pretty well back out of Europe, probably. It would not be a case of confessed scuttle, but you will find, I think, if that happened, that any push and drive of the present really promising program will disappear. Without energy of conviction and deep concern for the fate of Europe, we shall just peter out and leave it to roll on its own wheels to its own unbewept fate, congratulating ourselves that

---

[408] "Statement on Lend Lease," February 26, 1941, in 2 R. Taft, Works 229, quoted in C. Dueck, Hard Line: The Republican Party and U.S. Foreign Policy Since World War II (Princeton: Princeton U., 2010), 48.

[409] F. Burd, *supra*, 270.

[410] I. Berlin, Building: Letters 1960 to 1975 (H. Hardy and M. Pottle, eds., London: Chatto and Windus, 2013), 206.

[411] S. Morison, The Oxford History of the American People (New York: Oxford, 1965), 1076.

we have never been so corrupted by Communism."[412] As to 1952, it seems wildly inaccurate: a Taft presidency might have ended the Cold War in the era of Malenkov and his successors 45 years before 1989, by sparing the United States the intransigence of Eisenhower and John Foster Dulles.

His reaction to the Atlantic Charter was to declare that there was "no right to enter into any agreement" or to "disarm any nation by force" without an Act of Congress. Efforts to propagate the "Four Freedoms" he regarded as "an impossible policy and one which can only lead to the destruction of America." In 1941, he felt "confident that we can stand against the entire world and resist any effort to invade." "Nothing will end this war except an overwhelming delivery of airplanes from this country to England."[413]

In 1942, he declared, with complete accuracy, "you could forget the whole Office of Civilian Defense, save $108 million, and not lengthen the war by a single week."[414] Nearly ten years later, renewing his overestimation of airpower, he declared, "I would far rather spend money on the Air Force than on a program of bomb shelters and underground factories here at home."[415]

In 1946, he resisted a proposal that would have allowed President Truman to seize industries and draft workers; the proposal was rejected in the Senate by a vote of 70-13.

He voted against Lend-Lease, accurately forecasting that it amounted to a grant, the United States ultimately recovering about three cents on the dollar on British Lend-Lease and nine cents on the dollar on Russian Lend-Lease, but expressed a willingness to lend $2 billion to the then belligerent Allies, Britain, Canada, and

---

[412] Learned Hand to Bernard Berenson, February 17, 1952, in C. Jordan (ed.), Reason and Imagination: The Selected Correspondence of Learned Hand (New York: Oxford U., 2013), 308-09.

[413] RAT to HT, December 28, 1940, RAT Papers, Library of Congress, Box 25.

[414] Executive Club of Chicago, December 19, 1941, 2 R. Taft, Works 302.

[415] RAT to Clyde Meredith, July 25, 1951, in 4 R. Taft, Works 302.

Greece. "Lending war equipment is a good deal like lending chewing gum … you certainly don't want the old gum back."[416]

"The proposed credit did not represent a commitment of indefinite scope. It did not give the President the power as the Lend-Lease bill did to integrate the American economy with the British war effort. Nor would it tempt the chief executive to insure the safe delivery of goods to be lent or leased that might well lead to military involvement."[417]

Lend-Lease, he said, "combines all the faults of the worst New Deal legislation including unlimited delegation of authority and blank-check appropriations." "I don't see how we can long conduct such a war without being in the shooting end of the war as well as the service-of-supply end which this bill justifies.[418] "I am quite prepared to support without stint or qualification the wishes of the majority of the people declared by Congress, but I deny the right of the President to take us into war."[419]

He had no problem in identifying interventionists: "The war party is made up of the business community of the cities, the newspaper and magazine writers, the radio and movie commentators, the Communists, and the university intelligentsia."[420]

Even today, he is stigmatized by some who should know better as a "mercantilist and isolationist."[421] But Taft did not deny the theory of free trade, but was conscious, in a way that his interna-

---

[416] "Statement on Lend Lease," December 26, 1940, 2 R. Taft, Works 226.

[417] Congressional Record, 79th Congress, First Session, Part 5, May 29, 1941.

[418] N. Wapshott, President Roosevelt, the Isolationists and the Road to World War II (New York: Norton, 2015) 267; 87 Congressional Record, Part 1, 1588, 77th Congress, First Session.

[419] F. Burd, *supra*, 271.

[420] M. Radosh, Prophets on the Right: Profiles of Conservative Critics of American Globalism (New York: Simon and Schuster, 1975), 132.

[421] *E.g.*, J. Mathews, "What Trump Is Throwing Out the Window," New York Review of Books, February 9, 2017.

tionalist critics were not, of its possible adverse effect on high-wage economies, particularly those that do not improve their education systems. Taft's "isolationism" likewise was not doctrinaire; he was more responsible than any other Congressman for repeal of the Embargo provisions of the Neutrality Acts; he supported loans to Britain, Canada, and Greece, and ultimately supported Lend-Lease appropriations; he voted for the United Nations Charter; "After lend-lease was passed, I did vote for the first $7 billion in appropriations. I thought that all the troops needed would be obtained under a voluntary system."[422]

His suspicion of Bretton Woods rested in part on the perception, lost on many of his critics, that its provisions for early currency convertibility rested on American nationalism. He was doubtful about commitments in the Far East, a view in which he was vindicated by most historians: "If we are involved in protecting Singapore and the Philippines, much less aid and fewer airplanes are going to England."[423]

Anxious about favoritism and an aggrandizement of the power of the military brass, he objected to discretionary payments to dependents of soldiers over and above the congressional allowance.[424]

In a statement that resonates at the present day, he declared that "editors and columnists and professors who have never been in government or even a business seem to be more moved by war emotion than the plain average citizen who will have to do the fighting."[425]

He vehemently and successfully opposed proposals for the conscription of labor. "I am opposed to the Austin–Wadsworth bill

---

[422] RAT to Thomas Bowers, April 3, 1942, 2 R. Taft, Works 343.

[423] F. Burd, *supra*, 273.

[424] Allowances for the Dependents of Enlisted Men, May 1, 1942, 2 R. Taft, Works 356.

[425] F. Burd, *supra*, 274.

for drafting of every man and every woman in the United States."[426] In opposing Universal Military Training in 1944, he declared: "We are not fighting the war in order to turn the country into an armed camp. Furthermore, the President has already suggested that it ought to be combined with Civilian Conservation Corps (CCC) training. This would disrupt the whole educational system and give the government a chance to direct the education of all youths, a weapon which Hitler found so effective." He urged instead the provision of two three-month summer training periods to those who volunteer for them.

In February 1945, in response to complaints about the inadequate training of young draftees, he secured legislation[427] requiring six months' rather than three months' training for young draftees.[428] He also urged that officers' candidate schools be created for draftees with exceptional mental qualifications.[429]

In 1949, in response to the proclamation of the Truman Doctrine, he presciently expressed concern that "we might be prompted to go to war if Russia tries to force a Communist government on Cuba."[430] Earlier, he had observed: "I am a little troubled by this theory of exporting capital so that we own billions of dollars of property all over the world—haven't we experienced that this has created hard feelings? We have been absentee landlords and they are always accusing us of exploiting people. In Cuba, the fact that we have invested large sums of money ... is the principal argument of the tremendously growing communist movement there."[431]

---

[426] Ohio Federation of Republican Women's Organizations, May 7, 1943, 2 R. Taft, Works 432.

[427] 59 Stat. Part 1,166.

[428] Training of Draftees, February 27, 1945, 3 R. Taft. Papers 20.

[429] RAT to Isabel La Follette, February 27, 1945, in 3 R. Taft, Works 20.

[430] Patterson 370.

[431] New York Times, January 6, 1951.

"We can hardly object to the Russians continuing their dominance in Poland, Yugoslavia, Romania and Bulgaria [or] consolidation steps in Czechoslovakia—I know of no indication of Russian intentions to undertake military aggression beyond the sphere of influence that was originally assigned to them."[432]

This and other similar statements were jeered at as "remarkable" by the journalist John Gunther, writing in 1947,[433] the opening of the Soviet archives showed Taft to have been right.

In 1945, he voted for continuation of the draft, which passed by a majority of 78 to 20 in the Senate. He voted for continuation of the draft in 1950 and 1955.[434] He declared: "I have always been in favor of a conscription bill in time of war or in case war is threatened and voluntary methods failed."[435]

In March 1945, he opposed the Barkley bill, which would draft all men ages 18 to 45, describing it as "a system of forced labor in this country." He pointed out that military discipline could not be applied to workers living at home, and that employers would therefore be involuntarily afflicted with troublemakers.[436]

In opposing Universal Military Training, he said:

> "The plan to take a boy from home and subject him to complete government discipline is the most serious limitation on freedom that can be imagined ... An attempt to base a great permanent national policy on war emotion. My own opinion is that we need more initiative and more individual thinking with less discipline. If there is one place where morals will not be improved, it is in the vicinity of army camps. Military conscription is

---

[432] H. Berger, *supra*, 281.

[433] J. Gunther, Inside U.S.A. (London: Hamish Hamilton, 1947), 459.

[434] Patterson 385ff.

[435] W. White, *supra*, 151.

[436] Training of Draftees, *supra*.

essentially totalitarian, more the test of our whole philosophy than any other policy. We shall have fought to
abolish totalitarianism in the world, only to set it up in
the United States."

In a radio speech just after V-J Day in August 1945, he urged
discontinuation of conscription, abolition of the war manpower
regulations, tax reduction, and a coordinated program of public
works.[437]

The 80th Congress, over which he presided, despite being
derided by the Democrats as a "do-nothing" Congress, voted for
armed forces consolidation and creation of the Department of
Defense, foreign aid, extension of rent controls to 1949, civilian
control of atomic energy, extension of trade legislation, and the
draft. It rejected Universal Military Training, a minimum wage
increase, federal aid for housing and education, and a broadening of
social security. It also proposed the Twenty-Second Amendment,
limiting Presidents to two terms, of which a British commentator
wrote: "In view of subsequent abuses of Presidential power, this
revival of the two-term tradition looks a great deal wiser than it did
at the time ... a deliberate slur on the memory of Franklin Roosevelt." Taft's motives were purer than that, and as one contemplates
the consequences of the entrenchment of leaders such as Vladimir
Putin, Recep Erdoğan, and Benjamin Netanyahu, it clearly rests on
Lord Acton's accurate view that "power corrupts."[438]

"My quarrel is with those who wish to go all-out in Europe
who at the same time refuse to apply our grand program of strategy to the Far East. [In Korea] the administration refused to fight
with all the means at its disposal on the theory that we might incite

---

[437]   Radio Address, August 7, 1945, 3 R. Taft, Works 66.

[438]   H. Brogan, *The Penguin History of the United States* (Harmondsworth:
Penguin, 2d ed., 1999), 594.

Russia to start a third world war. But in Europe we have not hesitated to risk a third world war over and over again."[439]

He took a dim view of American paramilitary activities abroad: infiltration was "not in accordance with American tradition and is no part of a permanent foreign policy."[440] In August 1947, he expressed concern about American aid to the military in Latin America.[441]

In September 1947, he told Los Angeles County Republicans that "[d]rafting everyone into the army was even more totalitarian than the existing law—a dictator over every industry and every laboring man in the United States. We were determined that there not be fastened on this country permanent government price fixing, rent fixing, or wage fixing."[442]

Demobilization

Price controls were abolished in November 1946, after a prolonged fight. In August 1945, immediately after the end of the War, Truman, asserting that peace relieved labor shortages, suspended wage controls but not price controls. In November 1945, Taft charged that OPA "price fixing is based on the profits of the largest manufacturers so that many others are forced to sell at a loss ... we have profit control and not price control ... The Price Administrator cannot take the [wage] increase into account until after a test period of six months after the increase has been made. By the time the Price Administrator got around to granting an increase, if he

---

[439] RAT, quoted in J. Spanier, The Truman–McArthur Conflict and the Korean War (Cambridge: Harvard U., 1959), 141-42.

[440] Patterson 492.

[441] RAT to Grenville Clark, June 13, 1947, 3 R. Taft, Works 289.

[442] Address to Los Angeles Republicans, September 16, 1947, R. Taft, Works 320ff.

ever did, there would be a full year of operation on increased wages and no increase in price."[443]

On February 14, 1946, the Truman administration eliminated the six-month "test period" before allowed price increases. A bill to renew the OPA was heavily amended by Taft in the Senate by allowing manufacturers their 1941 profit levels and was vetoed by President Truman on June 29, 1946. On July 25, 1946, Truman signed a new price control bill containing a watered-down version of the Taft amendment which decontrolled meat prices until at least August 20. An attempt at re-imposing meat price controls resulted in shortages, prompting their abandonment on August 20, 1946. "OPA had lost its grip on the economy."[444]

His controversial and successful insistence on prompt de-mobilization after World War II echoed Hoover's views expressed after World War I: "many men came to believe that salvation lay in mass and group action … they have forgotten that permanent spiritual progress lies with the individual."[445]

Following the Republican victory in the Congressional elections, almost all controls were ended by the president on November 9, 1946.[446]

In February 1948 Taft told the Lincoln Club of Denver that the Army needed greater promotion by merit in place of the seniority system: "the greatest essential for defense is brains and organizing ability … an overlapping of roles and missions has been deliberately permitted by the Secretary of National Defense." He criticized Navy-Air Force rivalry over control of aviation.

He also made a proposal for creation of an intelligence reserve, in place of Universal Military Training, which would have served

---

[443] Commercial and Financial Chronicle, December 13, 1945, quoted in B. Bernstein and A. Madhouse, *supra*, 59ff.

[444] W. Manchester, *supra*, 489.

[445] H. Hoover, American Individualism (New York: Doubleday, 1922), 30-31.

[446] B. Bernstein and A. Madhouse, *supra*, 61-85.

the United States well in places like Korea, Vietnam, Iraq, and Afghanistan where it had few men with foreign language competence. He called for a "completely efficient and coldly practical intelligence service [which would] assist young Americans to undertake studies which would fit them for an intelligence reserve, rather than to spend ten times that amount of money giving them infantry training on an obsolete model ... reserve officers' scholarships to maintain necessary but unprofitable educational facilities [for] technical and intelligence skills which are sorely needed." Taft referred as a model to the Navy School of Oriental Languages established in December 1940. Recent fitful efforts by the State and Defense Departments to stimulate foreign language study in colleges are no substitute for this proposal.

In August 1948, he assured a correspondent that he would "undermine general propaganda for militarization."[447] In successfully limiting the scope of the Defense Production Act adopted in response to the Korean War, he declared: "[The President] wants the right to license every business in the United States and to revoke such licenses [and] have the government go into any business it wants to go into ... the power to grant subsidies ... I don't favor Congress granting any powers that aren't needed for immediate use ... once you let prices go up, it is almost impossible except in a few cases to roll them back without tremendous injustice."[448]

Congress refused to give the President rollback authority.

During the Korean War, he called for "a Congress which will investigate the vast government[449] expenditures for the Armed Forces, what has happened to the vast sums of money already spent."[450] He took the view that "the only indispensable things were to protect American liberty [from] the nationalization of all

---

[447] RAT to Robert Floss, August 10, 1948, 3 R. Taft, Works 457.

[448] Defense Production Act, July 2, 1951, in 4 R. Taft, Works 294.

[449] RAT to Ferdinand Mayer, August 6, 1952, in 4 R. Taft, Works 409.

[450] W. White, *supra*, 98.

industry and all capital and all labor … a Socialist dictatorship."[451] He favored "military readiness based almost wholly on the sea and air arms … it was to him a terrible thing to vote to put a boy upon a muddy field of fire."[452]

In a Senate speech in early 1951, he conclusively renounced what was left of his prewar isolationism: "Taft announced to his colleagues that he was opposed to Truman's dispatch of troops [to Europe] presently, but he refused to rule out the future stationing of U.S. forces in Europe. More importantly, however, Taft rejected Herbert Hoover's advice that the U.S. withdraw to the Western Hemisphere. Instead, he fully accepted the extension of foreign aid to America's allies and declared that he was ready to go to war if Russia attacked any member of the NATO alliance. As to foreign aid, he thought that "assistance to foreign nations justified by the desirability of creating a friendly feeling for the United States among other peoples and preventing the development of hostile alliances, which, if stimulated by poverty and hardship, may lead to the development of aggressive military dictators."[453]

In the course of his speech, the Ohio Republican also asserted that "although he did not object in principle to sending more U.S. troops to Europe, he believed that any such action required Congressional approval."[454]

He opposed an alliance committing American military aid in advance, believing that it "would inevitably produce a counter-alliance that would make war more likely,"[455] but declared in July 1949

---

[451] W. White 150.

[452] W. White 155.

[453] RAT, "An Alliance for Peace," New York Times Magazine, February 6, 1944, 8.

[454] J. Malsberger, From Obstruction to Moderation: The Transformation of Senate Conservatism, 1938-52 (Selinsgrove, PA: Susquehanna U. Press, 1999), 239. *See also* 2 G. Best, Herbert Hoover: The Post-Presidential Years, 1933-64 (Stanford: Hoover Institution, 1983), 345.

[455] F. Burd, *supra*, 290.

that "I favor the extension of the Monroe Doctrine under present conditions to Western Europe." A similar suggestion as to Britain alone had been made by the American diplomat Lewis Einstein as long ago as 1913.

In 1952, he condemned President Truman's seizure of the steel industry, a position in which he was vindicated by the Supreme Court decision in *Youngstown v. Sawyer*.[456] He had previously joined with the liberal Democrat Claude Pepper, a frequent adversary, in filibustering a proposal of President Truman to seize the railroads to avert a strike in 1946.[457] Allowing the seizure, he said, would "make it possible for any president to make himself a dictator—no statutory authority. There is no undefined residuum of power which the President can exercise because it seems to him to be in the public interest."[458]

Drafting strikers offends "not only the Constitution, but every basic principle for which the American Republic was established. Strikes cannot be prohibited without interfering with the basic freedom essential to our form of government."[459]

During his campaign against Eisenhower for the 1952 Republican nomination, he happily quoted from a statement the general had made on June 3, 1952: "Don't, in hysteria and bewilderment and fear, don't vote sums when you are frightened." He was worried that Eisenhower would be a spender: "no one can plan to spend so many billions abroad without yielding to very much the same spending instinct here at home."

With the advent of the Eisenhower administration, when his influence was at its maximum, he successfully pressed for a new set of Joint Chiefs committed to massive deterrence in place of those

---

[456] 343 U.S. 579 (1952).

[457] F. Burd, *supra*, 223, citing 93 Congressional Record, 80th Congress 4886 (1946).

[458] Seizure of Steel Industry, April 15, 1952, 4 R. Taft, Works 368.

[459] W. Manchester, *supra*, 493-94.

who conducted the Korean War, and secured the appointment of Admiral Radford and others.[460]

The Cold War and Economic Controls

He urged the immediate end of wage and price controls. Wage controls were ended on February 6, price controls were allowed to expire on April 30, and rent controls were extended, but only until October 30 rather than July 1 as urged by Taft.[461] He was instrumental in striking from an Eisenhower administration bill, by a Senate vote of 45 to 41, a provision for standby wage and price freezes, which he characterized as "absolutely contrary to the whole theory of a free economy … an acceptance of the philosophy of the Truman Administration and of socialism," which "ought not be put in a Republican bill."[462] He successfully urged a tight lid on foreign aid and defense spending, and heavy reliance on atomic airpower. He opposed universal military training, securing in its place a two-year draft with many exemptions, and supported air force expansion from 55 groups to 70.[463]

In an article written before the 1948 election he charged that President Truman "opposed a seventy-group air force because the brass hats in the Army and Navy refused to recognize the fact that modern war will be decided in the air."[464]

He fought off House Republicans who wanted drastic reductions in taxes, but was disappointed by the Eisenhower

---

[460] W. White, *supra*, 252.

[461] RAT to Dwight Eisenhower, January 8, 1953; 4 R. Taft Papers 449.

[462] "Senate, 45-41, Bars Stand-By Controls," New York Times, May 20, 1953.

[463] S. Hartmann, Truman and the 80th Congress (Columbia: U. of Missouri, 1971), 169.

[464] "The Case Against President Truman," Saturday Evening Post, 1948, in RAT Papers, Library of Congress, Box 736.

administration's failure to reduce spending as much as he hoped. An Eisenhower aide nonetheless quoted the president as saying: "I think I'm going to get along well with Taft and if things work out the way I hope, Taft might be available to us as a candidate for the top job in 1956."[465]

In seeking reductions in defense spending, he urged "complete reconsideration by the best military people who are not committed … why, for example, should the U.S. be paying for a land army in Germany when no one expected to fight a land war there?" Eisenhower's biographer Stephen Ambrose noted that "Eisenhower could not hear anyone who was advocating less spending on national defense than he was partly because the clamor from the other side demanding more spending on the military was so much louder, partly because Eisenhower was who he was." Of Taft's vehemence on this question, Eisenhower observed: "I do not see how he can possibly expect to influence people when he has no more control over his temper [than that]."[466]

After his death, with the advent of the Kennedy administration with its stress on conventional weapons, graduated response, and a fictitious "missile gap," defense spending exploded. He represented, it has been said, "an older tradition of small-town, Midwestern, conservative nonintervention whose passing was not altogether beneficial to the United States."[467]

A sympathetic critic of his foreign policy views observed: "He misjudged Hitler's intentions. He misunderstood the impact of air power. He didn't understand the spirit of total war. He (along with others) did not anticipate Communist postwar successes. He was concerned with the underlying and long-term implications of law

---

[465] E. Slater, The Ike I Knew (Privately published, 1980), quoted in 2 S. Ambrose, Eisenhower.

[466] 2 S. Ambrose, Eisenhower (New York: Simon and Schuster, 1984), 86-87, quoting Eisenhower's diary for May 1, 1953.

[467] C. Dueck, Hard Line: The Republican Party and U.S. Foreign Policy Since World War II (Princeton: Princeton U., 2010), 84.

and the U.N. when short-term foreign policy questions were dominant. He may have been unduly worried over Russian fears. He applied the questionable theory that armaments lead to war ... It is understandable that his judgment was questioned."[468]

However, in the perspective of an additional 45 years, Taft was not "unduly worried over Russian fears." The creation of NATO, which he criticized, was followed, as he forecasted, by creation of the Warsaw pact. Opportunities for disengagement were forsworn by the Western powers, and the division into rigid blocs fostered the Soviet interventions in Hungary in 1956 and in Czechoslovakia in 1968.

Robert Taft's attitude toward international relations was significantly shaped by his experience working under Herbert Hoover in the Food Administration in the aftermath of World War I. (For his services, he was decorated by the Polish, Finnish, and Belgian governments.) He deplored the fact that no hearing was given to the Germans in connection with the Versailles peace settlement, and the secrecy of the proceedings. He disliked the continuance of the British blockade after the armistice (it was not lifted until March 1919), and thought that many of the territorial disputes should have been judicially settled according to declared principles rather than determined at Paris. His attitude toward aid to Britain both before and after World War II was founded in part on a conviction that the British had brought their troubles on themselves. In his early career, he supported establishment of a League of Nations, which should be restricted to the sole function of preventing war, without intervention in internal governance.[469]

"I believe [Wilson] would accept almost anything if it was called a League of Nations, whether it had any force in it or not. I am not convinced that an international police force or executive would work, but a League without an agreement to use force, military and

---

[468] F. Burd, *supra*, 329.

[469] Patterson, 79-80.

economic, against anyone who makes an aggressive war, would be worse than useless."[470]

He adhered to the view that "[t]here is no principle of subjection to the Executive in foreign policy."[471]

In 1939, he declared: "we cannot well impose embargoes to starve them [Germany, Italy, and Japan] into submission. We cannot tell them what form of government they can have, unless we are prepared to join a world conflict. No nation can take methods short of war unless it is prepared to carry through the war to which such measures inevitably lead."[472] This proposition is lost on today's sponsors of economic sanctions on Cuba, North Korea, Iran, Syria, Russia, and Venezuela.

In 1941, he decried the idea of "a right and duty to interfere in foreign wars because of the character of government adopted by some of the belligerents. [This view] was not based on sentiment or any ostrich isolationism. Europe's quarrels are everlasting. There is a welter of races. National animosities are traditional and bitter. Only in this nation have they been laid aside."[473] He could not say that today, when both American political parties exploit "identity politics."

In April 1941, he declared: "we should not undertake to defend the ideals of democracy in foreign countries ... no one has ever suggested before that a single nation should range over the world like a knight-errant, protect ideals of democracy and good faith, and tilt, like Don Quixote, against the windmills of fascism."[474] "War is

---

[470] RAT to WHT, January 5, 1919, 1 R. Taft, Works, 12ff.

[471] Patterson 197.

[472] Memorial Day Speech, Arlington, May 30, 1939, in 2 R. Taft, Works 37.

[473] RAT, "Our Foreign Policy," 6 Vital Speeches 348 (March 1940), Address to the National Republican Club, New York Times, March 3, 1940.

[474] Patterson 198, citing Congressional Record, January 2, 1939, A253.

nothing but horror and mechanical destruction. It leaves the victor as exhausted as the vanquished."[475]

He feared the nationalization of industry, capital, and labor.

In 1942, he wrote: "I am also inclined to favor a division of the world into economic regions, each to be as self-sufficient as possible."[476]

The United Nations, in his view, should be an association of sovereign nations, established only after territorial disputes were resolved. "A crusade by its very nature is an act of aggression." In 1943, he opposed the Ball–Burton–Hatch–Hill ("2B-2H") world government resolution, believing it to be premature until victory was achieved.[477] In a radio address in 1943, he urged withdrawal of the President's authority to devalue the currency, and opposed an international stabilization fund.[478]

In 1943 at Cincinnati he noted that "[i]t may be possible to establish customs unions establishing free trade among certain groups of nations," but that in any all-encompassing organization "any question regarding our standard of wages we would be out-voted 10 to 1 under any conceivable plan of representation."[479]

The recent proliferation of regional, as distinct from world-wide, trade treaties in part vindicates his view. He did not oppose a United Nations organization: "I see no loss of sovereignty in a treaty binding us to send our armed forces abroad on the finding of an international body. Being sovereign, we could refuse to keep our promises. Being Americans, we would not refuse." In a speech to the American Bar Association in 1943, he espoused Taftian legalism: "Any policy based primarily on alliances is an abandonment of the

---

[475] Patterson 199.

[476] RAT to Robert Vanderhoof, May 6, 1942, 2 R. Taft, Works 369.

[477] 2 R. Taft, Works 421, April 7, 1943.

[478] Radio Address, April 19, 1943, 2 R. Taft, Works 426.

[479] Address at Cincinnati City Hall, May 22, 1943, in 2 R. Taft, Works 440ff.

ideals on which the American Republic was founded. It substitutes force for a rule of law ... Interference in domestic policies would be more likely to make war than to prevent it." He took the view that "[t]he old balance of power policy was not a successful insurer of peace."[480]

He initially supported the UN Charter, the Connally Resolution, and the Import-Export Bank, as well as UNICEF,[481] but opposed the World Bank, predicting defaults followed by a depression, as well as the International Monetary Fund, by reason of skepticism about foreign aid generally: "I see no reason why we should entrust our money to a board controlled by our debtors ... No people can make over another people."[482]

He had misgivings about the UN, centering chiefly on the fact that the American delegate was exclusively under presidential control and could commit the United States without congressional authorization; he also did not like the veto, viewing it as inconsistent with his ideas about the rule of law, and considered that the Security Council had too much power to impose economic sanctions. These misgivings (except for those about the veto) were not misplaced; President Truman entered the Korean War with UN authority but without formal Congressional support, and both the UN and United States have been promiscuous in their use of essentially destructive economic sanctions, in fulfillment of the "don't just stand there, do something" syndrome.[483]

---

[480] "What Foreign Policy Will Promote Peace?," June 8, 1944, 2 R. Taft, Works 552.

[481] RAT to Kenneth McKellar, August 28, 1950, 4 R. Taft, Works 195.

[482] Congressional Record, July 12, 1945, 7441.

[483] RAT to Richard Nielsen, January 30, 1946, 3 R. Taft, Works 124.

"That Taft had a constitutional point was illustrated in 1950 over the Korean War when only President Truman had the power to direct the U.S. delegates at the U.N."[484]

He pointed out that the U.S. act implementing the UN Charter authorized American troops only pursuant to an agreement with the Security Council "which shall be subject to the approval of the Congress by an appropriate Act or Joint Resolution."[485]

On June 28, 1950, he declared: "I would say that there is no authority to use armed forces in support of the United Nations in the absence of some previous action by Congress dealing with the subject and outlining the general circumstances and the amount of the forces that can be used."[486] Later, the historian Arthur Schlesinger Jr. was to endorse Taft's position: "When Senator Robert A. Taft proposed a joint resolution sanctioning military intervention. Truman was persuaded by Dean Acheson, his Secretary of State and an eminent lawyer, that congressional approval was unnecessary. This idea of inherent presidential power to send troops into combat was unwisely defended at the time by some historians, including this one. In its acquiescence, Congress surrendered the war-making power to the executive and has never reclaimed it since."[487] "If the President can intervene in Korea without Congressional approval," Taft said at the time, "he can go to war in Malaya or Indonesia or Iran or South America."[488] Even more prophetically, Taft observed,

---

[484]   G. Matthews, "Robert A. Taft, the Constitution, and American Foreign Policy, 1939-53," 17 J. Contemporary History 507 (1982).

[485]   "Great Debate," Speech in the U. S. Senate, January 5, 1951, in 4 R. Taft, Works 230ff.

[486]   Senate Speech, June 28, 1950, RAT Papers, Library of Congress, Box 256.

[487]   A. Schlesinger, The Cycles of American History (Boston: Houghton Mifflin, 1986), 280.

[488]   J. Doenecke, Not to the Swift: The Old Isolationists in the Cold War Era (Lewisburg: Bucknell U., 1979), 191.

Taft and Vandenburg

the president could try to "establish a vast Garden of Eden in the Kingdom of Iraq."[489]

He approved of two UN Charter modifications secured by his Republican colleague Senator Arthur Vandenberg: those providing for the codification of international law (the all-but-forgotten Article 13 giving rise to the General Assembly's recently revived International Law Commission) and for freedom of debate in the General Assembly.[490]

"The open forum provided for the discussion of public affairs is a useful thing in spite of the platform which it gives the Communists to state their case."[491]

He later described the General Assembly as "a town meeting of the world in which disputes can be brought into the open and

---

[489] R. Taft, A Foreign Policy for Americans, *supra*, 33.

[490] Speech to the Economic Club of Detroit, February 23, 1948, in 3 R. Taft, Works 400.

[491] RAT to George Rosenfeld, May 6, 1952, in 4 R. Taft, Works 375.

peaceful means urged to prevent war,"[492] sharing Churchill's view of it as a place where the small birds can sing.

The UN "does have many methods by which, through peaceful persuasion, it can defer or prevent war."[493]

He criticized the Nuremberg trials as ex post facto in nature and as using "the forms of justice to carry out a pre-determined policy ... the spirit of vengeance—a blot on the American record which we shall long regret."[494] "I had no objection to the Allied governments even without a trial, shutting these men up for the rest of their lives as a matter of policy and on the ground that if free they might stir up another war. That was the basis for the imprisonment of Napoleon."[495] "Today the [Nuremberg] court regards itself in many respects as the maker of policy—no maker of policy can command respect for impartial administration of justice ... The trial of the vanquished by the victors cannot be impartial, no matter how it is hedged about with the forms of justice ... Our whole attitude in the world for a year after V-E Day, including the use of the Atomic bomb at Hiroshima and Nagasaki seems to me a departure from the principles of fair and equal treatment which has made America respected throughout the world before the Second World War. Today we are cordially hated in many countries. We should view the future with more hope if even our enemies believed that we have treated them justly in trials, in the provision of relief aid, and in the fair disposal of territory."[496]

In his notes for the speech he expressed the view that "[t]he future nationalist leader is not likely to abandon a proposed aggressive war with all that it means for him in the immediate future because in the distant future if he fails and if he is caught he may

---

[492] "Taft Won't Budge in His Korean Stand," New York Times, June 2, 1953.

[493] W. White, The Taft Story (New York: Harper, 1954), 135.

[494] Patterson 328.

[495] RAT to Westbrook Pegler, October 14, 1946 in 3 R. Taft, Works 215.

[496] Speech at Kenyon College, October 5, 1946, in 3 R. Taft, Works 192.

be hanged. Human nature just doesn't work that simply."[497] He most assuredly would not have been a supporter of the ineffective International Criminal Court at The Hague.

He was not enchanted by Bernard Baruch's editing of the Acheson-Lilienthal plan for nuclear disarmament: "Of course, I think that Mr. Baruch is greatly over-rated. It is easy to propose great theoretical plans depending on all kinds of controls if you know that no one can possibly try them under conditions in the world today."[498]

Later, after supporting the Rio Pact for the Americas in 1947, he opposed the creation of NATO: "we are ringing them [the Soviets] about with armies for the purpose of taking aggressive action when the time comes. War becomes an instrument of public policy rather than its last resort." He sought to eliminate any provision for arms aid and was willing to support the treaty as a guarantee treaty, a security umbrella like the Monroe Doctrine (which the diplomat Lewis Einstein once proposed be extended to Great Britain), but was doubtful about its automatic involvement of the United States in disputes generated by other nations.[499] Taft's response to proposals for creation of NATO was to declare that "we seem to be stepping from the welfare state into the garrison state."[500] "Taft thought that NATO was a provocation of Russia, that the inclusion of Portugal made a sham of its pretense to defend democracy and that it would become a constricting millstone for decades."[501]

"He cannot send troops abroad if the sending of such troops amounts to the making of war ... The President cannot commit

---

[497] RAT Papers, Library of Congress, Box 862, Folder "War Crimes Trials (Nuremberg) 1946-48."

[498] RAT to Kendall Gillett, January 7, 1948, in 3 R. Taft, Works 383.

[499] J. Doenecke, Not to the Swift: The Old Isolationists in the Cold War Era (Lewisburg: Bucknell U., 1979).

[500] Patterson 480.

[501] J. and G. Kolko, The Limits of Power (New York: Harper, 1972), 500.

American troops in peace to an international army."[502] The recent call by Turkey for NATO support after it shot down a Russian airliner lends credence to his view. When the effort to eliminate arms aid failed, 74-21, he was one of 13 Senators to vote against the treaty. In 1951, he urged that "by reasonable alliance with Britain, France, Holland, Australia and Canada, the control of sea and air can establish a power which can never be challenged by Russia."[503]

His oft-stated premise was that "effective aerial attack cannot be made over any considerable distance."[504]

After the war, he was one of 18 Republicans to oppose the British loan, which he thought unnecessary, and which he erroneously thought would never be paid (it was paid, though in depreciated dollars).[505] He took the view that "the British loan has been used largely to maintain a higher standard of living in England than was absolutely necessary and ... machinery and other goods for rehabilitation have been neglected."[506] This corresponded to the view later expressed by the "revisionist" British historian John Charmley. "He indicated that he would support a reduced bill to finance British relief but would not endorse a program intended to subsidize what he considered to be the delusion of fully convertible, multilateral, trade." He opposed the Bretton Woods agreement on the same reasoning.[507]

---

[502] Senate Speech, March 8, 1951, in RAT Papers, Library of Congress, Box 1287, Folder "Senate Speech, March 8, 1951."

[503] "Great Debate," Speech in the U.S. Senate, January 5, 1951, in 4 R. Taft, Works 230ff.

[504] RAT, "Our Foreign Policy," 6 Vital Speeches 348 (March 1940), Address to the National Republican Club, New York Times, March 3, 1940.

[505] RAT to R. Blessing, April 25, 1946, 3 R. Taft, Works 146.

[506] RAT to Hoover, July 11, 1947, 3 R. Taft, Works 301.

[507] R. Foreland, The Truman Doctrine and the Origins of McCarthyism (New York: N.Y.U. Press, 1970), 62-63.

Unlike Churchill, he did not look forward to "an Anglo-American alliance perpetually ruling the world."[508]

He supported American aid to Greece after the war, although he saw no threat of Russian interference, thought aid would be ineffective, and questioned the fairness of Greek elections. "I do not regard this as a commitment to any similar policy in any other section of the world."[509] "Neither do I fully understand yet what the implications of this policy are in Germany, China and South America."[510] "I don't like the Greek–Turkish proposition but I do recognize that perhaps we should maintain the status quo until we can reach some peace accommodation with Russia."[511]

He was unenthusiastic about the Marshall Plan, though favoring some foreign aid. He was afraid that it would artificially stimulate demand for American exports, creating a fool's paradise for the American economy. "No Marshall Plan benefits are worth the return of price controls."[512]

His amendment to reduce the first year of Marshall Plan aid from $5.3 to $4 billion failed by a vote of 56 to 31 with half of the Senate Republicans voting against it. Later, he denied the urgency of aid: "People don't completely collapse, they go on living anyway."[513] He was unalarmed by the communist coup in Czechoslovakia in March of 1948.[514]

---

[508] R. Radosh, Prophets on the Right (New York: Simon and Schuster, 1975), 128.

[509] Patterson 370ff.

[510] Greece and Turkey, March 12, 1947, 3 R. Taft, Works 260.

[511] D. McCoy, The Presidency of Harry S Truman (Lawrence: U. Press of Kansas, 1984), 122.

[512] RAT, Address to the Ohio Society, November 10, 1947, Congressional Record, A4252.

[513] J. Doenecke, supra, 115ff.

[514] Congressional Record, March 12, 1948, 2643-44.

He correctly perceived that Russia was gravely damaged by the war: "I have never given the same importance to the Russian military position as have many other Americans ... gradually communism itself will be driven back into the borders of Russia and liberty will again become the ideal which it was in the nineteenth century."[515]

He thought that the Russians would not employ their own troops, as distinct from satellites and foreign political parties, against the West.[516] The brief opening of the Soviet archives after 1989 gave support to this view.[517] Nonetheless, he concurred in one object of Marshall Plan policy: "There should be a European confederation, certainly economic and if possible political."[518]

Like Senator Vandenburg, he did not criticize the Italian and Balkan peace treaties, which allowed "some basis other than military occupation."[519]

He was initially doubtful about the appointment of General Lucius Clay rather than a civilian administrator under the State Department, since "military men are too much inclined to treat war as in the regular course of business."[520] Clay had to be restrained by civilians after the start of the Russian Berlin blockade.

The French multi-party system greatly weakened France; in Germany "the U.S. pays the reparations by increased food shipments."[521]

---

[515] Patterson 475, citing Taft to A.J. Muste, March 8, 1951.

[516] RAT, "Peace and Politics," 25 American Bar Association Journal 139 (1943). J. Doenecke, Not to the Swift: The Old Isolationists in the Cold War Era (Lewisburg: Bucknell U., 1979), 191ff.

[517] J. Haslam, Russia's Cold War (New Haven: Yale U., 2012).

[518] RAT to Dorothy Thompson, May 31, 1947, 3 R. Taft, Works 285.

[519] RAT to Julia Brambilla, July 16, 1947.

[520] RAT to M. Cooper Judy, January 26, 1948, 3 R. Taft, Works 373.

[521] Statement on European Trip, December 1948, 3 R. Taft, Works 471.

In March 1949, he had not made up his mind about NATO but urged that U.S. troops be kept away from the Norwegian–Soviet border.[522]

"I think the deliberate arming of other nations by one great nation is a direct violation of the spirit of the U.N. Charter." "Every armament race in history has finally ended in war." Except for Greece and Turkey, "there won't be any great amount of military aid for anyone else at this session of Congress."[523]

He was one of 13 Senators to vote against ratification of the NATO treaty, saying that it "necessarily divides the world into two armed camps" and would "promote war in the world rather than peace. All kinds of circumstances may arise which will make our obligation most inconvenient. The government of one of these nations may be taken over by the Communist Party of that nation." "They may well decide that if war is the certain result, that war might better occur now rather than after the arming of Europe is completed." Earlier, he had said "if we assume a special position in Greece and Turkey, we can hardly object to the Russians continuing their domination in Poland, Yugoslavia, Romania and Bulgaria."[524] His central objection to the Treaty was that, if un-amended, it would allow the U.S. delegate to the UN to commit American troops without Congressional approval.

In his relation to Senate Republicans in this period, he was said by Hans Morgenthau to be part of "a vacillating center, which hearkened back to isolationism but would almost, but not quite, admit that isolationism was beyond the reach of a rational foreign policy. Senator Robert Taft was the most eminent spokesman for this group."[525]

---

[522] Speech on NATO, March 30, 1949, 4 R. Taft, Works 58.

[523] RAT to Henry Hazlitt, April 24, 1949, 4 R. Taft, Works 67; Radio Address on NATO, July 24, 1949.

[524] C. Dueck, Hard Line: The Republican Party and U.S. Foreign Policy Since World War II (Princeton: Princeton U., 2010), 73.

[525] H. Morgenthau, Truth and Power (London: Pall Mall, 1970), 90.

In December 1950, he summarized his attitude: "I never felt the Nazis were a threat to us, particularly after they became involved in a war with Russia.... With extended air power and the atom bomb, it is possible for the Russians to attack us. I doubt the practicability of defending Europe. However we can hardly be isolationists any more, since the Second World War involved us in the occupation of both Germany and Japan."[526]

In December 1950, he wrote: "I believe that the U.S. should go to war with Russia if it undertakes to attack Western Europe." The Germans should be allowed to re-arm "with such limitations as may be necessary to protect the French."[527]

It has been observed that "Taft's resolution failed overwhelmingly [opposing permanent stationing in Europe]. As subsequent events would reveal, however, NSC-68 was in place and the symmetrical rather than asymmetrical [favoring Europe] concept would prevail in American defense policy."[528]

It has been observed that Truman's aides "with good reason doubted Taft's ability to become the new Vandenberg on matters of foreign policy. In addition, there was the Ohioan's contempt for Dean Acheson. The administration was, therefore, unwilling to try out the Senate's Republican leader."[529]

In January 1951, in connection with the so-called Great Debate in the Senate, he said: "no one ever maintained that [the Atlantic Pact] committed us to send more American troops to Europe ... I do not see any conclusive evidence that [the Russians] expect to start a war with the United States." "Control over the air over Germany and Japan was the decisive factor in the winning of the war ... Whether war can be ended by air power alone may be

---

[526] RAT to Titus Crasto, November 24, 1950.

[527] RAT to Wilhelm Taft, December 14, 1950, 4 R. Taft, Works 224.

[528] R. Woods, Fulbright: A Biography (Cambridge: Cambridge U., 1995), 166.

[529] D. McCoy, The Presidency of Harry S Truman (Lawrence: U. Press of Kansas, 1984), 122ff.

open to question ... Now we are talking about providing 25 percent of all the foot soldiers involved in the European defense army. The [Russians] may even make a Dunkirk impossible [by wrecking ports]."[530] "No matter how defensive an alliance may be, if it carries the obligation to arm it means the building up of competitive offensive armaments ... the more [the Europeans] can find arms to undertake action which may be considered aggression in the colonies."[531]

In March of 1951 he wrote A.J. Muste to express views that were far more astute than those of the U.S. intelligence services, then or later: "I think that Russia is much weaker today than most people think, that it is having great difficulty with its satellite countries and that it is having great difficulty with its transportation and manufacturing programs."[532]

In a radio address in June of 1952, he emphasized the extent to which Western army and air forces were outnumbered in Europe. His ultimate warning was not heeded, leading to the Hungarian tragedy in 1956: "It would be criminal to attempt today to foment national revolts in Russia and her satellite countries since that would produce only the murder of the anti-Communists by the Communist secret police."[533]

Like George Kennan, he urged a form of disengagement in Europe: Churchill and the French "would be willing to assume that zone of influence gladly ... in return for some cut in armaments, freer trade, and a promise to behave in the future."[534]

The historian John Lewis Gaddis, generally an adherent of the "Washington Consensus," fairly summarized Taft's views: "the first principle of military strategy is not to fight on the enemy's chosen

---

[530] "Great Debate" Speech in the U.S. Senate, January 5, 1951.

[531] H. Berger, *supra*, 184-85.

[532] RAT to A.J. Muste, March 8, 1951, 4 R. Taft, Works 266.

[533] Radio Address on Foreign Policy, June 1, 1952, 4 R. Taft, Works 379.

[534] W. White, The Taft Story (New York: Harper, 1954), 132ff.

battlefield where he has his greatest strength." No nation could "be constantly prepared to undertake a full-scale war at any moment and still hope to maintain any of the other purposes for which nations are founded." "An unwise and overambitious foreign policy, and particularly the effort to do more than we are able to do, is the one thing which might in the end destroy our armies and prove a real threat to the liberty of the people of the United States."[535]

In 1948, he ruefully observed to Felix Morley "a man who is against war when everyone else is for it becomes very unpopular indeed."[536] It was said that "it was the unique contribution of Taft to have maintained a critical position in an era when criticism of U.S. foreign policy had been all but abandoned."[537] But it also was said that "warnings about the limits of American power might by themselves seem prophetic in post-Vietnam America; they were hardly in keeping with the relative world position of the United States after World War II."[538]

Taft had questioned the wisdom of economic sanctions that might force the Japanese to exert pressure on the Philippines.[539] There is no doubt that he agreed with Herbert Hoover's observation on the day after Pearl Harbor: "I have felt that this constant sticking of pins into rattlesnakes would produce just such a result … if this had not been done, Japan, from her internal exhaustion, would have totally collapsed without the loss of a single American life."[540] Both George Kennan and his frequent correspondent the historian John Lukacs regarded the American war with Japan as an unnecessary and avoidable war.

---

[535] J. Gaddis, Strategies of Containment (New York: Oxford U., 1982), 118-20.

[536] RAT to F. Morley, March 23, 1948, quoted in R. Radosh, *supra*, 157ff.

[537] R. Radosh, *supra*, 144.

[538] D. Reinhard, *supra*, 111.

[539] Patterson 246.

[540] Hoover to RAT, December 8, 1941, in 2 R. Taft, Works 302 n.1.

On December 19, 1941, he told the Executive Club of Chicago: "We might well investigate whether Secretary Hull told Secretary Knox the contents of the note which he had submitted to the Japanese Government ten days before requiring them to withdraw from China and which was not published until after the attack on Hawaii."[541]

"By 1973, a prominent historian could write (with possible exaggeration) that the majority of his colleagues probably viewed the war with Japan as one that could have been avoided."[542]

Taft referred to Justice Holmes' decision in *Frowerk v. United States*[543]: "we do not lose our right to condemn either measures or men because the country is at war."

In the spring of 1945 he suggested modification of the unconditional surrender policy by letting the Japanese keep Formosa as a means of ending the Pacific war without an invasion of the Japanese home islands.[544] He deprecated the concessions made to induce Russia to enter the war against Japan: "Japanese armies in Manchuria would never have been an important factor after the homeland was occupied and their emperor had surrendered."[545]

In the wake of the fall of China to the Communists, he urged U.S. naval defense of the Chinese Nationalists on Formosa.[546] "Aid to Burma and Indochina was infinitely less practical and more expensive and difficult than maintenance of an independent Formosa."[547] In November 1949, he along with Senators William Knowland and

---

[541] 2 R. Taft, Works 302.

[542] J. Denice, Not to the Swift: The Old Isolationists in the Cold War Era (Lewisburg: Bucknell U., 1979), 86ff, citing the introduction to W. Kimball, FDR and the World Crisis, 1937-45 (Lexington, Mass: Heath, 1973).

[543] 249 U.S. 204 (1919).

[544] Patterson 251.

[545] Economic Club of Detroit, February 23, 1948, 3 R. Taft, Works 402.

[546] Patterson 442.

[547] Statement on Formosa, January 11, 1950, 4 R. Taft, Works 122ff.

H. Alexander Smith urged preservation of Formosa for Chiang Kai-Shek and the use of the Seventh Fleet in the Formosa Straits to this end.[548] After the outbreak of the Korean War in June 1950, the Truman administration sent the Seventh Fleet.[549]

He thought that the effort to bring about a rapprochement between the Nationalists and Communists was a foredoomed mistake: "While I did not agree with Senator McCarthy's charges of conspiracy and treason against General Marshall, it seemed to me that General Marshall's stupidity was undoubtedly responsible for the calamity which we suffered in China and led directly to the Korean War."[550]

He opposed any effort to impose a Pax Americana: "It is based upon the theory that we know more about what is good for the world than the world itself. It assumes that we are always right and that anyone who disagrees with us is wrong."[551]

After initially endorsing action in defense of Korea in 1950 "wholeheartedly and with every available resource," though noting that "the new policy is adopted at an unfortunate time and involves the attempt to defend Korea, which is a very difficult military operation indeed,"[552] he criticized the Truman administration's failure to secure Congressional approval of it,[553] "a direct violation of the

---

[548] R. Freeland, The Truman Doctrine and the Origins of McCarthyism (2d ed.) (New York: N.Y.U., 1985), 341.

[549] R. Freeland, *supra*, 350.

[550] RAT to Albert McCartney, July 10, 1951, 4 R. Taft, Works 300.

[551] S. Kinzer, The Brothers: John Foster Dulles, Allen Dulles and Their Secret World War (New York: Times Books, 2013), 91, quoting J. Bagman, Henry R. Luce and the Rise of the American News Media (Baltimore: Johns Hopkins, 2001), 135.

[552] J. Denice, Not to the Swift: The Old Isolationists in the Cold War Era (Lewisburg: Bucknell U., 1979), 191. *See* Congressional Record, 81st Congress, 2d Session, 9319-23, excerpted in B. Bernstein and A. Madhouse, *supra*, 439-42.

[553] Patterson 454.

statute which specified that Congress must pass on the troops to be furnished the U.N., under the Charter."[554]

Secretary of Defense Louis Johnson declared: "we were scared of the Hill on this thing. If we tried to put ground troops in at the beginning, there would have been a good deal of trouble."[555]

In the same speech, Taft said, "I believe that we should increase our land army regardless of European commitments to 1,250,000 men." "From the beginning we should have insisted on a general peace negotiation with China including a unification of Korea under free Koreans and a pledge against further expansion in Southeast Asia ... I have never felt that we should send American troops to the Continent of Asia ... it would bring about complete exhaustion even if we were able to win."[556] "We have been seduced into something that was more than we could undertake."[557]

In his last speech in 1953 he again called for negotiations with the Chinese for a united Korea and prophetically observed: "If we once make this present truce, no matter what we put in the agreement about further negotiations for a united Korea, it is no more likely to occur than a united Germany."[558]

It was said of him after his death that he was "the only American statesman who really understood the role of Congressional prerogative and the danger of an omnipotent Presidency—the one man who could have foreseen the end of the long road running from Pusan to My Lai—was mourned on the Hill by politicians who by their very expressions of grief revealed how little they understood

---

[554] Speech to the Ohio Society of New York, January 15, 1951, in RAT Papers, Library of Congress, Box 1287.

[555] G. Paige, The Korean Decision (Glencoe, IL: Free Press, 1968), 177, 264.

[556] W. White, The Taft Story (New York: Harper, 1954), 135.

[557] Id. 166.

[558] National Association of Christians and Jews, May 26, 1953, in 4 R. Taft, Works 480.

him."[559] In July 1940, in decrying American resistance to Japanese expansionism in Southeast Asia, Taft had declared that no American mother was ready to have her son die "for some place with an unpronounceable name in Indochina."[560]

In his initial statement after U.S. intervention in Korea, on June 28, 1950, Taft said: "I believe the general principle of the policy is right … [there is] no pretense of any bi-partisan foreign policy about this action, no pretense of consulting the Congress. There is no legal authority for what he has done." Nonetheless, Taft would vote for an approving resolution if one was sought. The president was "usurping his powers as Commander in Chief, funds were only given for internal security [of Korea]. He noted the changes in policy toward Indochina and Korea: I approve of the changes now made in our foreign policy. Any Secretary of State who has been so reversed by his superiors … had better resign."[561]

In a letter in November 1950, Taft observed: "It seems to me we must still do our best to defend Japan, Formosa, and the Philippines." He supported ratification of the Japanese peace treaty notwithstanding the American commitments contained in it.[562]

"With regard to the atomic bomb, I think it would be a tragic error to use it against China, and I don't believe it would be successful in a land war operating over a 200-mile front. If we use it and it fails, we would be inviting Russian aggression in Europe."[563]

Later, he did not exclude the use of tactical nuclear weapons in wars of the Korean type.[564] He later noted that he had questioned

---

[559]   1 W. Manchester, The Glory and the Dream (Boston: Little Brown, 1974), 815-16.

[560]   New York Times, July 8, 1940, quoted in 1 W. Manchester, The Glory and the Dream (Boston: Little Brown, 1974), 267.

[561]   Korea Crisis, June 28, 1950, 4 R. Taft, Works 167.

[562]   Leffler, *supra*, 449.

[563]   RAT to B. Edwin Hutchinson, November 29, 1950, 4 R. Taft, Works 220.

[564]   RAT to Marilyn Lifschitz, January 3, 1952, 4 R. Taft, Works 344.

the legality of the Korean action under the UN Charter since Article 27 requires "concurring votes" of the five permanent members, not merely absence.[565] "We could not have a better lesson than has been taught us in Korea. Where there is complete disregard for human life, even the best weapons and equipment will fail to overcome that disadvantage in manpower." He also expressed reservations about the National Emergency Proclamation that accompanied American intervention in Korea.[566]

"He has no right to declare war whether a national emergency or not. It follows inevitably that he has no right to engage deliberately in military or naval action equivalent to war except when the country is attacked." In January 1951, he observed: "I am inclined to agree with you that we should get out of Korea at once. After we had captured the North Korean capital we could well have stopped. There was nothing along the northern edge except the power developments of particular interest to the Chinese communists"[567]

His suspicion of military alliances was reflected in his observation in a later letter that "there has never been a case until Korea when the President sent troops into one country to defend it against the attack of another country."[568]

In April 1951 he observed that "[a]n invasion of China is an impossible policy. We do have to agree that we are not going to make an appeasement peace."[569] In July, he noted: "Probably it is better to have a stalemate peace at the 38th parallel than a stalemate war at the 38th parallel under a policy which forbids our armies to go beyond that point or to win the war."[570] By June 1952, he concluded

---

[565] RAT to W.E. Bradford, December 10, 1950, 4 R. Taft, Works 225.

[566] Leffler, *supra*, 403.

[567] RAT to John Chapple, January 10, 1951, in 4 R. Taft, Works 253.

[568] RAT to Bertha Putnam, February 19, 1951, in 4 R. Taft, Works 261.

[569] American Policy in the Far East, April 27, 1951, 4 R. Taft, Works 277.

[570] To Merryle Rukeyser, July 28, 1951, in 4 R. Taft, Works 309. *See also* Taft to McArthur, August 9, 1951, Box 898, Library of Congress, Taft Papers,

that "[a]t the present time, I would try to complete an armistice in Korea because our weakness in the air is such that we could not hope to resume a successful war until many months of improvement in our air power. I do not think that as a permanent policy we should ever station troops on the continent of Europe or the continent of Asia."[571] When a Korean cease-fire was obtained by the Eisenhower administration, he found it to be "extremely distasteful … a condition likely to bring war at any moment" which gave China the freedom to attack Vietnam.[572]

Although he was cautious and prudent in discussing American involvement on the Asian continent, following the Republican defeat in the 1948 election, he was unrestrained in using the alleged loss of China and the stalemated Korean War as sticks with which to beat the Democrats. "[I]n 1949, Taft's aversion to Truman's domestic policies mounted and his misgivings about the benefits of bi-partisanship increased. Republicans got little credit for foreign policy successes, yet they could not take advantage of the Democrats' failures … they yearned to launch a full assault on Truman's foreign policies. With Dewey defeated and Vandenburg dying of cancer, they took control of the party … Taft was animated by his desire to kill Truman's farm and health insurance bills. Through the China issue, the Ohio Republican hoped to embarrass the administration. The State Department, Taft declared, was 'liquidating' the Nationalists and handing China to the Communists. The U.S. Navy, he insisted, should protect Taiwan."[573]

Foreign policy became a political weapon in his hands: "We cannot possibly win the next election unless we point out the utter failure and incapacity of the present Administration to conduct

---

quoted in J. Denice, Not to the Swift: The Old Isolationists in the Cold War Era (Lewisburg: Bucknell U., 1979).

[571] Radio Address on Foreign Policy, June 1, 1952, 4 R. Taft, Works 379.

[572] W. Manchester, *supra*, 813.

[573] M. Leffler, A Preponderance of Power: National Security, the Truman Administration, and the Cold War (Stanford: Stanford U., 1992), 342.

foreign policy and cite the loss of China and the Korean war as typical examples of their very dangerous control. We certainly can't win on domestic policy."[574]

Although much of what Taft said was demagogic, his criticism did encourage the Truman and Eisenhower administrations to protect Taiwan during the period of its maximum vulnerability, and it developed into a prosperous state and one not without influence on the economic course later followed by mainland China. Acheson's announcement of a U.S. fleet deployment was said to be due to "strong advocacy by such Republican leaders as Taft and Hoover ... Without reference to domestic politics, it is difficult to explain the emphasis placed by Acheson on publicly announcing the Formosa intervention."[575]

Taft's general attitude was "it is not nearly so dangerous to become involved in a war in the Pacific as in a European War ... a war in the Pacific is even more to be avoided while a war exists in Europe."[576]

Of the Republicans in the 1950s, it was said that "many left behind the more rational conservative aspects of Taft's foreign policy outlook and moved to a more militant anticommunist posture. Taft himself showed signs at the end of his career of veering in this direction, especially in his Far Eastern policies. Taft and the Vietnam protesters did share the conviction that the limitation of dissent in the name of unanimity in foreign relations can lead to the creation of tyranny abroad and the destruction of liberty at home."[577]

---

[574] RAT to J. Thomas Baldwin, July 31, 1951, RAT Papers, Library of Congress, Box 1187.

[575] R. Foreland, The Truman Doctrine and the Origins of McCarthyism (New York: N. Y. U. Press, 1970), 350.

[576] RAT, "Our Foreign Policy," 6 Vital Speeches 348 (March 1940), Address to the National Republican Club, New York Times, March 3, 1940.

[577] H. Bergen, "Bipartisanship, Senator Taft and the Truman Administration," 90 Pol. Sci. Q. 221 (1975).

Asked about policy toward Iran in 1951, Taft observed, in terms that still have resonance: "In my opinion, the policy of the U.S. must be one of refraining from a land war on the continent of Asia, certainly in any such remote spot as Iran, I do not quite see what the United States can do about it."[578]

He later wrote an Iranian "I do not think that any people can rise above their present condition without a tremendous effort on their own part, and I do not feel that the problems of any people can be solved by charity from outside the country ... I do think the Iranians are entitled to a far better share of the natural resources that are contained within Iran."[579]

A historian fairly summarized his views: "Isolationism scarcely described any important segment of American opinion, certainly not the views of the Taftites. Taft's personal views were complex. Troubled by the rise of a huge military establishment and the threat it posed to personal liberty and national solvency, Taft was obsessed with fighting Communism both abroad and at home. Taft's approach to foreign policy, part of a tradition reaching back to the beginnings of the Republic, is thus best expressed as 'unilateralist'":

> "First: no entangling alliances ... Some Republicans (not Taft himself) regarded the U.N. with outright disdain.
>
> Second, a foreign policy that stressed the Pacific region and Asia over Europe.
>
> [Third], America should never get bogged down in a land war on the Asian continent."[580]

Taft's view of the relative importance of the Far East vis-à-vis Europe was not fashionable in the fifties, though the rise of China,

---

[578] RAT to Tom Horn Jr., May 15, 1951, 4 R. Taft, Works 286.

[579] RAT to Khelil Teleghani, August 7, 1951, 4 R. Taft, Works 307.

[580] C. Alexander, Holding the Line: The Eisenhower Era, 1952-61 (Bloomington: Indiana U., 1975), 1-5.

Japan, India, and the Southeast Asian countries as economic powers has since given it greater force. It was Taft's misfortune that "the
urban unrest and economic decline that fueled the New Right back-
lash in the 1970s was nonexistent. His reform ideas were unsuited
to a complacent age."[581]

His central concern was once stated at length: "The first principle of military strategy is not to fight on the enemy's chosen battle-
ground, where he has his greatest strength. There is a definite limit
to what a government can spend in time of peace and still maintain
a free economy without inflation and with at least some elements
of progress in standards of living and in education, welfare, housing,
health and other activities in which the people are vitally interested.
The effort to do more than we are able to do is the one thing that
might in the end destroy our armies and prove a real threat to the
liberty of the people of the United States."[582]

A Career Summarized

Robert Taft did not have his father's benign personality, nor
his assured position in political society. For all but little more than
two years of his career, he was in opposition, not in government.
His party in his time was not the dominant party, either politically
or intellectually. The society in which he acted was undergoing the
great upheavals of depression and war. Given these limiting factors,
his role in American history was a substantial one. As the leader
after 1938 of a reduced rump of the Republican party, he restored
Congress' role in the making of domestic policy, and that of the
Republican Party as a coherent force with a coherent philosophy.
His successful opposition to nationwide secondary boycotts and

---

[581] M. Bowen, The Roots of Modern Conservatism (Chapel Hill: U. N.C.,
2011), 8.

[582] RAT, quoted in J. Gaddis, Strategies of Containment (New York:
Oxford, 1982), 120.

Taft Summer Home

Taft Cottage, Murray Bay

nationwide collective bargaining spared postwar America "the British disease" and restored a free labor market with mobility and low unemployment. Over great resistance, he at least somewhat limited the growth and influence of the American military, chiefly by repeatedly denying it direct control over the civilian labor force. He fostered, for a while, a culture in which national debates centered on issues, not on personalities. In the age of the dictators, these were not small achievements.

The French writer Andre Maurois stated a typical European view of Taft: "The Taft family has for a great while symbolized respectability mingled with culture and a love for tradition in the City of Cincinnati as the Lodge family had in Boston ... Filled with sincerity and an undeniable civic courage, Taft stood up for the old American liberties against all these dubious novelties, these plans, subsidies, and international engagements. In a word, he would have liked to live in 1900 and it was to be living in 1946."[583]

Another writer said: "Senator Taft's ideal was the preservation of the late 19th century political and economic system to which he attributed this country's greatness." "He made our foreign policy planners think twice before reaching for the moon."[584]

His overall view was that "[w]e have got to break with the corrupting idea that we can legislate prosperity, legislate equality, legislate opportunity. All of these things came in the past from free Americans freely working out their destiny ... That is the only way they can continue to come in any genuine sense."[585]

He was a devoted family man, whose favorite form of recreation was a family picnic at the family compound on the St. Lawrence River, which burned to the ground in the late 1950s, where he

---

[583] A. Maurois, From the New Freedom to the New Frontier (New York: McKay, 1962), 260.

[584] J. Armstrong, "The Enigma of Senator Taft and American Foreign Policy," 17 Review of Politics 206 (1955), 209.

[585] Quoted in E. Goldman, The Crucial Decade (New York: Knopf, 1956), 55.

Taft Memorial and Carillon

sponsored games of hearts, giving out five-cent candy bars as prizes to members of his extended family. "I look at that man," an Idaho Taft delegate declared at the 1952 convention, "and I see everything which my father taught me to hold good."[586]

---

[586] *Id.* 54.

HELEN TAFT MANNING (1891-1987)

Helen Taft, William Howard Taft's daughter, was the sister of Robert Taft and Charles Taft. Her father encouraged her to excel academically, and after graduating from Bryn Mawr, she took an M.A. degree there in 1917 and a Ph.D. at Yale, and was made Dean of Bryn Mawr, a position she held until 1941, thereafter serving as Professor of History until 1957. She twice served as Acting President of Bryn Mawr, the first time in 1917, when she was only 26. At that time, her father wrote her to say:

> "Your taking your M.A. degree and your election as Dean of Bryn Mawr constitute one of the great joys of my life and gives me the greatest pride. They open for you a career of great usefulness and great distinction. It is quite probable you will marry, though you may not. But now, whatever course you take, you will take it because you prefer it after due consideration and judgment uninfluenced by a duress which in so many cases has brought unhappiness."[587]

Three years later, he wrote in similar vein to say:

> "I have been very proud of the success you have thus far attained and perhaps my feeling in the matter has been colored by my ambition for a career for you so conspicuously begun. Your marriage will probably end that career if your married life is as happy as I hope it may be. You have a right to welcome married life. It is probably wiser for you to insist on it. Certainly you can and ought to be the arbiter of your own future in this regard. I hope you are not unconsciously stimulated in your enthusiasm for this marriage by the thought that

---

[587] WHT to Helen Taft, July 3, 1917, quoted in I. Ross, *supra*, 302.

you are approaching 30 and yearn for the happiness of family life. You are a woman of poise and level-headed and I cannot think this."[588]

In her youth, Helen, unlike her mother, was a champion of women's suffrage and was a supporter of the garment workers after the Triangle fire in New York; her father held back from endorsing support of women's suffrage until just before its enactment. In 1930, she actively opposed plans to merge a classical high school in Philadelphia into a comprehensive school.[589] She was said to have "confidence to set out on an independent path … exceedingly thoughtful and gentle, blissfully uninterested in fame." "A nice girl and very intelligent, without being a prude."[590] In addition to her Ph.D., she acquired a law degree from George Washington University at the age of 46.[591]

In April 1939, she parted company with her brother Robert by endorsing an appeal for 10,000 American visas for German refugee children.[592]

Three days later, she expressed views about an arms embargo: "Any threats of American embargoes against aggressors or promises of economic help to victims would not serve to prevent a war but might precipitate an outbreak of war on the part of the totalitarian states, which felt they must win quickly before American aid could count. The issue is whether we should throw over the national tradition of a hundred and fifty years and attempt by a system of

---

[588] WHT to Helen Taft, January 13, 1920, quoted in I. Ross, *supra*, 319-20.

[589] "Battle on High School Stirs Philadelphia," New York Times, May 4, 1930.

[590] C. Anthony, Nellie Taft: The Unconventional First Lady of the Ragtime Era (New York: Morrow, 2005), 10, 298.

[591] C. Anthony, Nellie Taft: The Unconventional First Lady of the Ragtime Era (New York: Morrow, 2005), 370.

[592] New York Times, April 19, 1939.

diplomatic intrigue and open threats to affect the issue of events in other parts of the world."[593]

"I believe that the policy of arms embargo is more likely to promote war than to prevent it. I proposed repeal of the arms embargo as early as April 25, 1939 ... It favored large nations ... continental powers ... warlike nations. It favored the aggressor as against the peaceful nation."[594] Later, she signed a letter in support of Lend-Lease while her brother Robert was still opposing it.[595]

Helen Taft Manning

In November 1950, she wrote: "The real threat to present civilization is that communism has been taken over by primitive peoples who have no concept of individual rights and responsibilities. [These were] saved not perhaps by victory in war but by the vitality of the group who cherish them in the face of disaster. [Individual rights] owe much to the teachings of the Christian church with its doctrine of the survival of the soul."[596]

She briefly studied law at George Washington University, and after her mother's stroke served as White House hostess in the last days of the Taft administration. At the age of ten, while her father was Governor General of the Philippines, she was introduced to Pope Leo X at the Vatican. Helen married Frederick Manning, a

---

[593] "Supports Ban on Arms Exports: Cash and Carry for Other Commodities," New York Times, April 22, 1939.

[594] RAT, "Our Foreign Policy," 6 Vital Speeches 348 (March 1940), Address to the National Republican Club, New York Times, March 3, 1940.

[595] C. Anthony, Nellie Taft: The Unconventional First Lady of the Ragtime Era (New York: Morrow, 2005), 279.

[596] "Barbarism Revival Seen," New York Times, November 5, 1950.

Professor of History at Yale who taught at Swarthmore following the marriage.

She was the author of two books on British colonial history which revealed a keen political intelligence. The first of these, *British Colonial Government After the American Revolution, 1782-1820*, appeared in 1933;[597] the second, *The Revolt of French Canada, 1800-1835*, was published after her retirement, in 1962.[598]

In the first book, she noted the paradox that the secession of the American colonies gave rise to tighter control of the remaining Empire from London. Ministers and the public remained attached to the Empire, although the anti-imperialist teachings of the radicals were unanswered in print. "The actions of governments almost never keep pace with the intellectual movements of the day and are usually under fire from the advanced guard of political and economic thinking." The abolitionists "had no cure for the evil against which they inveighed save the control of every detail of colonial government from London."[599]

The age she wrote about was in her view one of transition: "England had outgrown the limits of her own colored empire in the search for new markets and new sources of raw materials. If the eighteenth century was the age of the self-sufficient empire and the nineteenth the age of systematic (and unsystematic) colonization, the period of transition from one to the other might be given a name of its own—the age of the strategic post."[600]

One consequence of the American Revolution was "[t]he general recognition that Englishmen must submit to a second period of education in the language and customs of the races they were to govern." It was considered "not only unwise but dangerous to confer any local powers of self-government on colonists of an alien race."

---

[597] (New Haven: Yale U., 1933).

[598] (New York: St. Martin's Press, 1962).

[599] *Id.* 3, 6, 7, 13.

[600] *Id.* 286, 289.

At the same time, as with the Quebec Act of 1774, there was greater respect for local customs: "the retention of the French civil code, the feudal system of land tenure, and the authority and privileges of the Roman Catholic clergy."[601]

There was recognition that "no colonial militia could be of any service unless the settlers from whom it was drawn were loyal and satisfied with their government ... [F]ormer French officers [were taken] into British employ to enlist the Canadian military in British interests."[602]

"The ministers probably felt that they could count on the support of the anti-slavery party in denying any measure of self-government to colonists who were also slave-owners ... [T]he days when it could be taken for granted that every British colony should as a matter of course be governed by a governor, council, and assembly were gone never to return."[603]

In general, "government by the Crown tended to be far more arbitrary and inflexible than government by the House of Commons could ever be. The issue of slavery was to blind the British liberals for half a century to the need for greater autonomy in those parts of the colonial world where the interests of the black race were deeply involved, but in Canada and Australia the support and interest of Englishmen both in and out of Parliament was as great a factor in winning local self-government for the colonists as were their own efforts across the seas."[604]

Her book on French Canada noted the "resemblance between the movement in the St. Lawrence valley and the revolutionary movements on the continent of Europe which culminated in the Revolutions of 1848. To take a single example, that of Hungary, there is the same emphasis on language, the same desire for education and

---

[601] Id. 295, 299, 300.

[602] Id. 306, 322.

[603] Id. 437.

[604] Id. 540.

self-improvement and the same close study of constitutional precedents … the French Canadians knew that they must look to the
precedents of English constitutional history to gain their ends."[605]

Summarizing, she observed: "The chief contribution of the
French Canadians to the evolution of the British Commonwealth is
that they have demonstrated that a large and ever-increasing group
can live peacefully and happily within the boundaries of the Empire
without abandoning their own laws or language or their traditional
way of living. The other contribution of the French Canadians was
to the cause of colonial self-government in general. The assembly in
Quebec was the first representative body in British North America
to assert the right to be the controlling force in the government of
the province and the first to establish effective relations with individuals and groups in Parliament."[606]

Charles Phelps Taft II (1897-1983)

Robert Taft's brother Charles was, by Taft standards, a relative
liberal. He graduated from Yale College and law school, winning
the Gordon Brown Prize, was a law partner of his brother Robert
from 1922 to 1938 and prosecuting attorney in Cincinnati in 1927-
28, having served in the army in World War I. He was defeated
for re-election as prosecutor after losing a case against a notorious
gangster who won an insanity acquittal and was released six months
later. As he embarked for Europe, his father wrote him, paying tribute to "your fine character, your purity of soul, your high ideals, your
spurning of the low and unmoral."[607] Like many youngest children,
in his youth he was regarded as the clown in the family; perhaps in
consequence, he had a less hard edge than his brother Robert and

---

[605] H. Manning, *The Revolt of French Canada* (New York: St. Martin's,
1962), xiv.

[606] *Id.* 374-75.

[607] WHT to CT, December 19, 1917, quoted in I. Ross, *supra*, 305.

a more emollient personality. He had been twice around the world with his parents by the time he was eight years old, he gave interviews to the newspapers and posed for photographers at every stop, and once, with a friend, pasted spitballs on a portrait of President Jackson so as to give him warts.

He had enlisted as a private and after attending artillery school emerged as a first lieutenant. He was a member of the Cincinnati City Council from 1938 to 1942 and was a leader in the Charter reform movement in Cincinnati, which controlled the Mayoralty from 1926-37, 1953-54, 1972-76, 1978-80, and 1982-84. He was the author of several books: *City Management: The Cincinnati Experience* (1933); *You, I and Roosevelt* (1936); *Why I Am for the Church* (1947); and *Democracy in Politics and Economics* (1950). In 1936, he drafted much of the Republican platform. "We must not yield to the stand-patters' idea of policy. We cannot sit back and let people starve, and no more can we let individual human beings live in hopeless squalor." The platform as he drafted it was socially progressive and constitutionally and economically conservative. He accepted social security but urged that most other new programs be administered by the states, and joined his brother Robert in opposing the Reciprocal Trade Agreements Act. The campaign fell under die-hard influence, but he stuck it out to the end; Landon is said to have wanted to make him Solicitor General had he been victorious.[608]

He held several wartime posts in the Roosevelt administration, Director of the Office of National Economic Affairs in the State Department and Director of the Office of Transportation and Commercial Policy; later he was Director of the Division of Health and Welfare of the Federal Security Agency and a member of the War Relief Control Board.

The last agency was established by President Roosevelt in 1942 and abolished in 1946 by President Truman at the Board's request; its mission was the consolidation of over 700 private relief

---

[608] A. Schlesinger, The Politics of Upheaval (Boston: Houghton Mifflin, 1960), 547, 613-16.

Charles P. Taft

agencies into 100, the elimination of confusing and overlapping appeals, and the licensing and limitation of private relief agencies, which among them raised more than $1 billion. Joseph E. Davies, Roosevelt's late 30s Ambassador to the Soviet Union was the Chairman; the third member in addition to Taft was Frederick Koppel until his death and then Charles Warren.[609]

After the war, he again became a member of the Cincinnati City Council, where he served until 1977 and served as Mayor of Cincinnati in 1955-57, presiding over the construction of the Riverfront Stadium. He unsuccessfully sought the Republican nomination for Governor in 1952 and 1958.[610]

He was a co-founder of the World Council of Churches and was the youngest President of the International YMCA. In 1948, he was the President of the Federated Council of Churches of Christ in America and wrote an article for the *New York Times Magazine* about the initial meeting of the World Council of Churches. In it, he expressed the hope that the new organization would "find a single voice to speak to the common man and give him the courage and the sense of direction he needs to find his way in this increasingly baffling world … We must arouse the same enthusiasm that characterizes the devotees of secular movements."[611] In August 1954 at the Second Assembly of the World Council of Churches, he urged deletion of a reference to Christian evangelism to the Jews in the

---

[609]   War Relief Control Board, Voluntary War Relief During World War II: A Report (Department of State Publication 2566 (Washington: GPO, 1948).

[610]   H. Segal, "The Taft Brothers of Ohio: A Study in Contrasts," New York Times, November 18, 1951, E9.

[611]   C. Taft, "Why the Bells are Ringing Today: They Call for Religious Unity as Churches of All the Continents Meet Together in Amsterdam," New York Times Magazine, August 26, 1948.

message to the churches, urging that "the reference would make for bad interfaith relations," and prevailed by a vote of 195 to 150 "through the votes of Coptic and Orthodox delegates motivated by very different, even opposite, considerations."[612] He enumerated three areas of possible activity for the new organization: chaplaincies, inter-church aid, and refugee assistance.

Late in his career, he was a member of two organizations opposing racial discrimination, Republicans for Progress and Republicans Advance. His brother Robert once said of him "the truth with Charley is that he takes the opinions of any group of people with whom he is thrown."[613]

More recently, the historian Stephen Hess called him "a dilettante, a brilliant Roman candle whose shafts of light scattered across the landscape."[614]

He was proud to be known as President Taft's son, but his wife did not get along with Helen Taft, her mother-in-law. She was the former Eleanor Chase, daughter of the President of the Ingersoll Waterbury Company, a watch and clock manufacturer. She was described as "a quiet idealist, deeply religious and interested in social service. Gentle in manner, she was strong and steady in her convictions and sympathies, with an inflexible will ... Her interests lay in church work, international relief, and municipal affairs."[615]

He had worked in favor of the renewal of the Reciprocal Trade Agreements Act of 1934 and was a member of the Committee for a National Trade Policy. For him, trade "provided a little pressure that

---

[612] W. Herberg, Protestant, Catholic, Jew: An Essay in American Religious Sociology (New York: Anchor Books, 1960), 245, 252 n.32.

[613] R. Woods, A Changing of the Guard: Anglo-American Relations, 1941-46 (Chapel Hill: U. of North Carolina, 1990).

[614] S. Hess, America's Political Dynasties: From Adams to Clinton (Washington: Brookings, 2016).

[615] I. Ross, The Tafts: An American Family (Cleveland: World, 1964), 350, 388.

forces economies in production and cheaper necessities of life."[616] In 1955, he testified at a Senate hearing that opponents "are professional pessimists and their wails of anguish are heart-rending," leading Senator Eugene Millikin, formerly one of his brother Robert's close associates, to say without a smile that "It's rather lurid language to come from the mouth of a Taft."[617]

He was a supporter of Lend-Lease, the military draft, the British loan, and the Bretton Woods Agreement.

He found some lessons in totalitarian states: "First, there is the belief in leadership. That's what the YMCA is based on. In the dictator states, of course, they go too far and believe that their leaders are Gods. Second is a community feeling, the sense of belonging to something. The people know that when their leader succeeds, they succeed. That's something we've lost in this country, but we're getting it back to some extent through such organizations as the YMCA, the community funds, etc."[618]

He served as attorney for the Cincinnati branch of the Amalgamated Clothing Workers from 1928 to 1940. He was a trustee of the Carnegie Institute and the Twentieth Century Fund, of the Taft School, and of several business corporations, including Farrar Straus, the publisher.

His activities in charter reform gave rise to employment of a City Manager and to proportional representation in City Council elections, assuring minority party representation. Cincinnati was the first major American city to adopt the City Manager system.[619]

He observed of this: "A citizen organization can establish a good local government and maintain it permanently on a business basis without patronage, without yielding to either national party

---

[616]   *Id.* 42.

[617]   A. Drury, "Attack on Tariff Act Foes by C.P. Taft Stirs Dispute," New York Times, March 19, 1955.

[618]   "Charles Taft Finds Value in Dictatorships," Milwaukee Sentinel, February 11, 1939.

[619]   Obituary, New York Times, June 25, 1983.

and without injuring either. England, with two national parties far more compact and disciplined than ours, has no local machines of jobholders, corrupt or otherwise." He acknowledged, however, that "no independent movement in any community can succeed unless it carries with it the leadership, or some leadership, important leadership, of the dominant political party. The permanence of the two national parties is grounded not in their policies or platforms but in local patronage machines.[620]

In his book on Roosevelt,[621] he declared: "I can't and won't [damn FDR and all his works] and some of the Republican candidates who do give me an acute pain in the neck."[622] If they produce "a platform of a miscellaneous assortment of political lumber, glued together by the spittle of hate, the Republicans are beaten before they begin."[623]

A liberal party, in his view, had to work with left-wing groups who are adverse to compromise; the Republicans as a business party understood compromise. He declared that "legislation under the whip of the patronage power is not democracy. It is the absence in fact of discussion and debate which brings about unanticipated petty tyrannies of the kind that developed under the NRA ... reform without education is an unmitigated evil because it produces ultimately an extreme reaction."[624]

He was equally critical of the AAA: spending powers "should be subject to the limitations of the Tenth Amendment." His brother Robert took a more generous view of the General Welfare clause: federal spending was permissible if not conditioned on state regulations. He favored "purchase and withdrawal of marginal lands ...

---

[620] C. Taft, City Management: The Cincinnati Experiment (New York, Farrar and Rinehart, 1933), 5, 235-36.

[621] C. Taft, You, I and Roosevelt (New York: Farrar and Rinehart, 1936).

[622] Id. 4.

[623] Id. 8.

[624] Id. 82.

measures for erosion restoring fertility by cover crops. [The] U.S. cannot regulate tenancy or erosion … but [can provide] grants in aid or direct subsidies for desirable crops."[625]

As for housing, he favored "insistence on condemnation by the United States … the only sane way to resolve the constitutional issue." Railroads were reproached for failing to adequately provide for depreciation or obsolescence; he urged simplification of utility structures and that Republicans should be committed to "a successful regulation of business in the public interest."[626]

He regarded Carter Glass' work on the Glass–Steagall Act, separating commercial and investment banking as "one of the most amazing legislative feats in our history."[627]

Unlike his father, who fostered postal savings and feared perverse incentives, he regarded deposit insurance as a "good alternative to branch banking." Later Republicans were to afflict the nation with both. He also considered that corporate office "should be a matter of public trust like a public office instead of an opportunity for private profit and stock jobbing."[628]

He thought that "industrial unions [were] the only sound solution," but had "no objection to company unions if they are really independent self-governing organizations and if they have a really independent board set up to pass on grievances and other questions." The ban on them in the Wagner and Taft–Hartley Acts and President Clinton's veto of a bill that would have relaxed it denied American labor the benefit of German-style works councils at the plant level. "A well conceived and thoroughly organized union can do a good many things for the employer. It can help him in his production problems and in some cases can furnish financial assistance necessary to keep his concern going and his people at work. The

---

[625] *Id.* 55ff.

[626] *Id.* 59.

[627] *Id.* 64.

[628] *Id.* 68.

employer and the public must recognize without condoning violence that a picket line and a strike are not a pink tea. A man with
a family striking for improved working conditions is bound to have
some feeling. The rights of working men cannot possibly be protected except on the basis that strikers must be taken back when
the strike settles unless they have committed some serious offense
against community standards."[629] The law is still otherwise, and not
only in the proper case of public employee unions like the air traffic
controllers.

He shared Quesnay's view, also the view of some modern economists like Elinor Ostrom, that "if a number of individuals work
together to achieve a common purpose, a harmony of interest will
develop among them to which each will willingly subordinate his
self-interest." He decried, "Ricardo [who] was a London stockbroker
who took the teachings of the humane Adam Smith and invented,
from his country estate with his rich wife, that imaginary economic
man who was moved solely by a logical self-interest … Karl Marx
reaches the same result by a different approach and is just as bad
as (but no worse than) Ricardo … the instinct of human association in achieving a common purpose constantly leads men to yield
their material incentives."[630] His equal dislike of economist fanatics
of both right and left is not familiar in the American academy of
our time.

He was a supporter of minimum wage laws, his rationale being
similar to that once tendered by Learned Hand: "the first lien upon
the gross earnings of any company is a living wage for its employees. If the business is such that it cannot pay a living wage, then
the sooner it quits, the better." As for the rewards of management:
"Management should be compensated in accordance with its ability, but any man who thinks that he is worth a million a year has
a bad case of expanded ego. I have no sympathy with the current

---

[629] Id. 72-75.

[630] C. Taft, Democracy in Politics and Economics (New York: Farrar
Straus, 1950), 37-38.

demagoguery that would limit salaries to $8500 a year or less, but there is to my mind a very definite limitation upon the amount a trustee should pay himself for his services."[631]

He shared his brother Robert's view, eventually reflected in the Taft–Hartley Act, that "the [labor] rules ought to be statutory and not judicial [and] ought to be enforceable by the representatives of the public and not in a private action by one of the parties to the dispute."[632]

On the other hand, he was a critic of the right-to-work laws authorized by the Taft–Hartley Act: "I am interested in the freedom of the individual worker, but I see every reason why he should pay something for the representation he receives when the union lawfully designated by vote of the workers bargains for him. I see no excuse for the 'free rider.'"[633]

Taft decried the Roosevelt administration's abuse of patronage in the WPA, pointing out that competitive government positions decreased by 12,000 and noncompetitive ones increased by 240,000. He saw an attempt to "operate social security measures as adjuncts of political parties … How could you build a viaduct or a road or a post office with relief labor?" Work relief, he thought, was appropriate only at the local level.[634]

In the postwar period, he decried abuses by Congressional investigating committees, and was the sponsor of a resolution adopted by the National Council of the Churches of Christ declaring that "no committee should circulate on its letterhead, over the signature of its members or employees, unsupported charges against

---

[631] C. Taft, "A Theory of Living," Randolph-Macon College, June 12, 1934, in C. Taft, Why I Am for the Church (New York: Farrar Straus, 1947), 1, 10.

[632] C. Taft, "Thinking Versus Swearing in Labor Relations," State Bar of Michigan, September 18, 1937, in C. Taft, Why I Am for the Church (New York: Farrar Straus, 1947), 38-39.

[633] G. Dugan, "Slum Fight is Tied to Racial Tension," New York Times, June 18, 1958.

[634] You, I and Roosevelt, *supra*, 81.

individuals or organizations which it has made no effort to investigate or substantiate."[635]

There was no doubt about Charles Taft's commitment to limited government. "[Hegel's] followers believe that the State is the final judge of conduct and opinion, who by this rational exaltation of sovereignty can elevate spirituality. They conclude that the State is entitled to choose its own means, peaceful or otherwise, to maintain its own supremacy. That is the opposite of democracy." His brother Robert wrote of him: "Charley has always been somewhat New Dealish, but not in any extreme way, and has always considered himself a Republican."[636]

The journalist John Gunther said of him: "Basically, Charles is a do-better and a man of warmth and charm."[637]

As for foreign policy, he was an anti-imperialist: "we are reaping today in Japan and Germany and Italy what nineteenth-century imperialism sowed … the defense of the Philippines by force is practically impossible."

Further, in terms that have continuing pertinence: "When a treaty has been ratified, we have sat back and let it ride, [not] planning what to do in case of trouble … [The Foreign Service] lacks a college to train even career men, such as we have in the staff colleges for the army and navy. We need to train our ordinary politicians in foreign affairs." He decried the fact that the various peace societies were ethnically insulated and neglected Catholics and unions.[638]

In 1937, he was an anti-interventionist and even an appeaser: "I believe that these dictatorships that threaten our peace today have in them the seeds of their own destruction, and that no outside

---

[635] "Churchmen Assail Congress' 'Abuses' in School Red Hunt," New York Times, March 12, 1953.

[636] RAT to Dr. H.H. Banc, February 20, 1946, RAT Papers, Library of Congress, Box 872, "Demobilization 1946 File."

[637] J. Gunther, Inside U.S.A. (London: Hamish Hamilton, 1947), 473.

[638] RAT to Dr. H.H. Banc, February 20, 1946, RAT Papers, Library of Congress, Box 872, "Demobilization 1946 File," 42-45.

force from us or anyone else can bring the return of democracy any more quickly than it is coming anyhow. I believe that a large measure of that sense of injustice that sustains those dictatorships and breeds war, can be eliminated by peaceful methods."[639]

By January of 1941, however, he decried pacifism, and condemned Anne Morrow Lindbergh's *The Wave of the Future*: "One of the very fine women of our country says that some new conception of humanity is pushing up through the crust of custom in Germany and Italy and Russia and that it is in its essence good. Great ideas, we are told, enter into reality with evil associates and with disgusting alliances. That view destroys all moral judgment." As for Versailles: "Perhaps the worst error was the effort to divide Europe on the basis of nationality, with no restraint upon nationalism. But we all believed in it then. At that it might have worked if the plan for a moral organization to limit sovereignty had been made to create a real European community. Even so, there was no possibility of war until the Rhineland was re-fortified in 1936. After all, the major object of the treaty was to prevent war, and if enforced in that respect, it would have done so."[640]

He did not share his brother Robert's fears about the impact of war on American democracy: "the real democracies, of three centuries' standing, have gone through and come out of many wars in the last hundred years, and no permanent dictatorship has developed yet." In December 1946, he presciently observed: "The absolutism of the extreme Zionist and of the extreme Arab nationalist is bound to end in conflict, and can even produce condemnation of its own

---

[639] C. Taft, "What Can a Man Do?," Rochester University, June 21, 1937, in C. Taft, Why I Am for the Church (New York: Farrar Straus, 1947), 26, 31.

[640] C. Taft, "A Christian Choice of Evils: If War Comes," The Christian Century, January 1, 1941, in C. Taft, Why I Am for the Church (New York: Farrar Straus, 1947), 68, 70-71.

best leaders when they seek sensible solutions, as witness the recent attacks on Chaim Weizmann."[641]

He favored separation of ordinary and capital expenditures in budgets: "It is obviously proper to make capital expenditures and pay for them out of borrowed money, as Al Smith pointed out. But such capital expenditures should be paid for either by serial bonds or by term bonds and a sinking fund. The bonds should always be for considerably less than the life of the improvement and the improvement ought to be a really necessary one. The first essential of good governmental bookkeeping is to separate capital expenditures from operating expenses. There has hardly been an attempt to do so." He decried the effects of urban renewal projects and the interstate highway program in "stirring up the worst race feeling outside the South," saying that the relocation of minority groups has "taxed our ability to hold our towns together."[642]

He had seven children, two sons and five daughters. His papers, like those of his father and brother, were left to the Library of Congress rather than "a mausoleum someplace else."[643]

WALBRIDGE TAFT (1885-1951)

Walbridge Taft, eldest son of Henry W. Taft, graduated from Harvard Law School and married an heiress, Helen Draper, in Hopedale, Massachusetts. In 1917, they were later divorced and he married M. Elizabeth Clark in 1923.[644] He served as a captain in World War I and later joined his father's firm, Cadwalader,

---

[641] C. Taft, "The People in the Pews," Federal Council of Churches, Seattle, December 6, 1946, in C. Taft, Why I Am for the Church (New York: Farrar Straus, 1947), 89, 97-98.

[642] G. Dagan, "Slum Fight Is Tied to Racial Tension," New York Times, June 18, 1958.

[643] New York Times, June 9, 1960.

[644] New York Times, June 9, 1960.

Wickersham and Taft. He unsuccessfully ran for Congress in the 16th District of New York in Manhattan in 1916, losing to Peter J. Dooling.[645] He was one of a group of New York lawyers led by Emory Buckner who successfully agitated for repeal of New York's heart balm laws, perceived as tools of blackmail,[646] a cause that also interested his father.

WILLIAM H. TAFT II (1887-1952)

William H. Taft II, youngest son of Henry W. Taft, graduated from Yale in 1909. He worked for several brokerage firms and was Subscription-Circulation Manager of the *New York Times* from 1923 to 1929. He married Marguerite O'Neil and served as a Captain in the Field Artillery during World War I. From 1934 onward he worked for the Bank for Savings and its predecessor Central Savings Bank, retiring as Assistant Vice President and Secretary.

---

[645] Ogdensburg, NY, Republican-Journal, November 3, 1916, p. 2.

[646] A. Glassman, "I Do! Do I? A Practical Guide to Love, Courtship and Heartbreak in New York," 12 Buffalo Women's Law J. 47, 68 (2003).

THE FOURTH GENERATION

The 13 grandchildren, 6 boys and 7 girls, of William Howard Taft's three remarkable children had difficult acts to follow. Among them were a Senator from Ohio; a physicist who became Dean of Yale College, an Ambassador to Ireland and member of the Policy Planning staff of the State Department, a prominent Cleveland lawyer who narrowly lost a hopeless race for Mayor of Cleveland because he refused to play "the race card," and an environmental lawyer who became Assistant Attorney General of the Lands Division of the U.S. Department of Justice. The women included the head of the Criminal Division of the Manhattan Legal Aid Society, two prominent economists, and a teacher of music. In keeping with family tradition, almost all had excellent academic records at leading institutions. In this generation, the old school tie was definitely helpful; all six men graduated from the Taft School and from Yale College.[1]

Their careers were necessarily made largely within bureaucracies, the contours of post–World War II American society having largely been defined by the time they attained adulthood.

HELEN TAFT MANNING HUNTER (1921-2013)

Helen Taft Manning Hunter, the oldest daughter of Helen Taft, was a graduate of Smith who took a Ph.D. in economics at Radcliffe and became a professor of economics at Swarthmore for most of her career, and married a professor of economics at Haverford.

---

[1] Obituary, New York Times, February 11, 1952.

Caroline Manning (1925-2020)

Caroline Manning, Helen Taft's youngest daughter, was born in 1925 and graduated from Bryn Mawr. She became a teacher at the Manhattan School of Music and then at Bryn Mawr and married a professor of mathematics at Bryn Mawr.

Seth Taft (1922-2013)

Seth Taft attended the Taft School and was a Phi Beta Kappa graduate of Yale who stood near the top of his class at the Yale Law School; his wife Frances, a Vassar graduate held an M.A. from Yale and taught the history of art at the Cleveland Institute of Art. He spent most of his career with the Jones, Day law firm in Cleveland. He ran unsuccessfully for the Ohio Senate in 1962. He lost a close race against Carl Stokes for Mayor of Cleveland in 1967, steadfastly refusing to play the "race card." As observed by the historian William O'Neill:

> "The Democratic candidate for Mayor was Carl B. Stokes, a Negro who won the primary despite the machine's opposition. While Cleveland's voters were overwhelmingly Democratic, this did not insure his election. No Negro had ever been elected Mayor of a great city. The backlash ran strongly in Cleveland, a city whose ethnic minorities had never melted, and who, as in Boston, feared and resented the blacks, and all the more so as Negroes comprised more than a third of the population. Stokes' Republican opponent, Seth C. Taft of the famous Taft family would ordinarily have stood little chance in a place where Democratic registrations out-numbered Republicans 5 to 1. But as the only alternative to a black mayor, his position was greatly enhanced. Taft ran a very upright campaign. He neither sought nor wanted the racist votes. He got them anyway. 80 percent of the city's

white voters cast their ballots for him. But a crucial minority voted for Stokes, who slipped in by 1,644 votes out of nearly 260,000 cast."[2]

Seth Taft

He was a Cuyahoga County Commissioner from 1971 to 1978 and in 1982 was defeated by Clarence Brown in a Republican primary for Governor of Ohio.

Seth Taft had four children: Frederick I. Taft (1945-), a graduate of Phillips Exeter Academy, Yale College, and Yale Law School, and a partner in a Cleveland law firm, who has been active in local politics and is the author of an atlas of health care reform options.[3] Thomas Taft (1948-), a graduate of Yale College and the Yale Management School, Director of Finance of Germantown Academy after retiring from the investment business. Cynthia Taft (1950-), who holds a Ph.D. in American Studies from Yale and is a lecturer at MIT. S. Tucker Taft (1953-), a summa cum laude graduate of Harvard College and a developer of the Ada computer programming language.

PETER RAWSON TAFT III (1937-)

Peter Rawson Taft III graduated from the Taft School and from Yale, magna cum laude. He served on the *Yale Law Journal* and became law clerk to Judge Richard Rives of the United States

---

[2] W. O'Neill, Coming Apart: An Informal History of America in the Sixties (Chicago: Quadrangle, 1971), 179-80.

[3] F. Taft, "Atlas of Health Care Reform," 7 Law and Health 73 (1992), *see also* F. Taft, "Detention of the Unconvinced in Patna, India," 5 Case Western Reserve J. of Intl. Law 155 (1971).

Peter R. Taft

Court of Appeals for the Fifth Circuit and served as Law Clerk to Chief Justice Earl Warren at the 1962 term. Thereafter he practiced at Williams and Connally in Washington and at Munger Tolles and Olsen in Los Angeles. He ran unsuccessfully in 1971 for the Board of Trustees of the Los Angeles Community College, losing to an arch-conservative descendant of Senator Robert M. La Follette who was a supporter of Governor Reagan. He declared: "People don't appreciate what they have here. It's the best educational system in the country but they're sacrificing it without knowing what they have."[4]

He thereafter served as Assistant Attorney General for the Natural Resources Division from 1975 to 1977 and argued a Clean Air Act case, *Union Electric v. EPA*,[5] in the U.S. Supreme Court. He also negotiated a $54 million settlement on behalf of various Indian tribes in the state of Maine. Asked why he did not make his career in Ohio, he observed: "I once got an absentee ballot at school and there were four Tafts on it."

His tenure with Edward Bennett Williams was an unusual experience for a Taft. He represented various gangsters as well as the editors of the left-wing *Ramparts* magazine. Williams is said to have "hired Peter Taft after sitting across from him at a Georgetown dinner party." Williams for a time treated him as a surrogate son, sharing hotel suites, dining, athletic exertions, and copious drinking. He had astute reservations about Williams' political judgment; he was "terrible at the pulse of the electorate. Washington's not the best place for developing political judgment. It's so isolated. What the hell did Ed know about farmers." Eventually, he got restive and

---

[4] "A Taft Meets a La Follette in Election on Coast," New York Times, May 3, 1971.

[5] 427 U.S. 246 (1976).

left Williams and Connally for Los Angeles: "I think Ed told me I was a partner, but how would you know? Ed controlled everything."[6]

Cynthia Taft (1928-2013)

Cynthia Taft was paralyzed with polio (from which her twin sister Rosalyn died) in 1941, but that did not prevent her from graduating (on crutches) from Vassar and the London School of Economics and obtaining a Ph.D. from Yale. She married Donald R. Morris, a Foreign Service officer and served as a policy consultant to the State Department in 1963 and later as a Professor of Economics at Smith College and American University. She was the co-author of an important study of differential wage rates, for which she provided the statistical work as well as much material from British and French sources. Her summary chapter concluded that "wage differentials of every kind—occupational, inter-firm, inter-regional, inter-industry—are considerably wider in the United States than in the European countries ... the U.S. wage structure reflects the turbulence of a market economy as yet only partially harnessed by collective bargaining and other types of deliberate control."[7] William Howard Taft had also championed differential wage rates, condemning some unions for forswearing them.[8]

Cynthia Taft had four children. Eleanor ("Nonie") Taft (1918-2004), a Bryn Mawr graduate, married Dr. Donald Hall of Seattle. Sylvia Taft (1920-2008) graduated from Vassar and received an M. Ed. from the University of Rochester before teaching at the Germantown Friends School; she married Dr. William Lotspeick of Rochester; they had a daughter and two sons. Lucia Taft (1924-1955),

---

[6] E. Thomas, The Man to See: Edward Bennett Williams (New York: Simon and Schuster, 1991), 305-06, 385.

[7] L. Reynolds and C. Taft, Evolution of Wage Structure (New Haven: Yale U., 1956).

[8] See Obituary, Washington Post, August 8, 2013.

a Vassar graduate and teacher, committed suicide after a period of depression. Rosalyn Taft (1930-1941) died of polio in 1941.

Robert Taft Jr. (1917-1993)

Robert Taft Jr., the second of Robert A. Taft's four sons, graduated from Yale and the Harvard Law School and served in the Ohio House of Representatives from 1955 to 1962 and served as majority floor leader there. In World War II he served as a naval officer on an attack vessel, taking part in landings on Guadalcanal, Okinawa, Salerno, and Normandy.[9]

He was a delegate to the Republican National Convention in 1956, 1960, 1964, and 1972. He served as a Congressman from Ohio from 1963 to 1965, lost his seat in the 1964 Johnson landslide, and then served again from 1967 to 1971. He wrote a liberal trade policy plank for the 1960 Republican platform. He was elected to the U.S. Senate in the 1970 election, serving one term until his defeat in 1976 in the first post-Watergate presidential election year, when his candidacy was also hindered by reported health problems.

As a Senator, he compiled a record that was somewhat more liberal than that of his father, but one that was distinguished by undemonstrative work on issues that later became important. In 1971, he addressed himself to emergency labor legislation to deal with the strikes prompted by the Nixon administration's wage-price controls. He favored 30-day injunctions at the instance of the government but not private employers, and a procedure involving selection by an arbitrator between the final offers of union and management, the theory being that this procedure would narrow differences; it is doubtful that his father would have gone so far in support of arbitration. He also favored legislative curbs on unproductive work rules, with a proviso that reductions in force be carried out by attrition and the resulting savings shared evenly between

---

[9] M. Hunter, "Son of 'Mr. Republican,'" New York Times, May 7, 1970.

unions and management.[10] His father had resisted restraints on featherbedding in deference to the collective bargaining process.

Robert Taft Jr.

He opposed a "bailout" of the Lockheed Aircraft Corporation.[11]

He took a keen interest in legislation to reform private pension plans, favoring vesting, and prohibitions against self-dealing, an interest carried on by his nephew John G. Taft. He would not allow credits for contributions to social security, which operate to exclude many lower-paid workers from the full benefits of pension plans.[12]

In 1972, he strongly supported the War Powers Act, quoting some of his father's writings on the role of Congress in foreign relations in doing so. He observed:

> "This growing centralization of power in the Executive accompanied as it has been by a similar centralization of domestic power in the Federal Government has created a deep sense of frustration among the people, who increasingly despair that they lack control over their own destinies. There is a demand for participatory democracy in foreign affairs as well as on the domestic scene. Just as means must be found to strengthen local governments in dealing with matters of domestic importance, so must we increase the participation of the elected representatives of the people in the foreign policy determination process, particularly as it applies to matters of war and peace. Of course, Congress did appropriate funds for the [Vietnam] War, but there is a great difference between appropriating funds for troops already committed to battle and

---

[10] 117 Congressional Record (92nd Congress, 1st Session) 40844ff.

[11] 117 Congressional Record 26793-96.

[12] 117 Congressional Record 19848-50.

deciding initially that such a commitment is proper. The 'guns and butter' strategy produced a ruinous inflation. It would also seem to have generated a considerable degree of psychological and economic vulnerability. I am hopeful that this [Act] might turn into what I would term a 'new scepticism' where we no longer would feel a compulsion to intervene in every brush fire around the world."[13]

His nephew John T. Taft was to share these concerns.

He was a serious student of military affairs, preparing a monograph in 1978 entitled "A Modern Military Strategy for the United States" with Democratic Senator Gary Hart and William S. Lind. In it, he deprecated the strategy of forward response in Europe, taking the view that the United States was a sea, not a land, power and sharing his father's perhaps exaggerated view of the utility of airpower. The existing policy in his view reflected the "traditional orientation of the southeastern part of the United States towards the Army" as well as the "infatuation of the Office of the Secretary of Defense with quantitative as opposed to conceptual analysis."[14]

He spoke on a minimum wage bill, decrying youth unemployment and urging an 80% minimum wage for youth unencumbered by the certification requirements that labor unions had attached to the existing 85% youth wage; he also opposed, partly on constitutional grounds, the extension of the minimum wage to domestic servants.[15]

He opposed the extension of the Equal Employment Opportunities Act to state governments unless the enforcement powers over them were vested in the courts and not a federal administrative agency.[16]

---

[13] 118 Congressional Record 11135-36, 11142-43, 11961-62.

[14] A copy appears in WHT IV Papers, Library of Congress, Box 73.

[15] 118 Congressional Record 23959-63.

[16] 118 Congressional Record 1837-39.

He urged the tax deductibility of private school tuitions to the extent of 50% of tuition or $400, whichever was less, with a phase-out for higher income taxpayers.[17]

He supported a bill providing funds for training of day care workers which was opposed by his usually like-minded colleague Senator William Brock as a discrimination against families with stay-at-home mothers.[18]

He voted against closing debate on a bill to curb school busing for purposes of racial balance, confining his objections to inter-jurisdictional busing; his father would probably have been more protective of local interests.[19] His position was vindicated by the subsequent Supreme Court decision in *Milliken v. Bradley*.[20]

In the same year, he supported the Nixon administration's mining of the harbor of Haiphong, expressing the hope that it would lead to greater involvement of the Russians in helping to end the Vietnam War.[21]

In the following year, he delivered eulogies of Presidents Truman and Johnson, lauding the former for his foreign policy realism and the latter for his Civil Rights Acts.[22]

He supported a proposal for amnesty for Vietnam draft resisters performing three years of alternative civilian service.[23]

"It could do something to regain the confidence of millions of Americans, especially among our youth, who love their country but have not agreed with a course it has followed."[24]

---

[17] 118 Congressional Record 14647.

[18] 118 Congressional Record 21390-9.

[19] 118 Congressional Record 35319-26.

[20] 418 U.S. 717 (1974).

[21] 118 Congressional Record 16388.

[22] 119 Congressional Record 3499, 2071.

[23] 119 Congressional Record 42386-87.

[24] R. Taft Jr., "On the Matter of Amnesty," New York Times, January 8, 1972.

He opposed judicial appointment of a special Watergate prosecutor on separation of powers grounds, the position of the Nixon administration.[25]

On the other hand, he supported a compromise proposal that would have limited executive authority to impound appropriations to across-the-board cuts affecting all discretionary appropriations: "One of Congress' primary functions is to set the nation's budgetary priorities. A congressional compromise of this function, in the name of controlling inflation or any other cause, would create a serious imbalance between the powers of the legislature and the executive branch."[26]

On January 1, 1976, he supported the U.S. supply of defensive weapons to Communist China to enable it to resist Soviet pressure.[27] Earlier, he had declared: "We should carefully examine inclusion of China under the Nixon Doctrine providing her with the opportunity to acquire the material she needs to defend herself against aggression."[28]

In 1974, he again opposed the extension of the wage and hour laws to domestic servants, and again refused to cut off debate on a measure to curb school busing, though voicing his hope, ultimately gratified, that the Supreme Court would not compel inter-jurisdictional school busing. "Greater emphasis must be placed on the repeal of restrictive zoning laws, the creation of equal opportunity housing programs and the construction of educational institutions geographically situated to insure equal educational opportunity."[29]

---

[25] 119 Congressional Record 41028-30.

[26] 119 Congressional Record 34874.

[27] New York Times, January 1, 1976.

[28] R. Taft Jr., "Detente, With Caution," New York Times, June 30, 1974.

[29] 120 Congressional Record 5278-80 (domestic servants), 14911-13 (busing).

He opposed the Mansfield amendment to withdraw troops from Europe, which his father might well have favored.[30]

He supported the extension of the National Labor Relations Act to nonprofit hospitals, though with restrictions against strikes, and would have modified a Supreme Court decision invoking the Eleventh Amendment to insulate states against claims for damages by welfare recipients.[31]

On the other hand, he opposed creation of a federal agency for consumer advocacy, which he thought would breed litigation.[32]

He supported Amtrak's exploration of a West Coast corridor, decrying sprawl development as "dis-economical, inconvenient, and generally downright ugly."[33]

In 1975, he opposed any American involvement in Angola: "I have long held the view that we pretty much ought to stay out of Africa and African affairs."[34]

He urged temporary federal aid to localities losing property tax yield because of the bankruptcy of railroads, urging railroad deregulation as the long-term cure;[35] it came about three years later with enactment of the Staggers Act.

Along with 11 other liberal Republicans, he sponsored crime legislation, offered in reaction to Nixon administration proposals, which would have doubled federal expenditures on crime prevention and would have guaranteed federal prisoners annual parole and probation hearings, with counsel; provided compensation for federal and state crime victims; imposed sanctions on states not paying prison labor and allowing it social security credits; and studied

---

[30] 120 Congressional Record 18043.

[31] 120 Congressional Record 12943-46 (hospitals), 29471-72 (welfare).

[32] 120 Congressional Record 25195-202, 31858-61.

[33] 120 Congressional Record 27420-22.

[34] 121 Congressional Record 41202.

[35] 121 Congressional Record 31920.

decriminalization of victimless crimes including drug, alcohol, and prostitution offenses.[36]

In 1976, he opposed the Helms Right to Life amendment to ban all abortions, declaring that "the proper level of government for the consideration of the abortion issues should be the State legislatures. Under our legal system, family and related criminal laws have traditionally been state matters. The controlling Supreme Court decision is unfortunate and leaves more questions unanswered than answered."[37]

He voted to sustain a presidential veto of a bill relating to day care, preferring a system of block grants for day care services.[38]

Finally, in what may have been his most far-reaching and influential proposal as a member of either house of Congress, he presented a fully worked-out proposal for the indexing of standard deductions, personal exemptions, and tax brackets, he being the sole sponsor. He pointed out that a low-income wage earner gave up 4% to 5% of his income to federal income taxes in 1950 as against 9% to 10% 25 years later, because of "bracket creep." In this, he was ahead of his time. "'Bracket creep' might not have been heard of outside of economics departments, but almost every taxpayer felt its effects. Democratic governors like Michael Dukakis of Massachusetts and Jerry Brown of California knew what a rightward pull it was having on Democratic voters."[39] A similar proposal became law about six years later during the Reagan administration.[40]

Following his departure from Congress, in reflecting on the 1984 elections, he made the rather startling assertion that "[h]ad

[36] "12 Liberal Republican Senators Offer Prison Reform Legislation," New York Times, April 13, 1972.

[37] 122 Congressional Record 11577.

[38] 122 Congressional Record 12684.

[39] E. Fawcett and T. Thomas, America, Americans (London: Collins, 1983), 169.

[40] 122 Congressional Record 19175-76.

my father been nominated [in 1952], MacArthur was his 'odds on favorite' for vice president, which leads me to speculate as to what a 3½ year MacArthur presidency would have been like and what its impact might have been on history."[41] This surprising statement by Robert Taft might have been due to MacArthur's last-minute appearance to endorse Taft at the 1952 convention.

In the same article, Robert Jr. renewed his grandfather's and father's commitment to party regularity and the value of party deliberations: "One of our difficulties today is that the party process has become weak. As a result, an increase in individual candidacies with single-issue approaches, rather than a party program, seems likely to continue. A run-off or approval voting system might very well bring improvement and give the proper emphasis to the party's convention role once again. We should remove present limits on contributions by political parties, while still keeping a maximum expenditure limit on individual campaigns." He thought that there should be four regional presidential primaries, to reduce the interminable length and great cost of presidential campaigns. He expressed misgivings about Supreme Court free speech doctrines allowing unlimited contributions by millionaires, suggesting that a constitutional amendment might be appropriate to give Congress the power to regulate national elections.

He was married to Blanca Noel, who died of cancer in 1968 at the age of 51. Thereafter, he married Katherine Longworth Whittaker, the widow of a distant cousin David G. Taft; they were divorced in 1977. In 1978, he married Joan McKelvy (1926-2015).

Robert Taft Jr. had four children. Sarah Butler Taft (1943-), while at Radcliffe married Winfield Jones II in 1963; he is a Harvard College and Law School graduate and a New York lawyer while she graduated from Columbia Law School and became the head of the Criminal Defense Division of the Manhattan Legal Aid Bureau. In personality and attitude, she has been described to some extent as a

---

[41] 122 Congressional Record 19175-76.

child of the late sixties. Deborah Taft Boutellis (1946-), who married a French sculptor, Jean Boutellis, and now lives in Cincinnati. His sculpture Aggregation de l"Espace adorns Cincinnati's Central Parkway and is locally referred to as "The Cootie." Jonathan D. Taft (1954-), a graduate of MIT and the University of Chicago Law School, who was a lawyer in Chicago with the Sonnenschein firm before retirement. Robert Taft III (1942-), discussed in the Fifth Generation chapter.

WILLIAM H. TAFT III (1915-1991)

William H. Taft III, Robert Taft's eldest son, was a graduate of the Taft School and Yale and acquired a Ph.D. in English from Princeton. He had an unusual career, in that he became a career member of the Foreign Service after serving as Ambassador to Ireland from 1953 to 1957. During the war, having been rejected by the military services, he served in an intelligence position in the Pentagon. Thereafter, he taught English at Yale where he learned Gaelic and spent three years in Ireland as a Marshall Plan administrator before being named ambassador. The inclusion of Ireland in the Marshall Plan notwithstanding Ireland's neutrality in World War II and lack of direct war damage was, Taft said, political: "they have spent their time on Capitol Hill."[42]

He resigned as ambassador because "there was not all that much to do and I thought it would be a bad thing for my continuing moral fiber." He turned down the ambassadorship to Sri Lanka thinking that the development of civil war there made appointment of an expert appropriate, only to see the post awarded to Maxwell Gluck, an underwear manufacturer, who embarrassed himself at his confirmation hearings by being unable to name the then Prime Minister. He served on the Policy Planning Staff of the

---

[42] See his Oral History interview with Charles Stuart Kennedy, April 30, 1987, at www.loc.gov/resource/mfclip2004taf02/?sp=178st=text.

William H. Taft III sworn in as Ambassador to Ireland

State Department from 1957 to 1960 under Gerard Smith being principally concerned with Africa, and thereafter served as Consul in Lourenco Marques, Mozambique from 1960 to 1962, and in the new Office of Oceans and International Scientific Affairs. He then resigned from the Foreign Service in the hope of obtaining another political appointment to an ambassadorship, but was unsuccessful in doing so. As ambassador, he became a personal friend of John A. Costello, the Taoseich (President), and organized Costello's visit to the United States in 1956. His wife Barbara Bayfield, a graduate of the University of Michigan who took a Ph.D. at Bryn Mawr, was an historian.[43]

They had four children: Maria Taft Clemow (1943-), a graduate of Bryn Mawr College and a recipient of an M. Litt. Degree at Trinity College, Dublin, where she also received a teaching diploma. She married a French chemistry graduate and pharmaceutical

---

[43] Obituary, Washington Post, November 23, 2007.

executive of Toulouse, France.[44] William H. Taft IV (1945-   ), whose career is discussed in the next chapter. Martha Taft Golden (1947-), a graduate of Bryn Mawr College, who received an M.Sc. Degree at St. Andrews University in geology, and worked for a time as a geologist. She married a Scottish geologist.[45] They live in Cranleigh, Surrey. John T. Taft (1950-), who also is discussed in the next chapter.

HORACE DWIGHT TAFT (1925-1983)

Horace Taft, Robert Taft's youngest son, was a physicist who joined the Yale faculty in 1956 and served as Dean of Yale College from 1971 to 1979, having previously served as Dean of Undergraduate Studies in Physics. He made important contributions to research on sub-atomic particles. As Dean of Yale College, he was caught up in the turbulence of the 1970s, first announcing that failing grades would no longer be included on transcripts, although "withdrawal will continue to be required where the number of failures is inconsistent with satisfactory progress,"[46] only to conclude five years later that "our transcript would be more credible if Fs were recorded."[47]

He was considered "a very strong possibility" for President of Yale when Kingman Brewster retired in 1977, the post going instead to A. Bartlett Giamatti.[48]

He had served in the Army from 1943 to 1946, received a B.A. from Yale in 1950 (which he attended on the G.I. Bill) and master's

---

[44] New York Times, December 9, 1971.

[45] New York Times, September 21, 1971.

[46] New York Times, October 16, 1972.

[47] "Yale Students to Have Their 'F's' Recorded Again," New York Times, January 28, 1976.

[48] "Yale Ponders a New Kingman: At Yale the Talk Is of Succession," New York Times, February 20, 1977.

and Ph.D. degrees from the University of Chicago, where he studied with Enrico Fermi.[49]

He was married to Mary Ann Badger, a graduate of the School of Applied Arts in Zurich. They had three children, discussed in the chapter on the Fifth Generation: John G. Taft (1955-) of Minneapolis; Hugh B. Taft-Morales (1957-) of Washington; and Horace D. Taft-Ferguson (1963-) of New Haven.

Horace Taft

Lloyd Bowers Taft (1923-1985)

Lloyd Taft, the third of Robert Taft's four sons, was a graduate of Yale and the University of Michigan. In his youth, he served as a newspaperman and radio executive, eventually becoming the head of a stockbroking firm in Cincinnati.[50]

---

[49] Obituary, New York Times, February 14, 1983.

[50] Obituary, New York Times, October 23, 1985.

The Fifth Generation

The 25 or so members of the fifth generation of Alphonso Taft's descendants entered a more competitive, less deferential, and more bureaucratic postwar world. Given these obstacles, they must be judged to have given a good account of themselves. William H. Taft IV, in his opposition to the so-called "torture memorandum" in the second Bush administration, an opposition that cost him his job, can be characterized as a bureaucratic hero. Governor Robert Taft III, despite an indiscretion that blemished his record, upheld the cause of fiscal moderation at a time when it had been abandoned by both Democrats and Reagan Republicans; this, more than his indiscreet golf games, was the cause of his political undoing. John G. Taft, a financial executive, was a champion of both fiscal stewardship, for which he gained national prominence, and of moderate Republicanism. John T. Taft, a television producer, wrote two meritorious and still timely books decrying the student excesses of the 1960s and America's over-extended foreign policy in the third world. Others contributed to computer science, geology, nursing and the arts, or had meritorious careers in the law. Virtually all had fine academic records at leading universities and contributed to educational causes.

As a group, their task was helping to curb and discipline excesses arising from the postwar garrison state and the nationalization of political controversies. They stood for the maintenance and restoration of older civilities, and set themselves against the loss of a moral compass in politics.

Robert Taft III (1942-)

Robert Taft III graduated from the Taft School, and Yale College, and then took a master's degree at Princeton and a law degree

Robert Taft III

at the University of Cincinnati. After service in the Peace Corps, he served in the Ohio House from 1977 to 1981, as a Hamilton County Commissioner from 1981 to 1990, as Ohio Secretary of State from 1981 to 1880, and as Governor of Ohio from 1999 to 2007. As Governor, he adhered to a fiscally conservative policy that made him equally unpopular with liberal Democrats and Reagan Republicans. He won election in 1998 against Lee Fisher, receiving 50% of the vote to his opponent's 45%. In 2002, he was overwhelmingly re-elected, receiving 58% of the vote as against 38% for Tim Hagen, his Democratic opponent. During his second term, he sponsored a Third Frontier program involving state assistance to the biomedical, advanced propulsion, and alternative energy industries, totalling $681 million over the period 2003 to 2008. The state also awarded $28 million to a Center for Stem Cell and Regenerative Medicine. His administration invested $10 billion over 12 years in school construction. He also sponsored a modest program of private school vouchers. The state enjoyed steady improvement in test scores, particularly in math and science. He sponsored "tort reform" legislation limiting non-economic damages to $350,000 and shortening a statute of limitations. His highway program included a skyway in Toledo, a beltway in Cleveland, and a bypass in Wilmington. In 2003, responding to a recession, he sponsored a 1% state sales tax, half of which was rescinded in 2005, when phase-out legislation relating to the corporate franchise tax and tangible personal property tax were enacted. At the time, the head of the Ohio AFL-CIO acknowledged: "we get along with him better than with [former Governor George] Voinivich. He's a more honest person."[1]

---

[1] New York Times, July 11, 2004.

He unsuccessfully vetoed legislation requiring that weapons be carried in plain sight. Capital punishment was revived; there were 24 executions and one commutation during his tenure. He vetoed blanket legislation prohibiting jail terms for nonviolent offenders.[2]

He signed legislation barring "gay" marriage, but expressed misgivings about a proposed constitutional amendment to the same effect.[3]

He became involved in a "scandal" concerning his acceptance of 45 golf games and other gifts valued at a total of $5,800 from a rare coin dealer, Tom Noe, who was found to have sold fraudulent investments to the Ohio state pension fund and the Governor pleaded guilty to a misdemeanor offense relating to acceptance of gratuities for which he was fined $4,000 and reprimanded by the Supreme Court of Ohio, though retaining his office.[4]

As pointed out by his first cousin, William H. Taft IV, after discovering he had not reported his golf outings, "he acted immediately to bring it to the attention of the ethics committee and corrected it, which is exactly the right thing to do."[5]

The then Ohio rules required reporting of all gifts valued at more than $75. Ironically, the most recent draft of the Principles of Government Ethics promulgated by the American Law Institute exonerates from liability gifts motivated primarily by a personal relationship that do not have "more than $3,000 cumulative value within any twelve month period."[6]

---

[2] New York Times, July 11, 2002.

[3] New York Times, February 27, 2004, October 15, 2004.

[4] A. Salvato, "Ohio Governor Fined Over Unreported Gifts," New York Times, August 19, 2005; B. Brichaus, "Court Reprimands Ohio Governor Over Gifts, " New York Times, December 28, 2006.

[5] J. Lemer, "Governor's Criminal Conviction Contradicts a Legacy of Integrity," Toledo Blade, August 28, 2005.

[6] American Law Institute, Principles of Government Ethics, Preliminary Draft No. 2, April 13, 2015, sec.204(2).

He served as a delegate to the 2004 Republican convention, and he subsequently directed a Center for Educational Excellence encouraging science studies at the University of Dayton.

He was married to Hope Rothert.

WILLIAM HOWARD TAFT IV (1945-)

William Howard Taft IV attended the St. Paul's School before receiving a B.A. in English from Yale and a law degree from Harvard. He then became a "Nader's Raider," producing a critical study of the Federal Trade Commission,[7] and became an attorney-advisor at the FTC in 1970. From 1970 to 1973 he served as principal assistant to Casper Weinberger at the Office of Management and Budget. He married Julia Vadalla in 1974. He served as Executive Assistant to the Secretary of Health Education and Welfare, Casper Weinberger, from 1973 to 1976, and briefly as General Counsel to that department in 1976. There he was initially concerned with the new federal student loan program, taking the view that "[i]t is wiser to let private capital meet the demand for loans while the federal government conserves scarce budget resources for other forms of student aid."[8] Attention to this advice would have limited extravagant later tuition increases, crushing amounts of student debt, and the risk of massive defaults.

Later, he commended to the attention of Secretary Weinberger a Yale program making loan repayments contingent on income, like the Australian "graduate tax and recent British legislation."[9]

---

[7] E. Cox, et al, The Nader Report on the Federal Trade Commission (New York: Grove Press, 1970).

[8] WHT IV to Mrs. WHT III, March 28, 1973, WHT IV Papers, Library of Congress, Box 67, Folder 2.

[9] WHT IV to Weinberger, April 19, 1973, WHT IV Papers, Library of Congress, Box 67, Folder 3.

The loan programs were ultimately completely federalized during the Obama administration and, together with the fact and promise of "loan forgiveness" programs, have given rise to huge contingent liabilities.

His reaction to the early stage of the Watergate crisis was summarized in a file memorandum, "Two Thoughts on the Watergate," written in May 1973:

William Howard Taft IV

"We must continue to build the structure of world peace, pursuing detente with Russia and China and solidifying the tenuous peace in Indochina. We must promote further economic expansion but take great care to control inflation. We must take advantage of a revitalized federal system and develop new ways of dealing with emerging problems which can only be effectively met at the state and local level. If the Watergate were permitted to cripple our constructive energies at this challenging moment in our history, that would be the greatest scandal of all."[10]

Writing in August 1973 about racial affirmative action, he observed of Nixon: "He is not against quotas because they are numerical but because they are required," to which Weinberger rejoined "the heavy and exclusive reliance on numbers I object to."[11]

A memo in July 1973, prompted by the *Lemon v. Kurtzman* Supreme Court decision on aid to private schools, contained echoes of his forbear Alphonso's attitude on church-state matters: "How do you know that the closing of private schools is 'unavoidable'? I doubt it. At the very least, we should have some data. The memo is inadequate in that it does not once mention to the President the dangers inherent in the government's 'excessive entanglement' with

---

[10] May 5, 1973, WHT IV Papers, Library of Congress, Box 67, Folder 3.

[11] WHT IV to Weinberger, August 2, 1973, in WHT IV Papers, Library of Congress, Box 67, Folder 3.

religious institutions—a consideration no less important now than 200 years ago."[12]

In a speech before a private school PTA in February 1974, he described the advantages of private schools as "Diversity, Freedom of Choice, Religious Preference, Peer Pressure for Academic Excellence, Keep Them [the public schools] Honest," and their disadvantages as "Economic [cost] and Lack of Exposure to Representative Social Environment."[13]

His attitude toward the school busing controversy was nuanced. In July 1974 he observed to Secretary Weinberger: "Even if nothing else comes of it, you can add busing and school district consolidations to that long list of modern developments which are causes (effects?) of the disintegration of the family."[14]

Two years later, he told the Alabaman Secretary Mathews, Weinberger's successor, that "[t]wenty years after *Brown*, not only our schools but our entire society has a totally different attitude toward racial differences. Twenty years from now, the change will be still more marked. The integration of the schools now will multiply the rate of change we have experienced in society as a whole over the last five years."[15]

This view proved overly sanguine.

After the departure of Terrell Bell, whose work he respected, he took a jaundiced attitude toward the Office of Education: "It has long been impossible to get a grammatical sentence out of OE and it is even longer since any new idea surfaced there. What is next to be

---

[12] WHT IV to Weinberger, August 2, 1973, in WHT IV Papers, Library of Congress, Box 67, Folder 3.

[13] Address to Norwood School PTA, February 21, 1974, in WHT IV Papers, Library of Congress, Box 68, Folder 4.

[14] WHT IV to Weinberger, July 2, 1974, in WHT IV Papers, Library of Congress, Box 67, Folder 7.

[15] WHT IV to Mathews, March 24, 1976, in WHT IV Papers, Library of Congress, Box 68, Folder 4.

feared is a complete absence of information as to what is happening. This will occur if a few more mid-level managers find the jobs they have long been looking for and if the vacuum at the top persists."[16]

Much of his time and energy while at HEW were devoted to dealing with a "swine flu" epidemic requiring the negotiation of difficult problems involving the cost of and liability for vaccines. He negotiated a deal with vaccine manufacturers pursuant to which the government provided the public with warnings of possible side effects and liability of manufacturers was limited by requiring damage actions to be brought against the government under the Federal Tort Claims Act with limits on jury trials, punitive damages and contingent fees and requirements of exhaustion of administrative remedies. This approach was upheld by the courts.[17]

More than 40 million people were vaccinated when the program was discontinued, the epidemic not having spread beyond a single military base and a small number of persons having suffered serious side effects from the vaccine.[18]

One person died from the disease at Fort Dix and 13 were hospitalized. The vaccine resulted in 25 deaths and 500 cases of Gillian-Barre syndrome, or about one for every 100,000 persons vaccinated, but the incidence of claims was such that $3.5 billion was paid in compensation. At the crucial point of decision, it was Taft's view that "[t]he chances seemed to be 1 in 2 that swine flu would come."[19]

---

[16] WHT IV to Mathews, May 4, 1976, WHT IV Papers, Library of Congress, Box 68, Folder 6.

[17] Sparks v. Wyeth Labs, 431 F. Supp. 411 (W.D. Okla. 1977); Wolfe v. Merrill Natl., 433 F. Supp. 231 (N.D. Tenn. 1971).

[18] A. Silverstein, Pure Politics and Impure Science (Baltimore: Johns Hopkins U., 1981), 90, 95; H. Fineberg and R. Neustadt, The Swine Flu Affair (Washington: GPO, 1978).

[19] H. Fineberg and R. Neustadt, The Epidemic That Never Was (New York: Vintage, 1983), 263.

He was mildly egalitarian in his attitude toward taxation: "One may or may not like the idea of redistributing income. I think it is healthy, but only up to a point." To the President, he observed: "I would strongly urge that the low income population be generously included in any tax reduction proposal."[20]

After the defeat of President Ford, he began to write a manuscript tentatively entitled "A Social Welfare Policy for Americans" in memory of his grandfather Robert Taft's *A Foreign Policy for Americans*. He sent a proposal to Doubleday, but did not find a publisher and did not finish the book. Its concluding passages, however, summarized his political philosophy: "In too many instances, the federal government has encouraged or at least acquiesced in efforts to discredit intermediate institutions ... state and local governments, health and educational institutions, voluntary organizations and the family have all had their authority eroded. Restraining the abuse of authority should not, however, require dismantling the abusing institutions. It wasn't necessary to pay any price at all. Intermediate institutions tend to reinforce individual responsibility; the federal government to diffuse it."[21]

In his transition memorandum to the incoming Secretary Joseph Califano, he predicted that the Supreme Court would invalidate the Hyde Amendment restricting the availability of federal funds for abortions that his office had defended, a prediction that proved to be mistaken when the Supreme Court decided *Harris v. McRae* in favor of the government.[22]

With the advent of the Carter administration, he joined the Leva Hawes firm in Washington where he remained until the advent of the Reagan administration, in which he was appointed

---

[20] WHT IV to Weinberger, December 11, 1973, in WHT IV Papers, Library of Congress, Box 67, Folder 3; WHT IV to Ford, December 30, 1974, WHT IV Papers, Library of Congress, Box 67, Folder 8.

[21] WHT IV Papers, Library of Congress, Box 84, Folder 8.

[22] WHT IV to Califano, January 18, 1977, in WHT IV Papers, Library of Congress, Box 69, Folder 6.

General Counsel to the Department of Defense under Secretary Weinberger, becoming Deputy Secretary of Defense in 1984, with only Senator Barry Goldwater opposing his confirmation. [23]

In July 1981, taking issue with Rudolph Giuliani, then a Justice Department official, he opposed legislation that would have increased military involvement in the war on drugs, referring to tense situations that could arise if troops accompanied law enforcement officials. This mission, he thought, would detract from preparedness, impair the historic separation between civilian and military activities, and possibly endanger civil liberties. He preferred a Senate bill that excluded DOD personnel from operation of equipment in missions involving arrests.[24]

As General Counsel, he promulgated policies relating to curbs on enlistment of recruits carrying the AIDS virus.[25]

He also ruled that the permission of next of kin was required for organ transplants after death of a service member.[26]

He noted that "[i]f you have the confidence of the Secretary, you tend to get better connections with the services."[27]

As Deputy Secretary, he promulgated new rules requiring inactive reservists to report for duty for one day a year so that their whereabouts could be ascertained and their skills assessed.[28]

---

[23] "Taft Confirmed as Deputy, Only Goldwater Opposes," New York Times, February 5, 1984.

[24] S. Taylor Jr. "Pentagon Balking at Joining Drug War," New York Times, July 4, 1981.

[25] "Pentagon to Test All Recruits for Possible Sign of AIDS Virus," New York Times, August 31, 1985; "Pentagon Extending Its Aids Curbs to ROTCs," New York Times, December 14, 1986.

[26] New York Times, November 3, 1986.

[27] W. Biddle, "The Lawyer Who Oversees the Military Budget," New York Times, October 19, 1984.

[28] New York Times, November 21, 1985.

He was also concerned with improving equipment guarantees and parts purchases.[29]

He authorized acquisition of the controversial Osprey tilt rotor aircraft, though noting that the contract provided for "program cancellation with minimum penalty to the government."[30]

In 1987, he was Weinberger's choice to succeed him as Secretary of Defense, the administration instead appointing Frank Carlucci.[31]

He served as Acting Secretary of Defense from January through March 1989, essentially as a caretaker referring matters to White House aides Brent Scowcroft and Richard Darman,[32] thereafter as Permanent Representative to NATO until 1992. When the Democrats assumed office, he returned to Leva Howes. At the start of the George W. Bush administration, he was named Chief Legal Advisor to the Department of State, serving there with his wife, who had been Assistant Secretary for Population, Refugees and Migration by appointment of President Clinton since 1997.

On January 11, 2002, having learned of the so-called "torture memorandum" sent to the White House by Justice Department Officials Jay Bybee and John Yoo with the connivance of Vice President Chaney, he prepared in one night a lengthy answering memorandum, which was not released by the Bush administration, describing the Yoo memorandum as "seriously flawed," "incorrect as

---

[29] "Pentagon's Watchdog Office to Monitor Parts Purchases," New York Times, December 7, 1984, p. 22; "Parts Purchasing Reform Is Working Out," New York Times, June 2, 1984, p. 29; C. Mohr, "Pentagon's Rules Where Guarantees," New York Times, March 15, 1984; R. Halloran, "Pentagon Says Military Readiness Has Improved Sharply Since 1981," New York Times, May 16, 1984, p. 18.

[30] "U.S. Authorizing Tilt Rotor Plane," New York Times, May 3, 1986.

[31] "Washington Talk: Praise for Two Men, Taft Weinberger's Choice for Successor," New York Times, November 9, 1987.

[32] A. Rosenthal, "Pentagon Decisions Await a Leader," New York Times, February 14, 1989.

well as incomplete," and "contrary to the official position of the US, the UN and all other states that have considered the issue." "In previous conflicts, the United States has dealt with tens of thousands of detainees without repudiating its obligations under the [Geneva] Conventions. I have no doubt we can do so here, where a relative handful of persons is involved ... Your position is, at this point, erroneous in its substance and untenable in practice. Your conclusions are as wrong as they are incomplete." Memoranda in 2003 by the senior law officers in each of the armed services, Marine Brigadier General Kevin Sandkuhler, Army Major General Thomas J. Romig, and Air Force Major General Jack Rives concurred in his view that suspension of the Geneva Convention was "legally flawed and procedurally impossible."

On January 25, 2002, Presidential Counsel Alberto Gonzales asked the President to declare both Al Qaeda and the Taliban outside the coverage of the Geneva Conventions. A memorandum by Taft transmitted by Secretary of State Powell dated February 2, 2002, urged that the plain language of the Geneva Conventions and 50 years of practice was to the contrary, as was the language of U.N. Security Council Resolution 1193 relating to the war in Afghanistan. "A decision that the Conventions do not apply to the conflict in Afghanistan in which our armed forces are engaged deprives our troops there of any claim to the protection of the Convention in the event they are captured and weakens the protections afforded by the Conventions to our troops in future conflicts." Further, "the provisions [of the Geneva Conventions] apply to all persons involved in that conflict. If the Conventions do not apply to the conflict, no one involved in it will enjoy their protection, as a matter of law." "On further consideration, we determined that the conflict with Al Qaeda could be viewed as distinct from the conflict with the Taliban and came to agree with the Attorney General that the Conventions did not apply to it."[33]

---

[33] W. Taft, "The Bush (43rd) Administration: William H. Taft IV," in M. Scharf and P. Williams, Shaping Foreign Policy in Times of Crisis: The Role

On February 7, 2002, President Bush held that the Conventions do not apply to the conflict with Al Qaeda, and asserted the right to suspend the Convention as to the Taliban but decided not to do so at that time, but declared the Taliban ineligible for trial by military tribunals and excluded the State Department from further discussions of the issue.[34]

Thereafter, almost all limitations on questioning were evaded as a matter of policy.[35]

"Taft ... was shunned by the lawyers who dominated detainee policy, officials said. Although Mr. Taft had served as the Deputy Secretary of Defense during the Reagan Administration, more conservative colleagues whispered that he lacked the constitution to fight terrorists. 'He was seen as ideologically squishy and suspect,' a former White House official said. 'People did not take him very seriously.'"[36]

---

of International Law and the State Department Legal Adviser (Cambridge: Cambridge U., 2010), 127, 129.

[34] N. Lewis and E. Schmitt, "The Reach of War: Legal Opinions; Lawyers Decided Bans on Torture Didn't Bind Bush," New York Times, June 8, 2004; T. Golden, "Threats and Responses: Tough Justice: After Terror, A Secret Rewriting of Military Law," New York Times, October 24, 2004; M. Allen and J. Mintz, "Bush Grants Taliban Detainees Geneva Convention Protections," Washington Post, February 8, 2002. The pertinent documents are a letter from Attorney General Ashcroft to President Bush, February 1, 2002, and a memorandum from Taft to Alberto Gonzales, February 2, 2002, at www. nytimes.com/packages/html/ politics/20040608.Doc.pdf. Taft's memorandum is reprinted in 37 Case Western Reserve Journal of International Law 615 (2006). See Taft's comments in W. Taft and N. Buchwald, "Preemption, Iraq and International Law," 97 Am. J. Intl. Law 557 (2003).

[35] See "Lawyering the Treatment of Detainees in the War on Terrorism," ch. 16 of M. Scharf and P. Williams, Shaping Foreign Policy in Times of Crisis: The Role of International Law and the State Department Legal Adviser (Cambridge: Cambridge U., 2010), 181, 187.

[36] N. Lewis and E. Schmitt, "Threats and Responses: After Terror, A Secret Rewriting of Military Law," New York Times, June 8, 2004.

Taft later observed: "I am convinced that if we had been involved and our views considered, several conclusions that were not consistent with our treaty obligations under the Convention against Torture (CAT) and our obligations under customary international law would not have been reached. Later, in 2004, when we worked with the Department of Justice on the revision of the memorandum on the CAT that had been withdrawn earlier in the year, we were able to reach agreement on a very respectable opinion."[37]

After Colin Powell was succeeded by Condaleeza Rice as Secretary of State following the 2004 elections, Taft was replaced as Chief Legal Advisor by John Bellinger. His role had been revealed in an article in the *Washington Post* for June 24, 2004. He returned for a time to Leva Howes and in 2007 became Warren Christopher Professor of International Law and Diplomacy at Stanford. In May of 2005 it was disclosed that Taft had thwarted an effort by John Bolton, then Undersecretary of State for Arms Control, to have one of his subordinates removed from the State Department.[38]

On September 12, 2006, he publicly condemned the Bush administration's attempted redefinition of Common Article 3 of the Geneva Convention; he previously had supported an administration-opposed proposal subjecting CIA interrogations to the standards set out in the Army Field Manual.[39]

He was not a tribune of the people. He had the Taft dryness and, in speech, the Taft accent. He saw the unifying characteristics of his family as being interest in education and "awkwardness in the limelight." To invoke the language of Learned Hand in his eulogy of Justice Cardozo, the Tafts were not "foolish, tawdry moths flying

---

[37] W. Taft, "The Bush (43rd) Administration: William H. Taft IV," in M. Scharf and P. Williams, Shaping Foreign Policy in Times of Crisis: The Role of International Law and the State Department Legal Adviser (Cambridge: Cambridge U., 2010), 130.

[38] D. Tell, "Ex-CIA Official Says Bolton Interfered," Washington Post, May 7, 2005.

[39] New York Times, December 13, 2005.

into publicity's consuming fire." He took pride in the fact that his family had provided the endowment for the nation's largest classical library, two deans of leading colleges, and the founder of a leading boarding school.

John G. Taft (1955-)

John G. Taft, oldest son of Horace Dwight Taft, graduated from the Taft School in 1972 and from Yale, magna cum laude, in 1977. After working briefly for the *New York Times* and the Lowell (Massachusetts) *Sun*, he settled in Minneapolis and ultimately became Chief Executive Officer of RBC Wealth Management, the seventh largest retail brokerage firm in the United States and an affiliate of the Royal Bank of Canada. In 1978, he married the former Martha McPhee, a summa cum laude graduate of Yale;[40] the couple had three children, but the marriage ended in divorce, attributed by him to workaholism. Taft subsequently married a Quebecois with two children. He was led to support the "gay rights" movement by a child and step-child who were gay.

He is an advocate of a federal fiduciary standard of care for corporate directors, and is the author of *Stewardship: Lessons Learned from the Lost Culture of Wall Street*,[41] and the editor of a collection of essays on similar themes published in 2015, *A Force for Good: How Enlightened Finance Can Restore Faith in Capitalism*.[42]

In October 2013, following the downgrading of U.S. bonds due to the failure of Congress to promptly raise the limit on national debt, he wrote a letter to the *New York Times*,[43] published under the title "Cry of the True Republican," in which he observed:

---

[40] New York Times, December 11, 1977 (engagement), June 11, 1978 (marriage).

[41] (Philadelphia: John Wiley, 2012).

[42] (New York: Palgrave Macmillan, 2015).

[43] New York Times, October 22, 2013.

"The Republican Party is, or should be, the Stewardship Party. The Republican Party is, or should be, about responsible behavior. The Republican Party is, or should be, at long last about decency. What a long way we have yet to go."

John G. Taft

He was nonetheless described by one of his relatives as "practically a Democrat."

In his book on Stewardship, Taft reviewed the reforms carried out by the Dodd–Frank law and was encouraged by four of the reforms, those creating a Financial Stability Oversight Council to identify systemic risks, providing resolution authority and "living wills" for all financial institutions, requiring that derivatives be traded on regulated exchanges or through more transparent swap execution facilities, and requiring that originators of most mortgages retain unhedged exposure to at least 5% of the originated mortgage.[44]

He minimized the significance of the "Volcker rule" barring banks from trading for purposes unrelated to service of clients and the creation of a new Consumer Financial Protection Bureau.[45]

He found much hope in the new Basel II capital requirements for banks and related reforms having to do with capital quality, leverage, liquidity coverage and counterparty credit risk.[46]

As chairman of the Securities Industry and Financial Markets Association Private Client Group Steering Committee he urged the adoption of a fiduciary rather than suitability standard of care for broker-dealers and others giving investment advice to individual

---

[44] J. Taft, Stewardship: Lessons Learned from the Lost Culture of Wall Street (Hoboken, NJ: Wiley, 2012), 63-66.

[45] *Id.* 67.

[46] *Id.* 58-63.

investors,[47] a proposal ultimately adopted by the Labor Department, but for retirement accounts only. A proposed SEC rule of a broader nature met with opposition and, though authorized by the Dodd–Frank Act, has been delayed.[48]

In a section comparing the business cultures of the United States and Canada, he expresses a preference for Canadian values, in many respects the values of the Tafts:

> "Never change something that works
> Keeping what you have is preferable to searching for
>   something better
> Plan ahead for the future
> Incremental change is best
> Doing nothing is a perfectly acceptable course of action
> Never bet more than you can afford to lose."[49]

He announced his retirement from RBC in January 2016, effective as of May 31, 2016.[50]

JOHN T. TAFT (1950-)

John T. Taft, a son of William H. Taft III, graduated from the St. Paul's School (New Hampshire) and Yale and received master's degrees from Oxford and Johns Hopkins. He is married to Christine Jordan, a graduate of Brown and the University of Virginia, who was formerly a legal historian at the U.S. Supreme Court.[51]

---

[47] T. Bernard, "U.S. Plans Stiffer Rules Protecting Retiree Cash," New York Times, April 14, 2015.

[48] *Id.* 77-83.

[49] *Id.* 47-49.

[50] Idzelis, "RBC's Wealth Management Chief John Taft Is to Retire," Wealth Management.com, January 15, 2016.

[51] New York Times, June 29, 1990.

He is the author of *Mayday at Yale*,[52] an account of civil disturbances there in the late 1960s, and of *American Power: The Rise and Decline of American Globalism*,[53] a history of American twentieth-century diplomacy faulting American intervention in the Third World, particularly in Vietnam, which as a television producer he made into two television series: *After the War* and *America's Century*. His book on the disturbances at Yale was written at Oxford "on a father fellowship and with the continuing astute advice of my mother."[54]

He was sharply, though judiciously critical of Yale President Kingman Brewster's handling of the disturbances: "A university is an open place where visitors and strangers are free to come and go. An official welcome, in effect a betrayal of academic neutrality, in order to pacify a political assemblage, seems less than courageous. The formal decision to 'open up' Yale on May Day can only be explained as submission to extreme fear and pressure. Brewster's statement of skepticism about the possibility of a fair trial was at variance with his earlier call for academic neutrality. Academic principles shifted to the back of his mind temporarily as he made his retreat in the face of a physical threat ... He was willing to compromise the ideal of what a university should be in order to do what he believed necessary and expedient."[55]

His conclusions about the student movement were equally trenchant: "The American student movement disrupted campus and community for more than six years. A product of the soaring birthrate after World War II and the great increase in public and private money for education in the 1960s, the movement was instigated and sustained by black activists and the frustrations of the Vietnam War ... Not only is the United States too large and diverse

---

[52] (Boulder, CO: Westview, 1976).

[53] (New York: Harper, 1989).

[54] *Mayday*, *supra*, iv.

[55] *Id.* 29-30, 88-89, 95.

to be seriously affected by student politics, but the students of the sixties had neither extreme inequities to complain of nor a strong radical tradition to sustain them ... The 'marginal elements' that dominated American campuses in the sixties were often inspired by a sense of decency and compassion. But no movement succeeds because of the virtue of its motives. In action, student radicals exhibited so much self-indulgent intolerance that their reforms were transitory, their allies were estranged, and their entire generation was diminished."[56]

WILLIAM HOWARD TAFT V (1978-)

William Howard Taft V, a son of William Howard Taft IV, received a degree in history from Yale and graduated from the Yale Law School, thereafter serving as law clerk to Mr. Justice Alito in 2004-2005. Previously, in 2000-2001, he worked as a researcher for the RAND Corporation, writing a monograph entitled *Conventional Coercion Across the Spectrum of Operations: The Utility of U.S. Military Forces in the Emerging Security Environment*, published in 2003. He is a partner in the Debovoise law firm in New York. In 2005, he married Begum Bengu, a Turkish bridge architectural designer who is a Yale graduate with an M.A. from Harvard.[57]

HUGH B. TAFT-MORALES (1957-)

Hugh B. Taft-Morales, of Washington, the second son of Horace Dwight Taft, graduated cum laude from Yale and received an M. Phil. Degree from the University of Kent at Canterbury. He

---

[56]   *Id.* 1, 174ff.

[57]   New York Times, November 5, 2005.

is now a minister with the Baltimore Ethical Society and the Ethical Humanist Society of Philadelphia[58]

HORACE D. TAFT-FERGUSON (1963-)

Horace D. Taft-Ferguson, of New Haven, the youngest son of Horace Dwight Taft, attended the Taft School and Hamline University.

LLOYD B. TAFT (1962-)

Lloyd B. Taft, of New York, the only son of Lloyd Taft, is a graduate of Hampshire College and the Yale Architectural School. Some of his work can be viewed on a biog., BuildingSpirituality.org. He practices in Ridgefield, Connecticut.

JULIA TAFT JONATHAN (1958-2013)

Julia Taft Jonathan, a daughter of Lloyd Taft, graduated from the Taft School and Yale College. After teaching at the Hamden School and a related camp, she returned to Yale to take a nursing degree, and became associated with the Yale New Haven Orthopedics Group.[59]

VIRGINIA TAFT CARABINE (1950-)

Virginia Taft Carabine, another daughter of Lloyd Taft, was a graduate of Radcliffe, the Stanford Law School, and the University

---

[58] Idzelis, "RBC's Wealth Management Chief John Taft Is to Retire," Wealth Management.com, January 15, 2016.

[59] Geni.com/people/Julia-Jonathan, accessed February 4, 2018; Obituary, New Haven Register, January 31, 2013.

of Kent at Canterbury where she took a master's degree in English literature. Her husband was a lecturer in English literature at that university. She briefly worked for the legal services program of the Office of Economic Opportunity.[60]

Louise Taft Cooke (1949-)

Louise Taft Cooke, a third daughter of Lloyd Taft, graduated from Mount Holyoke and was married in 1970 to Carlton Perry Cooke III, then a medical student.[61]

Rhonda Taft Jones (1984-)

Rhonda Taft Jones, a fourth daughter of Lloyd Taft, remained in Cincinnati. Her career details are unavailable.[62]

Patricia M. Taft (1984-)

Patricia M. Taft, a fifth daughter of Lloyd Taft, received a degree cum laude from Vanderbilt University and an M.A. in Interior Design. She married Christopher Swaine and runs the Patricia Taft Studio in Santa Monica, California.

---

[60] Wedding Announcement, New York Times, September 15, 1974.

[61] Engagement notice, New York Times, July 28, 1974, Wedding notice, September 15, 1974.

[62] Wedding notice, New York Times, December 20, 1970.

Conclusion

There are some remarkable commonalities among the Tafts, now America's longest-lived political dynasty. They were united by unusual family institutions: Sky Farm in Cincinnati, at times inhabited by more than one nuclear family; the compound on the St. Lawrence in Quebec; the Taft School; and Yale College. They also had distinctive family values: the cultivation of academic excellence in each generation, among both men and women; a penchant for marrying highly intelligent women; abstention from alcoholic and sexual overindulgence. The values they stood for in politics also were of a piece: limitations of great concentrations of power, public and private; respect for localism, and for what Judge Learned Hand called "the preservation of personality"; protection of the rule of law, as distinct from a political agenda; suspicion of an over-aggressive foreign policy; a humane regard for those at the bottom of society, together with a determination that their plight should not be used as a fulcrum for the creation of monolithic state institutions. As President Taft put it in his *Liberty Under Law*:

> "We can waste money in helping individuals to a habit of dependence that will weaken our citizenship … We must stop attempting to reform people by wholesale. It is the individual upon whom our whole future progress depends. In giving and securing scope for his ambition, energy and free action our constitutional system has its chief merit, whatever would-be reformers say."[1]

In the intellectually complacent liberal climate that followed the New Deal, these ideals did not resonate. A review of a biography

---

[1] WHT, Liberty Under Law, *supra*, 42.

of Robert Taft by Elting Morison in 1954 self-indulgently described Taft as "so fully engaged in his own ideas that only imperfectly and with reluctance was he made aware of what was going on … he as a Middle Westerner liked to believe that America was an island unto itself … a receiver for an insolvent faith [with] no refreshing ideas upon which his followers could unite for constructive action,"[2] though conceding that he was "honorable, shy, able, decently ambitious and wholly courageous … He possessed, what most of his colleagues had lost, a desire to make the thing work."

Eighteen years later, Wilson Carey McWilliams, long an editor of the left-wing *Nation*, reviewing the Patterson biography of Taft in a more chastened America took a more generous view: the Tafts were "part of the old middle class, a social and political world radically different from the world of the Babbitts and the organization men.… Taft hated rule by interest groups generally, by bureaucracy, by centralized government … Taft never recognized that the law 'rules' only in a society of atomized individuals, each unable to affect the whole and secure in the knowledge that neither can anyone else." They "never aped the style of the socialites, [adhering to] a severe atmosphere which demanded that individuals work hard and excel—on their own, sticking it out confident that effort, honesty and character would win through … The Tafts respected education and the mind: it would be difficult outside New England to find an equally wealthy family with so many Ph.D.'s."[3] One of their descendants, John T. Taft, referred to "a tradition of going into politics, the judiciary, the military or public administration with relative honesty and dedication … perform[ing] the essential task of keeping the ship of state going without as much favoritism, greed, or lust for power as many other people."

---

[2] E. Morison, Book Review of W. White, The Taft Story, New York Times Book Review, April 11, 1954, 1.

[3] W. McWilliams, Book Review of J. Patterson, Mr. Republican, New York Times Book Review, November 19, 1972, 1.

A recent study, following upon Francis Galton, found that class position varied little across generations of prominent families, the thesis being that genetic kinship and wise marriages sustained existing social positions.[4] While the Tafts married carefully, Robert Nisbet is probably right in saying that their distinction "may and probably does argue something in favor of genetic transmission, but it much more visibly and incontestably argues something in the way of the continuity of cultural patterns: patterns of incentive—recorded achievement to serve as example; of the kind of training and instruction that can come only from someone who is emotionally close, indeed persistently close, and of the discipline, encouragement, and emulation which are so vital in the formation of personalities, good or bad, gifted or sterile."[5]

"Taft's fight against modernity," McWilliams wrote, "was brave, but a little sad, a little foolish. And there is something equally plaintive in the shy boy, fearful of failure and ridicule, savagely self-punitive, who tried to cover his sensitivity by abruptness, assertiveness, and an air of certitude. But his followers, so much like him, saw through the mask to the love within; it, as much as his role as their champion, won their hearts. And whatever his faults, we will miss him in a time when character, integrity and courage exist only as memories in the world of politics." The Catholic historian Carroll Quigley similarly regarded Taft as a spokesman for a declining old middle class, attributing its decline largely to post–World War II prosperity: "The child who grows up in affluence is more difficult to instill with the frustrations and drives that were so basic to the middle-class outlook. For generations, even in fairly rich families this indoctrination had continued because of continued emphasis

---

[4] G. Clark, The Son Also Rises: Surnames and the History of Social Mobility (Princeton: Princeton U., 2015).

[5] R. Nisbet, Twilight of Authority (New York: Oxford, 1975) 256-58.

on thrift and restraints on consumption … middle class self-discipline and future preference provided the savings and investment."[6]

The family history belies the statement of Arthur Schlesinger Jr.: "We have no aristocracy in the British sense; how can we expect to enjoy aristocratic leadership? For better or worse, our upper classes base their position not on land or tradition or a sense of social responsibility but on the folding stuff. They constitute not an aristocracy but a plutocracy."[7]

The Tafts' history assuredly manifests what Bertrand Russell called "many elements which have hitherto been associated with aristocracy, such as fearlessness, independence of judgment, emancipation from the herd, and leisurely culture." They were also relatively free from what Russell called "the typical aristocratic vices, limitation of sympathy, haughtiness, and cruelty for those outside a charmed circle." Russell thought there were three conditions necessary to make the positive qualities widespread in an industrial community: "first, a more even distribution of the production of labor, second, security against large-scale wars, and third, a population which is stationary or nearly so."[8] For many, Senator Robert Taft is the most problematic of the Tafts, but in his instinctive acceptance of progressive taxation and his hostility to foreign wars and large-scale immigration, his vision of an ideal society was not far removed from Bertrand Russell's.

In their approach to education, they favored the traditional liberal arts and the law, as distinct from micro-economics and "public choice" theory. Robert Taft Sr. repented scattering his college courses among disciplines, rather than majoring in English

---

[6] C. Quigley, Triumph and Tragedy: A History of the World in Our Time (New York: Macmillan, 1966), 1252, 1237.

[7] A. Schlesinger, The Politics of Hope (London: Eyre and Spottiswoode, 1964), 75.

[8] B. Russell, "Things That Have Moulded Me," The Dial, September 1927, 181-86, reprinted as "Introduction" Selected Papers of Bertrand Russell (New York: Modern Library, 1927), xv-xvi.

literature; William Howard Taft III and William Howard Taft IV both became English majors. For those contemplating public life, English and History are not self-indulgent choices; they involve the study of how human beings behave in fact, not about the ways in which economists and "political scientists" would like them to behave or assume they behave.

To a surprising degree, the Tafts' policy causes continue to have relevance, and need to be revived, not forgotten. They upheld the separation of powers that is the foundation of American government. William Howard Taft's cures for the concentration of wealth did not include measures of confiscation such as the "wealth taxes" being fostered by some of today's Presidential candidates. He and his son Robert were mindful of the fate of state intangible property taxes, which were easily evaded and found to be unenforceable. Instead, he favored measures, both in private and public law, which would foster the fragmentation of estates, including shortening of the rule against perpetuities (some states today have moved in the opposite direction by abolishing it), forced heirship, i.e., equal division requirements on the model of the Napoleonic Code for the very largest estates, and graduated inheritance taxes in place of estate taxes. These methods do not seize property from the living, but ensure its fragmentation after death. He was similarly hostile to large philanthropic foundations with perpetual lives, a concern not shared by today's redistributionists, who like the left-wing causes fostered by "philanthropoids" in the foundations.

Another favored cause of William Howard Taft was "industrial education," which he sought to foster in his frequent meetings with Booker T. Washington and during his 18 years on the Board of Directors of the Hampton Institute. This cause suffered during his time from the opposition on W.E.B. Du Bois and other "civil rights" leaders, North and South, who stressed professional education for the "talented tenth" of blacks at the expense of education in occupations requiring manual labor, which were thought of as a continuation of servitude. Today, there is renewed appreciation of the value and importance of vocational education and admiration for the German apprenticeship system, with its recognition of the dignity of labor and its appreciation of the fact that not all persons have the aptitudes or home backgrounds fitting them for conventional college education.

Taft's opposition to sumptuary legislation manifested in his newspaper writings opposing the Volstead Act resonates in this era of reaction against the excesses of the drug war. Similarly, his resistance to "defined benefit" pension plans has continuing resonance.

Both William and Robert Taft shared three attitudes toward the making of war. First, it should not be undertaken without support from Congress. This underlay President Taft's non-intervention in Mexico and his son's withholding support for the Korean War after the Truman administration failed to seek its endorsement by Congress. Second, it should be restricted to causes where the American interest was clear, and required deliberation: 'a war that cannot stand the test of delay is a war best not embarked upon.' This was reflected in Senator Taft's delineation of an American sphere of interest largely confined to North, Central, and Northern South America and the Caribbean Third, when force was used, overwhelming force should be employed.

On this basis, President Taft, like Theodore Roosevelt, opposed the armistice in World War I, believing that German militarism needed to be decisively broken and likewise favored the sending of a large force to Russia to strangle Bolshevism in its cradle, Taft describing Wilson's limited intervention at Murmansk as being equivalent to being "a little bit pregnant." His son Robert, no military expert, lay heavy emphasis on the use of air power. Even in domestic affairs, President Taft held to the same view, and was accused of bloody-mindedness in declaring at the time of the Pullman strike that six deaths of strikers were not enough. There is no doubt that had he been called upon to employ force in the American South, his response would have resembled President Eisenhower's deployment of airborne troops at Little Rock more than President Kennedy's sending of a scratch team of U.S. Marshals to Oxford, Mississippi.

There is increasing disillusionment today with the "consumer welfare" theory of antitrust policy, particularly of its use to uphold increasingly monopolistic control of the mass media. This renders President Taft's vigorous deployments of antitrust litigation to combat "private government" increasingly attractive.

Chief Justice Taft's wide recognition of a broad federal commerce power over economic questions to regulate but not spend would have spared the nation much constitutional controversy in the 1930s. His dislike of the use of the taxing and spending power to accomplish non-revenue objects, manifest in the child labor tax case, has enjoyed a revival in the recent *Sibelius* case curbing conditional federal spending power and protecting state autonomy.

Similarly, both Tafts, though upholding the powers of the federal judiciary, were prepared to curb abuses of power by the bench. President Taft was prepared to completely prohibit the use of temporary restraining orders; Senator Taft did not challenge the restrictions placed by the Norris-La Guardia Act on the seeking of labor injunctions by employers

The Tafts were united in their belief in representative government and their hostility to "direct democracy." The vices of party primaries, as opposed to the convention system, were decried by both William Howard and Robert Taft. Since it became dominant in 1960, the quality of Presidential nominees has measurably deteriorated, and a similar deterioration has taken place in Great Britain, where party leaders are no longer chosen by parliamentarians who know them but by an electorate of enrolled and fanatical party activists. As for ballot initiatives and plebiscites, the recent California experience and the Common Market and Scottish Independence referenda in Great Britain give force to the Tafts' forebodings.

Modern conceptions of both executive and judicial power are in large part the work of William Howard Taft. His *Myers* decision defines Presidential removal power except over administrative agencies; he was deemed by Henry Stimson to be the best administrator of the six Presidents he served: Theodore Roosevelt, Taft, Coolidge, Hoover, Franklin Roosevelt, and Truman. Taft protected the investigative power of Congress in *McGrain v. Daugherty*.[9] The modern authority of the Supreme Court rests on the discretion in selection of cases and the rule-making power that he secured from Congress as Chief Justice.

Many of Robert Taft's causes have contemporary pertinence. Few propose revival of the price, wage, and rent controls that he fought so bitterly. In his speech in opposition to President Truman's "socialized medicine" proposal, he urged funding of school health examinations, medical practices in poorer areas, and community health clinics, all causes that would benefit from greater attention. Community clinics have recently been expanded at the instance of Senator Bernie Sanders; the other two proposals await sponsors. Senator Taft also urged that military expenditures should be paid for, at least in part, by increased taxation. This cause was later fostered by the Budget Reconciliation Act, since eroded by lobbying by the military. The little-noted provision of the UN Charter contemplating codification of international law, inserted at the urging of Senator Taft, has recently received belated attention at the UN.

His most important contributions were his preservation of the Republican Party as a coherent political force: its revival after the Roosevelt landslide in 1936 did not begin until his arrival in the Senate in 1938. His efforts to assert Congressional war powers are now more appreciated. Although stigmatized as an isolationist, his was the most influential voice in the repeal of the embargo legislation signed by President Roosevelt in 1939—a repeal that made possible the cash-and-carry purchases that sustained Britain for the first two years of the war until shifts in public opinion made possible the enactment of lend-lease. He would have required means-testing for new welfare programs; programs of general applicability like medicare and the student loan program required federal taxes and controls and their third-party payment systems were an impetus to inflation in costs, there being no market checks on inflation.

---

[9] 223 U.S. 134 (1927).

Robert Taft Jr's once lonely advocacy of indexing of tax brackets, deductions, and exemptions to avoid constant automatic extensions of the resources and role of the federal government has become an accepted part of our law. William Howard Taft IVs insistence on compliance with the *posse commitatus* act and on interrogation standards for the military and CIA have had a beneficial influence on today's practices. Few other contemporary politicians have emulated the efforts of Governor Robert Taft III, both in and out of office, to foster high school science education, a tremendous national need, and few private citizens have displayed John G. Taft's interest in fostering fiduciary responsibility in the investment industry

The Tafts, in politics, have shown a capacity to see beyond the immediate fashionable causes of the moment, and have at times displayed a willingness to oppose such causes, as with John T. Taft's critiques of post-war American foreign policy in the Third World and of student activism, the surrender of college administrations to it, and their malign consequences.

A currently serving U.S. Senator, on being informed of this project, observed that William Howard Taft in his judgment was one of the five outstanding U.S. Presidents. This is not a fashionable judgment, but a very defensible one. Recent works by Jeffrey Rosen[10] and Dolores Kearns Goodwin[11] have elevated President Taft's popular standing. The present writer's own list would include Presidents Washington, Jefferson, and the two Roosevelts, all, like Taft, aristocrats of a sort. There are other worthy Presidents, some from humbler backgrounds like Harry Truman, who fit within Edmund Burke's definition in the *Appeal from the Old to the New Whigs* of "natural aristocrats": "to be bred in a place of estimation; to be taught to respect one's self, to have leisure to read, to reflect,

---

[10] J. Rosen, William Howard Taft: The 27th President (New York: Holt, 2017).

[11] D. Goodwin, The Bully Pulpit: Theodore Roosevelt, William Howard Taft, and the Golden Age of Journalism (New York: Simon and Schuster, 2013).

to converse; to be habituated in armies to command and to obey; to possess the virtues of diligence, order, constancy and regularity." It is astonishing how little attention is paid today to the early family background and undergraduate education of Presidential aspirants.

The Tafts tended in matters of religion to be Unitarians and Episcopalians; of the "varieties of religious experience," these are not the most intense. Their common creed could be summarized in two quotations, one from the author and colonial Governor General John Buchan (Lord Tweedsmuir); the other from the diplomat Lewis Einstein, summarizing the beliefs of Justice Holmes. Both these writers forswore equality of condition, even as an ideal; Buchan observed:

> "In such a world, everyone would have leisure. But everyone would be restless, because there would be no spiritual discipline in life. Some kind of mechanical philosophy of politics would have triumphed and everyone would have his neat little part in the state machine. Everybody would be comfortable, but since there could be no great demand for intellectual exertion, everybody would be also slightly idiotic. Their shallow minds would be easily bored and therefore unstable. Their life would largely be a quest for amusement. The raffish existence led today by certain groups would have become the normal existence of large sections of society.
>
> Some kind of intellectual life would no doubt remain, though the old political disputes would have cancelled each other out, and the world would not have the stimulus of a contest of political ideals, which is after all a spiritual thing."[12]

---

[12] J. Buchan, Pilgrim's Way (Boston: Houghton Mifflin, 1940), 289-90, quoted in J. Lukacs, A New Republic: A History of the United States in the Twentieth Century (New Haven: Yale, 2006), 198. Cf. Eric Hobsbawm to Eugene Genovese, undated, 1992, quoted in R. Evans, Eric Hobsbawm: A Life in History

Lewis Einstein wrote of Holmes:

"His own lack of belief was very far from being a mere negation. It carried with it the thought that life was in itself an end, but that real life must always result in a struggle either of the mind or of the body, for nothing that one came by easily was ever worth having. No man despised materialism more, and he felt little sympathy for any future world that was 'cut up into five acre lots and having no man upon it who was not well fed and well housed' unless this future world was also prepared to understand 'the divine folly of honor, the senseless passion for knowledge' and the pursuit of ideals that could never be achieved but which made life worth living."[13]

(Boston: Little Brown, 2019), 598: declaring that "radicalization, mindless, libertarian and often basically individualist (i.e., anti-social) ... 1968 radicalism provided and provides no basis for progressive politics."

[13] L. Einstein, Preface to J. Peabody (ed.), Holmes–Einstein Letters (New York: Macmillan, 1964), xix, xxlv.

Dramatis Personae

Benedict, Katherine Taft (1909-2001) Daughter of Hulbert Taft.

Clemow, Maria Taft (1943-) Daughter of William H. Taft III, M. Litt, Trinity College, Dublin, resident in France.

Golden, Martha Taft (1947-) Daughter of William H. Taft III, geologist.

Hunter, Helen Manning (1921-2013) Daughter of Helen Taft Manning, Professor of Economics, Swarthmore College.

Manning, Caroline (1925-2020) Daughter of Helen Taft Manning, teacher, Manhattan School of Music.

Manning, Helen Taft (1891-1987) Daughter of William Howard Taft, Professor of History, Dean, and Acting President, Bryn Mawr College, author *British Colonial Government After the American Revolution* (Yale, 1935), *The Revolt of French Canada* (Macmillan, 1962).

Semple, Louise Taft (1879-1961) Daughter of Charles Taft, benefactor of Classics Department at University of Cincinnati.

Sinton, Anna (1850-1931) Wife of Charles Taft, department store heiress.

Taft, Alphonso (1810-1891) Ohio Circuit Judge, Secretary of War, Attorney General, Minister to Vienna and St. Petersburg.

Taft, Charles (1843-1929) Half-brother and financial supporter of William Howard Taft, publisher of *Cincinnati Times-Star*, Congressman from Ohio.

Taft, Charles II (1897-1983) Son of William Howard Taft, leader of Cincinnati Charter movement, Mayor of Cincinnati, unsuccessful candidate for Governor of Ohio, head of wartime agencies in Roosevelt administration, author *You, I and Roosevelt* (Farrar and Rinehart, 1936), *City Management: The Cincinnati Experiment* (Kennikat Press, 1971).

Taft, Cynthia Bradley (1950-) Daughter of Seth Taft, lecturer, Massachusetts Institute of Technology.

Taft, Cynthia Herron (1928-2013) Daughter of Charles Taft Jr., Professor of Economics, Smith College, labor economist.

Taft, David (1916-1962) Son of Hulbert Taft, officer of Taft Broadcasting.

Taft, Deborah (1946-) Daughter of Robert Taft Jr.

Taft, Eleanor Kellogg (1918-2004) Daughter of Charles Taft Jr.

Taft, Frederick I. (1945-) Son of Seth Taft, Cleveland lawyer.

Taft, Helen Herron (1861-1943) Wife of William Howard Taft, author of *Recollections of Full Years* (Dodd Mead, 1914), *see* C. Anthony, Nellie Taft (Morrow, 2005).

Taft, Henry (1859-1945) Special Assistant to the Attorney General, leader of the New York Bar, President, Japan Society, author *Occasional Papers* (Macmillan, 1920), *Opinions, Literary and Otherwise* (Macmillan, 1934), *Legal Miscellenies* (Macmillan, 1941).

Taft, Horace Dutton (1861-1943) Founder of Taft School, author *Memories and Opinions* (Macmillan, 1942).

Taft, Horace Dwight (1925-1983) Physicist with Enrico Fermi, Dean of Yale College under of Taft School.

Taft, Hulbert (1877-1959) Publisher *Cincinnati Times-Star*.

Taft, Hulbert Jr. (1907-1967) Officer of Taft Broadcasting.

Taft, John G. (1955-) Oldest son of Horace Dwight Taft, Head, American branch of Royal Bank of Canada, author of *Stewardship* (Wiley 2012), *A Force for Good* (Palgrave Macmillan, 2015).

Taft, John T. (1950-) Television producer, author *May Day at Yale* (Westview, 1976), *American Power: The Rise and Decline of American Globalism* (Harper, 1989).

Taft, Jonathan D. (1954-) Son of Robert Taft Jr., lawyer in Chicago.

Taft, Lloyd (1923-1985) Son of Robert A. Taft, head of stockbroking firm, Cincinnati.

Taft, Lloyd B. (1962-) Son of Robert Taft III, architect.

Taft, Lucia C. (1924-1955) Daughter of Charles Taft Jr., suicide.

Taft, Martha Bowers (1891-1958) Wife of Robert A. Taft.

Taft, Peter Rawson (1785-1867) Member Vermont legislature, Vermont Circuit and Probate Judge.

Taft, Peter Rawson (1846-1889) Son of Charles Taft, Valedictorian at Yale.

Taft, Peter Rawson III (1937-) Law Clerk to Chief Justice Warren, partner in Williams and Connally, Assistant Attorney General for Lands Division, partner Munger and Tolles, Los Angeles.

Taft, Robert (1640-1725) Emigrated from Russia 1678.

Taft, Robert A. (1889-1953) Majority leader, Ohio House, Congressman and Senator from Ohio, *see* J. Patterson, *Mr. Republican* (Houghton Mifflin, 1972), author *A Foreign Policy for Americans* (Doubleday, 1951).

Taft, Robert Jr. (1917-1993) Congressman and Senator from Ohio, author (with Gary Hart and William Lind) "A Modern Military Strategy for the United States."

Taft, Robert III (1942-) Hamilton County Commissioner, Ohio Secretary of State, Governor of Ohio.

Taft, Rosalyn (1930-1941) Daughter of Charles Taft Jr.

Taft, Sarah Butler (1943-) Daughter of Robert Taft Jr., Chief, Criminal Defense Division, Manhattan Legal Aid.

Taft, Seth (1922-2013) Cyahoga County Councilman, unsuccessful candidate for Mayor of Cleveland and Governor of Ohio.

Taft, Sylvia Bradley (1950-) Teacher, Germantown Friends School.

Taft, Thomas (1948-) Son of Seth Taft, Director of Finance Germantown Academy.

Taft, Walbridge (1885-1951) Eldest son of Henry Taft, New York lawyer, opponent of Heart Balm statutes.

Taft, William Howard (1957-1930) Prosecuting attorney, Judge, Ohio Circuit Court, Solicitor General in Benjamin Harrison Administration, Judge, Federal Court of Appeals for the Sixth Circuit, Governor general of the Philippines, Secretary of War, President of the United States, Professor of Law at Yale, Chairman of the Board of Hampton Institute, Chief Justice of the United States, author *Liberty Under Law* (Yale, 1922), *Popular Government* (Yale, 1914), *The Antitrust Act and the Supreme Court* (Harper, 1914), *The President and His Powers* (Yale, 1914), *see* H. Pringle, *William Howard Taft* (2 vols. Farrar and Rinehart, 1939), A. Butt, *Taft and Roosevelt* (2 vols. Doubleday, 1930), J. Lurie, *William Howard Taft* (Cambridge, 2012), A. Mason, *William Howard Taft: Chief Justice* (London: Oldbourne, 1964), D. Goodwin, *The Bully Pulpit* (Simon and Schuster, 2013).

Taft, William H. II (1887-1952) Younger son of Henry Taft, Assistant Vice President and Secretary, Bank for Savings, New York.

Taft, William H. III (1915-1991) Ambassador to Ireland, foreign service officer, Mozambique, Policy Planning Staff, State Department.

Taft, William H. IV (1945-   ) General Counsel, Department of Health and Human Services, Deputy Secretary of Defense, Legal Adviser, State Department.

Taft, William H. V (1978-   ) Law Clerk to Justice Alito, Partner, Debevoise and Lieberman, author *Conventional Coercion Across the Spectrum of Operations* (RAND Corporation, 2003).

Taft-Carabane, Virginia (1950-   ) Lecturer, English literature, University of Kent at Canterbury.

Taft-Jonathan, Julia (1958-2013) Daughter of Lloyd Taft.

Taft-Morales, Hugh B. (1957-   ) Minister, Baltimore Ethical Society.

Titus, Margaret Taft (1913-2008) Daughter of Hulbert Taft, horsewoman and licensed pilot, benefactor of American Indian and Classical studies.

Bibliography

C. Abbott, Population, Economic Thought and Occupational Structure: Three Middle Western Cities in the Ante-Bellum Decade, 1 J. Urban History 175 (1974).

C. Alexander, Holding the Line: The Eisenhower Era, 1952-61 (Bloomington: Indiana U., 1975).

O. Alfonso, Theodore Roosevelt and the Philippines (Manila: U. Philippines, 1970).

S. Alinsky, Rules for Radicals (New York: Random House, 1971).

S. Ambrose, Eisenhower (New York: Simon and Schuster, 1984).

American Law Institute, Principles of Government Ethics, Preliminary Draft No. 2, April 13, 2015, sec. 204(2).

J. Anderson, William Howard Taft: An Intimate History (New York: Norton, 1981).

R. Anderson, "Building National Consensus: The Career of William Howard Taft, 68 U. Cincinnati L. Rev. 323 (2000).

D. Andrews, William Howard Taft: A Conservative's Conception of the Presidency (Ithaca: Cornell U., 1968).

C. Anthony, Nellie Taft: The Unconventional First Lady of the Ragtime Era (New York: Morrow, 2005).

J. Armstrong, "The Enigma of Senator Taft and American Foreign Policy," 17 Review of Politics 206 (1955).

T. Arnold, The Folklore of Capitalism (New Haven: Yale, 1937).

J. Bagman, Henry R. Luce and the Rise of the American News Media (Baltimore: Johns Hopkins, 2001).

C. and M. Beard, The Beards' Basic History of the United States (New York: Doubleday, 1946).

H. Bergen, "Bipartisanship, Senator Taft and the Truman Administration," 90 Pol. Sci. Q. 221 (1975).

H. Berger, "Senator Robert A. Taft Dissents from Military Escalation," in J. Paterson, Cold War Critics (Chicago: Quadrangle, 1971).

I. Berlin, Building: Letters 1960 to 1975 (London: Random House UK, 2013).

G. Best, Herbert Hoover: The Post-Presidential Years, 1933-64 (Stanford: Hoover Institution, 1983).

A. Bickel, The Judiciary and Responsible Government, 1900-21 (New York: Macmillan, 1985).

W. Biddle, "The Lawyer Who Oversees the Military Budget," New York Times, October 19, 1984.

C. Black, FDR: Champion of Freedom (Washington: Public Affairs, 2005).

R. Bork, The Antitrust Paradox (Glencoe, IL: Free Press, 1993).

R. Bork, "The Rule of Reason and the Per Se Concept: Price Fixing and Market Division," 74 Yale L.J. 775, 779 (1965).

M. Bowen, The Roots of Modern Conservatism (Chapel Hill, U. N.C., 2011).

J. Bradley, Imperial Cruise (Boston: Back Bay, 2010).

E. Brandeis, History of Labour Legislation in the United States: Labour Legislation (New York: Macmillan, 1935).

D. Brody, Visualizing American Empire (Chicago: U. of Chicago, 2010).

M. Bromley, William Howard Taft and the First Motoring Presidency, 1909-13 (Jefferson, NC: McFarland, 2003).

M. Brown, The Roots of Modern Conservatism: Dewey, Taft, and the Battle for the Soul of the Republican Party (Chapel Hill: U. of North Carolina, 2011).

O. Bullough, "The Great American Tax Haven: Why the Super-Rich Love South Dakota," The Guardian, November 14, 2019.

F. Burd, Robert A. Taft and the American Understanding of Politics (Chicago: University of Chicago, Thesis T 17276, 1969).

J. Burnham, The Managerial Revolution (New York: John Day, 1941).

D. Burton (ed.), Collected Works of William H. Taft (Athens, OH: Ohio U. Press, 2004).

D. Burton, Taft, Holmes and the 1920s Court (Teaneck, NJ: Fairleigh Dickinson U., 1998).

D. Burton, Taft, Wilson and World Order (Teaneck, NJ: Fairleigh Dickinson U., 2003).

A. Butt, Taft and Roosevelt: The Intimate Papers of Archie Butt (New York: Doubleday, 1930).

J. Carpenter, Ulysses S. Grant (New York: Twayne, 1970).

A. Castillo-Freeman and R. Freeman, "When the Minimum Wage Really Bites," in G. Borjas and R. Freeman (eds.), Immigration and the Workforce (Chicago: U. of Chicago, 1992).

J. Chamberlain, Review of Pringle, William Howard Taft, New York Times, October 29, 1939.

Countess de Chambrun, Shadows Like Myself (New York: Scribner, 1936).

W. Churchill, Book Review of P. Drucker, The End of Economic Man, Times Literary Supplement, May 27, 1939, 206.

G. Clark, The Son Also Rises: Surnames and the History of Social Mobility (Princeton: Princeton U., 2015).

J. Cole, Ainsworth Spofford and the Copyright Law of 1830," 6 J. Library History 34 (1971).

P. Coletta, The Presidency of William Howard Taft (Topeka: U. Press of Kansas, 1973).

Commission on Immigration Reform, Final Report (Washington: GPO, 1997).

Commission on the Future of Worker-Management Relationships, Report (Washington: GPO, 1994).

A. Cooke, Generation on Trial (New York: Knopf, 1950).

D. Cooper, Darling Monster: The Letters of Lady Diana Cooper to Her Son John Julius Norwich (New York: Ovatham, 2014).

E. Cox, et al., The Nader Report on the Federal Trade Commission (New York: Grove Press, 1970).

A. Craitu (ed.), Tocqueville on America After 1840: Letters and Other Writings (Cambridge: Cambridge U., 2009).

R. Cramton, "The Supreme Court and the Decline of State Power," 2 J. Law and Econ. 175 (1959).

B. Cushman, "Inside the Taft Court," 2015 Supreme Court Review 345.

D. Daniel , Shadow of Slavery (Urbana: U. of Illinois, 1990).

R. Davies, "Mr. Republican Turns Socialist," 73 Ohio History (Summer 1964), 135.

T. Dennett, "President Roosevelt's Secret Pact with Japan," Current History, October 1924.

R. Divine, The Illusion of Neutrality (Chicago: U. of Chicago, 1962).

J. Doenecke, Not to the Swift: The Old Isolationists in the Cold War Era (Lewisburg: Bucknell U., 1979).

P. Drucker, The End of Economic Man (New York: John Day, 1939).

C. Dueck, Hard Line: The Republican Party and U. S. Foreign Policy Since World War II (Princeton: Princeton U., 2010).

H. Duffy, William Howard Taft (New York: Milton, Baulch, 1930).

R. Engs, Educating the Disadvantaged and Disinherited (Nashville: U. Tennessee, 1999).

R. Escalate, The Bearer of Pax Americana: The Philippine Career of William Howard Taft (Manila: New Day, 2007).

W. Eskridge and J. Ferejohn, A Republic of Statutes: The New American Constitution (New Haven: Yale U., 2010).

R. Evans, Eric Hobsbawm: A Life in History (Boston: Little Brown, 2019).

C. Fairman, Five Justices and the Electoral Commission of 1877 (New York: Macmillan, 2009).

C. Fairman, History of the Supreme Court of the United States, Part 2 (New York: Macmillan, 1987).

E. Fawcett and T. Thomas, America, Americans (London: Collins, 1983).

H. Fineberg and R. Neustadt, The Epidemic that Never Was (New York: Vintage, 1983).

H. Fineberg and R. Neustadt, The Swine Flu Affair (Washington: GPO, 1978).

O. Fiss, Troubled Beginnings of the Modern State (New York: Macmillan, 1993).

R. Foreland, The Truman Doctrine and the Origins of McCarthyism (New York: N. Y. U. Press, 1970).

F. Frankfurter, "Child Labor and the Court," The New Republic, July 26, 1922.

F. Frankfurter, "The Same Mr. Taft," New Republic, January 18, 1922.

F. Frankfurter and N. Greene, The Labor Injunction (New York: Macmillan, 1930).

M. Freedman, Roosevelt and Frankfurter: Their Correspondence: 1928-45 (London: Bodley Head, 1967).

M. Friedman and A. Schwartz, The Great Contraction, 1929-33 (Princeton: Princeton U., 2008).

T. Friedman, "If I Ruled the World," Prospect, February 2017.

T. Fryer, "Business Law and American Economic History," in 2 S. Engerman and R. Gallman, The Cambridge Economic History of the United States (Cambridge: Cambridge U., 2000).

J. Gaddis, Strategies of Containment (New York: Oxford U., 1982).

C. Glenn, The Myth of the Common School (Amherst, MA: U. of Massachusetts, 1988).

C. Goldin, "Labor Markets in the Twentieth Century," in 3 S. Engerman and R. Gallman, The Cambridge Economic History of the United States (Cambridge: Cambridge U., 2000).

E. Goldman, The Crucial Decade (New York: Knopf, 1956).

D. Goodwin, The Bully Pulpit: Theodore Roosevelt, William Howard Taft, and the Golden Age of Journalism (New York: Simon and Schuster, 2013).

J. Gottlieb, "Guilty Women," Foreign Policy and Appeasement in Inter-War Britain (Basingstoke: Palgrave Macmillan, 2015).

L. Gould (ed.), My Dearest Nellie: The Letters of William Howard Taft to Helen Herron Taft, 1909-1912 (Lawrence, KS: U. Press of Kansas, 2011).

L. Gould, President to Chief Justice (Topeka: U. Press of Kansas, 2014).

H. Graff, American Imperialism and the Philippine Insurrection: Testimony of the Times, Selections from Congressional Hearings (Boston: Little Brown, 1969).

M. Gratke, In Sickness and in Health: Conception of Disease and Ability in Presidential Bodies," www.scholarship.claremount.edu 23828.

C. Gregory, Labor and the Law (2d ed.) (New York: Norton, 1961).

J. Gunther, Inside U.S.A. (London: Hamish Hamilton, 1947).

P. Hales, Revolution and Intervention: The Diplomacy of Taft and Wilson with Mexico, 1910-17 (Cambridge: MIT Press, 1970).

L. Halle, "Looking Backward," in A. Campbell, Expansion and Imperialism (New York: Harper, 1970).

S. Hartmann, Truman and the 80th Congress (Columbia: U. of Missouri, 1970).

J. Haslam, Russia's Cold War (New Haven: Yale U., 2012).

W. Herberg, Protestant, Catholic, Jew: An Essay in American Religious Sociology (New York: Anchor Books, 1960).

S. Hess, America's Political Dynasties: From Adams to Clinton (Washington: Brookings, 2016).

S. Hess, "Big Bill Taft," 17 American Heritage No. 6 (1966).

W. Hesseltine, Ulysses S. Grant, Politician (New York: Ungar, 1935).

T. Hicks, William Howard Taft: Yale Professor of Law and New Haven Citizen (New Haven: Yale U., 1945).

H. Hoover, American Individualism (New York: Doubleday, 1922).

M. Howe (ed.), Holmes-Pollock Letters (Cambridge: Harvard U., 1961).

P. Hutchcroft. Autonomy in the American Philippines, 1900-13, 59 J. Asian Studies No. 2 (2000), 279.

H. Ickes, "Not Guilty Richard A. Ballinger: An American Dreyfus," Saturday Evening Post 212, May 25, 1940.

Japan Society, Celebrating a Century, 1907-2007 (New York: Japan Society, 2007).

J. Jenkins and S. Milkus, The Politics of Major Policy Reform in Post-War America (Cambridge: Cambridge U., 2014).

C. Jordan (ed.), Reason and Imagination: The Selected Correspondence of Learned Hand: 1897-1961 (New York: Oxford U., 2013).

L. Jorgenson, The State and the Non-Public School, 1825-1925 (Columbia: U. of Missouri, 1987).

S. Karnow, In Our Image (London: Century, 1990).

W. Kimball, FDR and the World Crisis, 1937-45 (Lexington, MA: Heath, 1973).

S. Kinzer, The Brothers: John Foster Dulles, Allen Dulles and Their Secret World War (New York: Times Books, 2013).

E. Kirkland, Industry Comes of Age: Business, Labor and Public Policy, 1860-97 (Chicago: Quadrangle, 1967).

G. Kolko, Main Currents in Modern American History (New York: Harper, 1976).

J. and G. Kolko, The Limits of Power (New York: Harper, 1972), 5.

P. Kramer, The Blood of Government: Race, Empire, the United States and the Philippines (Chapel Hill: U. of North Carolina, 2006).

A. Krock, Memoirs (London: Cassell, 1968).

P. Kurland (ed.), Felix Frankfurter on the Supreme Court (Cambridge, MA: Belknap Press, 1970).

W. La Feber, The American Search for Opportunity, 1865-1913, 2 Cambridge History of American Foreign Relations (Cambbridge: Cambridge U., 2013).

M. Leffler, A Preponderance of Power: National Security, the Truman Administration (Stanford, CA: Stanford U., 1983)

N. Lemann, "Progress's Pilgrims," New Yorker, November 18, 2013.

L. Leonard, Life of Alphonso Taft (New York: Hawke Publishing, 1920).

W. Letwin, Law and Economic Policy in America: The Evolution of the Sherman Antitrust Act (Chicago: U. of Chicago, 1965).

E. Levi, Book Review of G. and R. Hale, Market Power: Size and Shape Under the Sherman Act, 26 U. Chi. L. Rev. 672 (1959).

G. Liebmann, Diplomacy Between the Wars: Five Diplomats and the Shaping of the Modern World (London: I.B. Tauris, 2011).

A. Lindbergh, The Wave of the Future (New York: Harcourt, 1940).

B. Linn, The Philippine War, 1898-1902 (Lawrence: U. Press of Kansas, 2000).

W. Lippmann. A Preface to Politics (2d ed.) (Ann Arbor: U. Michigan, 1914, 1962).

R. Logan, The Betrayal of the Negro (New York: Macmillan, 1964).

T. Lowi, The End of Liberalism (New York: W.W. Norton, 1969).

J. Lukacs, A New Republic: A History of the United States in the Twentieth Century (New Haven: Yale, 2006).

J. Lurie, William Howard Taft, The Travails of a Progressive Conservative (Cambridge: Cambridge U., 2012).

J. Malsberger, From Obstruction to Moderation: The Transformation of Senate Conservatism, 1938-52 (Selinsgrove, PA: Susquehanna U., 2000).

W. Manchester, The Glory and the Dream (Boston: Little Brown, 1974).

H. Mannheim, Criminal Justice and Social Reconstruction (London: Kegan Paul, 1946).

H. Manning, British Colonial Government After the American Revolution (New Haven: Yale, 1933).

H. Manning, The Revolt of French Canada (New York: St. Martin's, 1962).

A. Mason, William Howard Taft: Chief Justice (London: Oldbourne, 1964).

J. Mathews, "What Trump Is Throwing Out the Window," New York Review of Books, February 9, 2017.

G. Matthews, "Robert A. Taft, The Constitution, and American Foreign Policy, 1939-53," 17 J. Contemporary History 507 (1982).

A. McClure, The Truman Administration and the Problems of Post-War Labour (Teaneck, NJ: Fairleigh Dickinson U., 1969).

D. McCoy, The Presidency of Harry S. Truman (Lawrence: U. Press of Kansas, 1984).

D. McCullough, The Path Between the Seas: The Creation of the Panama Canal, 1830-1914 (New York: Simon and Schuster, 1977).

R. McKay, "The Rapid Rise and Fractious Fall of Taft Broadcasting," Cincinnati Magazine, July 1987.

W. McWilliams, Book Review of J. Patterson, Mr. Republican, New York Times Book Review, November 19, 1972, 1.

R. Mennel and C. Compston (eds.), Holmes and Frankfurter: Their Correspondence 1912-34 (Hanover, NH: U. Press of New England, 1996).

R. Merry, President McKinley: Architect of the American Century (New York: Simon and Schuster, 2017).

S. Milkie and J. Miler, Progressivism and the New Democracy (Amherst: U. of Massachusetts, 1999).

N. Miller, Benevolent Assimilation: The American Conquest of the Philippines, 1899-1903 (New Haven: Yale U., 1987).

Z. Miller, Boss Cox's Cincinnati: Urban Politics in the Progressive Eram (New York: Oxford, 1968).

H. Millis and E. Brown, From the Wagner Act to Taft-Hartley (Chicago: U. of Chicago, 1950).

R. Minger, "William Howard Taft and Cuba," in A. Campbell, Expansion and Imperialism (New York: Harper, 1970).

P. Mooney, The Organic City, 1880-1920 (Lexington: University Press of Kentucky, 1987).

T. Morgan, Reds: McCarthyism in Twentieth Century America (New York: Random House, 2004).

H. Morgenthau, Truth and Power (London: Pall Mall, 1970).

E. Morison, Book Review of W. White, The Taft Story, New York Times Book Review, April 11, 1954.

S. Morison, The Oxford History of the American People (New York: Oxford, 1965).

E. Morris, Theodore Rex (New York: Random House, 2001).

A. Nevins (ed.), Hamilton Fish: The Inner History of the Grant Administration (New York: Dodd Mead, 1937).

R. Nisbet, Twilight of Authority (New York: Oxford, 1975).

M. Northrop, A Grave Crisis in American History, 62 Century Magazine 923 (1901).

T. Olson, "William Howard Taft," in J. Tarrant and L. Leo, Presidential Leadership: Rating the Best and Worst in the White House (New York: WS Books, 2004).

W. O'Neill, Coming Apart: An Informal History of America in the Sixties (Chicago: Quadrangle, 1971).

J. Peabody (ed.) The Holmes-Einstein Letters (London: Macmillan, 1964), 73-74.

S. Perlman and P. Taft, History of Labour Legislation in the United States: Labour Movements (New York: Macmillan, 1935).

G. Perrett, Days of Sadness, Years of Triumph: The American People, 1939-1945 (New York: Penguin, 1974).

R. Post, "Taft's Epochal Opinion in Myers v. U.S.," 45 Journal of Supreme Court History 167 (2020).

H. Pringle, William Howard Taft (New York: Farrar and Rinehart, 1939).

M. Radosh, Prophets on the Right: Profiles of Conservative Critic.

C. Quigley, Triumph and Tragedy: A History of the World in Our Time (New York: Macmillan, 1966).

P. Rego, "William Howard Taft: The Constitutionalist as Critic of Progressivism," in L. Bailey and J. Miler, In Defence of the Founders' Republic: Critics of Direct Democracy in the Progressive Era (New York: Bloomsbury, 2015).

D. Reinhard, The Republican Right Since 1945 (Lexington: Kentucky U., 1983).

L. Reynolds and C. Taft, Evolution of Wage Structure (New Haven: Yale U., 1956).

S. Ricard, "Anti-Wilsonian Internationalism: Theodore Roosevelt in the Kansas City Star," in D. Rossini, From Theodore Roosevelt to FDR: Internationalism and Isolationism in American Foreign Policy (Staffordshire: Keele U., 1995), 40.

M. Rodgers, The Impossible H.L. Mencken (New York: Doubleday, 1991).

T. Roosevelt, "The Trusts, the People, and the Square Deal," 99 Outlook 654 (1911).

J. Rosen, William Howard Taft: The 27th President (New York: Holt, 2017).

I. Ross, The Tafts: An American Family (Cleveland: World Publishing, 1964).

K. Rove, The Triumph of William McKinley (New York: Simon and Schuster, 2015).

R. Rovere, "Taft: Is This the Best We've Got?," 196 Harper's 289 (April 1948).

R. Rovere, Senator Joe McCarthy (New York: World, 1960).

R. Rovere, What Course for the Powerful Mr. Taft," New York Times Magazine, March 23, 1953.

B. Russell, Marriage and Morals (New York: Liveright, 1929).

F. Russell, The Shadow of Blooming Grove, Warren Harding and His Times (New York: McGraw Hill, 1968).

M. Scharf and P. Williams, Shaping Foreign Policy in Times of Crisis: The Role of International Law and the State Department Legal Adviser (Cambridge: Cambridge U., 2010).

A. Schlesinger, Crisis of the Old Order (Boston: Houghton Mifflin, 1957).

A. Schlesinger, The Cycles of American History (Boston: Houghton Mifflin, 1986).

A. Schlesinger, The Politics of Hope (London: Eyre and Spottiswoode, 1964).

W. and M. Scholes, The Foreign Policy of the Taft Administration (Columbia: U. of Missouri Press, 1970).

R. Scylla, "Experimental Federalism, 1789-1914," in 2 S. Engelmann and R. Gillman, The Cambridge Economic History of the United States (Cambridge: Cambridge U., 2000).

H. Segal, "The Taft Brothers of Ohio: A Study in Contrasts," New York Times, November 18, 1951, E9.

E. Severeid, Not So Wild a Dream (New York: Knopf, 1946).

A. Silverstein, Pure Politics and Impure Science (Baltimore: Johns Hopkins U., 1981).

J. Simon (ed.), The Papers of Ulysses S. Grant (Carbondale, Southern Illinois U., 2005).

M. Sklar, The Corporate Reconstruction of American Capitalism, 1890-1916 (Cambridge: Cambridge U., 1988).

T. Smith, America's Mission (Princeton: Princeton U., 1995).

T. Smith and R. Taft, Foundations of Democracy: A Series of Debates (New York: Knopf, 1939).

J. Spanier, The Truman–McArthur Conflict and the Korean War (Cambridge: Harvard U., 1959).

D. Spivey, Schooling for the New Slavery: Black Industrial Education 1868-1915 (Westport, CT: Greenwood, 1978).

K. Stampp, The Era of Reconstruction, 1865-1877 (New York: Vintage, 1965).

C. Taft, Democracy in Politics and Economics (New York: Farrar Straus, 1950).

C. Taft, Why I Am for the Church (New York: Farrar Straus, 1947).

C. Taft, "Why the Bells Are Ringing Today: They Call for Religious Unity as Churches of All the Continents Meet Together in Amsterdam," New York Times Magazine, August 26, 1948.

C. Taft, You, I and Roosevelt (New York: Farrar and Rinehart, 1936).

F. Taft, "Atlas of Health Care Reform," 7 Law and Health 73 (1992).

H. Taft, A Century and a Half at the New York Bar (New York: Privately Printed, 1938).

F. Taft, "Detention of the Unconvinced in Patna, India," 5 Case Western Reserve J. of Intl. Law 155 (1971).

H. Taft, An Essay on Conversation (New York: Macmillan, 1927).

H. Taft, Japan and America: A Journey and a Political Survey (New York: Macmillan, 1932).

H. Taft, Japan and the Far East Conference (New York: Macmillan, 1927).

H. Taft, Kindred Arts: Conversation and Public Speaking (New York: Macmillan, 1929).

H. Taft, Legal Miscellanies: Six Decades of Change and Progress (New York: Macmillan, 1941).

H. Taft, Memories and Opinions (New York: Macmillan, 1942).

H. Taft, Occasional Papers and Addresses of an American Lawyer (New York: Macmillan, 1920).

H. Taft, Opinions, Literary and Otherwise (New York: Macmillan, 1934).

H. Taft, Our Relations with Japan (New York: Japan Society, 1920).

H. Taft, Recollections of Full Years (New York: Dodd, Mead, 1914).

J. Taft, American Power: The Rise and Decline of American Globalism (New York: Harper, 1989).

J. Taft, A Force for Good: How Enlightened Finance Can Restore Faith in Capitalism (New York: Palgrave Macmillan, 2013).

J. Taft, Mayday at Yale (Boulder, CO: Westview, 1976).

J. Taft, Stewardship: Lessons Learned from the Lost Culture of Wall Street (Philadelphia: Wiley, 2012).

R. Taft, "An Alliance for Peace," New York Times Magazine, February 6, 1944, 8.

R. Taft, "The British Loan," Vital Speeches XII, June 5, 1946, 501-02.

R. Taft, "Laying Ghosts of Ignorance," in S. McCall, For the Honor of the Nation: Patriotism of the American Jew Hailed by Christian Historians (New York: Plymouth Editions, 1939).

R. Taft Jr., "On the Matter of Amnesty," New York Times, January 8, 1972.

R. Taft, "Our Foreign Policy," 6 Vital Speeches 348 (March 1940).

R. Taft, "Peace and Politics," 25 American Bar Association Journal 139 (1943).

R. Taft Jr., "Detente, With Caution," New York Times, June 30, 1974.

W. Taft, "The Future of the Republican Party," Saturday Evening Post, February 14, 1915.

W. Taft, The Influence of Hampton, Report of the Department of the Interior, Bureau of Education, Bulletin 23 (1923), 3-4.

W. Taft, Liberty Under Law (New Haven: Yale U., 1922).

W. Taft, Popular Government (New Haven: Yale U., 1914).

W. Taft, "Mr. Wilson and the Campaign," 10 Yale Review 1, 19-20 (1920).

W. Taft IV, Memorandum on Torture, 37 Case Western Reserve Journal of International Law 615 (2006).

W. Taft IV and N. Buchwald, "Preemption, Iraq and International Law," 97 Am. J. Intl. Law 557 (2003).

W. Taft V, Conventional Coercion Across the Spectrum of Operations: The Utility of U.S. Military Forces in the Emerging

Security Environment (New York: RAND Corporation, 2003).

S. Taylor Jr. "Pentagon Balking at Joining Drug War," New York Times, July 4, 1981.

M. Teague (ed.), Mrs L: Conversations with Alice Roosevelt Longworth (London: Duckworth, 1987).

E. Thomas, The Man to See: Edward Bennett Williams (New York: Simon and Schuster, 1991).

C. Tomlin, "Labour Law," in 3 S. Engerman and R. Gallman, The Cambridge Economic History of the United States (Cambridge: Cambridge U., 2000).

L. Troy, Twilight of the Old Unionism (Armonk, NY: M.E. Sharpe, 2004).

H. Uppendahl, "Intergovernmental Relations in the Federal Republic of Germany," in A. Norton (ed.), The Present and Future Role of Local Government in Great Britain and the Federal Republic of Germany (London: Anglo-German Foundation, 1985).

M. Urofsky and L. Levy (eds.), The Letters of Louis D. Brandeis (Albany: SUNY Press, 1978).

J. Valtin, Out of the Night (New York: Alliance, 1941).

J. Vivian (ed.), William Howard Taft, Collected Editorials, 1917-1921 (Westport, CT: Praeger, 1990).

N. Wapshott, President Roosevelt, the Isolationists and the Road to World War II (New York: Norton, 2015).

War Relief Control Board, Voluntary War Relief During World War II: A Report (Department of State Publication 2566 (Washington, DC: GPO, 1948).

G. White, The American Judicial Tradition (3d ed.) (New York: Oxford, 2007).

W. White, A Puritan in Babylon (New York: Macmillan, 1938).

W. White, The Taft Story (New York: Harper, 1954).

C. Williams, Life of Rutherford B. Hayes (Boston: Houghton Mifflin, 1914).

R. Woods, A Changing of the Guard: Anglo-American Relations, 1941-46 (Chapel Hill: University of North Carolina, 1990).

R. Woods, Fulbright: A Biography (Cambridge: Cambridge U., 1995).

C. Wunderlin (ed.), Papers of Robert A. Taft (Kent, OH: Kent State U., 2001).

D. Wyman, The Abandonment of the Jews (New York: Pantheon, 1984).

H. Young, "William Howard Taft and Hampton Institute," in K. Schall (ed.), Stony the Road: Chapters in the History of Hampton Institute (Charlottesville: U. Press of Virginia, 1977).

INDEX